GOD IN CHRISTIAN
PERSPECTIVE

GOD IN CHRISTIAN PERSPECTIVE

George Newlands

T&T CLARK
EDINBURGH

T&T CLARK LTD
59 GEORGE STREET
EDINBURGH EH2 2LQ
SCOTLAND

First published 1994

ISBN 0 567 09657 2 HB
ISBN 0 567 29259 2 PB

British Library Cataloguing-in-Publication Data
A catalogue record for this book is available from the British Library

Typeset by Trinity Typesetting, Edinburgh
Printed in Great Britain by Redwood Books, Trowbridge, Wiltshire

Contents

I. God in Creation

II. God in Reconciliation

Preface

God in Christian Perspective is concerned with the substance of the Christian understanding of God. It explores the sense of the presence of God as a hidden presence, appropriated in the response of faith. God is known always as creator and reconciler simultaneously, identified with his creation in its joy and its suffering, characterised always by the self-giving love of Jesus Christ, active as spirit in the Church and in the world. This is what faith struggles to express in speaking of the reality of God.

This study has developed over several years, from a consideration of the doctrine of God, to a reflection upon the relation between creation and reconciliation, and the consequences of reconciliation. It has become to all intents and purposes a systematic theology. If there is one thinker upon whom I have tried to reflect more than others over the last decades it is Dietrich Bonhoeffer. But the reader will find almost no direct citation. And though I have tried to avoid recourse to 'cheap grace' in relation to God, Church and world, I do not imagine for a moment that I have been entirely successful.

I have been lucky enough to have been able to try out sections of it in various guises and in various places and before audiences believing and less believing, notably my students, who have suffered more than most. Thanks are due, too, to my son Stewart for help in preparing the text for printing, and to my wife Elizabeth for her love and support.

Glasgow, 1994

vii

I. GOD IN CREATION

1

Introduction

1

'God is love; he who dwells in love is dwelling in God, and God in him. There is no room for fear in love; perfect love banishes fear' (1 John 4:17, 18). God is in his essential nature love, love characterised precisely and uniquely in the self-giving of God to humankind in the events surrounding the life, death and resurrection of Jesus of Nazareth.

There is no point in recommending the concepts of traditional theism simply for their own sake. A living God does not need to be preserved in archaic thought patterns. And certainly there is no point in defending hallowed misconceptions. The intention is to work out a modern restatement of the Christian doctrine of God.

In the history of humankind there have been many gods. Divinities great and small have appeared, been feared, loved, despaired of, discarded, deposited in museums of ethnic antiquities. In Europe and America, and in countries influenced by European thought, belief in God has long been subject to serious doubt. Renewals of interest in transcendent values and transcendental religion together with resurgence in national religions often linked with political movements, have done little to repair the shattered fabric of belief. Within the religions and especially in the case of Christianity, focus on the elucidation of particular issues of doctrinal debate has often tended to obscure the great underlying issue of the nature of the concept of God, and the basic uncertainty surrounding the subject of faith and belief.

Awareness of the variety of transcendent values in the

3

pluralism of the modern world, and also the experience of evil on a previously unheard of scale in modern wars, have tended to reinforce intellectual objections to traditional doctrines. This mood was brilliantly captured by the Jewish philosopher Martin Buber in writing of the eclipse of God in our time. It was personified in the figure, to our generation the somewhat uncomfortable figure, of the martyr Dietrich Bonhoeffer, in poetry and prose and in the daily cost of discipleship.

It has often been said that modern theology talks about anything and everything but God. If this is true, then there are many good reasons for reticence. In the recent past 'God' was a word that passed too easily on men's lips. God was taken in vain, and the result was eclipse of God and holocaust. In addition, the philosophical problems involved in explaining the classical Christian doctrine of God are truly formidable. The deeper the issues are probed, the more complex they appear.

Studies of God as God are far outnumbered by books on aspects of Christology, God and hermeneutics, God and meaning, God and society and the like. None of these issues is irrelevant to talk of God. Yet there must always be attempts, however incomplete, to spell out in detail a reflective account of the character and activity of God as creator and redeemer. Such accounts are of course no substitute for a tradition of life lived in trust in God and prayer to God as part of the Christian contribution to the understanding of all human society as God's humanity. It is entirely right that we should place great value upon the Bible and the rich heritage of Christian thought about God through the ages. We must also continue to think seriously about God in our own time. We may well judge that some modern theological reconstruction has resulted in a disastrous weakening of the classical Christian claims about the nature and activity of God. If so, our remedy will lie in praying for the grace to persevere, and to encourage others to take up where we have left off with a clearer vision.

2

Here is a brief summary of the first part of this study. In Chapter Two, Faith After Faith, I deal with the nature of faith in the

Christian God in the modern world, the questions faith raises for society and the questions which society in turns asks of faith. How is faith lost, sustained, recovered, deepened?

Chapter Three discusses the understanding of God in contemporary theology. Where are we now, how have we got to this point, and how are we to move forward? The method of development of the cumulative rational case from the sources and norms of theology is set out in Chapter Four. Chapters Five and Six are on the transcendence and immanence of God, and the cosmological and existential dimensions of human experience of God. This leads naturally in Chapter Seven into reassessment of what it means to speak of God as being, as person and as personal being.

Chapters Eight and Nine consider divine personal involvement in the contingency of history through Jesus Christ, in his life, death and resurrection. How are we to distinguish sense from nonsense in talk of the crucified God? In what respects may we say that God is Spirit? Then there is Chapter Ten on God as Trinity. In Chapter Eleven we return to the cosmological dimension of our understanding of God, as creator of heaven and earth, and so, in Chapters Twelve and Thirteen, to providence and the great question mark over all theology, evil. Trust in God should lead us to a new sense of a purpose in God's humanity in new creation. Part Two deals with Christology and the sphere of the Spirit in Church and society.

This book develops further the direction of earlier studies. In *Hilary of Poitiers* I examined the relation between scripture, tradition and the pressures of contemporary culture, especially in theology and philosophy, in doing theology. In *Theology of the Love of God* I attempted to work out a programme for theology, relating theoretical issues of method to the actual process of exposition of the substantive issues of doctrine. In *The Church of God* I suggested the richness of the devotional tradition of the life of the Christian Church in prayer, worship and service. Without both the questions and the devotion of others the theologian is lost in self-reflection. *Making Christian Decisions* examined the contribution of Christian theology and practice to some of the important ethical issues which are of vital concern to contemporary society. Here I return to the basic internal content of Christian theology, the concept of God. This then leads to a reconsideration of Christology.

In exploring the substance of concepts of God we shall inevitably refer to rules, methods and guidelines in theology. Rules are guidelines, to enable one to be constructive – not to be restrictive, stuck in a sectarian conceptual fundamentalism. It is all too easy to construct theologies which appear to be impressive only because they reinforce the prejudices and interests of particular ecclesiastical factions or academic fashions.

Yes, but what then is positive in your own method? it may be asked. I see my work as a developing reflection on the proposition that God's love is the centre of theology. Christians find this love spelled out in their imaginative reflection on the biblical narratives, within the tradition of the Church, in the past and in the present. There is a reciprocal illumination here of text and context. The biblical story, of creation and redemption, centred on the life, death and resurrection of Jesus, remains the centre. Here we learn of the character of Christ as the character of God. Nothing can separate us, nothing can separate all mankind, in time and eternity from God's love.

Here we reconsider the meaning of God, and its implication for creation and redemption, in the light of the long history of Christianity's wrestling with this issue, with the aid of philosophy and other related academic disciplines, up to and especially in the present.

Focus on God's love is a necessary but not a sufficient condition for an adequate approach to theology. Though it remains the underlying reality for Christian faith, it must be reflected on with all the resources of reason, revelation and experience, building up a cumulative rational case in the light of the history of doctrine and its exposition in contemporary theology.

How do we judge between conflicting suggestions for love's consequences? By asking which frameworks, in exegesis and philosophy, most faithfully say what we want to say and most positively exclude what we don't want to say. What is doctrine? It is the formulation, with the maximum possible precision, of the significance of the Christian gospel. Constructive critical theologies are produced in numerous different ways.

> A good theologian does not live in a house of ideas, principles and methods. He walks right through all such buildings and always comes out into the fresh air again. He remains on the way.

This comment, in a letter of Karl Barth to Heiko Miskotte of 12 July 1956, and to Marcus Barth 21 April 1956, seems to me to be one of the best pieces of advice ever given in theology, and I endorse it without qualification.

This does not mean of course that Barth had no theological method. Of course he had, otherwise he could not have produced those thirteen tightly written volumes. He concentrated on the exposition of the word of God, which he regarded as the centre of theology. It included a precise appraisal of the relation between scripture and tradition, between faith and philosophy, between the various strands of the Church's tradition and theories of revelation in previous theology.

Explicit discussion of method in this study is mainly confined to Chapter Four: the role of Christology in theology, the central facts to be included in consideration of God, the question of analogy in language about God, the role of the Bible, the indispensable things in scripture and tradition, the Church in its response to sociological and other pressures, and any other relevant data. A cumulative rational case uses each of these strands in different ways in dealing with specific problems – issues of transcendence, immanence, the sense of the presence and absence of God, hiddenness, suffering, spiritual reality, personal being, Christology, the Holy Spirit and the Trinity, creation and divine action, grace and history.

Trust in God should lead us to a new trust and sense of purpose in God's humanity in new creation. Not the confusion of mankind but the unity of mankind as the children of the loving God may become a symbol of the creation of confidence and the gradual erosion of fear in our society. God's love is the basis of human freedom and mutual concern in human life at every level.

No useful purpose can be served by pretending that the questions are less complex than they really are. In this sense the verdict of the 'man in the street' is no better and no worse in theology than in any other subject of vital concern in human society, whether in medicine, law or whatever. Still there is no reason why the basic themes of research should not be explained in plain language without distortion or loss of intellectual rigour. This is particularly the case where we are concerned with the background to the Christian gospel which is for all humanity. We should try to eschew the mystique of pseudo-intellectual jargon which so easily creeps into theology. There is in the gospel a strangeness, an ascetic chord, a refining fire. Beyond the fire there is however the constant purpose of God's sustaining love, not indeed to sustain all we regard as desirable for as long as it suits us, but to guide us into the mutual dependence and illumination of the freedom of the children of God.

2

Faith After Faith

1. Faith and Grounds for Trust

Faith in God means trust in God for all things. Trust does not involve an exhaustive knowledge of the subject of trust. It would be plain silly to trust in someone for the most serious matters of life unless one had grounds for thinking that the trust was well placed. It would be sad if the absence of definitive information made it impossible for us ever to trust anyone at all. The Christian gospel is an invitation to trust in God. Our concern is with the character of God and the grounds for trusting in him.

Thinking about God and having faith in him need not always overlap, though often they do. There are people who think about God a great deal without ever feeling that they have anything like faith in him. There are others whose faith appears to be a blind obedience involving only minimal reflection. There are various sorts of combinations of these.

We live in community, and faith and thought about God are formed in life within society, in the various religious communities of mankind. In universities and similar places, thought about God, whether or not accompanied by faith in God, takes place within the framework of an academic discipline. But faith in God usually arises within the life and thought of a religious community, for Christianity in the life of the Church in the midst usually of an increasingly secular state.

It is then from religious experience which is not an isolated factor but part of our experience of life that faith is first formed and then sustained. This is experience, Christians claim, not

9

simply of experience but of God. Faith includes the component of experience. It is based also upon reflection on experience, ours and that of others throughout history. Faith also includes information about historical events, at least it does in a religion like Christianity which includes historical claims among its central affirmations. Reflection then leads to other logical and metaphysical beliefs about the nature and activity of God. It may also lead to reflection about the ways in which we come to have faith with a specific content, that is, to theories of revelation. Experience, reason and revelation are all components of faith as trust. They are also, in various forms, the basic building blocks of theological methods and construction.

Faith in God as the transcendent creator of the universe means trust in one who is in important respects mysterious to us. It involves elements of doubt and uncertainty as well as trust and confidence. Thinking about God involves a constant process of construction, criticism and reconstruction. Lines of argument come up which count against the existence and activity of such a God. Others count for. The long history of the dialogue between faith and reason is the story of this internal and external critique of belief in God. This is a process which Christians should welcome, though anxiety sometimes leads them to shrink from it. Similar dialogues take place in other cultures and religions.

Critical thinking about God in the European tradition of course predates Christianity and goes on in a continuous intellectual stream from the presocratic philosophers to the present.[1] What is the nature of rational enquiry? Does exploration of the understanding of God help us to judge between the various conflicting accounts of the nature of critical rationality available to us? At some stages in the great dialogue between faith and reason it was thought that there was one agreed understanding of the doctrine of God, supported by revelation, and that on the other hand philosophical theories of the nature of truth and knowledge

---

[1] Cf. W.K.C. Guthrie, *The Greek Philosophers*, or in succinct form A.H. Armstrong's excellent *Introduction to Ancient Philosophy*. It would be hard to underestimate the value of the legacy of Greek philosophy to European civilisation.

were subject to controversy and speculation. At other stages
the reverse has been true. Sometimes the rational framework
has been thought to be agreed, while the area of talk of God has
been held to be mere insubstantial speculation. 'Consign it
then to the flames', in the words of the great anti-magician,
David Hume. Today there is in most places an understandable
caution in the face of all such general theories. We need not
abandon the doctrines of traditional religion without reflection.
But equally, the achievements of the past do not relieve us of
the need to continue to think in the present.

2. The God of Christian Faith

Christian faith in God generally arises within the Church as
faith in God through Jesus Christ. It may be a simple faith in
God as saviour. Reflection will then lead us to the conclusion
that all God's activity in creation and reconciliation overlaps
and is simultaneous. Such faith, expressed in the biblical
imagery of God as the Almighty is still some way away from the
omnipotent, omniscient being of the theology of the high
Middle Ages. The medieval framework has however been an
important intellectual support to faith, in both Catholic and
Reformed traditions, for seven hundred years.

Faith in God through Jesus Christ is traditionally understood
as based on reason, revelation and experience. Revelation,
once understood with the aid of a form of Platonic intuition,
is today seen more often as deriving from a basis in historical
events and their interpretation in the common experience of
the Christian community. It need not be thought of as contrary
to reason, but may in principle go beyond what is accessible to
the everyday world of empirical experience without becoming
unintelligible. Such an approach may at least be understood by
theists and non-theists alike. Basil Mitchell has spoken of
revelation as indicating things which men claim to know about
God, which they could not have discovered for themselves.
Anthony Kenny has commented: 'Certainly it would be wrong
to argue that one could never be justified in accepting something
as a message from X unless one had independent evidence for
believing in the existence of X; a message from Mars might

make one believe in the existence of living beings on Mars which there was no other reason to suspect.' In both cases the search for rational grounds remains a continuing task.[2]

In some modern versions of Christian faith the connection between Jesus and God is much weaker than in traditional Christianity. Jesus is God's servant, who points to a new direction in human society. In traditional classical theology God is identified with Jesus in a form of strict identity, such that the creator enters into the contingency of human life fully. He is involved in the life and death of one particular individual, and in the resurrection of Jesus takes this experience into his own eternal being as God.[3]

Sometimes this identity in the strongest possible sense is expressed in the suggestion that Jesus is God and that all our talk of God may be replaced by talk about Jesus. This usage is common in modern evangelical Christianity. At other times the notion of Jesus Christ as the unique self-expression of God is central, notably in the theology of Karl Barth. There is a constant danger of reduction. God the creator may be perfectly expressed through his involvement with Jesus Christ.[4] Yet through the life of Jesus he remains the creator. We shall see similar problems arising in the notion that God is expressed definitively on the cross, in opposition to the claims of philosophical theism.

---

[2]Basil Mitchell, *The Justification of Religious Belief,* 156; Anthony Kenny, *The God of the Philosophers,* 128.

An excellent dicussion of the relations between faith and reason has recently been provided by Ingolf Dalferth in his *Theology and Philosophy.* I have compared his approach to the classic British discussion in John Baillie's *The Sense of the Presence of God,* in *Christ, Church and Society* ed. D.A.S. Fergusson, T&T Clark, 1993. Cf. too F.S. Fiorenza, *Foundational Theology,* esp. 285-311, which closely approaches, from a different tradition, the appeal to a cumulative case argued by Basil Mitchell.

[3]In this text God is sometimes spoken of as 'He', following traditional usage. This does not mean that God is to be regarded as male rather than female. Feminist theology rightly points here to an imbalance in traditional imagery concerning God. This imbalance has often had undesirable consequences when used without regard for the limitation on all anthrompomorphic imagery in theology.

[4]Karl Barth, *Church Dogmatics* 2.1.

Understanding the relation between God, maker of heaven and earth, and Jesus Christ, constitutes the central problem of Christian theology. It is a mystery, God's mystery. How to steer a median course between rationalisation and mystification is an important decision in Christian understanding of God. In the light of the Church's understanding of the Bible we may come to see God as the supremely loving God, for whom to be is to love, in the pattern of self-giving as self-affirmation spelled out in the life, death and resurrection of Jesus Christ.[5]

God in Christian understanding is uniquely and distinctively personal. He related to humanity in creating personal relationships with himself. God is personal, not in the sense of a humanoid 'superperson' but as the source and ground of authentic personhood. In classical Christian theology he is understood as the trinitarian God, as three persons, Father, Son and Spirit. The persons exist together in perfect personal relationship, both internally and in relation to mankind. That is how God is. At the same time, he is also truly person in his oneness. God is, and he acts towards us as one integrated person. All models of his nature are bound to be inadequate. Yet there is understood to be in God genuine personality and relationship, relating to us through the person of Jesus and in the action of the Holy Spirit in the created order.

As a personal God acting in the characteristically self-giving, self-affirming manner indicated in the life of Jesus through the creator's participation in the vulnerability of creation. God is understood as love, in his essential nature, self-giving love. God is understood to care for, sustain, protect and nurture all human life. To be able to act in particular providence in this manner raises the most difficult of questions concerning the nature of divine action. These are central to our assessment of the so-called divine attributes of omnipotence, omniscience, foreknowledge, freedom and determinism. At the centre lies the problem of evil. Can the divine love be reconciled with evil in the world, natural evil and evil caused by human action? The theoretical problems of how to conceive God's perfections are considerable. Yet a doctrine of God which denies God this wide

---

[5]Ibid. 4.1, 175ff.

range of concern for his creation falls far short of the Christian vision.

3. God in Perspective

God in the Bible and in the Judaeo-Christian traditions is the Maker of heaven and earth. His love is all-embracing. He is the ground of the universe. God has brought the created order into being, from disorder into order. This conception has been developed in the doctrine of *creatio ex nihilo*, and remains of central importance. God sustains, directs and protects all life. Without his sustaining grace the created order would collapse. Such a claim about God is of overwhelming magnitude. It is hardly surprising that it has been much modified. It has often been explained as being poetic or symbolic in nature, as referring to anything but the physical order of creation to which it was originally applied. It is clearly not necessary for a community which holds a living faith to affirm all that has been said in the past about that faith. Yet reduction of the claim for God's sovereignty over the created order turns the basis of Christianity into something other than it was in the Bible and in much of the history of the Church. I want to suggest that this claim can be maintained, and that there is evidence to indicate the coherence and rationality of this belief.[6]

To understand God as the creator of the structures of the universe is in my view basic to Christian faith. We need not however regard the Genesis narratives as some sort of divinely inspired scientific account of creation. When it comes to understanding the processes of the development of matter and of life we must turn to the appropriate scientific expertise. Christians understand God as at once hidden in the processes of natural order and as intimately involved in the lives of all individuals in history. Here we may begin to appreciate the

---

[6]P.C.W. Davies offered an imaginative account of the relation of cosmology to theology in *God and the New Physics*. On the important question of the relations between science and theology, cf. especially the writings of A.R. Peacocke and John Polkinghorne. Cf. too T.F. Torrance, *Space, Time and Incarnation*.

wonder and complexity of divine action. Both extremes of deism and interventionism are ruled out. God is not aloof from but deeply and personally involved in his creation. God is not present exactly as one human being may be present to another, so that each is familiar with the other's sphere of work and daily engagements diary. God's presence is a hidden presence, not at our disposal for our particular and often self-centred convenience. This is a presence reflected in the numerous world religions, and for Christianity centred in the presence of the risen Christ.

The history of theology since the eighteenth century is largely the history of attempts to offer a new and satisfactory intellectual justification for religious belief. Critical re-examination has resulted in a salutary stripping away of elements of superstition and misapprehension, and unnecessary doctrines which now seem to be at best peripheral to the gospel. It has inevitably led to doctrinal reconstruction of a minimising nature. These have not been satisfactory, either as adequate accounts of Christian faith or as apologetic to enable the outsider to entertain belief as a viable option. The process has not been entirely negative, for it has helped to pin-point the central issues. It is through such a history of discussion that scholarly advance takes place.

It may be thought that a defence of anything like traditional theism must fail. Such patterns are bound to traditional orders of society, indeed to outdated conceptions of the role of authority and of institutions in society. Much of the Marxist critique of religion, developed in the writings of critical theory in recent years, is directed especially against the Christian doctrine of God. As I understand it however, the authority of God must not be confused with any sort of authoritarian appeal by one group of people against the rights, dignity and freedom of any other group.

4. God's Presence

In thinking of a God who is present as a living reality to his creatures we cannot hope to offer 'God's presence and his very self' as a higher gift than grace, but as a focal point which may help to link together reflection on an assortment of diverse observations about God, all of which are pretty familiar to you.

Christians understand God as at once hidden in the process of natural order and intimately involved in the lives of all individuals in history. God is creator of heaven and earth. He is independent of space and time except as he chooses to be involved in space and time. Modern cosmological study can make no difference to central affirmations about God as creator, we may say. Yet it is more difficult to conceptualise notions of God's providential care in a universe which appears to be infinite, but in which each galaxy has a fixed and finite term of existence.

Awareness of this vastness of scale may help us to form a new conception of the divine transcendence. The cosy familiarities of a local dignitary with his clients are not the appropriate model for such a God. God's love works on a scale in which the span of human life on earth, indeed of the existence of our planet, is a mere fragment. On such a scale particular providence may seem unthinkable. But precisely here we may perhaps grasp some heightened awareness of God's grace, so that in St. Paul's words, 'nothing can separate us from the love of God through Jesus Christ'.

It follows from our earlier discussions of God's hiddenness that belief in providence, in God's creative activity within the created order, is 'against the odds', and belief in God's victory over evil is focused on the events concerning Jesus. God acts, in the manner appropriate to self-giving love. How he acts is left to the imagination of faith to work out. In human life commitment to love means endless different sorts of responses, not all identifiable by a simple direct association with 'love' as the obvious motive.

The actions of God take place in, with and under the tradition of experience of communities and societies. They remain the actions of the hidden God, to be apprehended in faith. What would it mean to say that God is a God for whom historicality is part of his very being? This is in the first instance a reference to the incarnation.

The historicality of God is intimately related to the spirituality of God. It is as a self-focused presence, as one who has acted decisively in history in the events concerning Jesus and now is present to mankind through the spirit that God sustains mankind with his grace. That presence is the presence to faith of the Spirit of God.

5. Father, Son and Spirit

Reflection on a God who is present as a living reality to his creation helps us to bring into focus most of the main areas of this perspective on God. The Christian God is personally concerned for all mankind. He allows space to his creation. God is not meaningless, nor even totally unknown. His action is not merely a master act which sets creation in motion. His concern as Father, Son and Spirit is expressed in providence and in particularity, and it has an eschatological dimension. God is present now through Jesus Christ, *Christus praesens*, and a hidden presence in experience but not only through experience. There is no point, as in some theological reflection, in playing off concepts of God as Word against concepts of God as Spirit. Both are central to Christian theological reflection. This reflection also embraces the sphere of the many religions of mankind.

God acts in grace in creation and in reconciliation. His self-giving love is present in creation through the action of the Spirit. God's action in history is not seen so clearly by mankind before and after the incarnation. Yet the incarnation, the life and teaching as well as the death and resurrection of Jesus, is the ground for affirmation of all God's action. Spiritual creativity is the sphere of self-giving love. God is not wordless. The incarnation is of self-giving love, and is not simply a concept born of anthropomorphism. The hiddenness of God's love is not absence or indifference to mystery as such, but is precisely love, infinitely complex yet central.

There is indeed much that we do not know about God. God is a mystery, not totally but largely. At the same time, we must speak of what we know. Neither pure symbolism nor benevolent deism is adequate. Here there is something to be learned from St. Thomas, with his insistence on residual mystery in God, and from Luther, with his stress on Christ as the key to God's nature. In the nineteenth century people thought that they knew a great deal about biology. Now biologists reckon to know much more, and much less. Similar considerations apply in theology.

In Christian thought the hiddenness of the presence of God is often related to suffering, and this is quite right. But God is present where there is good as well as where there is evil. God delights in the created order. Our uncertainties about God in a suffering world can sometimes be a too-easy reflection of the plausibility criteria of the age. How to speak of God as the ultimate spiritual reality without confusion with the contemporary equation of spirit with spookiness is one of the major contemporary problems of Christian communication.

The name of God is constantly trivialised, by critics and devotees alike. In thinking of ultimate reality we cannot rest content with a simple biblicism, a bored liberalism, a retreat into patristic romanticism, or any such fashionable response. We cannot deify nature and call this God. Nature's cruelties are unpleasant enough without exalting them. The idea that God intends endless unnecessary suffering in human dying, in malnutrition and in natural disaster is monstrous. God is not indeed a life principle as such, but God is love. God has been present in history wherever there is joy, goodness and love in human life as well as in contexts of suffering.

The love of God has often been particularly well expressed in incarnational theologies, but it has also been profoundly suggested in Judaism, and in non-incarnational liberal theology. All depends on the quality of the reflection. We experience the presence of God in our relationship with other people, through the Spirit. The action of the Spirit does not however take place in a sphere beyond, above or in spite of suffering, as in some idealist thought, but precisely through identification in suffering love. The Spirit is not to be thought of as in contrast with the world but within the world. God as spirit is not in opposition to God incarnate. God's presence is his own presence, as the Spirit of the crucified and risen Christ.

Reflection upon God often occurs in prayer. This again is not a retreat from but a summons to the world. Self-giving has psychological, sociological, political and economic aspects.

This is a consequence of the incarnation of God. Such reflection requires awareness of academic disciplines. It may be true that when six million Jews were gassed the Churches did all too little to help. Yet not all was silence. Bonhoeffer was struggling with a new ethics, and others were actively in revolt. There is no point in the western intellectual liberal tradition, to which civilisation owes a great debt, dying in self-generated embarrassment. What is needed is more critical thought and action, not less. And somewhat as experience of God is not only individual but social in character, so is the need for collective thought and action.

At different times in history theologians have perceived different problems as central. There is need for a balance which takes account of the present, in the light of the concerns of different periods in history. Neither Troeltsch nor Kant nor Einstein, neither a characteristically patristic or a medieval consciousness can set the agenda for thought about God. Problems of history, of modern historical consciousness, are especially important in post-Enlightenment thought. But this does not mean that we need over-react, for example, to the point which the historical tradition of the *magnalia Dei* was making about the divine sovereignty as the centre of creation. God is as near to one generation as to another, though different generations face different obstacles to reflection on God. To know who he is, as Hans Frei has well said, is to believe in his self-focused presence. Such a presence has different manifestations in different cultural contexts, yet centres upon the expression of self-giving love as focused in Jesus Christ. [7]

[7]Despite over-use in the theology of the 1960s, I regard Bonhoeffer's theological work as of lasting value for the interpretation of the Christian gospel in a secular world. It is in the context of reflection on the *Letters and Papers* that this chapter is written. On the presence of God, Hans Frei's *The Identity of Jesus Christ* is always instructive, as is Emil Fackenheim's study, *God's Presence in History*.

The question of the nature of ultimate spiritual reality has been asked sharply in recent writings by Don Cupitt, and his solutions to the problem have been much criticised, notably by Keith Ward (cf. Don Cupitt, *Taking Leave of God*, and Keith Ward, *Holding Fast to God*). It seems to me that Cupitt has shown an awareness of the serious nature of the questions raised by our secular culture about the Christian tradition on God. His own solution, that God is a name for human self-consciousness, does not commend itself to me. However, it is too easy for theologians to mount a logical argument against Cupitt, and then believe that the problems to which Cupitt draws attention have simply vanished. The exposition of an understanding of God as a hidden reality of loving presence seeks to take seriously both the felt absence of God's presence within the consciousness of modern society and the Christian affirmation of God as the creator and reconciler of the universe, active as personal being. It is true that the 1980s saw the arrival of militant religious consciousness in Islam, in the Moral Majority in the USA, and elsewhere. There is a tendency for theologians to retreat into the exclusive backwater of the religious sect, whether in Protestant or Catholic form. But if Christianity is not for all humankind then in my view it is misunderstood. I am not greatly attracted to Alistair Macintyre's vision of quasi-Benedictine oases in the midst of a society too easily given up as lost to faith (cf. his *After Virtue*).

3

The Christian God

1. Contemporary Explorations: Ebeling and Barth

How is a new study of the doctrine of God to be constructed? God as the self-giving, self-affirming God characterised definitively through the events concerning Jesus is the ground of all reality. God does not offer us an authorised theological method. Nor indeed are we in a position to regard a particular theoretical framework as the only fruitful way. However, and this too must be emphasised, this does not leave us without a perfectly clear and rational method of procedure. In opting for a method based on an affirmation of the central emphases of Christian theology, in the events of creation and redemption, rather than an affirmation of infallible methodological rules, we seek to avoid the constriction which produces that paralysis of the theological imagination which has had a disastrous effect, not least in the liberal Protestant tradition in which this study stands.

Academic theology is often necessarily preoccupied with escaping from fundamentalism. However, in escaping from the bondage of biblical or ecclesiastical fundamentalism theologians are all too prone to fall into conceptual fundamentalism, and to have minds as irrevocably closed as those whose naiveté they are so delighted to censure.

How is contemporary theology to be done through faith after faith? At this point I want to examine an important recent attempt to take up the theological consequences of the situation of faith after faith, reflected on in a way not dissimilar to our own. I refer to Gerhard Ebeling's three volume classic, *Dogmatik des Christlichen Glaubens*.

21

Ebeling's *Dogmatik* is firmly in the tradition of Schleiermacher, but with important variations reflecting the theological scene of a century and a half later. Theology is primarily concerned with experience, and with personal relations, relations of the individual with God and between individuals in community.

Beings are constituted through their relationships. God in self-giving gives being to mankind and to the created order, and this being is authentic only as it relates in response to God its creator. But the reality of the world, *coram homine*, is a reality of absence of God and strained relationships, individual and social. It is through grace that wholeness may be restored. Therefore the whole secular consciousness through which we live in society is to grace as the law is to the gospel. Life is to be interpreted through the basic distinction, from Luther, between the law and the gospel. Through faith men and women understand themselves as redeemed through Christ, and live in the world, the same secular world, as those who try to follow in the way of discipleship. It was not for nothing, of course, that Ebeling had been a member of Bonhoeffer's illegal theological college in Finkenwalde.

Ebeling was of course well aware of the traditional objections to theologies of personal relationship and existential encounter, and he introduces important developments. Though he fully endorses Luther's objection to the substantialism associated with St. Thomas, and insists that God is properly experienced as relation, experience is basically related to God through prayer. God is encountered as ultimate reality, not as an abstract being but as the subject of prayer.

Through participation in the Christian tradition of prayer, we come to understand ourselves and our world, to have trust in God, against the appearance of things.

Central to this perspective is Christology, belief in God as the redeemer of the world. In Christ, we see the incarnation of God, the death of God and, through resurrection, the life of God. Central to the life of Jesus of Nazareth is his *exousia*, his indirect power, expressed in his word and his actions. This word, in language and conduct, is an invitation to response in faith, and it is self-authenticating, creating the response for which it calls. Jesus enables us to ask for and to receive forgiveness, and so to dedicate ourselves to God. The greatest sign of his power is not his miracles but his acceptance of powerlessness, at the end in crucifixion. Christology is then reflection upon the contemporary response of the believer to Jesus' *exousia*.

The response of faith in relationship to God is not a purely individual but a corporate response. This is brought out well in the third volume on the Spirit and the Church.

In Ebeling's work all the elements which we have mentioned in earlier pages, the contemporary world in which we find ourselves and where we have to begin, the biblical narratives and the tradition of Christian life and thought in the Church, and the intellectual environment in which we must think out our theological arguments, are brought together in a construction which, though clearly in a particular tradition, makes a contribution to any Christian thinking about God.

Ebeling's theological programme has been trenchantly criticised by George Lindbeck, as an example of the expressivist-experientialist approach to theology which he believes to be inadequate. Lindbeck's own theory has in turn come in for much critical comment, much of which appears to me to be justified.[1] In my view there is a real danger, in the flight from the modern to the post-modern, of failing to appreciate the real gains made by theology in the nineteenth century and in the liberal tradition in the twentieth century. At the same time, a realistic assessment of the failures of the liberal theological tradition is essential if there is to be genuine development. Paradoxically, it appears to have been the intolerance of the liberal tradition, its inability to learn from alternative perspectives, which prevented it from developing as it should. At its worst such openness leads to a fudging of every issue which guarantees that nothing is treated in depth. At its best there may be a cross-fertilisation which produces a new engagement with the subject. In classical theology much of the

---

[1]The course of the debate on George Lindbeck's proposals on the nature of doctrine may be followed e.g. in *Modern Theology*, Jan.1988, in D.Z. Phillips, *Faith after Foundationalism*, and in A.E. McGrath, *The Genesis of Doctrine*.

strength of Augustine and Aquinas derives from such a capacity. For modern writers, I have written elsewhere of John and Donald Baillie as remarkable examples of an ability to combine the liberal and the evangelical, the catholic and the protestant, in a classic reappropriation of the mainstream of Christian thought. In the next chapter we turn to a reconsideration of the basic axioms of an understanding of God in a theology of the love of God.

A quite different, but equally illuminating approach to faith after faith, was made by Karl Barth. Barth's concept of God is based not on the possibility of there being a God but on the Christian tradition of the reality of God as creator, sustainer and saviour of the universe. There is room for neither negative nor positive speculation. God is known only through grace, mediated through his revelation in Jesus Christ. He is not a solitary being with added attributes in relation to creation such as omniscience, omnipotence, etc. He is personal, in the threefold personhood of Father, Son and Holy Spirit.

God is a living God, dependent on nothing, free and self-existent. He is the one who loves in freedom. His attributes or perfections can only be understood as the perfections of the divine love. As perfect love he is for ever constant, faithful, concerned without end or limit. Eternity involves constant involvement in temporality, rather than solitude and immutability. These are paradoxical affirmations, arising out of the nature of the subject, which we just have to live with, while always seeking deeper understanding.

God is being and is personal. He is transcendent and immanent. He is self-giving love and is self-sufficient. He cannot be known through rational theology but his self-revelation can be rationally discussed. We may think here that God's grace may work in, with and under the human response, not instead of transcendent action but as part of it, overcoming human frailty because it is sheer grace. This thought does not alter the substance of the concept of God, but opens up the way to wider searching for rational grounds for faith, as well as to a sympathetic approach to non-Christian reflection on God as the source of creation and salvation.

God is the one who loves in freedom. For Barth, God's being and action are integrally related. Being involves becoming and vice versa, for it is precisely the being of self-giving love. Such a love is self-sufficient, and can produce true freedom in the creatures which it supports, creating uniquely free independent beings (a view stressed also by Karl Rahner). The traditional attributes of God become the perfections of the divine love in freedom. Because the living God has taken death in the death of Jesus into his own being from all eternity, grace is effective beyond evil and death to all eternity.

God's love is merciful and is patient. He is neither one nor three in numerical order, but acts in a unique triune unity. He is omnipresent because he creates space. He is not immutable in an Aristotelian sense but he is constant in his perpetual self-giving. His omnipotence is the power that has triumphed through suffering and death. This is an eschatological victory, and has nothing to do with temporal power. God's omnipotence has nothing to do with contradiction of the laws of thought, nor of the possibilities, negative and positive, which the created universe offers. His power is not self-limited, but he remains weak and in sorrow in the face of evil and disaster in the world. Evil and suffering are not a necessary condition of eschatological peace, but they remain a contingent feature of the temporal order. The resurrection of the crucified one remains the chief clue to a future of eschatological fulfilment

This understanding of divine love in action is formally articulated in the doctrine of God in the early volumes of the *Church Dogmatics*. It is symbolically developed in volume four, in the Christology built on the parable of the prodigal son, of rejection and consummation.

2. Von Balthasar and Jüngel

Two theologians who continue to work at the consequences of God's love as the centre of theology are Hans Urs von Balthasar and Eberhard Jüngel. Balthasar has attempted to understand the whole of reality in the vision of a theological aesthetic.

The facts of revelation are perceived initially in the light of grace, and faith grows in such a way that it allows the self-evidence of these facts to continue to unfold according to its own laws and principles. Christ is the norm of true beauty and true goodness. In the light of faith the whole world is seen to point to the glory of the Lord in the pattern of the hidden Christ. Christ is the centre of the form of revelation. The form is mediated through scripture, Church and sacraments, notably through Mary and through the Johannine Christ. (See *The Glory of the Lord.*)

Where von Balthasar produces a Christocentric theology in which there is subtle complementarity between nature and grace, for Jüngel all natural theology is ruled out from the start. The concept of God follows from the Christian faith itself.

We start from revelation rather than from natural theology. There is a basic analogy for talk of God, but it is an *analogia fidei*. Jesus is God's supreme parable. He constitutes the humanity of God. This humanity of God is unfolded for our understanding in the telling of the story of Jesus. God is the mystery of the world in that he comes through Jesus, and in no other way, as an open secret. The appropriate human response to his coming is in the fruits of faith, hope and love, in which existence is restructured as being in Christ, rather than as having, as living for God rather than for self. This is a theology of God's love. God has defined himself as love on the cross. (*God as the Mystery of the World*, esp. p. 316ff.) In love we are changed from those who have into those who are. Then we can say that God is love. As love he is the mystery of the world.

We may well feel that Jüngel, like von Balthasar, offers an 'inside' view of faith that offers no explanation outside the language of the Christian community. If we who live in a pluriform society wish to enter into the genuine dialogue with those 'outside', sharing and wrestling with their perplexity, something more needs to be done. Jüngel's Christological answer may be central but it is somehow incomplete. How can we see the manifestation of God in Jesus without any prior notion of what God might be like? How is the concept of God in Christianity to be related to concepts of God and of transcendence in other religious and philosophical frameworks? What Jüngel takes as given are precisely the areas in which the problems are most pressing.

To such questions Jüngel would doubtless reply that we must

read his work more carefully. God is in no sense 'necessary' for modern man's self-understanding. Hence the talk of God's death from Hegel to Bonhoeffer. The turn to the thinking self in Descartes' philosophy as a new basis for metaphysics established the certainty of God at the price of positing his 'necessity' in dialogue with methodological doubt. Such a God is finally inconceivable. God can only be conceived in the struggle between being and non-being, between possibility and nothingness. God allows himself to be spoken of through his unity with perishability in Christ, in the story/parable of his humanity, which renews and transforms creation.

Both von Balthasar and Jüngel have succeeded in providing profound meditations on the heart of the Christian gospel. From an Anglo-Saxon perspective it may seem that their strengths are also their weakness, a sophisticated but at the same time unselfconscious vision of the communion of the Christian with God, unclouded by the secularising refraction of the British and American philosophical tradition. Jüngel's appreciation of modern philosophy, brilliant as it is, might turn out on closer inspection to be quite as selective as von Balthasar's, in its synthesising account of a number of quite different developments.

It is possible, clearly, to operate with different sorts of theology to achieve different sorts of explanation. But some attempt at critical dialogue is also called for. It may be that an account of fundamental theology such as that given by Gordon Kaufman in his recent essays, pallid though it appears in relation to the continental Christological concentration, could be related to the concerns of von Balthasar and Jüngel to produce a more comprehensive perspective. Von Balthasar offers a particular model of an intuitive knowledge of God, Jüngel a particular sort of understanding of existence and of historical contingency, Kaufman a particular pattern for a model of moral agency. None will provide the key to all theology. If we forget the vision of God, or God's engagement with historical particularity, or the importance of moral agency, our theology will be impoverished. God is, after all, involved in the history of the created order and in all human history, in general and in particular providence. He is his own unique hidden presence. God is involved in the Judaeo-Christian tradition, in the events concerning Jesus and in the history and influence of the Christian community in society. He uses human beings as the instruments of his love, constantly inviting response. Though God is indeed virtually inconceivable and in no sense 'necessary', yet the tradition of the gospel of Christ can be seen as open at least in principle to grounding in an account of the truth of the way things are. However that may be, von Balthasar and Jüngel certainly remind us forcibly once again of a number of weighty items on our theological agenda.

Jüngel holds that, apart from invocation of the Christological dimension, talk of God is indeed dead in the modern world. However, God's Word in Christ brings God to expression in the world, so that language becomes the all-important vehicle of grace. The incarnation is the basic *Sprachereignis* or language event which provides the basis, the sole and sufficient basis, for the theological enterprise. Indeed since the redemptive word is none other than the creative word, the ability to develop and explore the possibilities of language is central to the being of man made in the divine image. Jüngel's analysis of man *coram Deo* as a speaking, language-using being is ingenious and impressive. It could be criticised in a manner similar to that of Pannenberg's criticism of 'verbalisation of the Gospel' in Barth's theology of the word. But for Jüngel basic speech between man and God, and man and man, is not purely a verbal relationship, since word and act are combined in the essential nature of man.

It is when Jüngel offers an account of the relationship between theological discourse about God and other sorts of ordinary language discourse, whether about God or about anything in the created order, that things become less clear. For Jüngel, the hinge of theological discourse is provided by an *analogia gratiae* between God and man. What is difficult is the spelling out of accounts of the sorts of theological constructions which are and are not fruitful. For it is crystal clear that theology is illuminated by many different sorts of discourse, some of which are compatible with Jüngel's model of *analogia gratiae*, but very many of which are not.

Between Barth and Ebeling there are important similarities.

Both are in an important sense theologies of the Word. What divides them sharply is their different attitude to the significance of the Enlightenment for theology. For Ebeling the Enlightenment is a potential ally. Indeed he has argued that the historico-critical method of the interpretation of scripture corresponds to the *sola fide* of the Reformation faith. For Barth the Enlightenment brought a fateful turn towards a man-centred religion, resulting in the disaster, as he saw it, of nineteenth-century Protestant theology. His work may be seen as a massive attempt to turn theology back on to the right course, a course pursued by St. Paul and the Fathers of Chalcedon, and emphasised at the Reformation in stress on the sovereignty of God.

These issues are absolutely central to theology today. It is not then surprising to find in our second pair of theologians, von Balthasar and Jüngel, similar concerns. We noted that von Balthasar was sharply critical of the results of 'the historico-critical method'. Jüngel offered a brilliant reinterpretation of the history of doctrine, centred on the impasse reached by theology at the Enlightenment, as the key to progress in theology for the future. Others in the school of Barth have followed his lead. In order to assess this issue properly, to determine the best strategy for the construction of a theology for the real needs of the present, we must investigate the conflicting claims about the development of the legacy of the Christian intellectual tradition, and its challenge for the future.

The matter does not end here, however. For there has been a further important recent challenge to theology, which pinpoints precisely the intellectualism of Western Christianity as a reason for the weakness of contemporary theology. I refer to the whole area of Liberation Theology. Jon Sobrino may serve here as representative of many writers. Sobrino is echoed in the Marxist tradition, channelled in many ways, and notably through the Frankfurt school of philosophy. Sobrino has stressed the point, not of course unfamiliar to the classical Christian tradition, that the sources of theology must lie as much in reflection on life as it is lived in Christian community, as in the analysis of concepts in the history of ideas.

In Chapter Three we shall reconsider the sources, norms

and methods of theology in the scriptural Word, the worship
of the Church, as an empirical reality, for better or for worse,
rather than an ideal possibility, and in metatheological critical
perspective. From there we shall develop again the doctrine of
God. First however we turn to the classical Christian tradition
about God, to see what we must conclude about its true nature
and its future prospects.

3. God in Christian Tradition

God has been conceived of in the many religions of mankind
through the ages in countless ways, in polytheistic and
monotheistic forms, in personal and impersonal forms, in
analogies drawn from nature, from animal and human life.
Gods have been imagined with the powers of natural forces, as
local or universal creators, as protective powers who distribute
justice in more or less regular ways.

The Christian understanding of God was shaped decisively
by the Old Testament tradition, which itself developed in
interaction with various ancient Near Eastern concepts of
deity. The Old Testament tradition remained important for
the later Christian tradition, notably for the patristic period. In
the Old Testament God is understood through a great variety
of imagery. The central strand of this material is a conception
of God as the creator and sustainer of his creation. He acts in
providence. He is always with his chosen people, guiding them
in prosperity and adversity.

In the New Testament there is also a wide variety of reflection
upon God's nature. The Christian tradition saw here above all
a basis for the understanding of God's nature as love. This is the
story of God's self-giving in the sacrifice of his son, and of Jesus'
self-giving to God and mankind. God is identified with his
creature, man, through his presence in Jesus. God suffers,
shares in life and death, shares in Jesus' lot, somehow even
takes death overcome into his own nature as God. The question
of the identity of Jesus becomes central to the question of the
identity of God. Jesus of Nazareth, a man devoted to God whom
he understands as his father, and to his fellow man in thought
and action, becomes the decisive clue to the concept of God in

Christian perspective. The New Testament concentrates on the public ministry of Jesus and his teaching about God's Kingdom, on the Pauline reflection on his life, death and resurrection, and the Johannine reflection on Christ and discipleship.

In Christian reflection since New Testament times these biblical strands of God as creator and sustainer, father, subject of complete personal trust, redeemer and reconciler, have been developed in countless ways, in corporate and individual devotion, in theology and literature, in art, music and in practically every area of human endeavour.

For Justin Martyr, writing in the second century AD and echoing Philo of Alexandria's philosophical reinterpretation of the Old Testament, God is the creator of the universe, eternal and unchangeable, all-powerful and invisible. He has revealed fragments of his truth to all people, including the people of Israel, before finally revealing himself through his son Jesus Christ the logos, the light, the eternal reason. The relation of Christ the logos to God the Father then became the subject of endless discussion.

For the greatest of the Greek theologians, Origen, God is spirit, entirely without a body. Here as often elsewhere, Plato's legacy combines with biblical imagery. God is the one, the perfect incorporeal reality, the divine simplicity, the one over against the many. He lacks nothing. He is the highest good. He has always been the father and the creator. He has brought about the creation from nothing, out of his good pleasure. He is a perfectly simple intellectual existence. (*De Principiis*, i.1, cf. *Contra Celsum*.62-64).

The Fathers developed their understanding of God in controversy with various sorts of alternatives, provided by Gnostic, Stoic, Manichaean and other thinkers, and especially through Neoplatonism, which stressed the unknowability of God, a concept which had advantages and disadvantages for Christians. Discussion of Creator, Christ, Spirit were interrelated in the search for a deeper understanding of the Christian God. Augustine, representing in many ways the highest point of patristic thought, combines profound personal devotion with a strongly Platonic stress on the mysterious nature of the

creator (cf. *Confessions* 1.4.4, where God is addressed as
secretissime et praesentissime). Unlike some of the Fathers,
Augustine is always concerned with man and with human
psychology. But this is man in a God-centred universe, a rather
different perspective from modern anthropocentric theology.
'A te petatur, in te quaeretur, ad te pulsetur; sic accipietur, sic
invenietur, sic aperietur.' (*Confessions*, 10, 30; 13, 28).

4. God in the Middle Ages

When medieval scholars wrote about God they did so in
conscious continuity with a long tradition, stretching through
the Fathers to the Bible. Their knowledge of individual patristic
texts depended on the uncertainties of availability and
manuscript accuracy. Yet they were steeped in and committed
to the central themes of this classical Christian tradition. In the
West, this meant the tradition shaped and moulded by
Augustine. In both East and West the patristic exploration of
the relationship of the gospel to Plato and Aristotle was further
exploited in depth for a thousand years. Augustine's influence
both on technical discussion of concepts of God and on
religiously attractive images of God was enormous. The
Confessions stamped the whole eastern discussion at the latter
level, and the *City of God*, the work on the Trinity and the anti-
Pelagian writings especially at the former level. In his concept
of God the Neoplatonic emphasis on unchangeability and
complete transcendence was tempered by the equally Platonic
insistence that God the transcendent one was at the same time
the ground of ultimate reality in the temporal order. Though
he placed an important doctrinal emphasis on Christology and
on the Trinity as a community of loving persons, he did not
explicitly relate the notion of self-love to the formal character
of his God-concept. This somewhat austere formal
understanding of God was emphasised further by Boethius, for
whom Aristotle was a significant influence. For Boethius too
there was an important connection between theory and practice
in religion and it may well have been precisely awareness of this
connection which drove him to strive after the greatest possible
formal precision.

After Boethius the next really significant turn in development came with Anselm, though the intense debate between realist and nominalist doctrines of the eucharist prepared much of the ground for the new theology. Augustine and Plato are again crucial. Contrary to some recent interpretations, it is clear that Anselm expected to be able to prove the existence of God. Anselm stressed the unity of the divine attributes, in opposition to any suggestion that God's will could be treated independently of the rest of the doctrine of God.

With Gilbert of Poirée the Boethian influence was uppermost, in a stress on God's formal character as being itself. This formal Platonic approach was taken further in a Neoplatonic dimension in the school of Chartres, notably in the free speculative thought of Thierry. God was to become the perfect form of all creaturely being. Pantheism was now a danger, clearly recognised in the critique of Robert of Melun. One way of coping with this problem was to be found in the doctrine of analogy. The analogies between God and man are analogies of names and not of being. God is not the greatest of the beings or even the ground of being, but the creator of being, which he creates *ex nihilo* at his own pleasure. Creation is not necessary for God.

The most distinguished medieval thinker was of course St. Thomas Aquinas. Building on the work on Aristotle of Albert the Great, Thomas denied the basic Platonic thesis that man has a natural spiritual intuitive knowledge of God's nature. For Thomas, all knowledge of God comes through empirical deduction from the created order. Some of this process is possible only by revelation, enshrined within the created order by the Bible, the creeds and the authority of the church. Other aspects of knowledge are the product of rational critical reflection.

In the work of John Duns Scotus the Augustinian concentration on God's will, especially against Pelagius, again comes to the fore. Confidence in reason as a way to knowledge of God wanes. We simply must learn to obey God's will. Duns' work was carried forward in a creative and original manner by William of Occam, for whom the entire rational framework has now become suspect. We can say nothing of the divine attributes:

we can only obey his will. God is infinitely transcendent. Against this infinite qualitative distance came an Augustinian reaction in the writings of Thomas Bradwardine. Again, Duns thought of God as a being, a wholly other transcendent being. However, for Meister Eckhart God was not a being but pure thought. This line was carried forward by Nicolas of Cues. God is the explanation or ground of meaning, in which the many become the one, and through which in turn the one may be understood, through *coincidentia oppositorum*. Here is another aspect of the famous Neoplatonic dialectic, which runs such a varied and creative course through theology from Augustine to Barth, and which achieves a particular brilliance in the law/gospel contrast of perhaps the most creative heir of the nominalist tradition, Martin Luther.

In the East, though there were translations of Augustine, the writing of Pseudo-Dionysius was the key factor. Again however the extreme mystical transcendence of the Neoplatonic tradition was to be tempered by other considerations, notably from the discussion of Christology, and Trinity, in the work of John of Damascus. The pure mystical strain was to surface more clearly in Gregory Palamas and the Heysychasts. Here again, notably in Nicholas Cabasilas, the eucharist contributes importantly, as part of the liturgical tradition, to the development of the concept of God. Perhaps the greatest contribution of the medievals to the concept of God was in the careful working out of the scope and limitations of analogy. Analogy could work at different levels.

God was the creator *ex nihilo,* greater than our thoughts of him. Yet we know, by revelation and by understanding ourselves as being made in his image, that personal analogies are not entirely inappropriate, if used carefully, to talk of God. But God remains the primary analogans, whether as pure thought, the ground of being or the perfect will who is the source of our will to respond to him in work and thought.

5. Reformation and Enlightenment

The Reformers, indeed all sixteenth-century theologians, were steeped in the work of Augustine. It is no surprise to discover that Luther's thinking about God was much concerned with the dialectic between the hiddenness and the revelation of God, between God in his awesome, inaccessible majesty, and God in his tender love for his creatures through Jesus Christ. Luther wrestles with the paradox that here is one and the same God, whom he could describe as a glowing oven full of love. God's revelation is made through faith, faith alone in Jesus Christ. Faith is itself God's gift. We are justified, brought into a loving relationship with God, by faith alone. But God is also hidden. There are two aspects of hiddenness, stressed in different ways at different times. God is hidden in that he is above all creaturely understanding as such. He is also hidden in that though he is openly and publicly revealed in Jesus Christ, yet we cannot see without grace. He is hidden in his revealedness, centrally on the cross. That is where we must come to recognise him. To be God is to be God on the cross. No one can recognise God in his majesty and glory until he has recognised him in the weakness and humiliation of his cross.

This profound but paradoxical insight of Luther was carried on by Melanchthon in the Lutheran tradition, and so into German theology, philosophy, literature, art and music for centuries to come. It was also carried on, as Brian Gerrish has recently emphasised, through the Reformed tradition from Luther through Calvin and Schleiermacher. To know God is to know God not simply as creator but precisely as redeemer. Knowledge of God is of God in cross and resurrection, through faith. This is theism without deism, trust rather than demonstration. It is a strength when rational arguments for a natural theology are under pressure, but it can also lead, as in John Paul, J.G. Hamman and Nietzsche, when the resurrection perspective is overshadowed by the cross, to a conviction that God is dead.

For Calvin and the orthodox theology of the seventeenth century the mighty acts of God in history, and the conviction of divine sovereignty, provided grounds for confidence. The beginnings of a new development in philosophy associated with Descartes, grounding certainty on personal existence, and the philosophies of Locke, Hobbes, Leibnitz and Berkeley, totally diverse though they were, appeared at first to offer theology a new rational grounding. Natural theology provided a scientific basis for what was known to faith through revelation. But as in the case of St. Thomas' magnificent synthesis, the shattering of confidence produced a deeper crisis than before. In the seventeenth and eighteenth centuries natural theologies, deistic concepts of God, were prominent. It was thought that the working of God could be deduced from observation of the natural world, if not easily at least with a modicum of faith in the Church's tradition. All things work together for good. Some such correlation rapidly came to be regarded as part of the minimum requirement for a reasonable faith. It was in any case available.

Against such presumptions and expectations the minus side, as it were, of the new philosophical impulse for faith came to be seen as having disastrous consequences, pulling down not only moderate rational theology but the whole intertwined edifice of revelation with it in its fall. Once the nominalists coming after St. Thomas could turn to obedience to the divine will revealed in scripture and tradition. Now Bible and Church alike were at the same time being shown by the philosophers' colleagues in the field of historical research to be the product of centuries of remarkably haphazard accretion of traditions, traditions of highly doubtful veracity.

We may begin to understand the reason for the analysis common to the Barth, Jüngel, von Balthasar tradition that the Enlightenment was the great disaster, the time when man, notably Descartes, turned from understanding God as the ground of his being to himself as the ground of his self-understanding. We can also understand the opposite position of Ebeling who believes that since we are justified by faith alone, we may and indeed must take the risk of exposing God's truth to every possible critical procedure, confident that we shall reach a deeper understanding of that truth. Truth, and seeking the truth, makes us free, free from the shackles of a misplaced and ultimately sceptical traditionalism, the classic form of bad faith.

Those who follow either of the above alternatives have their own interpretation of the Enlightenment, and the nineteenth-century theology to which it gave rise serves as a paradigm of its consequences, good or bad, according to prior judgement. Was nineteenth-century theology essentially a triumph of the Holy Spirit, of the freedom of the children of God from the dogmatic prejudice of the past? Was it a return to a man-centred religion, in which the objective perspective on God's creation was lost, deliberately ignored? We cannot even dismiss these theologies as a purely Protestant phenomenon, for they are now widely influential in Catholic and other theologians.

Most would allow that it involved elements of both, and other things as well. I would however want to go much further than this, and claim that the development of modern theology involved many inherently diverse developments, which cannot usefully be brought into any sort of umbrella concept. It is, indeed, of the nature of the revolution in knowledge in the modern world that it has not moved in step-by-step logical developments.

This revolution has had good and bad results for mankind. But these results are not directly correlated to the question of the way in which we have come to our present world. Because we cannot share the bold simplicity of the continental theologians we shall not be able to take up their prescriptions for a new basis for faith after faith, grounds for trust. That does not mean however that we may not learn many things from them, positively and negatively.

We have already acknowledged the need for theology to take firm cognisance of the community and society in which it is to be articulated, in response to criticism of the intellectualism of the European post-Enlightenment tradition. In fairness to that tradition it may be allowed however that the contemporary theologies of the Word are centrally concerned not just with words and concepts but with the Word incarnate in human history, and there is at least one theology of history which is at once penetrating and comprehensive in the work of Pannenberg.

I come back to the development of concepts of God in the modern era. Descartes' development of a theory of knowledge based on awareness of the self was indeed a critical step. But the type of empiricism which it stimulated was very different from the speculation of the school of Leibnitz and his successors, on

whose natural theology deism was largely dependent. Kant is
sometimes held to have overcome the dichotomy between
empiricism and rationalism, but this is itself something of an
idealist interpretation. From Kant philosophy – and theology
– could proceed in various directions. Though Kant learned
from and adapted ideas from Hume, Hume's thought provided
grounds for much more direct confrontation with theology
than Kant had done.

Schleiermacher we noted was one who played a pivotal role
in the response of theology to the modern world. His concept
of God was to be based primarily on religious experience. This
concept was soon perceived to raise great difficulties –
experience is always susceptible to self-deception, individual
and collective. Yet his overall contribution, a theology based
firmly on trust in Christ the redeemer, but entirely open to
critical dialogue with modern scholarship in every relevant
field, was an important step forward. Though the philosophical
genius of Hegel made possible interpretations which
incorporated again all the richness of the tradition, notably the
classical trinitarian doctrine, Schleiermacher had opened up
the subject.

I have long considered that though the Enlightenment
made legitimate demands on theology for explanations, it
should not be regarded as rewriting the agenda for theology.
That remains the articulation of the gospel of the life, death
and resurrection of Jesus Christ as the revelation of God's
salvation. That is why I have spent some time on the medieval
period. Here we see a similar proliferation of new impulses, but
no grounds for a new gospel. The difference with the modern
period is that here the concept of God comes into question in
a much more final way.

Hegel is often seen as the father of modern speculative
philosophy of religion, e.g. in the work of Tillich, Troeltsch
and Process thought. More recently his influence on the
school of Barth has been recognised. It is worth pausing to
reflect that the incisive critique of the Enlightenment's influence
in theology by a scholar of the considerable stature of Eberhard
Jüngel is itself a distinguished product of precisely that tradition.
Of course Jüngel develops the tradition against itself, as

Kierkegaard criticised Hegel, with important substantial results. My point is that Olympian detachment is simply not possible in theology. What then is to be done? We must accept the consequences of the cultural relativity of our thinking, learning from modern sociology of knowledge. But that is clearly not enough. Cultural relativity is not cultural relativism. We are in no way absolved from the need to continue to press forward to specific choices and specific substantial proposals about the Christian understanding of God. Precisely because the context of God in Christian perspective is the context of God as creator and redeemer of all mankind, past, present and future, we are committed to try, however cautioned by and mindful of the development of analytical philosophy, to produce constructive reconstruction of Christian doctrine in the light of Christian faith. Nowhere is this task more urgent than in the doctrine of God.

4

Revelation as Love

1. The God Who Loves

God in the Christian tradition, though sometimes defined as the absolute or the ground of being, is often characterised as being in his essential nature love. Love is not just one of God's attributes, such as power, wisdom and holiness. It is the central characteristic of God in himself and in relation to the created order. The grounds for this affirmation lie in reflection throughout the Christian tradition that the biblical teaching about God is a narrative best understood as a witness to love. Love is a notion which enables us to deepen our appreciation of the divine nature as it is in itself. Here I should like to explore further consequences of this affirmation for the nature of the understanding of God.

We may recall the narrative dimension of Christian theology.[1] God in the Old Testament, conceived of in a variety of ways, remains always the sustainer of creation, looking after his people. All our human experience helps us to recognise the character of God's concern. The reference to God as creator suggests dimensions in God which go beyond our own experience. The basis of Christian understanding of God's love has been an interpretation of the New Testament in terms of God's self-giving in the sacrifice of his son, and in Jesus' self-giving to God and mankind. God is identified with his creation

---

[1]Cf. George Stroup, *The Promise of Narrative Theology*, cf. too Newlands, art. 'Love' in *Dictionary of Pastoral Theology* (SPCK).

through his presence in Jesus Christ, suffering, sharing in life
and death, bringing life and reconciliation out of death and
disaster.

Jesus of Nazareth identified himself through his actions and
teaching with the lives of people around him. His love for his
fellow-men was expressed in specific teaching about the nature
of God and his relation to mankind. It was expressed in
concern for particular individuals, with a distinct bias towards
the poor and the disadvantaged. It brought him into conflict
with the religious and political authorities of the day. He was
crucified. Central to classical Christianity is the affirmation
that death, identification in suffering, was not God's last word.
Through the resurrection of Christ God's love has in a profound
and mysterious way overcome evil. Nothing can now separate
us from God's love.

The understanding of God as love, of God's purpose for the
created order as leading to fulfilment in love, has sweeping
implications for individual and social ethics, and for the life of
the Christian community, the Church. Love is to be the
informing principle, not just in special cases but in all human
social life. Here is the perennial relevance of an impossible
ideal.

Christian reflection on love has developed over the centuries
in dialogue with ancient Greece. The spiritualisation of love,
with its attendant advantages and disadvantages, reached a
climax in the Neoplatonic ideal of the highest love as a purely
spiritual contemplation of a perfectly incorporeal God. This
tradition had a deep influence on Christianity, notably in
emphasising ascetic and monastic love of God at the expense
of love between the sexes.

Christianity is concerned for loving relationships between
people at every level. As a religion of incarnation it resists
devaluation of the material world in favour of ideas. Love
between persons is often expressed appropriately in sexual
terms. Love for society means feeding the hungry with real
food rather than benevolent sentiment. Yet Christianity
also has a true spiritual dimension and does not regard
perfect union as always quasi-substantial physicality. Love
includes allowing the other space, letting be, encouraging

independence. The clue remains the self-giving love of God in Jesus Christ.

What are the basic implications of this concentration on God's love for theological method? Focus on God's love is a necessary but not a sufficient condition, in my view, for an adequate approach to Christian theology. It will not guarantee success, but it ought to point in the right direction. Though God's love as a reality in itself is the centre, there is no single corresponding theological method, offering an authorised single theological epistemology. However, we are emphatically not then left with a framework of philosophical positivism which simply lets us say nothing about God. That is a perfectly safe theological method, but in practice it proves to be perfectly useless for constructive theology. This is a point which cannot be emphasised too often, for it has brought paralysis and sterility to much recent theology. God's love remains the underlying reality for Christian faith. It can be reflected upon through the traditional framework of the interaction of reason, revelation and experience. In all of these spheres considerable progress in understanding continues to be made, not so much by slogans as by careful scholarly analysis. The dynamic which brings such procedures to exciting fruition is not the methods in themselves but the hidden love of God which is there to be appreciated in every generation.

2. Critical Reflections

Doctrinal criticism, properly deployed, is a thoroughly positive and constructive procedure. The last twenty years have seen a considerable interest in systematic theology, and an appraisal of Christian doctrine which has sought to be at the same time critical and constructive. In Britain the influence of linguistic philosophy has contributed to a distrust of general theories and grand systems of doctrine. The approach is more often one of building up a cumulative rational case on the basis of analysis of the various components of a given doctrinal affirmation. Realisation that 'metaphysics' may not always be a bad thing has been coupled with caution. On the Continent there was from at least the time of Albrecht Ritschl a parallel attack on metaphysics. This has in no way deterred scholars in all ecclesiastical denominations from producing comprehensive doctrinal systems, often with the metaphysical structure implicit and so, often, unexamined. Genuine dialogue between British and continental scholars is limited, though there are some signs of hope.

A good example of this cross-fertilisation of methods without abandoning critical rigour is to be found in David Tracy's *The Analogical Imagination*. Tracy considered doctrine under the image of the classic, a work of art or an event in which persons express themselves in a manner which has universal significance. The classic provokes new insights and leads to decisions. The Christian classic is God's self-manifestation in Jesus Christ. Through reflection on the pluralism of approaches to the events concerning Jesus we may reach a different understanding of the divine presence in the world. Tracy's work provides support for the suggestion that doctrinal criticism is important both for its own sake, and for its place in the continuing human search for a deeper understanding of God's salvation. Doctrinal criticism may lead to doctrinal construction, which in turn will provoke further questioning of previous assumptions.

Our understanding of this critical function will depend on what we mean by doctrine. In the New Testament dogma can refer to a decree, or to the Old Testament law. If we were to regard this as normative for our understanding, we should already be taking a doctrinal decision, which would in turn be a proper subject for doctrinal criticism, in order to produce the best available rational basic for our doctrinal choices.

Doctrine overlaps with faith, information, worship, the philosophy of religion, apologetics, personal faith, historical tradition. But it coincides with none of these. We may perhaps regard it as the formulation with the maximum possible precision, of the significance of the Christian gospel. Its sources lie in the Bible and in the tradition of the Church, in personal faith, in the contemporary Christian community, and in the development of reason through the experience of and reflection upon modern society. Understanding of God is always a gift of God. Yet it is human doctrine, with all its provisionality and possibility of error. As the study of human response to the gospel, it is something which Christianity cannot do without.

3. Analogy and the Range of Language

Theology which is critical and constructive at the same time is already flourishing in various parts of the world and even in Britain. One need only recall some of the more imaginative writers of the last twenty years to realise that a great deal of theology is being produced and that attempts to regulate what may or may not be done have been quite unsuccessful. In the work of such scholars as James Barr, Don Cupitt, John Hick, and John Macquarrie we have a remarkable diversity of constructive theologies, written not in isolation from each other but in imaginative and independent construction. It would be hard to find agreement between these writers on a particular theological method. Yet all of them have illuminated aspects of the reality of God in Christian perspective in striking ways.

It need not surprise us to be constantly made aware of the variety of approaches to theology. God is not part of his creation, an object in the world of objects. This has absolutely fundamental consequences for our procedures. I return to one basic strand, perhaps the basic strand, of theological procedure, the way in which we use words with reference to God. We have seen that Jüngel seeks to avoid 'natural theology' where Balthasar wishes to employ both natural theology and Christology in complementarity. This debate about natural theology centred on the question of the use of analogy in theology, a matter much discussed in continental theology since Barth's notorious comments that he would be a Roman Catholic were it not for *analogia entis*. Without offering a whole chapter on analogy, I should like to stress the importance in my view of the fact that theologians can and do use analogies in different ways in theology, and need not feel bound to a single usage.

Let me recall some traditional distinctions. In an analogy of proper proportionality, it is held that a word in one conceptual framework plays a role that is syntactically identical with the role played by an analogous word in another framework. For example, the word 'exists' plays an analogous role in quite different conceptual frameworks in such cases as the Prime Minister exists in Downing Street, and Hamlet exists in *Hamlet*. Further up the scale, the three persons of the Trinity exist in mutual interpenetration and subsistence, we may say. The differences between the conceptual framework of this and the other examples is now much greater, since the transcendent sphere of operation is unique. We cannot show how the persons of the Trinity exist. We are claiming, rather, that the expressions can be used in a syntactically identical way. It may be objected that we are saying no more than that the Prime Minister is Prime Minister-like and Hamlet is Hamlet-like as the Trinity is Trinity-like. This tells us nothing.

In an analogy of attribution it is held that a word or expression in a particular conceptual framework is implicitly defined in terms of another expression within the same conceptual framework. The frameworks are judged to be the same on the basis of say a causal relationship between the two subjects. Now if we speak of intrinsic attribution we hold that an analogical relationship holds between two words or expressions in the language we use to make the claim. In the somewhat inelegant scholastic standard example, urine is defined as healthy on the basis of an underlying causal relationship to the 'health' of the person concerned. Things in the world can be seen by God to be good, on the basis of their relation to his own goodness, on the basis of his creative intentions.

It's not so easy to move from our language to God, however. Not everything in our world may be appropriately attributed to God: we would probably not want to way that he is perfectly boring, arrogant and corrupt, though we would want to claim that he is perfectly loving and just. For talk of God we need an analogy of extrinsic attribution. When we say that in our language the 'goodness' of the world is related to the goodness of God by the analogy of extrinsic attribution we claim that there occur in God's language proper expressions of the perfections of the world, and that these perfections are defined implicitly in terms of God's perfection, based on a causal relationship in terms of God's perfection. What is happening here is that the analogies of proper proportionality and attribution are combined. To say that two expressions in one conceptual framework are related by analogy of extrinsic attribution is to say that their analogies in another conceptual framework are related by the analogy of intrinsic attribution. In the above example, a corollary is that we deny that goodness means for God the same as it means for us. We claim only an analogy.

Victor Preller, in discussing analogy along these lines,[2] suggested that whenever Thomas Aquinas uses the analogy of intrinsic attribution he is speaking hypothetically from God's point of view. At these moments he is being most radically a theologian. When he uses the language of intrinsic attribution he is stressing the limitations of our knowledge of reality. And when he speaks in the language of proper proportionality he is emphasising that we do not have access to the language of God. This is in sharp contrast to the tendency to unite everything into a single doctrine, corresponding to proper proportionality, which is a result of Cajetan's confusion of proper proportionality and intrinsic attribution. The doctrine of analogy is not then a means of knowing God but an analysis of the words we use to name God. There is an analogy of being from God's side, but our proofs for the existence of God are our way of confessing our ignorance of its true nature.

4. Theological Method

The role of analogy is a central axis in any consideration of theological method. Though there are important differences in culture which in turn affect theology profoundly, there are also important similarities in the development of Christian theology at different periods.

I have suggested that reflection on theological method acts like Warfarin on the imagination of theologians. Sometimes it is good for them, reducing pressure on the overheated dogmatic

---

[2] V. Preller, *Divine Science and the Science of God.*

consciousness. Often it is noxious. It thins their notions of the substantive content of theology so far that they lose their grasp of distinctions between form and content, confusing programmes with results. It leads to discovery of the perfect method, after which they are incapable of producing anything. Perfectly safe from criticism, they become perfectly useless. This is the special fate of those mesmerised by the baleful glare of logical positivism. It leads also to a new post-liberal intolerance, a view of correct thought saved by egoism from realisation of its own eccentricity. Conscious reflection on theological method theology owes largely to Schleiermacher. Yet Schleiermacher is not to be blamed for what others have done with his work. Indeed his best interpreters provide striking examples of a theological praxis which is at once professional and profound – a good example is Brian Gerrish's superb short study of Schleiermacher. [3]

There are significant lacunae in Schleiermacher's vision, indicated for example by Barth's theology of the Word, by Rahner's ecclesiology, by Liberation Theology's struggle for social justice. There is also much of enduring merit. Theology in this tradition is not an esoteric craft designed for obscure technicians with ink-stained fingers but for all thoughtful Christians. Christian life is expressed equally in worship, action and in thought.

Why Schleiermacher? He is one of a handful of great theologians, an eminently practical theologian, and a theologian firmly in the Reformation tradition. He is the father of modern hermeneutics. The contrast between feeling and intellect, issuing from his Moravian years, is charmingly focused on the Christmas dialogue. Genuine theological reflection takes place within a life of spontaneous piety, in the network of human relationships. Schleiermacher was a liberal evangelical.

Christ is the centre of Christianity. But the accumulated debris of tradition is not to be venerated unthinkingly. Doctrinal criticism is an urgent task. What do we actually know about

---

[3] B.A. Gerrish, *Schleiermacher, a Prince of the Church.*

Christ? History brings questions as well as answers. Faith is to
be grounded on the consciousness of God's presence in Christ
in the present. The basis lies in inward rather than external
grounds: interiority is decisive. How does God act, and what is
meant by the sense of God? God does not intervene in specific
events, for all action already has its source in him. Awareness
of God as God is open to all, and is mediated for Christians
through Christ. Religion and community, God and Christ are
inextricably linked. Schleiermacher is a church theologian, a
prince of the Church.

Schleiermacher, like all thinkers, had his limitations. He
does not provide the answer to the problems of theology a
hundred and fifty years after his time. As one of the giants of
the Christian tradition he is neither to be copied slavishly nor
to be wilfully misunderstood, but to be listened to within the
communion of the saints.

5. Christian Identity

That the tradition of Schleiermacher is at least potentially as
fruitful as the tradition of St. Thomas for stimulating fundamental
reflection on the basis of Christian though about God is clearly
seen in the seminal study of the sources of theology, *The Identity
of Christianity*, by Stephen Sykes. What is the essence of
Christianity? Sykes' first concern is with the Identity and Conflict
in Christianity, the Tradition of Inwardness, and Power in the
Church. From the earliest times Christian communities
developed in different ways. Christians differed about the true
identity of the faith, its intellectual formulation, and the life and
worship which it ought to promote. This was inevitable, for the
core of the faith was of an inward and personal nature. It was
indeed impossible to be certain of Jesus' own thoughts and
motivations, and especially of the relationship to God around
which his life revolved. Jesus was recognised as the source of
authority and power. But the sociology of power, in the early
communities as in today's communities, was complex, and its
manifestations not always edifying.

How then is the internal conflict about the identity of
Christianity to be resolved? There is here a careful and rigorous

analysis of debate and research about the centre of the gospel
in important nineteenth- and twentieth-century theologians.
Schleiermacher's investigation of the essence of Christianity is
compared with Newman's analysis of the Idea of Christianity.
This is followed by a study of the crucial issues of the debate
between Loisy and Harnack. Deeper dimensions of research
are included by Troeltsch, with his awareness of the complexity
of the epistemological problems raised, not least through the
presence of cultural relativity. Then against much of the
prevailing wisdom Barth raised the famous challenge of his
theology of the Word.

Sykes concluded that there is something odd about the
definitions of the essence of Christianity being left to the most
powerful theologian of the day. Systematic theology is necessary,
vitally necessary, but not sufficient. The choices to be made
among concepts which are essentially contested concepts
should be guided through the corporate worship of the Church.

> The constant rehearsal, therefore, of what in a previous
> chapter I called the formal definition of Christianity (the
> deeds of Jesus, set in the context provided by creation
> beliefs and eschatology) is the natural substance of the
> rituals of worship. So too is the bodily enactment of the
> sacrificial self-dedication of Christ at the last supper with his
> disciples 'on the night in which he was betrayed' by one of
> them. (281)

Only within this context can creative doctrinal conflicts be
entered. Such conflict is not an end in itself, but a means of
drawing all things into a unity with Christ. The basis of the unity
is not a generalisation to which none can decently object, but
Christ himself.

Unity is to be sought in deeper understanding, sometimes
through conflict, never in shallow compromise. It might be
thought that for Christians peace is a more central word than
conflict. But Sykes is wary of a peace which is the peace of
convenience rather than the peace of God. It might also be
thought that the social dimensions of worship in relation to
other human activity, notably bias to the poor, need to come
more explicitly to expression. It is too easy to be at ease in Zion

when all around suffer deprivation. For Sykes this dimension of identity also arises out of the sphere of worship, in which we seek first the Kingdom of God. Not any sort of worship will do: we are referred back constantly to the deeds of Jesus, done on the plane of public history.

Christian theologians, we may reflect, are committed to the belief that Christ is the way, the truth and the life. The gospel is itself an invitation to be open to all criteria of public truth, to all assistance from the development of modern thought. This does not mean that they will attempt only to construct the most logically coherent doctrine of God from a strictly empirical point of view. They are committed to think out the implications of faith in the tradition of the gospel, the tradition, evangelical and catholic, of the Christian community. Faith in the truth of the gospel encourages exposure to critical discussion in the search for a deeper Christian understanding.

6. The Biblical Stream

Something more should be said here about the role of the Bible in the Christian understanding of God.[4] For convenience I want to divide recent discussions of the problem into two groups of writers. In the first group may be placed these who still see the Bible as an autonomous, or practically autonomous, centre of authority for Christian theology. These include conservative evangelical and neo-orthodox theologians and their latter-day descendants. They would include John Stott and James Barr, William Abraham, Brevard Childs, Peter Stuhlmacher and Paul Ricoeur. The second group would include more modernist scholars, e.g. David Kelsey and

---

[4] G.M. Newlands, *Hilary of Poitiers*, 166ff., *Theology of the Love of God*. Problems of text and interpretation are usefully discussed by Werner Jeanrond in *Text and Interpretation as Categories of Theological Thinking*. There is a good analysis of the Ricoeur's critique of the debate between Habermas and Gadamer.

Cf. too Hans Frei, *The Eclipse of Biblical Narrative*, and the voluminous discussion of this, esp. Garrett Green (ed.) *Scriptural Authority and Narrative Interpretation*. Also David C. Greenwood, *Structuralism and the Biblical Text*.

Edward Farley. A sub-group of the first would be the theologians of hope and promise, and the liberation theologians, though they also have some affinity with the second.

It is not always easy to see exactly what James Barr considers to be the constructive role of the Bible in theology, but he does regard the role of the biblical material as central. For Barr, if authority lies in a line of tradition, the main balance of this authority is in the Bible, at the beginning of the line, like the head of a comet (and we may hope that its substance turns out to be more useful than fragments of frozen ice). Barr is aware of the problems raised for talk of God by analytical philosophy, and so is wary of any sort of generalised concept of totality.

More classically Protestant and Reformed is Paul Ricoeur, for whom the action of the Word of God can be recovered by a new form of hermeneutics which owes much to Gadamer. 'Jesus Christ himself, exegesis and exegete of Scripture, is manifested as logos in opening the understanding of the Scriptures.'[5]

Death and resurrection receive a new interpretation through the exegesis of human existence. The 'hermeneutical circle' is already there, between the meaning of Christ and the meaning of existence which mutually decipher each other. We are the hearers who listen to the witnesses: *fides ex auditu.* This is not how it is but how it ought to be. As Mudge says in his introduction, we are deaf to the word today. Why? The root of the problem, for Ricoeur, lies in the general lack of sensitivity to symbolic language in modern western civilisation. The answer lies in a new Hermeneutics of Testimony, which should be based not on a philosophy of absolute truth but on faith in the resurrection of Christ.

This does indeed point to a key issue, if not the key issue. Our fathers in the faith preached sermons, expecting the Word of God to be effective. The congregation had the same expectations, and the word was a living, vibrant, effective word.

---

[5] P. Ricoeur, *Essays in Biblical Interpretation*, ed. L.S. Mudge, 52; cf. P. Stuhlmacher, *Historical Criticism and the Theological Interpretation of Scripture.*

Now we tend all to be dulled by the dead hand of Enlightenment and nothing ever happens.

In a similar situation Peter Stuhlmacher called for a 'hermeneutics of consent'. This is an attempt to find a *via media* between fundamentalism and an excess of historico-critical positivism. 'When we consciously begin from the basic principle of consent and hearing, we remain open to the church's experience that the biblical texts disclose a truth which awakens faith and does not lie within the scope of human possibility' (88). This openness is defined as 'openness to an encounter with the truth of God coming to us out of transcendence'. But suppose we are open, we consent, and then nothing happens. The proposal begins perhaps to seem a little like Schleiermacher's principle of the feeling of absolute dependence – it may have no specific content.

Between these lie the theologies of hope, promise, revolution and liberation. I mentioned Moltmann. Here the biblical concepts are part of the given, and they must then be applied to practice. For example, 'He hath put down the mighty from their seat, and hath exalted the humble and meek'. In general it would seem that Third World theology shares with continental theology confidence in biblical language as the starting point which is lacking in modern British and American theology, where philosophical analysis of concepts is a more common starting point.

In the second category of interpretation the basic suggestion is that though the Bible is important, the role of the Christian community, through the thought of its scholars and the life of its members (not mutually exclusive categories) shapes the biblical material in order to guide its life, believing and hoping that this process of interaction of text and context happens under the guidance of God and the influence of the Holy Spirit. So David Kelsey .[6]

'The results of exegesis of biblical texts taken as scripture are relevant but not ultimately decisive. They are themselves shaped

---

[6]D. Kelsey, *The Uses of Scripture in Recent Theology*, 201, 167f.

by a prior imaginative theological characterisation of theology's discrimen...'

Kelsey affirmed (*JAAR* 48/3. 1980: 385ff.) that biblical writings are scripture, and so normative, when and in so far as they function in the common life and thereby author new identities and, for that reason and on that basis, also function to authorise theological proposals. This is its *de facto* authority. He says of scripture (394), 'Its authority consists in its functioning to "author" or to shape decisively communal and individual identities.'

Kelsey's position is reaffirmed by the American scholar Edward Farley, in a joint essay with Peter C. Hodgson on 'Scripture and Tradition'. 'Like Kelsey we must speak of God "shaping", transforming, occasioning, making use of scripture and tradition.'[7] The thought then is that certain basic biblical themes influence Christian thought and action. This is a more conservative position than that of e.g. Denis Nineham, who loves to say that there are no norms and criteria of any sort for theology, and that the Church must make up the rules within its own tradition as it goes along, as indeed it has always done. One problem here is that the person outside that tradition may want to know why he or she should enter it in the first place, and on what grounds the tradition itself arose, and whether these grounds were then or are now justifiable. (These questions arise in a similar manner in regard to Pannenberg's stress on the apocalyptic tradition. Why this tradition rather than others?)

The issue was taken further in an interesting essay by Sean McEvenue.[8] This was basically an attack on Brevard Childs' theory of canonical exegesis, with the aid of Bernard Lonergan's theology. For McEvenue the Bible is emphatically not a collection of timeless truths or answers to our contemporary questions. 'The Bible, taken with all its diverse meanings, demands of its readers the wide range of vision which can be taken as Christian vision' (242). The current crisis in Biblical Theology has arisen because current western culture will not allow a

---

[7] In *Christian Theology I* ed. P.C. Hodgson and R.H. King, 60.
[8] S. McEvenue, 'The Old Testament, Scripture or Tradition', *Interpretation*, July 1981.

direct normative role for ancient documents in articulating current doctrines. Current western culture, understood in its best expression, does allow for the prophetic spirit to be awakened through Scripture and to lead theologians towards truths for today' (242). History for McEvenue, contra Childs, is a moving process, which cannot be caught and arrested in the norm of a 'canon' like a still shot from a moving picture.

Recent discussion of the category of narrative in biblical interpretation has also been divided between those who see narrative as normative for theology and those who do not. It has become clear that the narrative category has both advantages and disadvantages, and everything depends on specific applications. While some scholars see it as *the* central interpretative tool, others regard it as a useful instrument, which leaves the basic theological issues still to be determined. It may be regarded as supporting again the centrality of the text, or as tending to a 'tyranny of the text', which may mask basic issues about the understanding of God.

Clearly these two main positions, though they can be made to seem opposites, can and do overlap and may be complementary. For most Christian theology the Bible is more or less central, sometimes more, sometimes less, but it is not usually the only source of theology. (I think of the traditional triad of reason, revelation and experience.) Much depends on the particular theological exercise involved which may be the examination of particular philosophical concepts, involving issues of metaphysics or ethics.

If one looks at the works of half a dozen contemporary British or American theologians, it may seem at first that there is little direct use of the Bible at all, and there is little to choose between the more liberal and the more conservative writers. Even in a work like Shubert Ogden's *The Point of Christology*, which is much concerned with New Testament hermeneutics, there are few biblical quotations, and there certainly appears to be little attempt to use the Bible in theological construction. But, on the other hand, without the biblical material on 'the events concerning Jesus', Ogden's book could not have been written. The indirect role of the Bible may be greater than at first seems to be the case, even when there are as many interpretations of the material as there are interpreters.

I return in conclusion to something like my original position. Basic themes in the Bible function to illuminate Christian life and thought in different ways at different times. This is part of the action of God, Father, Son and Holy Spirit, in human life. I have tried to pick up one of these basic themes, the love of God, in *Theology of the Love of God*, and in writings on the Church and on ethics. But of course the theological use of the Bible in seeking to illuminate the meaning of human life is by no means confined to systematic theology.

7. Praxis: Church, Community and Society

The Bible is and has always been interpreted through the life and thought of the Christian community, the Church. There is a reciprocal relationship between scripture and tradition. But of course the Church in a given place is never an abstract ideal, as often in, for example, Schleiermacher's discussion, but is a highly particular manifestation. This is one reason why, without any suggestion of biblical fundamentalism, the biblical narratives perform an important task in setting the pattern of the events concerning Jesus constantly before the community.

In order to underline the importance of the Church in the past for the understanding of the Church in the present we may perhaps fittingly end this chapter with a slightly larger scale map of a tiny corner of the history of the Church. A closer inspection of any corner would produce similar results, of a vastly complex interaction between the Christian gospel and human society, in which different facets of the gospel strike different people in different ways, and men and women try to work out in their own generation the nature of Christian discipleship. A good example is the Oxford Movement, and its central figure John Henry Newman. This movement is not more central than any other movement to the history of the Church, but it contains most of the ingredients of the search for a more adequate understanding of the Church as a source of theology, with its strengths and weaknesses, in a given cultural environment.

The Oxford Movement was a movement within the Church of England, operating especially in the years 1833-45, centred in Oxford and aimed at the restoration of the 'High Church' ideals, as it saw them, of the seventeenth century and the early Church. It sprang on the one hand not from a philosophical programme but from concern at the progressive decline of church life and the spread of liberalism in all fields and especially in theology, and on the other hand from the impetus of the Romantic Movement which inspired a new interest in primitive and medieval Christianity. Among the more immediate causes – the Church has never lived in a vacuum – was the fear that the Catholic Emancipation Act (1829) would lead many Anglicans into the Roman Catholic Church, the anxiety caused by the passing of the Reform Bill and the plan to suppress the ten Anglican Irish bishoprics (Ireland has always been a delicate issue), which led to John Keble's Assize Sermon which marked the beginning of the Movement proper.

The aims, expressed in the *Tracts for the Times*, were to defend the Church of England, not for the sake of establishment or ecclesiology, but as the divine way to salvation, the successor of the Apostolic Church, the via media between the errors of Rome and Geneva. Without Catholic faith there is the alternative, not of an easy liberalism, but of complete scepticism. Hence the vital importance of defence, especially in an age of doubt, of an historic chain of succession with the apostles and of existential response in personal holiness to the nearness of God's presence in his Church. Stress on devotion, the sacraments, the visible ordinances of the Church, the link with the past through the bishop, these are the keynotes of Edward Pusey's enthusiasm. It has often been remarked how the Oxford men had learned from the Evangelicals not to be afraid of their emotions, though the outward expression was to be tempered by a doctrine of reserve.

The ancient Church was looked at as the undivided norm of Christian truth, and the true interpreter of the scripture, biblical criticism, was largely ignored. Deviation from patristic norms was to be dreaded. 'I saw myself in a mirror, and I was a Monophysite.' So Newman in 1839. *Securus iudicat orbis terrarum.* In time the notion of the *via media* faded. 'Every day

I begin to hate the Reformers more and more', said Hurrell Froude. Members of the movement attempted to move as close as possible to Rome without actually being received. Many took the next logical step.

The Movement's influence was greatest in the field of worship and piety, least in the field of doctrine. It exhibited some of the less reputable aspects of what Luther called *theologia gloriae*, and the image of the unique *via media* looks increasingly less convincing in the pluriform context of world-wide Christianity. Yet its concern was undoubtedly for the essence rather than the form of the gospel. Though it was too much hampered by chronic anachronism, it was aware too of a real feeling for tradition as an ally, rather than a hindrance, in the search for a flexible and creative approach to Christian community in the present.

8. Culture and Community

Wolfhart Pannenberg has emphasised that man is by nature an historical animal who learns to experiment in the future by looking at his experiments, collective and individual, in the past, and in this way stimulating greater creativity. It may be said that by reflecting on the richness of the tradition of the gospel in the past we too may come in the future not to close doors because of historical experiences, but to open them.[9]

Our example was from the western tradition. The richness of the gospel tradition encompasses the Christian East, the various churches of the Orthodox tradition. Here concepts of Church, God and society are linked together in an impressive and ancient synthesis. Kallistos Ware has characterised the Church in terms of the three ideas of the image or icon of the Holy Trinity, the Body of Christ, and a continued Pentecost. His accounts of the nature and history of Orthodoxy provide an excellent introduction to the subject. Here too is a great tradition of Christian life, thought and worship.[10]

[9]Pannenberg, *What is Man?* Cf. too his *Christian Spirituality and Sacramental Community*.
[10]K.T. Ware, *The Orthodox Church* and J. Meyendorff, *The Orthodox Church*.

If the Orthodox witness represents some of the most ancient living traditions, then the Latin American, African and Asian Churches represent, at least in their contemporary forms, some of the newest. Compared with the older Churches, their voices are only just beginning to be heard in the West. Yet the unity of the Church is the universal Church, and its achievement is linked with the unity of all mankind. In the history of the next two thousand years, these newer voices are likely to become increasingly important for the understanding of the service of Jesus Christ in the Church of God.

It is in this highly complex world, which is the world in which we find ourselves, of reason, revelation and experience, of biblical interpretation and ecclesiastical tradition, theological methodological debate and social critique of intellectual values, that the understanding of the Christian God is the subject of reflection. For the Christian faith is not concerned with an abstract deity, but with the God who is creator and reconciler of heaven and earth, not as it might possibly and theoretically be, but as it is in its present reality.

In reflecting on the God of Christian faith it is necessary to take account of the intellectual tradition of concepts of God, of the substantive content of doctrine through the ages, of the sources in the interaction of Bible, tradition and community, and of new developments in human knowledge, in the arts and the sciences. Each of the central strands of the faith of the community must be developed. But there is no order of procedure prescribed. What is done is based on the experience of the theological tradition, developed over two thousand years and passed on for the future. Ultimately it is by its fruits in Christian life and worship that such theology is judged, and becomes in turn a source of deeper reflection.

Notably in *The True Church and the Poor*, Jon Sobrino considered that theology begins with the reality of the Church as it is. 'Theology becomes practical because its motivating concern is not pure thought nor even pure truth but rather the building of the kingdom of God and of a Church that will be at the service of this kingdom.'

He analysed theological understanding in European and Latin American theology. In the latter case, 'The enemy of theology has been less the atheist than the inhuman.' The promotion of justice is an essential part of the gospel message. Jesus openly denounced the refusal to love. In the service of faith, justice is seen as the concrete embodiment of love. The Church of the Poor is the resurrection of the true Church, breaking away from traditional means of being Church. Here the Spirit is present, here are *oekumene,* catholicity and apostolicity. Here God is experienced, precisely in the communal experience of the oppressed community.

In Latin America the Church protests against the destructive consequences of injustice. Confession of faith as concern, concern for the Christianisation of the human, leads to martyrdom. Unity and conflict are in tension not only outside but also within the Church itself. 'It is not possible to speak of a single hierarchy, a single clergy or of *the* laity.' True unity combines the institutional with the prophetic and is an eschatological gift.

What then is the theological significance of the persecution of the Church? Is it an attack on the values of the Kingdom of God? The task of the Church remains evangelisation, through word, life and action. No one has greater love than those who give their lives for others. Christian faith is the foundation of the religious life, and it finds identity in its mission, through celibacy, poverty and obedience as a following of Jesus in the Third World. It is sometimes thought that Latin American theology is all right for the Third World, but can safely be disregarded in more enlightened society. This is a somewhat myopic view of the communion of saints.

How are the relations between theology, community and society to be understood? Certainly the problem of using the language of the New Testament in an entirely different particular culture today is a most important issue. What is a local theology? Robert Schreiter has suggested (in *Local Theologies*) that reflection on the missionary work of the nineteenth century produced a search for new means of communication, through translation, adaptation and contextual models. Local theology is always theology incarnate in local culture. Tools for listening to a culture are needed, including ecological, structuralist and semantic approaches.

Church traditions are themselves local cultures, and may be understood through the sociology of knowledge. The search for Christian identity involves dialogue between church tradition and local theology, between theory and practical action in community, between popular religion and official religion. This dialogue is complicated by the presence of syncretism and dual religious systems in many cultures. Good evangelisation should in turn bring about cultural change, though the pace of change is not to be forced.

9. God and Gender

For centuries the language of theology and of the Church has been expressed in male terms. God is habitually referred to in masculine pronouns, in theology and in worship. All human language in reference to God has a metaphorical and an anthropological element. If we are to speak of God as person, then inevitably we speak of God in human personal terms, and the Judaeo-Christian tradition has, for cultural reasons, used male terminology.[11]

For Christianity there is a further complication. The Word was made flesh . God became incarnate in a particular human being, That person had to be male or female, and was in fact a man. But there is no need to assume a Christological bias towards masculinity. Maleness was simply part of the cultural particularity of Jesus, and the New Testament records do not depict a modern macho figure. In theory, there are no insuperable problems.

Practice, however, is a very different matter. I suspect that the main source of the problem has been not so much theology as church life, though the one has powerfully reinforced the other. The history of humankind is in part the history of the subjection of some social groups to a position of inferiority by other social groups. Women have been and are subjected to

---

[11]Some of the best work in this area has been done by Elizabeth Schüssler Fiorenza, esp. *In Memory of Her*, and by Rosemary Radford Reuther, esp. *Sexism and God Talk*, Boston,1983.

oppression in many cultures. This has often been reinforced in cultures with a strong religious base – Islam and Christianity.

In much traditional reading of the Bible, men are thought to be superior in the order of creation to women. The Genesis narratives may be read to suggest that women are the source of sin, sin being thought of almost exclusively in the realm of sexuality. Jesus, it has been argued, chose only male disciples. Hence there can be no women priests. Any women ordained are invalidly ordained by definition. But in a Roman Catholic understanding of priesthood, to choose a difficult example, it may be said of the priest that 'He represents Christ the redeemer: he does not impersonate Jesus of Nazareth. What is important is the sacrament in humanity, which men and women share.'[12]

It is against this background of uncritical reinforcement of the cultural assumptions of Middle Eastern culture in the period of the Old Testament and the New Testament that language about God may need to be reviewed. The harmless use of masculine imagery, hallowed by tradition, may become an instrument of oppression. The difficulty about change is that a switch to feminine or female language may seem shocking, contrived, provocative. Yet a sharp protest may be needed to overcome centuries of complacency. In all of this a balance must be struck. There must be genuine commitment to the equality of men and women before God in all things. But it cannot be assumed that shock tactics will always produce the best way forward.

For the Judaeo-Christian tradition, God is neither male nor female, masculine nor feminine. The human personal attributes which we give, help us to understand God in personal relationships, Since God is in his essential nature self-giving love, these terms are properly used in inclusive rather than exclusive ways. Only evil is excluded by God's love, which overcomes evil. We can call God father or mother, male or female, masculine or feminine, provided that these terms are used to enrich rather than impoverish our vision of the scope of the divine compassion. Jesus Christ is the word and sacrament

[12]Editorial in *The Month*, February, 1977.

of God for all humanity. In Christ there is neither Jew nor
Greek, male nor female. All are included.

10. Actuality and Possibility

The last hundred years have brought momentous changes to
the human community. There has been great progress in the
technological and the social dimensions of human life. There
have been spectacular improvements in the quality of life for
great sections of humanity. To deny this is simply foolish. There
has also been murder and repression on a scale unheard of in
the ancient world. In Europe two world wars and their aftermath
brought millions of military and civilian casualties. In Russia
and China millions disappeared. In Africa millions died of
starvation, and in Latin America life for many of the inhabitants
of the subcontinent has been brutal in the extreme. Christian
theology is concerned not only with Christians but with all
humankind. How should it develop in response to the
contemporary world, not as it would like it to be but as it in fact
is?

My own perspective views the gospel as centred in the life,
death and resurrection of Jesus Christ, and in the Judaeo-
Christian tradition leading to and from this centre. Within the
community of whose who have faith in God in this tradition,
these central events are self-interpreting. They shine through
history and produce reconciliation in their own light, the light
of God's self-giving love. They give out this light even when they
have been very imperfectly understood, and transmitted by
Christian communities whose witness is gravely inadequate
and incomplete. That is to say, their efficacy depends solely on
God's grace, and not on particular ecclesiastical practices,
philosophical principles or world views. In other words, there
are no essential metaphysical principles of Christianity.

The events which are the focal points of a Christian
understanding of ultimate reality are sometimes said to
constitute God's story. The recent fashion for narrative theology
has had its advantages, in stressing the impact of the biblical
text upon human life. But, as one of its leading creators, Hans
Frei, was himself aware, the story concept may not be used to

favour a reading of the narrative which brackets out all questions of ultimate truth claims. It is the truth of these particular events by which the gospel stands or falls, and through which the gospel is appropriated in succeeding generations.

In *Theology of the Love of God* I suggested that it was appropriate to maintain a balance in Christian theology of epistemological scepticism with ontological confidence. It just is the case that the foundations of theology are many and various, and that in a pluralist society they will be developed in different ways by different Christian thinkers. A theology which seeks to reflect the concern of God for all humanity will seek to respect and benefit from this richness. It will build its structures as a cumulative case.

At the same time, faith in the hidden love of God is something which arises in Christian experience and which persists, establishing a view of ultimate reality in God which is definitive and is not negotiable. It is, indeed, open to falsification, and much counts against it. But the circumstances in which it would be appropriate to abandon the belief entirely are hard to specify, and indeed it is a main characteristic of faith that it is often 'against the odds' and it regards despair as a kind of capitulation to evil.

There has been much discussion in recent years of what constitutes foundationalist and antifoundationalist, fideistic and non-fideistic views of theology, often centred round widely varying interpretations of Rorty and MacIntyre, Frei, Lindbeck and not least Wittgenstein. I think that different theories do in fact lead to illumination of different aspects of Christian theology. But I stress here the importance of an inclusive rather than an exclusive approach to frameworks other than one's own, as a basic characteristic of response to a God who is equally present to and present for all humankind. This need not inhibit precision, definition and debate, provided that the overall purpose of Christian theology is not obscured in the process. It is the role of new approaches to open up doors, not to close them, to point to the manifold riches of the gospel, rather than to pull up the drawbridge.

Faith and experience, reason and revelation, the Bible and tradition, the Christian community in its internal reflection and in its external engagement with society, all are involved in theological construction. In the next section we shall turn directly to this construction, beginning with the fundamental notion of the divine transcendence.[13]

[13]I have not attempted, in the manner of Jüngel, Küng and others who have recently written on God, to offer here a theological critique of the history of modern European philosophy. Though such studies are instructive they are of limited value precisely in relation to both the modern question about God as absent and to the Christian response. Both question and answer have communal and practical as well as purely theoretical dimensions.

I have said nothing explicitly of the concepts of post-modernism or of deconstruction in this section. It may well be that theology has much to learn from these developments, but some care is necessary with their deployment. Appeal to deconstruction may not be used as a ground for the arbitrary dismissal of all traditional theology, and appeal to post-modernism may not be used as a ground for dismissing the immense contribution of the Enlightenment to theology. It is tempting, but in the end not always illuminating, to use such concepts, along with story, narrative and hermeneutic, as vehicles for repeating the traditional battles between conservative and liberal in theology.

Not all aspects of the tradition need be preserved. There are areas of the Christian tradition, of caring devotion to God and humanity, for which we must be truly thankful. There are other areas of tradition, for which we must ask forgiveness of God and man, a need which we have so far scarcely recognised. Not all areas of Enlightenment or post-modern thought are of equal merit. Clearly Kant would hardly have approved of the changes which Marxist bureaucracy made in his native Koenigsberg in turning it into Kaliningrad. Yet despite their mutual antipathy, the traditions of Kant and of Marx are both heirs of the Enlightenment. The development of philosophical theory in the twentieth century is examined with particular clarity by Christopher Norris in *The Contest of the Faculties: Philosophy and Theory after Deconstruction*. The sections on narrative theory, sense and reference, and relativity are especially helpful.

5

The Holiest in the Height

1. Divine Transcendence

The God of Christian faith is radically transcendent to the world. In his essential nature, love, God is the hidden divine external referent. On him the created order depends for its continuing existence. He works in, with and under the structures of creation, immanent in its structures as its sustaining force. Transcendence is manifested in his unique sovereign power over and freedom within the structures of the created order.

Transcendence can mean very different things.[1] Different religions understand God's immanence and transcendence in different ways. Neoplatonism in the ancient world carried the transcendence of God to a great degree of sophistication, denying in God any trace of contamination by the material world. Strict pantheist understandings of religion view God as entirely encompassed by the material world, with no residual spiritual dimension. The classical Christian understanding of God is that he is more transcendent than the God of Neoplatonism, because he has created the physical structure of the universe from nothing, *ex nihilo,* and he is not linked by any chain of orders or degrees of being to the created order. At the same time God is more intimately involved in the created order than pantheist conceptions of deity allow, for he

---

[1]Transcendence and immanence. There is a voluminous literature, cf. the arts., in Paul Edwards, ed., *Encyclopaedia of Philosophy* and in Hastings' *Encyclopaedia of Religion and Ethics.*

is the sole sustaining power of all that exists, immediately and directly.

God's transcendence is at once the clue to his unique nature as God and the source of many of the difficulties facing the human quest for understanding. Because of the peculiar nature of divine transcendence our theories are always underdetermined by the available empirical facts. There may be other sorts of facts of a transcendent and spiritual nature. There remains this central quality of transcendence, not reducible to other components. Transcendence is interpreted in relation to particular cultural dimensions within the theological traditions themselves. In this way a multiplicity of often conflicting perspectives arises at the heart of faith's reflection on God. Differences are not necessarily the reflection of obtuseness, insincerity or defective knowledge, but constitute the variety of experience. Faith is driven to deeper understanding among these various perspectives.

Understanding transcendence includes awareness of the various roles of transcendence in non-theological reflection. Between the radical divine transcendence of Neoplatonic mysticism and deeply pragmatic empiricism there lie numerous levels involving different sorts of transcendence. There is an important area of what is sometimes called this worldly transcendence – in all sorts of aesthetic experience – in music, art and literature, in the appreciation of moral and cultural values, perhaps especially in experience of and reflection upon personal relationships.

God is unique. There is then no possibility of moving from human to divine transcendence by an easy analogical step. Christians understand themselves to be given some clues to God's nature, including his transcendence through grace. Though God's transcendence is unique, our language about it is not. Here is the central paradox about talk of God.

Not all experience of transcendence may be understood in a religious context, even by religious people. Some of it is, and this may help our imaginative appreciation of divine transcendence operating in human life. Such transcendence may be linked directly to the understanding of God, or, in a non- theistic religion such as Buddhism, to the essence of the numinous. God's transcendence is understood by Christians as the transcendence of the divine love, and as such is understood in the light of Jesus Christ. This particularisation helps us to distinguish Christian concepts from other concepts of absolute transcendence in the history of philosophy and religion.

The grounds for this characterisation of transcendence lie within the areas of reason, revelation and experience. In the Judaeo-Christian tradition the prime source of understanding of divine transcendence is the Bible, and the experience of God in society, worship and individual imagination which this reflects.

Creation from nothing suggests at once the complete independence of God from his creation and the utter dependence of creation on God. The Old Testament offers accounts of God as the transcendent God who acted through a covenant relation with his chosen people Israel. Christians have come to trust in this transcendent God through seeing the subjects of the New Testament narrative as the providential culmination of this tradition. They have come to understand God as the transcendent, self-giving God, whose nature is characterised through the life, death and resurrection of Jesus Christ.

God's transcendence may be understood by individuals through reflection upon personal experience of God's grace. It may also be related to the experience of others. It may involve reflection on the manifold logic of fact and interpretation which is the basis of description in most subjects. For some people thought of God's transcendence may be a source of joy, gratitude and peace. For others, there may be a sense more of meaninglessness and disaster at the root of human society. A general theory of divine transcendence in relation to creation ought to take account of both ends of the spectrum, of quiet confidence in divine blessing and of weary despair perhaps in the face of mass deprivation.

Awareness of divine transcendence is sometimes seen as a state of serenity, characterised by a natural sovereignty over the natural order. Exceptions may be seen in the mystical experience of the blank wall, the concept of dread in

Kierkegaard and the existentialist tradition, and notably in Luther's relation of transcendence to the death and resurrection of Jesus.

Recent Jewish theologies of the holocaust have explored the transcendence of the suffering of God. God's transcendence overcomes the barrier of death, the Achilles' heel of most conceptions of other worldly transcendence. God who is self-giving love brings life out of death in the mystery of his eternal goodness. This is difficult territory, but is not on that account to be neglected.

God's transcendence is mysterious. The modern world seems to belie talk of mystery. The obvious solution is a compromise, talk of the semi-transcendence of a reasonably comprehensible deity. But of course we can be content neither with a restatement of the verities of the past nor with vacuous modern reinterpretation. God is in his essential nature love, love defined uniquely and precisely (though also in part mysteriously) in his self-giving, self-affirming engagement with the life, death and resurrection of Jesus Christ.

In speaking of God's transcendence I would want to speak of a metaphysical transcendence of God's being, of God as creator and redeemer of the physical structures of the universe and of human destiny within these structures. Ontology of love based on God's love has personal dimensions but includes a general ontology. As persons we exist, sustained through the being of the divine person.

God in the biblical narratives is free, sovereign, not limited by our temporal conceptions of what pertains to deity. He is not given to contravening the laws of thought. But he is free on behalf of and apart from man. There is nothing in the created order which God may not influence as he sees fit. Our theoretical concepts of omnipotence help us to explore this notion of freedom. God is able to act at any time in any way, against all possible obstacles. There remain problems, in relation to evil, suffering and the question of a finite universe.

God is personal but not a super-person. The tradition speaks more readily of personality in God than of the personality of God. The notion of a super-person acting in an infinite number of ways in organising an infinite number of individual and usually conflicting thoughts and experiences is bizarre. Such a notion of God is manifestly incoherent. We must conclude that freedom in God is in important respects unlike human freedom extrapolated to an infinite degree. We may conceive of God's freedom as consisting in the ability to do precisely what we cannot do, acting simultaneously on behalf of all his creatures, directing and caring for them. Grounds for this affirmation lie in judgement on the truth of the events concerning Jesus. The reference of the affirmation however is to God the creator. Confusion of ground and reference may lead to either Christocentric narrowing or to deism.

2. Creative Transcendence

The transcendent God is the creator God. Creativity is a universal and varied human activity. To speak of God as creator is to use the language of metaphor familiar in talk of the potter creating the pot. The creation of the pot is a matter of factual significance, except say when the potter creates the pot in his mind's eye when he lies in bed. Christians have been concerned to affirm belief in creation as implying God's activity, rather than simply human ideas about divinity. In discussion of the various strands of metaphorical reference such basic but crucial distinctions easily disappear. Here theologians may be grateful to G.E. Moore for rescuing common sense from hermeneutical mystification. The grounds for believing claims about God as creator to be true lie again partly in the experience of life, thought and worship in Israel culminating in the events concerning Jesus, and partly in the evaluation of this tradition in the present. The individual can scarcely claim credit for progress in theology, yet he cannot disclaim responsibility for what he himself affirms or denies.

God is not an object in the world of objects. God is independent of space and time except as he chooses to be involved in space and time. Modern cosmological study can make no difference to central affirmations about God as creator. Yet it is more difficult to conceptualise notions of God's providential care in a universe which appears to be infinite, but in which each galaxy has a fixed and finite term of existence.

Awareness of this vastness of scale may help us to form a renewed conception of the divine transcendence. The cosy familiarities of a local dignitary with his clients are not the appropriate model for such a God. God's love works on a scale in which the span of human life on earth, indeed the existence of our planet, is a mere fragment. Yet Christians affirm his close involvement with the life of every human being. On such a scale particular providence may seem unthinkable. Yet precisely here we may grasp some heightened awareness of God's grace, so that nothing can separate us from God's love.

In the Christian perspective heaven and earth are made for God's enjoyment and that of his creatures. Development of ecological, environmental and conservational programmes relies heavily on understanding mankind as stewards of nature, responsible to God for their use of it. There is movement towards new theologies of nature.

Here the importance of the principle that with God creation and reconciliation are simultaneous becomes clear. Environmental concern that preserves green belts, pure air and sparkling water in one area of a city at the cost of lower living standards, lack of employment opportunity and similar deprivation in another area can never be justified. In God's nature, love and justice are one. Reconciliation means love and equity throughout the created order as well as forgiveness for the individual. 'The introspective conscience of the West' may be partly attributed to the influence of the great Augustine. In the East fossilising tendencies of another sort led, with a few bright exceptions, to a state of perpetual stagnation. In the West the restless energy of Augustinian piety succeeded, almost in spite of itself, in producing fruits of an overlapping of creation and salvation in the development of natural science. So much for the belief that purity of method will always produce successful practice. The connections between theory and practice in the contingencies of history are scarcely straightforward. As creator, God is equally concerned with the welfare of all mankind. This is a basis for a theology of the world religions, for Christian social ethics, for commitment to all the human and physical sciences.

3. Hiddenness

Because we understand God as creator, it is less than easy for us to imagine him as playing a public and visible role in creation, like the works foreman on the shop floor. On such a model it is natural to reflect that there ought to be a definite correspondence between God's creative activity and human scientific discovery, between God's action and the laws of motion, and so on. But God's transcendence is a hidden transcendence. Divine creativity is neither an extension of human creativity nor of creative process in the natural order. God's creativity is not the first link in an infinite chain of causes. It is the basis of all creaturely activity, both separate from such activity and co-operating in, with and under all creativity in the created order. Such a state of affairs may seem to be a contradiction in terms. Either God's creativity is or is not related to creative activity deriving from the natural order. But there is a connection. An example may clarify the problem. In any civilised society individual families live and work within the infrastructure of local and national government. In a similar manner we may imagine God working in, with and under human activity without being involved in a causal-mechanistic manner. The problems are those of all talk of God, involving a unique transcendent being, and are not peculiar to the understanding of creation as such.

The hiddenness of God underlines a further crucial aspect of transcendence. On grounds of revelation we may be justified in speaking of positive characteristics of God's nature. Yet the fact that God is not an object in the world of objects renders all analogies from the natural world, including of course personal analogies, inadequate. This being the case, we appear to be left with the unpalatable alternatives of an unsupported appeal to revelation and some version of post-Kantian agnosticism.

Resolution of this issue requires a reconsideration of traditional distinctions between natural and supernatural theology. For St. Thomas, unlike much Thomism, there was no absolute distinction to be drawn between nature and supernature. Between nature and grace there was a complete interaction and complementarity. Later dualism, taken up on both sides of the Reformation, served to complicate matters further. However, we cannot go back today to the attractive theology of St. Thomas. For us the whole concept of a framework of nature, however related to grace, is problematic. Even if we have such a framework in mind, it will not provide us with explanations of the nature of God, man and the universe. It does not offer us an authorised version of theories of general and special relativity and the like. We must be content with a number of different approaches, and only parts of general theories. The results will depend entirely on the value of these specific judgements.

One of the more effective approaches to understanding God's hiddenness has been in the tradition of Martin Luther. This derived much from medieval mystical piety, but was crystallised in the work of Luther himself. For Luther God is revealed as the hidden God. He is *Deus Revelatus* and *Deus Absconditus.* God is revealed in Jesus Christ, though hidden except to the eyes of faith. In the created order apart from faith God's revelation is veiled in the guise of the law, which only exposes as worthless human attempts at understanding. In Calvin the law and the gospel are complementary rather than opposed. Now the gospel is interpreted even more one-sidedly than in Luther in the light of the law.

In the work of Rudolf Bultmann the hiddenness of God in creation is recognised in the refusal to develop a speculative theology of creation. Only in the realm of personal, existential encounter, around the pivot of the Christ event, is the experience of the hidden God possible. Karl Barth, dissatisfied with the Lutheran tradition, attempted again to relate the gospel to the structures of the physical order, seeing creation, with Calvin, as the theatre of the glory of God. In doing so he lost the intimate connection with the contemporary intellectual tradition which Bultmann had been at such pains to maintain.

It is of prime importance to maintain both the hiddenness of God and the intimate connection between theological understanding of the created order and non-theological analysis.

Defects in the existentialist tradition of talk of the hidden God have been amply demonstrated in the Anglo-Saxon philosophical tradition.[2] This tradition has in turn often been singularly lacking in appreciation of the particularity of history and the development of historical consciousness which existentialism has grasped. Once again, what is called for is not a dubious amalgam but a fresh development.

It is time to specify more precisely the different strands of meaning in talk of God's hiddenness.[3] First, the hiddenness of God refers to the virtual inconceivability of God the unique creator, to human minds. Secondly, this hiddenness is not a defect in God. Nor is it simply to be put down to human sin in being unable to see God. Often in human life we are unable to see things that demand our attention because we do not want to see them. There is an alienation from God, but this is not the centre of the picture. Thirdly, the hiddenness of God in his created order including man is there in the nature of the case. In revelation it is not entirely removed. The appropriate medium of relationship between God and men is faith, a unique but not entirely incomprehensible gift which God in his grace offers to men. Somewhat as in human relationships there remains an important residual element of mystery, so there is maintained between God and his creatures a measure of what is sometimes called 'epistemic distance'. Regarded in this way, the hiddenness of God may be seen as a part of what Barth called 'the shadowside of creation', part of what it is to be a creature living, in the language of the New Testament, between the times of faith and consummation.

[2]Summarised in Flew's short art. in *Epworth Review* for Sept.1980.

[3]Twentieth-century European thought on transcendence is of course much indebted to Hegel – even in opposition to Hegel, e.g. in Adorno.

The discussion of transcendence in the Fathers is often connected with stress on *Creatio ex nihilo*.

On the problem of hiddenness and faith, cf. St. John of the Cross, Luther, Bultmann, etc.

An existential understanding of creation was developed by Kierkegaard. On grace cf. Edward Yarnold, *The Second Gift*.

God's hiddenness is the hiddenness of presence.[4] It is the medium of the 'love that will not let me go'. Love's 'letting be' in epistemic distance is also love that will not let us go. Between sentimentality and cynicism this paradox may become a clue to understanding the hidden love of God. The appropriate response to God's hidden love is prayer, which involves talking to the hidden God.

Reflection on God's hidden presence may help us to distinguish some more and less successful moves in some recent secular theology. That the presence of God should be grasped by faith alone should come as no surprise in a tradition including Augustine's meditations on the mystery of God and Aquinas' hymns of adoration of the hidden saviour in the eucharistic elements. But it was precisely in the doubly secularised society of the twentieth century, secularised by widespread abandonment of belief in God and by human savagery on an unprecedented scale, that Dietrich Bonhoeffer came to understand God's presence in his hiddennness. Not every good idea is followed up in an intelligent way, and the history of Bonhoeffer's interpretation is by no means an illumination. Yet the dimension of faith's renewed apprehension of the presence of the hidden God is important. We may not have fideism, yet we need not regard faith as basically suspect until correlation with every last area of human intellectual endeavour has been checked out. Such mechanical analysis would be the death of all human relationships.

The hiddenness of God is not some independent attribute which may be dealt with in isolation and then forgotten. It runs as an important thread through the whole Christian understanding of God. The absence of certain empirical correlates need not be taken as a mark of the absence of God. God's hiddenness is manifested as the transcendence of the hidden God in his inconceivability. This becomes clear in God's engagement with the events concerning Jesus. Christology points to this metaphysical opacity of God in creation and redemption. It is not then from a particular abstract concept of transcendence but from the living faith of Christians that we may hope to develop models for understanding God. For this is the God who is trusted as the transcendent God.

[4]Cf. Bonhoeffer, *Letters and Papers*, passim.

6

Out of the Depths

1. Divine Immanence

God in Christian faith is not only transcendent but deeply immanent in his creation. This affirmation has sometimes led to fascinating speculation about the world as part of the being of God, about the necessity of their personal existence to the perfection of the creator, to various combinations of pantheism, panentheism and the like. Experience of God's presence and reflection on experience, is at once the most basic and the most ambivalent of criteria. If we have no experience of God, then God, it might reasonably be thought, is at best peripheral to our lives. But experience is often deceptive, and the history of mankind is full of discovery that the certainties of past experience are no longer the certainties that they were, in the light of developing knowledge.

Feuerbach's critique of all human experience as projection of human wishes led Karl Barth to abandon all the territory of human experience to the secular moralist and philosopher. Inevitably Barth came back into the field of experience, regarding our experience of divine presence as the special, *sui generis* gift of the Holy Spirit. The Holy Spirit is the most intimate friend of a proper human understanding of man. But by that stage a framework has been created in which the full force of the significance of God as active in, with and under human activity could not always be taken up. This is in a way all the more surprising, since no one has offered such detailed positive appreciation of God as creator and man as creature in our time as Barth. In Augustine and Aquinas the role of

Christology though central is limited. In Barth fear of anthropomorphism and neglect of historical consciousness leads to a failure to grasp the nettle of immanence.

Immanence without transcendence is problematic. But the scope of God, not as the absolute dialectic between immanence and transcendence but as the God of all grace, is all-embracing. Immanence without transcendence leads easily to the assimilation of God uncritically with contemporary structures of society. Transcendence provides opposition to a specific culture on necessary occasions, but lacks constructive engagement with cultural aspects of the theatre of redemption. The profound identification between nature and grace achieved through the events concerning Jesus Christ may lead us back to a new appreciation of the structures of creation and of human existence as the structures of God's reconciling presence. This situation was acutely perceived by Dietrich Bonhoeffer. Creation without reconciliation is nothing. Through God's hidden presence in Christ, the created order – Bonhoeffer's secular world – may again become the instrument of God's gracious love to men. To live *etsi Deus non daretur* is easy and is indeed part of the contemporary condition of alienation. To live *coram deo, etsi Deus non daretur* may be part of a particular form of Christian communication. We may not give up creation to the sphere of unbelief for the sake of the gospel, for all is sustained and held in being by the God of Jesus Christ. To speak of the action of God in Christ is to recall not an exclusive but an inclusive action. It should lead not to a weakening but to a strengthening of awareness of the importance of God the creator. As creator and reconciler God is immanent in all areas of his created order, distinct from but freely engaged in all action in the physical universe.

2. Immanence and Experience

Claims about experience, and especially religious experience, tend to be self-fulfilling. Self-deception is a danger. As is often noted, Buddhists' experience of transcendence tends to be focused on the Buddha, Roman Catholics' on the Blessed Virgin, others on various images of Jesus Christ, or on models of perfect humanity. Unanimity in the interpretation of experience, found in totalitarian groups in history, is itself a ground for caution. For Christians the sense of the presence of God is registered in different ways by different people at different times.

The sense of the presence of God is filled out for us in its objective pole, we may think, through reflection back upon the biblical experience of God as creator and redeemer. The subjective pole of Christian experience is in the sphere of forgiveness and reconciliation. As Schleiermacher recognised, the subjective colouring of experience is to be appreciated within a dialectic (though not a formal dualism) of sin and grace. Here is the perennial and crucial significance of Luther's insistence that experience of the Christian God is not to be grasped by faith as an undefined experience of a gracious God, whose presence is a forgiving and reconciling presence.

Presence is then the subjective correlate of the more objective affirmations made in the biblical narrative of the love of God incarnate. It would indeed be strange if there were not such an observed correlation between Christian theory and Christian experience. Experience of God as the reconciling God has an important psychological dimension. As such it may be anthropomorphised as an answer, or part of an answer, to needs for security, warmth and comfort. A God who did not meet such needs, ever, would be a strange sort of God. But the appropriate response in reflection on religious experience should not then be narrowed to a conception of God as simply the projection of these basic needs.

God is to be found in various religions and in various other sorts of reflection on transcendence. John Bowker has interestingly explored experience of God in a number of studies, notably in *The Sense of God*. How to distinguish such forms of religious experience from wider concepts of innerworldly transcendence remains a central question. For the Christian the core element of such experience remains the experience, however frequent or infrequent, intense or less intense, of the forgiving and reconciling grace of God in Jesus Christ. This experience is understood further as the presence of the Holy Spirit, the gift of God's peace.

3. The Absence of God

The sense of the presence of God is a natural consequence of the sustaining grace of the loving God, operating everywhere throughout the created order in self-giving, self-affirming love. But, all too often, men and women have lived and died in human history with at best a gravely fragmented, or at worst, perhaps most commonly, an entirely non-existent sense of God as a sustaining presence, especially in times of dire need. The problem of the nature of divine presence and action was classically explored in the ancient world already in the fifth century BC in the plays of the great tragedian Aeschylus. The question of divine action is already hinted at by the watchman in the opening words of the *Agamemnon*, 'Of the gods I ask deliverance from this toil.'

The belief that the gods were either indifferent to or actively hostile to men, and the absence of a concept of divine love for men, was characteristic of the Archaic age. The idea of *phthonos* implied that the gods were amoral in their dealings with men. This unsatisfactory situation then led to the insertion of a concept of justice into the supposed action of the gods. For Solon the *phthonos* fell especially on those who were led by wealth to insolence, and who then through greed committed acts of hubris, and therefore, passing the bounds of justice, were punished by the gods.

Against this background Aeschylus developed his own view of justice. In the *Persae*, the historical basis is the defeat and humiliation of the Persians at Salamis. Xerxes has made a bid for world empire, has bridged the Hellespont and destroyed the temples of the Greeks. Disaster occurs. For Xerxes, 'fate has turned against me'. For the messenger of the traditional *phthonos* is against the king. The ghost of Darius states the poet's view clearly, *Hubris* has created a seed of hate, which has brought about a harvest of annihilation. In destroying the temples Xerxes has brought about his own downfall, destroying justice through his arrogance. Here Aeschylus has implicitly denied Solon's view that good and evil men alike are liable to be destroyed suddenly.

A more explicit illustration of the poet's position is to be found at *Agamemnon* 75ff. The descendants of evil men will be evil and their house will perish, but the descendants of righteous men will not be destroyed. Agamemnon is predisposed to evil. But his crime is the deliberate decision on his part to kill Iphigeneia. Clytemnestra and Aegisthus also deliberately planned murder, and so must die. Again the dualism of divine retribution and human crime, which must itself be punished in turn, runs through the play. In the *Eumenides* Aeschylus works out the reconciliation of the objective claims of the Furies to the judgement of Zeus, and Orestes is acquitted. This reconciliation is represented historically as a permanent development of the influence of Zeus, and the function of the Furies is channelled through the court of the Areopagus. All is achieved through the plans of Zeus. He reigns supreme.

It is good to remember that people have puzzled about the nature of divine action and the problem of hiddenness for a very long time. Sometimes we are tempted to think of the 'good old days' when natural theology was perfectly natural, when every experience was of God, and there was no doubt where the history of salvation ran. Then came the Enlightenment, after which all was problematic and depressing. But Aeschylus came before the Enlightenment. What indeed are we to say of God's action on behalf of the millions of mankind who lived before the coming of Jesus Christ? There were some consolations in the tradition of Plato, and in the notion of the contemplation of the sovereignty of the good as a prefect ideal. But the tragic conflict depicted in Aeschylus and the bitter-sweet agnosticism of Euripides would not have permitted of idealistic solutions in the manner of later Platonism. (So much for generalisations about 'the Greek mind' and the like.)

Remarkable instances of a complete faith in human ability to have a certain knowledge of the nature of divine action are also to be found in the European pre-Enlightenment tradition. A splendid example comes to mind in John Knox's *History of the Reformation in Scotland*, in which the side he favours is always directly guided by the Holy Spirit, and the opposition are always fighting against God.

Not all Christians can be as certain as Knox was. The bad men are killed, the good always win. In any case, if we believe in the ultimate unity of creation and reconciliation we must assert the presence of the divine love even to those who had perhaps no belief in God, no sense of divine presence and consolation, even in the most desperate circumstances of total abandonment. Such a situation is graphically portrayed in Thucydides' description of the end of the Syracusan expedition in September, 413 BC. The prisoners suffered from heat, cold and malnutrition. 'Fleet and Army perished from the face of the earth; nothing was saved, and of the many who went forth few returned home. This ended the Sicilian expedition' (Jowett, I, 549).

We may recall here the analysis of the nature of divine action in modern theology, especially in the work of Eberhard Jüngel and Gordon Kaufman. God must be able simultaneously to suffer with those who are in distress and to rejoice with those who rejoice. A God who cannot do this is scarcely worthy of disbelief, not to speak of belief.

4. Presence in Hiddenness

The presence of God is mediated to mankind, and the action of God to man occurs, in space and time, and also in eternity. The ground of this historical basis is God's presence to mankind always through Jesus Christ. But God's presence is not directly accessible historically. This paradox is indicated by the doctrine of God as spirit. God's presence and action are hidden. God is neither purely temporal or purely eternal, being both outside time and involved in time. This creates special problems for understanding his being, action and presence.

Involved everywhere in countless acts, God cannot be conceived of by us as aware and conscious of every action as a personal agent might be. Such a concept of God is incoherent. God acts in different ways at different times, but all his actions are equally his actions, in general and in particular providence. God's actions in the world have eschatological dimensions. He is concerned for people in this life and beyond.

As self-giving, self-affirming love, God abhors all evil and suffers under evil when his creatures suffer. The existence of evil under God is part of the condition of the possibility of finite freedom. It is overcome eschatologically and is always opposed now by God, in suffering and in persuasion.

God's hiddenness is not then a purely Gnostic notion of pure transcendence, ineffable inaccessibility. (Not all mysticism is truly Christian in character.) God may be experienced as a hidden presence in Christian community. But even in the absence of experience he may be affirmed as one who is present in absence, as a compassionate and hidden presence, on the basis of historical events in the past and future reflection about the nature of reality as God's reality from these.

We return to the problem of the Athenians in Syracuse in 413 BC. As Christians we will want to affirm the identification of the loving God with them whether they experience this or not, in hope and in desolation. This presence is affirmed to them at worst eschatologically after death. They may or may not have had some sense of the divine presence. Often they don't appear to have had any sense of self-transcendence or anything of the sort that Karl Rahner has spoken of in thinking of anonymous Christianity.

How can a man be an anonymous Christian? 'Without reflection he accepts God when he freely accepts himself in his own unlimited transcendence.'[1] Later he may come to understand the transcendent self-communication of God through Jesus Christ in history. In the case of ancient Greeks, clearly such transcendence was not possible in this life. Possibly too there was no such self-acceptance in terms of unlimited transcendence. Possibly there was no sense of ultimate meaning. Possibly there was little if any awareness of love and compassion by other human beings. But if there was such a vacuum in their lives, then we must affirm that God abhors this tragic state too.

If God abhors such a state, then we can scarcely fail to ask why God did not intervene in such cases in particular providence. The answer, as far as we have one, must lie in the mystery of finite freedom. We may think, too, that the providential action in the incarnation availed eschatologically for them, bringing the peace of God. We shall want to say then that men and women may have faith in God's presence as a loving God, even in the absence of particular direct experience of loving presence in extreme situations. Such a claim is clearly

[1]Karl Rahner, *Theological Investigations* XVI, 55.

open to the charge of self-delusion. The ground for a rational argument on behalf of such a faith will lie in appeal to God's grace in history, and to revelation through historical experience, though not just revelation of experience. As in all Christian theology, reason is supported by the gift of faith, nature by the all-pervasiveness of grace. In seeing grace as the clue to God, we shall want to see the whole of Christian discipleship as the history of a tradition of experience of divine action, stemming from the life, death and resurrection of Jesus Christ.

5. Presence in Suffering

To speak of God's constant involvement in the depths of all human experience, in immanence within the created order, is to make a statement of very far-reaching consequences. I have spoken of the identification of God with all men and women in times of joy and in times of disaster, even when they have absolutely no sense of the presence of God, of self-transcendence or whatever. I have indicated that the apparently tough-minded argument from the apparent absence of God in the evils of the world to the non-involvement of God in particular providence is inadequate. It could indeed be that God is not involved in the world. But this argument is not a sufficient warrant for general conclusions.

Sometimes people have affirmed a sense of God's presence as loving presence in times of apparent desolation. Where this has been absent, Christians believe that this presence will be affirmed to them eschatologically after death. The grounds for this hope lie in the present, in reflection through faith in the nature of God the creator.

We may take further Pascal's thought that Christ will be in suffering till the end of the world. Wherever there is human suffering God is involved, even if his presence does not prevent the physical and mental consequences of such suffering. Here God is powerless indeed by his own choice, not intervening in the structures of his creation though present to and through them. Such powerlessness remains a scandal to anthropomorphic conceptions of an omnipotent deity. This powerlessness is emphasised in the parable, which is not just our parable but God's substantially enacted parable, of the experience of the creator with death in the cross of Jesus. Through suffering as through rejoicing, God brings eschatological reconciliation.

That most intractable of all theological problems, the problem of evil, is then closely associated with the mystery of the hiddenness of the divine presence in the depths of the created order. We may think of the case of Dostoevsky's Alyosha and the reply that no amount of eschatological bliss can ever begin to justify God's permitting the torture of one single child in this world. There are again no simple answers. The theological response is to point again to the cross where God abandoned himself in love to mankind, where love is crushed and at the same time released through human hatred. But, it may be argued, it is one thing to suffer oneself for others and quite another to permit others to be tortured. God however is God, he is there in suffering identification, in silent identification, wherever such suffering occurs. This dimension of God's presence has been well appreciated especially in the light of the disasters of the Second World War, by Kitamori in his *Theology of the Pain of God*. God both lets us be in making possible authentic human response, and yet will not let us go, in constant total concern.

To speak of God as suffering is to use language analogically. But not all elements of our talk of God are analogical, certainly not analogical in the same way. Once again the basis of the analogy is in an understanding of God as love based on the biblical tradition. This is the given clue to the nature of God as substantially involved in the temporal process though not engulfed in it. To speak of God as suffering is no more and no less intelligible than to speak of God as not suffering, not subject to change, not affected by happenings in the world. We cannot escape the anthropological pole of theology simply by resort to negative theology.

6. Faith and Paradox

There was a time, not so distant, when the centre of systematic theology in many ways was providence. Following Calvin's development of Augustinian and medieval doctrines of double predestination, seventeenth-century orthodoxy spent much time examining the biblical evidence for the divine decrees, and seeking to relate them to evidence for divine presence in the form of external supports from nature and miracle, as part of an all-embracing theology of providence. Rationalist examination of such claims led inevitably to increasing scepticism about particular providence. The next step was the rapid establishment of deist or almost deist views of God as the standard Enlightenment grid for assessing talk of God. Kant in turn building on Hume called in question any pretence to standard frameworks. He raised again sharply the questions of the difficulty of truth conditions regarding talk of God in himself. It then required the turn to Biblical Theology associated with Barth, a heroic but desperate device, to come back to anything remotely resembling the sort of understanding of particular providence to be found in the biblical narrative.

Accounts of providence in modern theology have tended to follow either the standard Enlightenment pattern or the lines indicated by the repristinating theology of the biblical revival. In the first case there was an appeal to providence so general that its affirmation or denial became almost inconsequential for the lives of individual human beings. In the second case there was no appeal to particular providence in a mould claimed to be uniquely and decisively Christian, but seen in almost identical form in recent militant revivals in Islam, Buddhism and in Neo-orthodox movements in Hinduism.

It seems clear that providence is central to the religious understanding of God, and reappraisal of providence is likely to be best undertaken through re-examination of the doctrine of God. If we think of God as a sort of super-object, then we are likely to face a choice between a remote deist deity and an interventionist God. Both are equally unpalatable and may then lead us to scepticism. There may be another way. The transcendent, constant God need not be an unchanging deity of the sort envisaged by Aristotle. Equally, a God whose hidden presence is definitively characterised by his involvement in history need not be the 'fruity pagan deity' of naïve anthropomorphism.

God is immanent in the created order in a manner which is in important respects unique and inexplicable. He remains the hidden sustaining presence, quite independent of any sort of created presence. Because he has created men and women within this order, he has made it possible for us to have a human understanding of this presence. This is the basis of human relationship with God. Christians find the central clue to God as the loving God in the historical events relating to Jesus. This specific presence in love provides a means of discernment for testing the visions of men, empirical and spiritual. Not every appeal to the vision of the spirit is legitimated in faith's understanding of the divine presence and action. The love of God is the basis for coolness and discernment in understanding the affairs of the world and God's relationship with mankind. The fires of enthusiasm and the complacency of rationalism are to be tempered and questioned at the same time.[2]

A profound study of the hiddenness of God in Luther and Calvin has been made by Brian Gerrish. Luther begins from the early lectures on the Psalms. Interpreting Psalm 18.11, 'And he made the darkness his hiding place', Luther gives a fivefold application. God hides in the darkness of faith, in light inaccessible, in the mystery of the Incarnation, in the Church or the Blessed Virgin, and in the Eucharist. God is spoken of, not as an unknown but as hidden (*absconditus*). Luther's interpretation has traced two aspects of this hiddenness, God as unknown, the God of the law, *deus absolutus*, God behind his revelation, and God as hidden *in* his revelation, where revelation and hiddenness coincide. There is the hiddenness of God apart from Christ, and the mystery of God in Christ, hidden in incarnation, crucifixion, suffering.

There is a residual dualism here, which leads Luther to a painful paradox. The entirely reasonable affirmation that we do not know all about God, even in faith, becomes a lingering doubt about the character of the creator. Both Luther and Calvin become lost in the problem of double predestination. In recent times Karl Barth has stressed that God really *is* what

[2]On religious experience cf. R.W. Hepburn, R.R. Niebuhr.

he has shown himself to be. The mystery of God is the revealed mystery of his grace. However, in human experience there may be the most anguished conflict between faith and doubt. In that sense faith is a move away from the unknown God to the known, a movement experienced through suffering by the redeemer himself.

Reflecting on Gerrish's account we may be fairly sure that Luther's interpretation of the Psalms owes much to his medieval predecessors and to the Augustinian tradition. It is precisely true, as Karl Barth emphasised, that God is really revealed as he is in himself, as the God who loves, through Jesus Christ. But it is also true, as Augustine emphasised. that the loving God is not always an immediately present reality to all of us. Our hearts are restless (*inquietum*) till they find rest in God. The hiddenness of God, the mystery to be resolved in the greater mystery of word and sacrament, belongs to the centre of our faith.

The tradition of Luther has been eloquently developed in the twentieth century by Rudolf Bultmann. 'God's action generally, in nature and history, is hidden from the believer just as much as from the non-believer. But in so far as he sees what comes upon him here and now in the light of the divine word, he can and must take it as God's action.' Christian faith can only say, 'I trust that God is working here and there, but His action is hidden for it is not directly identical with the visible event' (*Jesus Christ and Mythology*). 'This is the paradox of faith, that faith "nevertheless" understands as God's action here and now an event which is completely intelligible in the natural or historical connection of events.' There are obviously dangers in such an approach, to which critics have often drawn attention. But the affirmation of faith in the hidden presence of God, the great 'nevertheless', remains a central and vital element of the Christian understanding of the gospel.

7

Personal Being

1. God's Being

My concern here is with the being of God. The basis of talk of God as love lies in faith and revelation, and is shaped through the biblical narratives understood in the Christian tradition. This ground goes beyond but does not contradict critical rationality: it is a mystery which embraces and transforms critical discernment. Faith develops between critical caution and religious enthusiasm. God's love both lets us be and will not let us go. It is the foundation and at the same time an invitation to concern for all human welfare. Such love has been understood often in the past through the symbol of the crucible, the fire whose warmth is a gift of the Holy Spirit. It is also an invitation to the coolness of Christian discernment.

In speaking of transcendence and immanence we have already gone some way towards explanation of the meaning and reference of the statement that God is. It is often said that God does not exist, but simply is. There are important distinctions to be made here. These are not to be made at the expense of avoiding the propositional puzzles raised by talk of divine being. We may not use the perspective of religions perception and religious experience as a reason to avoid taking thought.

As I understand the matter God is, as the ultimate spiritual entity, the hidden presence, transcendent and immanent, who is simultaneously creator and reconciler of the created order. He is both creator and redeemer simultaneously. At all times he has also been involved substantively in the created order and in the temporal process. Such a God is not easy to conceive.

That God's existence has not been and cannot be proved is a rational conclusion shared by Christian and non-Christian alike. The grounds on which people have based their affirmation of God's reality have varied as much as their conceptions of reality have varied, and the form of their argument has been even more diverse. I have indicated my own preference for a cumulative case based on arguments from a number of sources. It would be very convenient if a complete case could be built up from a single source, but I am not convinced by any attempts to date. Appeal to diverse sources brings its own problems, but these are not in my view insuperable.

Christian trust in the existence of a loving God, creator and reconciler, is based in the first instance on the biblical narratives, as these have been interpreted and appropriated in the experience of the Christian community, in life and thought, over two thousand years. The philosophical implication of the statements in these narratives about God's relation to mankind involve assertions about historical events and transhistorical realities. Trust is created through faith's experience of the reality of God, and this in turn may lead to the creation of a further intellectual framework as the servant of faith and understanding.

Here we may recall Austin Farrer's dictum: 'We can trust God if he exists, but we cannot trust him to exist.' This is used by Farrer as an apology for a particular sort of natural theology. But of course part of the grounds for trust in God's existence is the ground internal to faith in Jesus Christ. Natural theology and grace, as St. Thomas and von Balthasar – to mention only two of many – have insisted, overlap and are not to be separated arbitrarily. Affirmation of God's existence is based partly on faith's perception of the hidden presence of God, and its trust includes affirmation of this presence in the past from biblical times. It is also based partly on rational considerations concerning the appropriate shape of a cosmos-explaining, creating and sustaining being.

Not every concept of God requires such an existent God who is creator of the physical structures of the universe. Deities in various traditions and in some versions of Christianity have aesthetic and symbolic significance which is not related to a realist interpretation of engagement with the world. For this analysis ontological frameworks are not required. But for classical Christianity the claims, problems and implications are inescapable.

Classical theologians have long followed St.Thomas in asserting that creation has a beginning in time and is not eternal. Augustine suspected however that creation did not take place in time, but that time itself is an aspect of the created worlds. How then are we to speak of the creator himself in relation to time? God is traditionally held to be timeless and eternal. But the notion of a timeless God has been cogently criticised as being both meaningless in itself and as failing to do justice to Christian views of God's engagement with the creation. God is then seen to be involved in time, subject to change. Such a temporal God may be thought to be quite as incomprehensible and incoherent as an eternal God, involved in a mind-boggling confusion of activities. Compromise suggestions of a God who is both involved in time and beyond time appear more satisfactory, though still including residual mystery.

On seeking an explanation it is worth bearing in mind what can and cannot be expected of theology. Because God's presence is a spiritual presence, at once a hidden reality and a reality tied to particular characteristic of event related to Jesus, there is no possibility of our being able to penetrate as it were into a grand, complex reality of divine action and being beneath the surface of things, with the structure of something like a spiritual equivalent of a DNA molecule, waiting for the advance of the molecular theologian. To hope for this is the delusion of Platonism, the great flaw in much systematic theology.

Another possibility is the state of affairs in which we can give only an exclusively and existential reponse to our own impressions, somewhat as in the kerugmatic theology of Rudolf Bultmann, in the wider tradition of experience associated with Schleiermacher. We may then feel constrained to speak only of our own direct religious experience, and to use this as the sole criterion for judging talk of God. In this way a valuable aid for thinking of God may become a severe handicap.

Having set up these two possibilities we may be tempted to regard them as equipollent, cancelling each other out and so leaving us only with the option of a benevolent scepticism. It is possible however that several, in some respects contradictory, avenues can be explored to yield a better understanding. God, it seems to me, is best conceived as both independent of time and as operating in time, not only in relation to creation but also in regard to the significance of the events concerning Jesus, in his own life. To speak of the life of God is also to use analogical language, but the centre of Christianity is the living God.

2. Divine Substance

Discussion of *ousia* and *hypostasis*, substance and accident in the theological tradition, may well seem light years away from the problems of how to speak of a living God who is both creator of time and active in times. Yet this uniqueness of God as a complex reality, the most complex of realities, has forced theology back again and again to the crucial question of its nature.

We know that God does not exist simply as objects in the physical universe exist. In any case the question of existence in the universe is far from simple, in the light of new advances in science and in the range of the scientific imagination as it contemplates new possibilities from microbiology to macrophysics. God is not some sort of quasi-physical spiritual substance, exhibiting the same properties as physical substances but on a spiritual plane. God is not a being of the male sex with a particular cultural and genetic background, like all human males. Yet in Christianity he is understood as involved in a manner decisive not only for mankind but also for his own being, in the events related to Jesus of Nazareth. In the face of these specifications it is small wonder that discussion of divine substance has been difficult. How to try to understand while attempting to do some justice to the complexity of the divine reality remains perhaps theology's first problem.

The problem of divine substance is comparatively easily stated but not easily solved. Drawing upon the exegesis of such central passages as the 'I am that I am' of Exodus and the Johannine 'I and my father are one', the earliest Christian theologians turned naturally to Greek philosophy and especially to Plato, the best and most sophisticated philosophy available to them, to spell out the theoretical implications of faith's claims about God. In doing so they entered into philosophical debates already of long-standing. A great deal of conceptual development had of course already taken place in which different approaches to such terms as *ousia* and *hypostasis* had been hammered out.

Christians were concerned with God as Father, as Son and as Spirit. Distinctions between the one and the many in philosophical tradition from the presocratics onwards were linked with different expressions for the understanding of God as Father, of Jesus and of the Spirit. Various versions of a trinitarian concept were produced, some stressing the unity of the Godhead, others the distinction between the expressions of God, which came to be understood as persons. The relations between the three and the one, and the three among themselves in relation to the one, were again variously interpreted. Hence an account of divine substance, not universally agreed in every detail, but excluding a single essence uncompounded of parts at one end of the scale, and three Gods at the other end, involving one substance and three persons, came to guide Christian thought about God. Without an appreciation of God as creator, reconciler and spirit, it came to be held, talk of the Christian God is seriously inadequate or at least only very partially explored.

How does the understanding of God as love affect the understanding of the divine substance? Substance was a concept approached from many angles in Greek and Latin philosophy and in the medieval world. The Reformers reacted against what they regarded as a false ontologising of the tradition, in favour of faithfulness as a key to understanding God's nature. The tradition returned to the metaphysical issues, reaching in Leibnitz's view of substance a new systematic perfection. Though Kant and Hume brought that particular tradition to an end, the issues have since been discussed in various guises quite as intensively as ever before.

We cannot describe God in the ways in which we can describe either physical objects or people in their psychological or biochemical characteristics. We can only describe him in so far as he makes himself known to mankind. This may include the dimension of personal existential encounter but the data go beyond this limit. As loving, God is perceived to be both author and sustainer of the physical structure of the universe as well as the sustainer of individual lives, through the pattern of love disclosed in the events concerning Jesus.

Though we have no blueprint for God's nature, patterns worked out in early discussion of substance and Trinity may still help us. God is the author of the cosmos yet involved in personal relationship within himself and in relation to men. How such a God could be directly engaged in vital relation with such an infinitesimal piece of the cosmic structure as mankind is virtually inconceivable. Yet if the Christian faith is true, this is true.

3. Substance and Being

Substance in our everyday usage tends to suggest to us either the essence of a thing like the chestnut inside its outer covering, or a kind of stuff, like a sticky substance coming out of an upturned tin of treacle. The various interactions in the long history of its usage have given rise to different sorts of explanation.[1]

Substance is often divided into questions concerning the four areas of individuation, identity, objectivity and questions of the foundations of knowledge. We may look at the nature of individuation, what it is that gives a substance its own distinctive shape, and the relation of qualities and attributes to things. Why should it be thought that there is more to a thing than the sum of its properties? We can look at the idea of a thing in itself, at notions of references and existence, at the nature of the identity of things and the question of things of ultimate or eternal significance.

---

[1] Cf. Anthony Quinton, *The Nature of Things.*

Such an analysis helps us to avoid some common misunderstandings in speaking of substance. Though Plato and Aristotle developed complex and varied views of substance, the legacy at a general level of the Platonic tradition, revised but also reinforced by Thomas's enshrining of Aristotle, has led much Christian piety to conceive of God as a spiritual existent being in the manner of objects in the physical world. The manifest absence of traces of such a solid figure in the world has led since the Enlightenment to agnosticism and in our own day to atheism.

Since the Enlightenment there have grown up new concepts of substance, in which substance is seen as a sort of shorthand for a bundle of properties arranged in conventional clusters. This has in some ways been helpful to theology, displacing the quasi-physical substantial conceptions of the medieval world. In turn it has left the impression that talk of God's being as an independent transcendent existent is quite meaningless. This position has been forcibly and, despite the scorn of theologians, tellingly made by Antony Flew.

God as creator is outside the world of created being. He has independent, individual existence as a complex independent entity. As such he may be called the ground of being, provided that in using this phrase we draw no automatic assumptions about the nature of being drawn from created being, and provided that we assume no causal progressions of an Aristotelian sort from the ground of being to being.[2]

In making these qualifications something may be gained from the long tradition of negative theology, which functioned in the early Church as a sort of necessary counter to Platonic ontologism. However, it should be underlined that the Christian God is not the Neoplatonic God of negative being. God as ultimate spiritual reality is the ground of all creaturely reality, and he is known as such in his self-giving love towards his creation at all times.[3] It is not known exhaustively how he is

[2]On the notion of a cosmos-explaining being, cf. J.J. Shepherd, *Experience, Inference and God.*
[3]On the theological understanding of time, cf. John Lucas, Hugh Mellor. For Augustine on time, cf. Lampey, *Das Zeitproblem in den Bekenntnissen Augustins.* There are classic discussions in Gadamer and Barth.

known. But this need not lead us from epistemological
perplexity to metaphysical agnosticism. Such a step might only
be a kind of naïve realism.

The notion of ultimate substance is not to imply that he is
changeless, though changelessness and substance often go
together in the history of ideas.[4] On the contrary, God as self-
giving love is sympathetic and affected by the sympathy for his
creatures in his actions towards them.

God is ultimate, transcendent, spiritual reality. It does not
follow however that God is spirit without remainder. God is
Father, Son and Spirit. He is word and spirit, presence and
even incarnate presence through Jesus of Nazareth. No single
quality, attribute or property exhausts his nature. Love is not
an attribute among others but the prime overall characteristic
of his being.

God is love: God is. I have indicated that there remains in
my view something residually unsatisfactory in the Thomist
understanding of God's being, even with a measure of
improvement and modification. More unsatisfactory because
more reductionist are post-Enlightenment deist or humanist
frameworks in which God is essentially either remote from the
world as a 'non-interventionist' God or a transcendent postulate
of human understanding and no more.

Rather different is the account of God's being in much neo-
orthodox theology, in both Barth and Bultmann. Here God's
presence is affirmed in loving action, but again little can be said
of God in himself, and little of how he acts in the world.

I would want to lay stress on real knowledge through Jesus
Christ of God in himself, and an openness of God's loving
action in the world. God's love is weak in the world and is
therefore hidden from our sight by moral evil and the
contingency of the natural order. At the same time I would
agree with Barth that this is a knowledge in faith. There is
another order of knowledge which is reserved for the
eschatological dimension, when God's love will be seen to be
fully effective. Here pre-Enlightenment understandings of

---

[4]For divine substance cf. G.C. Stead, and the useful review of this in *Philosophical
Review* for March 1980. Cf. too *Archiv fur Begriffsgeschichte* on 'Substance'.

God's being as open to rational deduction are precluded. God's being is a personal being and so must be explored through an ontology of persons as well as of being. God is hidden in his being, but is open to faith, as personal being, in the Judaeo-Christian tradition. Now we must explore further this concept of personal being.

4. Divine Presence

By far the most important concept for the articulation of concepts of the God of Christian faith has been that of person.[5] God is the God of Abraham, Isaac and Jacob. In the Old Testament God has revealed himself as person in encounter with persons, and in the New Testament supremely in the person of Jesus Christ. As person he is a living, speaking, acting, communicating being acting through events in human history. He has all the optimum personal characteristics of human beings with none of their disadvantages. God is the one person for whom to be is to love *par excellence.* As transcendent person he has all the capacities of the creator.

God is then fully personal and more than personal. He is also as creator the sustaining ground of the physical structures of the universe. He is the ground of being, in such a manner that though all depends on him, he is in no way dependent on the created order. When he chooses to participate in this order, this is of his grace rather than of any external necessity.

In speaking of God as person Christians speak naturally of God the redeemer through Jesus Christ. How may we best understand God as a personal creator? Here we can begin to appreciate the advantages and disadvantages of personalism. Because God is a personal god nothing in creation takes place without his personal loving will and act. Where there is evil and disaster this takes place against the love of God, and not in indifference to it. The universe is not subject ultimately to random chance occurrence or to some sort of mechanistic determination. Whatever the infrastructure, all is ultimately

---

[5]Persons, cf. B. Williams, *Problems of the Self*; Shoemaker, *Self Knowledge and Self Identity.*

under the guidance of God. Process theology in speaking of God's persuasive action in the created order may go some way towards helping us to understand here.

At the same time we need not move towards animistic concepts, in which the universe is itself a living part of God. The lives of creator and creation are interwoven but also quite distinct. A personal creator may operate through impersonal, natural structures in order to promote personal ends. (We need not indulge in misleading sorts of romantic fallacies of identification with personal agency and 'personalising' activity.) Understanding a fully personal God does not imply accepting all the ramifications of philosophical personalism: in some instances the reverse may be the case.

A further modification of familiar concepts arises from the realisation that though God is fully personal and in an important sense a person, he is not an isolated individual in the physical sense in which human beings are. He is one in three persons, the unity existing in the threeness. Use has been made here with some success of societal models of personhood. This leads us to the centre of the trinitarian question. It is worth noting here what trinitarian models can and cannot be expected to do for us. Talk of Trinity reminds us that in Christian perspective God is not a single monolithic source of being, either as an anthropomorphic super-person or as an impersonal substance. In himself and in relation to us he is differentiated, as Father, Son and Spirit. With God creation and redemption, universality and particularity are simultaneous and complementary. Contingent human experience is taken up through Jesus Christ into divine being.

In thinking of God in human experience we must remember the old adage 'opera trinitatis ad extra sunt indivisa'. Christian tradition regards experience of a personal divine presence as experience not of the members of the Trinity separately but of the personal totality of the Godhead. Here both anthropomorphism and mystical ineffability are equally misleading. This hidden, transcendent and immanent personal presence is the reference of Christian tradition about God, the source of prayer and devotion and service.

One of the things we cannot reasonably say is that the

problem of the complexity of God as person is resolved simply by reference to threeness. For God is more complex than three thousand million individual selves, not to speak of three. On the plane of the issues, real issues, of the unintelligibility of notions of God's involvement simultaneously in innumerable conflicting thought and actions, threeness is really no better than oneness as an explanatory tool.

A further somewhat doubtful implication of Trinity is the suggestion that talk of God as person is legitimated solely as talk around the parabolic words and actions of Jesus, as the one risen from death. Such a picture of Christological personal *Sprachereignis* is equally limiting. As the one who is in his essential nature self-giving, self-affirming love, and therefore a non-embodied but infinitely personal being, God is reconciler, spirit, creator, *totus simul.* For God it is true that a thousand years are but as a day, and perhaps even truer that two thousand years are but as a micro-second, even if an extremely important one, and our planet as a speck of cosmic dust. To speak of God as personal in such a perspective we need reason and analysis, myth and symbol, metaphor and existential commitment. We also need some confidence in the reality of God's grace.

5. Types of Person

What sort of concepts of person do we regard as fruitful for the understanding of the creator and reconciler of all mankind? People come in all sorts. There are alcoholics, living a twilight existence in the communities to which they belong. There are short-term prisoners in our jails, constantly returning to the inside because of inadequate social service provisions outside. There are dropouts and dossers. There are public schoolboys coming through the Oxbridge colleges into the higher echelons of Church and state. God does not partake of humanity in biological terms. Whom does he most resemble in character? What sort of personal presence do we have in mind?

> I was asked to Sheila's home on Sunday afternoon. It was a neat, polished house with a television set, tape recorder, etc. I met Sheila's mother, a small, plump and compact person

who did not know how to react to me and found it difficult to talk at first, speaking to me through Sheila and referring to me as 'the lady'. I found this most disturbing but Sheila appeared not to notice and the atmosphere was more relaxed after tea. (Mary Morse, *The Unattached*, 107)

Is God small, squarely plump, compact, in a neatly polished house with a record player? If not, why not?

Try another character. '"Your father is getting on very well with the president", the Provost said. "At our first meeting, when he came to talk to me about you, I discovered him to be decidedly a Kunstgeschichtler. It is the kind of learning with which not every practising artist of high distinction troubles himself, I am told." The Provost paused on this accolade. There were no doubt a dozen people at the dinner party to whom some specific civility of this kind had to be offered. "So we must consider", he went on, "the question of showing him our own paintings. My idea is to form a small group later, without breaking up the company. Would that be right?"' (J.I.M. Stewart, *Young Patullo*, 235).

How is God person and how is he available as personal presence to all sorts and conditions of human person? Don't we feel that God would really feel more at home in the Provost's Lodge? Surely God's personal presence is at least a more heroic presence than in the first example, self-giving, self-affirming, dying, not in geriatric disintegration but in youthful martyrdom? Obviously neither élitist prejudice nor liberal sentimentality will do. As creator God is able to identify with all his creatures in every way. But to care is not to identify simplistically with their individual and collective shortcomings. God's love is an effective love, centred not in ascesis but in fruitful new creation, for human beings inaugurated in this life and fulfilled after death.

God does not have a body. But many of the consequences drawn from this proposition by Christian Neoplatonists through the ages are just plain wrong. God has a mind, or something like it, which allows mental functions. He lives, plans, creates, fulfils, relates, communicates, supports. For these reasons it is convenient – even essential, for nothing else will do – for us to use the term person. This term is legitimated for us in the sphere of revelation, in the Old Testament and in the tradition of the Church as well as in the New Testament, and also in human reflection at large on transcendence in the religions of mankind.

As living source of life and being God acts. The ways in which he acts are mysterious to us, apart from certain clues. He may appear to act according to the pattern of the laws of physics which he has created. Christians see a specific clue to God's action as loving action in the events concerning Jesus. There appears to be no empirical evidence of God's activity at specific places and times in world history. This is no proof of course that God is not at work within the physical structure of our world in various ways. There is evidence, in human experience, of the presence of the grace of the hidden God, even if this is not strong enough to be sufficient evidence on empirical criteria, e.g. as Christians understand life in the context of prayer and the answer to prayer.

Talk of personal analogies brings us on to the central issue of the Christological dimensions of talk of the Christian God. Through the incarnation, by which I mean the mystery of God's presence in the widest and most profound sense, we learn that the creator of the universe has opened up a new dimension of relationship with mankind, based on his own characteristic presence as the presence of self-giving love. This love is the foundation of renewal in creation. This is the ground of promise that the human future in God is not of doom and gloom but of hope and joy. The personal sequel to the cry of dereliction is the sound of the laughter of the children of God in heaven. If this is not so, then we ought indeed to be taking leave of God. That it is so is the faith of the Christian tradition.

6. Personal Attributes

In modern theology there has been a reaction, a highly understandable reaction to the traditional treatment of the attributes of God. Somehow the recital of a list of physical properties seems inappropriate to characterisation of the God who is a living, personal being. God is love. If we have to consider these categories, let us at least consider them as dimensions of his essential nature as love. This is an approach with which I have considerable sympathy. To speak of God's omnipotence as the omnipotence of the divine love is at once more intelligible and more consonant with the Christian understanding of God than the mere affirmation of omnipotence, with all the implications of arbitrary power which this carries for us. Yet once we recognise the crucial difference which an understanding of God as God in Christ, a trinitarian God makes to these Aristotelian attributes for primary substances, we can benefit from the philosophical tradition as a check on a reduction into imprecision and sentimentality.

I come back then, to the tradition of the attributes. God has *omnipotentia*, God has the capacity to do everything. This is really a corollary of the confession that God is the Lord. If he is Lord of all, then he has power over all, he can do everything. Does this mean that God has absolute power, and if so, where then is the reality of the independence of the creature, it has been asked. The answer must be that we know that this is not the way in which he has chosen to make his supreme power work. On the contrary, we see in Jesus of Nazareth that the power of God is made perfect in weakness. It is part of God's nature to will to create man as a creature with a real independence in relationship to himself. This ability to create autonomy in his creature is something that only God can do perfectly in relationships. God's power is related to his love, and the nature of his love is to let the creature be himself, to let be, as modern writers, notably Rahner, Macquarrie and Hick have stressed. In loving, Jesus did not attempt to impose his power upon people, but to serve. So it is with the almightiness of God. Yet at the same time, since God remains the Lord of heaven and earth, nothing can happen in the universe which God does not allow to happen. God does not break in and demand submission. Always, God is the one who stands at the door and knocks.

Omnipresence appears at first sight to be a synonym for pantheism. God is everywhere, in everything, and you may then reflect that everything is God. Reflection on transcendence and immanence between creator and creation suggests a rather different conclusion. God is not limited to any one place. There is no place where God cannot be with us. 'Ubique es, et nusquam locorum es', said St. Augustine. Though there is a sense in which we can be near to or far from God, by our own choice, it is fundamental to faith that nothing can separate us from the love of God in Christ.

Omniscience suggests a similar path to understanding. God's knowledge is not bound to space and time as ours is. This does not however entail that man's freedom is limited because God knows in advance what will take place. God's knowledge is an informed knowing, and his concern for creation is an informed concern.

A further traditional attribute of God is eternity. God is creator of all. Therefore time too is of his creation. The temporal as such is not inferior to the eternal, as in Plato's thought, because it is in itself part of God's good creation. God becomes involved in the temporal in the incarnation, yet remains also the Lord of time. He is not timeless, but he is not limited by time, as he is not limited by anything that he has created.

The whole notion of God's involvement in time raises difficult philosophical problems, and has led many philosophers to regard God as timeless. Indeed the whole question of the nature of time, and the relationship between time and space, remains a matter of active debate. Theology cannot offer solutions to philosophical problems in themselves. But the Christian tradition has certain constant implications which may need to be expressed differently as our perception of the nature of time changes. Though not limited by the temporal process, God does not stand apart from it. God is always involved, always with mankind.

Since all the attributes refer to God they are interrelated. I wish to consider here the righteousness of God. Because God is righteous he gives every man and woman what is his or her due, namely final fulfilment in terms of his own purpose for the human race. This righteousness is not an innate quality in mankind, but is restored through reconciliation in Christ. Further, since in God's creation all share equally, there is an element of equality in God's righteousness. It includes justice. Righteousness is an element of the divine concern for humanity, an aspect of his love.

There are other attributes, in the biblical and in the philosophical traditions. For example the Bible speaks of God's glory. This has usually been seen as connected with God's majesty, the radiance of the divine light of God, which accompanies him because he is God. It refers to the honour due to God because he is who he is, as well as to the effect which his presence has, in producing light out of darkness.

There are the attributes of the simplicity and immutability of God. We have seen that these are brought into question by our understanding of God as personal being. We may see simplicity as affirming that there are no final contradictions in the nature of the Godhead. But the word is misleading if it seeks to support an inaccurate notion of the superiority of the uncompounded, of parts to that which is complex, in the Platonic tradition. Similar considerations apply to the notion of immutability. Theologians are sometimes reluctant to affirm that God suffers, and is affected by events in the created order. This reluctance has a sound basis in the conviction that God the creator is always superior to his creation. But it may mask the distinctively Christian affirmation that God chooses to allow himself to be affected, as part of the vulnerability of a true incarnation involving the entire Godhead. Here again the patristic tradition of immutability and impassibility becomes a hindrance to the explanation of the gospel.

God is perfect. Any change from that perfection must be a decline. Therefore God is immutable. And since this world is but a shadow of the form of the ideal world, God cannot be affected by matter: he is impassible, unaffected, not subject to any change. Patristic discussion, notably in the fight against Arius, tended to reinforce notions of impassibility, and these can still find defenders. But I believe that the involvement of the undivided Godhead in suffering is an essential aspect of the gospel. This need not lead us further into process philosophy without remainder, though process philosophy has helped many theologians to articulate God's suffering involvement in the created order.

Something should be said here concerning the will of God. Christians believe that the will of God is disclosed supremely in Jesus Christ. Through Christ we learn of the reconciliation of humanity to God. This is related to the ancient discussion of election and predestination. The whole notion of predestination conjures up in the modern mind a rather sinister notion of God taking mysterious decisions about the fate of individuals before they are born. The Christian perspective is that God saw from the beginning the fulfilment of his purposes in Christ. The incarnation was not an accident or afterthought, an emergency measure in reaction to disaster, but was anticipated. Creation was intended to be fulfilled in election, in the coming of Christ to put us back on the road to fulfilment. This confirmation of humanity's place in God's purpose could not have occurred at all without the incarnation and cannot be appropriated except through the grace of God. At the same time, it is received in free personal decisions, since God is the one who gives authentic freedom.

Discussion of the divine attributes underlines many of the issues underlying all talk of the Christian God. Divine omnipotence is not precisely the same as human omnipotence. But it is not an inverse mirror image. That too would be anthropomorphism. It is real, effective power to bring about change. But it is power manifested through the divine powerlessness. Human powerlessness is just weakness and is ineffective. God is not ineffective, and this is part of the uniqueness of God. There is an element of paradox in such conceptions, though not all paradoxes are illuminating. It depends on the specific aspect of paradox involved. This is particularly clear in consideration of God and evil, to which we shall return.

In conclusion it has to be emphasised again that God's attributes are aspects of his being as personal being, and discussion of his attributes is a way of discussing further the nature of divine personal being, the divine love in its transcendence and immanence, its breadth and scope. This is the sphere of holiness, compassion, constancy, unlimited concern.

7. Intelligibility and Coherence

We have seen that though God's action is seen supremely for Christianity through Jesus Christ, it is desirable for theology to consider the nature of divine action *remoto Christo,* in order to stretch our theological imagination as far as possible precisely in order to do justice to the difference that the Christological dimension makes. Similar considerations apply in the case of persons, beings and personal being. We need to discuss arguments for and against talk of God as being and as person in order to make our theological statements as clearly as possible. I want to refer here to two arguments on similar topics, by Keith Ward and Stewart Sutherland. Keith Ward argues from the intelligibility of being to God as the one who is necessarily existent, the creator, a rational being who has purposes, expressed in goodness in opposition to evil. Divine benevolence flows out from divine being.

> Such co-operating and sharing love is one of the greatest values, as it is only in transcending self and relating to others that one truly becomes a person, a developing, self-expressing being discovering itself in the forms of its social relationships. Thus God can become a person, in this sense, only as he creates some community of rational agents in relation to which his own perfection can be expressed. In creation, God determines his own being as interactive; in doing so, he actualises his own nature as one who is love, in particular, contingent ways. (*Rational Theology and the Creativity of God,* 141)

Stewart Sutherland on the other hand abandons the notion of God as personal, as being incoherent and ultimately incomprehensible. This is derived from an analysis of what it is for God to know and to act. Theological assertion, illustrated from Maurice Wiles, simply lacks adequate rational grounds. 'The idea of God as an individual has gone, and with it must surely go the power and weight of the anthropomorphisms of the imaginings and sayings of the theism of communal and individual piety' (*God, Jesus and Belief,* 199).

It must be agreed that a great deal of modern theology does indeed rest on extremely precarious foundations, that Sutherland's choices are rational and his arguments attractive. Sutherland recommends that we preserve the advantages for the moral life of transcendental theism without the intellectual impossibilities by constructing a vision of life *sub specie aeternitatis,* as a kind of counterweight to myopic concentration on the present and the immediate, while still making sense of the world. Within such a framework Jesus may serve as a pointer to the nature of true goodness. In making these moves, reductionist in an entirely respectable sense, Sutherland comes close, from a different approach, to the course recently advocated by Don Cupitt in a number of studies. Remove the basic problem of a personal God, and an intelligible faith to live by may again become possible.

It will be obvious that the argument developed in this study of the nature of God's being as love, love often hidden but always present, precludes acceptance of this proposal. The sort of God whose actions and attributes can be measured and found wanting is not the God of classical Christian faith. But, it may be thought, such an elusive deity easily dies the death of a thousand qualifications if he is not to be discussed in terms of public criteria of truth. I agree. My argument is that God in the nature of the case is in some respects to be assessed by the criteria appropriate to beings in the created order and in other respects not. That is what it is to be God. Of course, if there is no relation at all to empirical evidence in the widest sense then indeed there comes a cut-off point, beyond which there is no reason to suppose that we may not be in a realm of pure fantasy. But as a matter of fact, rather than of theoretical possibility, I believe that the basis of the Christian tradition of God-talk, in reason, revelation and experience, can be rationally, though not of course conclusively, taken as a pointer in the direction of a trinitarian God, in which Jesus is not only a pointer to goodness but also to the nature of what it is to be God.

On the human plane, the whole question of what it is to be a person, and the explanation of personal identity, are the subject of lively philosophical debate, debate stimulated by new medical research on the nature of the human brain, and the consequences of development in brain surgery. The recent discussion between Shoemaker and Swinburne exemplifies the problem: each gives a quite different but equally persuasive account of the nature of personal identity, one a dualist and the other a materialist account. Discussion of the personal identity of God leaves open even more possibilities. For example, we might take up Rahner's insight into the nature of God who creates responsive being out of self-giving, not dissimilar to Jüngel's notion of God's being as including perishability. God as person might originate action through will and purpose without generating the problems of the relation of the temporal to the eternal which might lead us to discard the tradition of a personal God. That this is so cannot be proved. We cannot even offer a theory of how such action might take place. But this sort of action is in principle the sort of action we might appropriately attribute to God, since whatever he is, he is precisely not a creature, and therefore accounts of God's action in anthropomorphic terms must require radical modification. This is not to discount the anthropomorphic model, for it has an indispensable role in building up a framework of perspective for the theological imagination. But it cannot be the final arbiter of the possible in God.

8

Through Jesus Christ

1. Incarnation and God

The role of Jesus Christ in the doctrine of God remains a matter of continuing dispute. Masterly accounts of God have been given by two theologians on opposite sides of this dispute, Aquinas and Barth. There is also a considerable amount of common ground between the contrasting approaches. It may be that there is no one correct solution to the problem. Each must make his or her own judgement of what constitutes the most adequate account of the place of Christology in the doctrine of God.

In British and American theology there is comparatively little recent treatment of the events concerning Jesus in the formation of concepts of God. In the tradition of Barth, mainly on the European continent, Christology and God's involvement with death on the cross of Jesus have remained the focal point and ultimate reference of all God-talk. To speak of God has almost been synonymous with speech about God incarnate, experiencing death and overcoming death in resurrection. New developments in doctrine will probably come through study of these traditions rather than in spite of them. But there is a very long way to go before anything remotely satisfactory can, it seems, be expected.

Creation and reconciliation are not consecutive but simultaneous. In correction it is then said that on the cross God in his nature has been revealed, as one for whom self-abandonment constitutes his essential nature. Yet this is only a facet of the whole. For both in creation and in reconciliation God is the giver of life, of love, concern, fulfilment, both in regard to man and to his essential nature. If love appears to be irrevocably associated with suffering, that is not how God is in himself but how the world is, and not how it is meant to be. It is not in avoiding death and despair that theology speaks most accurately to the human condition. But in all this nothing can separate us from God's love.

In God it is better to arrive than to travel, whatever lessons may be learned *in via*. The reality of goodness in God is in some ways more of a scandal than the existential poignancy of the situation of heroic despair. We can become so fascinated with God's epic struggle with death that we forget the astounding claim that in God the sovereignty of the good has been established from all eternity. To doubt this is all too human. To doubt it systematically is to understate a central dimension of the gospel. To maintain the sovereignty of divine love is not of course synonymous with an optimistic view of Church and society. It is to maintain however that God is always to be trusted, as effective in his love.

While creation and redemption characterise God in various religions, in this area we come to the most historically contingent aspects of Christianity. In order to grasp the distinction of the biblical tradition we must be aware of the material in its historical context. Theology today lays much stress on the element of cultural relativism involved sometimes in the context of a minimising account of divine action. Oddly however there has often been much rather shallow interpretation of the background, in the case of the biblical material and of the secular Greek and Latin societies against which much of the decisive early interpretation was hammered out, notably the secular literature of the patristic period.

2. The Crucified God

In the last decade there has been much debate about the role of incarnation in theology.[1] Without rehearsing this discussion

---

[1]Cf. part 2, on God in reconciliation.

it may be said that the word incarnation will not automatically provide illumination. But the loss of certain features traditionally connoted by the model 'incarnation' drastically reduces the significance of God in human understanding. Where it is borne in mind that God is in his essential nature love, it goes without saying that the initiative is with God. that he is deeply involved in his creation, that the centre of his initiative and involvement is Jesus Christ.

Any theology which takes full account of these elements may be described as incarnational in that sense, implicitly or explicitly. However, an explicitly incarnational theology, such as that of Oscar Cullmann, may be inadequate to the reality of incarnation, while such a theology as that of D.M. Baillie, formally less favourable to incarnation, may be satisfactory, even if not all who appeal to it are equally successful.

To speak of God incarnate is to speak of the identity of Jesus Christ. The philosophical problems attending talk of personal identity in individuals are formidable. When we speak of God the creator in identity with a man the difficulty of explanation is compounded. We ought to be able to say something of this identity, for we are concerned with the identity of God. This is not the only clue to the identity of the Christian God, but it is a most important one, in some circumstances the sole compelling clue. As I understand the matter, in revelation as in reason we are invited to consider a number of clues which point to and can be built up into a cumulative case and a cumulative pattern for the understanding of God. Each of these clues has been at different times blindingly illuminating by itself. It is important from time to time to consider the framework as a whole, or as far as we can go towards this. We can for example learn, in recent continental theology, both from the general frameworks advocated by Pannenberg and the highly particular approaches of Jüngel and Moltmann, with further modifications as required. Whether the result is a muddled compromise or a new step in thinking depends entirely on the nature of the analysis.

In speaking of the identity of Jesus Christ we are speaking of the identity of God. We are thinking of God's engagement with human life, particularly with human pain, suffering and death.

No one in modern theology has written more eloquently of the identity of God with human suffering than Jürgen Moltmann in his profound study *The Crucified God*. Talk of the cross of Christ is the centre not just of Christology but of theology. God is the crucified God, or he is not God at all. This is the centre of the Christian perspective on God. I have registered criticism of Moltmann's work elsewhere. Here I want to stress what I regard as the creativity of his work as a guide for the future of talk of God.

The cross of Christ is the foundation and criticism of Christian theology. The cross is not and cannot be loved. Yet only the crucified Christ can bring the freedom which changes the world because it is no longer afraid of death. Much of the official face of Christianity, liberal and conservative alike, is sadly irrelevant in the modern world. Christians must rediscover their true identity through identification with the cross of Christ, and so through solidarity with the poor and the oppressed in this world. Solidarity becomes radical only if it imitates the identification of the crucified Christ with the abandoned, accepts the suffering of creative love, and is not led astray by its own dream of omnipotence in an illusory future. In other words, he that doeth the will shall know of the doctrine.

Jesus is true God and true man. As the crucified one, the risen Christ is there for all. In the cross of the son of God, in his abandonment by God, the crucified God is the God of all godless men and those who have been abandoned by God. Jesus' death is death in God, though not the death of God. Theology has too often replaced Luther's God of the weakness of the cross with the God of the philosophers and the psychiatrists. We need a new exploration of the cosmic dimensions of the cross, which will generate a new metaphysics between theism and atheism. Like protest atheism, but unlike philosophical theism, the theology of the cross takes up seriously the mystery of evil in the world. The cross involved Trinity and eschatology. 'For eschatological faith, the Trinitarian God-event on the cross becomes the history of God which is open to the future and which opens up the future' (255). If not self-evidently meaningful, this is challenging at least. 'The Trinity is not an exclusive mystery which seals off the orthodox as a superior race, but an expression of God's identity with suffering. Even Auschwitz is taken up into the grief of the Father, the surrender of the Son and the power of the Spirit' (278).

How is this cross-centred, trinitarian concept of God to be related to questions about the nature of human existence in society? The connection is in the identification of the faith with the suffering of the poor and oppressed in our world. It is in the light of his solidarity with the weak and the broken-hearted that God through the cross makes sense, in relation to our understanding of the world. Faith and reason complement each other not in a Platonic harmony but in a Lutheran *theologia crucis*. God is not an impassible Constantinian monarch but a fellow sufferer with our pains. Clearly, a theology in which this key element is underestimated is a pale shadow of the Christian gospel.

This is theology of the sacrifice not just of Jesus but of God on the cross. God is the subject and object of sacrifice, through his own love destroying evil by abandoning himself, and at the same time coming through death in resurrection. This does not mean that God dies: not the death of God, but death in God is at the heart of the divine mystery. This is a radical modern theology, taking account of the historical reality of the life of Jesus and of the enormity of the problem of evil in our world.

Interestingly it moves in a direction opposite to that of much radical modern British theology, which sees the development of historical consciousness and the problem of talk of God in today's world as a basis for abandoning, or at least drastically revising, both key concepts of Moltmann's theology, incarnation and Trinity. Perhaps in conceiving of God as person we ought to begin from the personal presence of the crucified Christ. On the Continent there has been a great deal of further imaginative writing on God's involvement in death in the work of Rahner, in von Balthasar and Jüngel. Any theological understanding of God as the loving God must include the dimension of God on the cross. 'God is unconditional love, because he takes on himself grief at the contradiction in men and does not angrily suppress this contradiction. God allows himself to be forced out. God suffers. God allows himself to be crucified and in this consummates his unconditional love that is so full of hope.' To recognise God in the cross of Christ means to recognise the cross, inextricable suffering, death and hopeless rejection in God.

This is clearly important. However, it is possible to offer cogent criticism of this suggestion that the key to talk of the Christian God is to be found in the cross. In doing so it remains essential to maintain awareness of the profound value of Moltmann's line of thought. If one begins only from God *in genere* and then goes on to speak of God in Christ and then of the death of God on the cross, this death itself becomes a 'phenomenon of God'. We must begin from the cross in order to understand the meaning of the term 'God' for faith. It could be said however that the basis for talk of God's presence as love is wider than this. It is decisively expressed on the cross because of the nature of man rather than the nature of God. The God who is love expressed himself primarily in resurrection in which God's experience of involvement in death is a central factor. It is not the only factor. God remains the creator God, the living God who delights in the building up of his new creation. To use an example from common human experience, our own births, marriages and death may provide a framework for our activity, but not all our activity reflects these points in any direct sense. The experience of my own birth may reflect the pains of writing a book, but the imagination need not always be helpfully stimulated by this sort of symbolic parallelism and romantic mythology.

I have suggested that the essence of Christianity, if there be such a thing, is not the cross of Christ but the love of God. God's self-giving, self-affirming love is most decisively expressed on the cross because of the nature of man rather than because of the nature of God. The God who is love expresses himself primarily in resurrection and joy, the fullness of life.

Two further comments may be made here. Too often in history people have rushed into religious martyrdom, espousing death for the God who is near in death, when they ought simply to have reflected on the political incompetence of their leaders and turned them out at the ballot box. Worse, in the years since Auschwitz we have become positively blasé about mass extermination, domesticating the horror in glossy photographs. To see God as characteristically rather than exceptionally involved in such butchery, even as a victim, could lead paradoxically into acquiescence, and so become a final tribute to monstrous evil. God's love is not a beautiful solidarity in suffering but an identification which is utterly intolerant of the evil which is the opposite of love. Death is indeed the last enemy, and in the resurrection of Christ it is destroyed.

God is greater than our greatest thought of him. The last thing we need is a bland theology including a small element of the cross, a little resurrection, an innocuous balance of everything. In all the dimensions of God's love which we seek to explore, his joy, his suffering, his glory and his humiliation, God's gracious presence includes dimensions beyond all that we can ask or think. None of us can deal adequately with all or even any of these themes. That is why we must be grateful for a fresh and thorough exploration of some of the facets of any one of them. This may not be the whole picture, but it may afford us a marvellous opportunity to reflect again critically on one central area of the depth of God's love.

For Eberhard Jüngel, in the continental tradition of understanding God from the cross, 'The crucified one is the criterion for a possible concept of God. From the point of view of the world (that is, the world of post-Enlightenment thought and the secularised society), God is by no means necessary', and so all natural theology based on demonstrating such a necessity is futile. God can be thought of only from the word of the cross, in which he was involved in human death. The word is a self-authenticating word which creates its own convictions by faith alone. Rahner and von Balthasar, and the Jewish theologians Martin Buber and Eli Wiesel, have all taken up this theme of the eclipse of God and the revelation of God in death. As Rahner says, 'Through the death of Jesus our death becomes the death of the immortal God himself.'

3. Resurrection

Through Jesus Christ the nature of the hidden, mysterious presence of God is disclosed, through death but also through resurrection. In one sense resurrection may be thought to compound the mystery, for no human being has come through death to give us an account of the experience of resurrection. Jesus himself has, but this is a special case which will not answer all our questions. There is of course a long tradition about resurrection from the dead in Israel, and the post-resurrection communities drew on this experience and imagery to express their faith in the presence of their risen Lord. Still, it is immensely hard for us to conceive of what it could possibly be like to be dead and then to come alive again. We can look at the mystical traditions in other religions of reincarnations in other places as indicating the range of human imagination on the subject. We can look at accounts of dreams and sensations by people who have spent long periods in coma after accidents. We can consider the familiar daily process of going to sleep and waking up. But then we must admit that nothing in human experience remotely measures up to the sort of material we require to be able to begin to understand the involvement of the creator of the universe in human resurrection.

Once again the enormity of the conceptual gulf between talk of God and talk of human experience reasserts itself. Two thousand years of Christian tradition is precious little even in the scale of life on earth. Yet the particular contingent cluster of events which constitutes Jesus' resurrection is vital, for the divine presence is not a wordless and featureless mystery. To be God is to be involved in the destruction and reconstruction of life. The lines between living and inanimate organisms in chemistry are hard to draw and far from clear cut. The main point here is that God as person is involved in the destruction and reconstruction of a personal consciousness, whatever the biochemical constituents of such consciousness in living and dead specimens may be. The post-Easter proclamation 'I am the resurrection and the life' proclaims God, not as the source of a vitalist principle, but as the source of healing, recreation and renewal within the world of sentient, intelligent personality.

'Did he who made the Lamb make immunology?' It can be no part of the theologian's task to trace the hand of God in the technical process of the life sciences. We cannot even see God as a kind of organic source of matter, rather in the manner of some panentheistic thought. Rather, we may perhaps consider that in his involvement with the resurrection of Jesus God invites us to see him, not as part of the created order but as one in whom there is a personal power to heal and restore human personhood after it has been destroyed by the physical process of decay. Such is the character of the God of the resurrection. Further, this renewing facility is present in the eternal nature of God himself, so that he is constantly engaged in fresh creative and sustaining activity. Such a prospect is not quite the pattern of the divine energies in patristic thought, but rather of a personal affective consciousness of a dynamic quality virtually inconceivable to human experience. It is not that God is endlessly and frenetically busy, but that the resurrection clue characterised him as one who is constantly eliciting in creation newness of life, and brings it about, sometimes in the physical structures of creation, sometimes on an eschatological, spiritual plane, precisely in the midst of the processes of decay and destruction. God's love as resurrection love is effective because it is ultimately and ceaselessly active.

4. The Life of Jesus and the Understanding of God

Resurrection, death, life. The life of Jesus is and remains central to our understanding of the being not only of the man Jesus but of God, creator and redeemer. The significance for God-talk of the life of Jesus has been recognised in various theological traditions, though its development requires further thought. In the tradition of dialectical theology Emil Brunner in *Die Mystik und das Wort* pilloried the Catholic mystical tradition in the name of the living word. In Liberal Protestantism Don Cupitt has recently used the ironic languages and style of Jesus as the key to the understanding of religion, in *Taking Leave of God* and other books.

We must be very careful about how we use analogies in relating language concerning Jesus to language concerning God. We can and we must use personal analogies in religion. We can and we must use Christological analogy. But we have to be careful about how this is done. It will not do, either, to contrast analogies of being with analogies of grace. Being and grace are correlative: all depends on how the analogies are used. It has been shown that St. Thomas, for example, was much more circumspect in his various uses of analogy, than his critics often imagined. We may perhaps use the events concerning Jesus as paradigmatic clues given by grace to the understanding of God, and we must use our powers of reasoning, including comparison and argument, to understand these clues, We cannot however simply extrapolate from the man Jesus to the divine nature as if there were some authorised one to one correspondence, whether through analogy of grace or being. We may not say that because Jesus used parables all his language is parabolic and our understanding of theology is parabolic in the same way. We may not say that because Jesus was male God has hallowed maleness as the preferred human concept for understanding or receiving either God or redemption. Yet such arguments are constantly deployed in theology. We must bear in mind too the issues raised by various sorts of combination of relativism in relating concepts derived from the story of Jesus, a man at a particular place in a particular time, to the being of the eternal God.

The life-style, teaching and activity, all these make up the character of Jesus which is the basic clue to the Christian understanding of God. This we understand *par excellence* as the character of the divine love in human circumstances. Despite the fragmentary and varied nature of the evidence, most of us would agree that Jesus comes through the gospel tradition as the embodiment of self-giving, self-affirming love, devoted to God and man, intolerant of evil which is the opposite of love. Jesus is concerned for the poor, the oppressed, the exploited. God is concerned especially for his creatures who are in this position. This observation sometimes leads people to feel that God is less concerned for those who are less poor and less oppressed, but care is needed here. It would appear rather that God, whose being is expressed in love unto death because of the nature of man rather than of God, is concerned for the wellbeing and fullness of enjoyment of creation of all his creatures, rich and poor. The crucial point is that the poor are farthest from this condition, and so most urgently in need of effective loving concern and action.

The centre of Jesus' life is his devotion to his father in heaven. The forms of expression which this devotion took reflected the conventions and practice of the age. The central element I take to be this. God is a God who invites communication and community between himself and mankind. He is not content with a non-communicating situation in which he does his work and we do ours, but he encourages us to develop as human beings through the maturing of a spiritual relationship with him. This relationship is not fostered at the expense of other human relationships. It takes place in, with and under these. This is a further clue from the life of Jesus to the nature of the personal God. He is the source of and the answer to prayer. With all due regard for the analogical nature of language, he is a God who listens, who enters into a loving relationship which encourages maturity and freedom in human beings. As the stimulus and the answer to prayer he is in this dimension too the self-giving God.

The parables of Jesus, his life and his teaching are the central clues, for Christians, to self-giving love. God's kenotic self-giving is incarnation and service is the way of the cross. Through the suffering humanity of Jesus Christ in humiliation comes resurrection. God is compassionate and creates compassion in us. Jesus Christ is God for us, answering God's self-emptying in his own life of sacrificial love, a love eschatologically effective through resurrection. This perspective says more than a little about Jesus, about God and man, and the way of discipleship in the world. It is this God, the God who has made himself vulnerable in the contingency, whom Christians understand as the creator and reconciler of the cosmos.

9

God the Holy Spirit

1. God as Spirit

God is creator and redeemer, a mysterious hidden presence, understood by Christians in various ways as Father, Son and Holy Spirit. This state of affairs is reflected in trinitarian imagery throughout the ages. God is one, yet in a complex sense differentiated within himself. In talking of God we are talking of God as Spirit, as well as Father and Son. In this chapter we should like to explore further the dimension of God as Spirit. This has always been a central feature of Christian faith, articulated in various distinctive ways.

In previous chapters we explored the paradox which lies at the heart of Christian faith in the modern world and which in turn gives rise to a number of dialectical tensions. God is a living God. He is the centre of the faith and devotion of millions of people, day by day. Yet there is for millions of other intelligent people, a great question mark hanging over the very idea of God. The problem of evil raises more acutely than ever before the question of divine action. Why does God not do something about starvation and mass murder in our time? Why is evidence for his providential action so selective, so unpredictable, so miserably far short of what is urgently and immediately required?

It may seem that these are easily answered questions. If God acted as a person in the world of persons, putting everything instantly in order, there would be no scope for human freedom. Such a controller is not the God of Christian faith. We can also affirm that God moves in a mysterious way, his wonders to perform. Since such a claim is infinitely elastic it cannot be disproved. But of course it easily dies the death of a thousand qualifications, becoming an insignificant and trivial piece of folklore.

In the face of this continuing paradox, I believe that exploration of the Spirit of God may indicate ways forward. Of course mere invocation of the Spirit to decorate the arguments we have just mentioned will lead us no further. We may say that the Spirit produces concrete manifestations of God's power in particular cases, after the manner of medieval miracle stories. We may also say that the whole process is radically mysterious. taking refuge in spiritual ineffability. Neither course cuts any ice, nor should it.

Somehow, steering between the Scylla of fundamentalism and the Charybdis of pantheism, we want to think out the implications of affirmation of God's hidden love as at work everywhere in the created order, more present than any human presence, yet not open to our everyday criteria of success or failure. We want to think about the power of the Spirit.

It is often said that the doctrine of the Holy Spirit is the most neglected area of Christian theology. Yet in fact there is a vast amount of modern reflection on the subject. Karl Barth has written extensively of the Spirit as 'the most intimate friend of a proper human understanding of man'. Karl Rahner puts it this way. 'The essential nature of genuine experience of the Spirit does not consist in particular objects of experience found in human awareness but occurs rather when a man experiences the radical reordering of his transcendent nature in knowledge and freedom towards the immediate reality of God through God's self-communication in grace.'[1]

What we are concerned with here is the relation between thought and life, between Christian reflection and Christian expression of thought in community. In a fascinating article entitled 'Creator Spiritus, the challenge of Pentecostal experience to Pentecostal theology', Walter Hollenweger

---

[1] Karl Rahner, *Theological Investigations* XVI, 27.

criticised the Neopentecostals and charismatics in other denominations for neglecting the world of experience in theology. 'Their charisma does not lie in theological formulas but in theological experience.'[2] This is not simply a vague sense of excitement. It leads in turn to a new appraisal of theology, to a charismatic doctrine of the Trinity, a charismatic ecclesiology and a charismatic theology of the world. In other words, doctrinal appraisal must look forwards as well as backwards.

Let us consider briefly the understanding of the Spirit in the biblical narratives. Perhaps the most influential imagery in Christian devotion has been the imagery of St. John and St. Paul. In the Fourth Gospel the Father is present and at work in the Son, who continues to be present and active in the Spirit. For St. Paul, the Spirit is the source of strength and action. We do not even know how to speak to God in prayer. But in our weakness the Spirit comes to our aid. This Spirit is always the Spirit of Christ, crucified and risen.

The Spirit is the Spirit of Christ. Nothing, says St. Paul, can separate us from the love of God in Jesus Christ our Lord. The Spirit is not a third dimension which takes away from the centrality of the events concerning Jesus. The Spirit points us to the cross, not in a narrow sense but in an inclusive sense, as continuance. Christian love is anything but a bland tolerance of all that is done in the name of God.

2. Spirit and Holy Spirit

In speaking of God as spirit and God as Holy Spirit we are not referring to two separate entities. Our concepts for understanding spirit and Holy Spirit overlap. But there are important distinctions to be made. The relationship between the two is parallel to that of creation to new creation. Christians believe that God, through the Holy Spirit of the risen Christ, brings to expression and articulation that which is already present in the created order.

---

[2] W. Hollenweger in *Theology*, 1978, 32f.

The sense of the presence of God is affirmed throughout the major religions. Many who would not speak of God have been aware of a sense of transcendence which they regard as more than a product of their own self-consciousness. In Judaism there has been a long tradition of witness to the presence of God as a loving, suffering God who is present to his people, enduring with them throughout history. Religious people have understood the human spirit, and the recognition of self-consciousness, as itself as response to the Spirit of God its creator. The Holy Spirit is not the successor of all these things, but rather brings all such awareness of spirit to fulfilment.

Yet the fruits of the Spirit in Christian life are still only first fruits. To confuse the ultimate things with the penultimate is, as Bonhoeffer constantly recalled, a fatal mistake. We walk still by faith, and our vision remains limited.

3. Life in the Spirit

When Christians speak of God they often proceed by setting out the evidence for God's existence and activity, arguing carefully and seeking to build up the best possible cumulative case. But they have always understood that the awakening of faith, and the deepening of faith, is a matter not contrary to reason but including things beyond reason. Here is the proper role of the 'reasons of the heart'. Faith in this sense is a gift of the Holy Spirit. It is not however a self-contained spiritual dimension. It is faith in God through Jesus Christ. At the same time, it is not simply faith in the veracity of some parts of an historical narrative as such. It is a living faith, which creates its own relationship of response and reciprocity. This, Christians have affirmed through the ages, is part of the meaning of life in the Spirit.

It is not perhaps as easy to speak of the Spirit which is the subject of life in the Spirit as it is to speak of God as Father or as Son. We cannot here focus on a centre of activity in the same way that we can think of cosmic creation through the Father or redemption in a life lived in historical vulnerability by the Son. To that extent the Spirit is much more of a challenge to the Christian imagination. The notion of the Spirit as relation but somehow much more than a mere link between Father and Son, seeks to express this mystery.

It is then in the Spirit that all Christian life, thought and action is lived. But this need not be accompanied by any special extraordinary manifestations. The nature of the Spirit is precisely that it is free from the limitations of empirical reality, though it may make a great difference to empirical reality in the created order. However, this does not take away from the freedom of the Spirit to manifest himself within the structures of empirical reality if he chooses in his freedom to do so. But this freedom remains entirely a gift of God's grace, in no sense open to our disposal.

God invites mankind to become instruments of his love in service to all men and women. We may then venture to affirm that wherever there is concern shown for others, after the pattern of the love of the crucified Christ, there is the working of the Holy Spirit. Such love may be worked out in action in innumerable ways. Sometimes love may inspire dramatic action. At other times it is shown in almost imperceptible endless acts of compassion and care for our fellow human beings.

There are no bounds to the work of the Spirit. It is possible however to indicate distinctive but not separate areas of the Spirit's influence.

1. The Spirit of God, as the Spirit of the risen Christ, is promised in the New Testament to all believers. Through the Spirit Christians become aware of the presence of God as a personal presence. For various reasons, we may on occasion experience the absence rather than the presence, of God. But that God is present, that he is concerned for each particular individual, for every Christian and indeed for every human being, is a fact at the centre of the gospel. Without this the sea of faith becomes the faith at sea. There is a legitimate individual dimension in the presence of the Spirit, not to be swallowed up in the collective. But this individual element is not a licence for any sort of ego-trip.

> The man from Pretoria
> Whose sins grew goryer and goryer
> But by fasting and prayer

And some savoir faire
He now lives at the Waldorf Astoria.[3]

The Spirit is never given to the individual as a possession. Christians have always understood that the Spirit is a gift only received as it is poured out in concern for others.

2. The Spirit of God is experienced in relationship in the corporate community of Christ's body, the Church, in the fellowship of word, sacrament and discipleship. It is part of the paradox of faith that the Church, which is so full of imperfection and limitation at every level, does on occasion function as the instrument of God's love to humankind. Christians understand this effective ministry, despite almost all appearance to the contrary, as the action of the Holy Spirit. This is a process which continues in different ways throughout history. 'It is this historical character of Christianity which gives to the Church not only the mission of the Spirit but certain media of continuity through which the Spirit acts in the Church's common life: these media of continuity include the sacraments, the apostolic ministry and a tradition of teaching. The Church is thus not without visible shape, and this shape is itself a witness to the history of salvation. But while the Spirit uses this shape and the media which constitute it, the Spirit also acts in unpredictable ways, exposing, teaching, illuminating, judging, renewing.'[4]

3. The sharing in community which characterises the Church is not confined to the eucharistic fellowship. Community is open, the Church is there as the servant of the world for the sake of the gospel. Christians are called both out of and into the world. In this outward movement, from the outward facing circle, there is a giving on the part of the community of the spirit of the risen Christ. The distinctive character of the gift of Christian life in worship and service should not be underestimated.

---

[3]Martin and Mullen, *Strange Gifts*, 161.
[4]Michael Ramsey, *Holy Spirit*, 86.

4. In the encounter between Christians and non-Christians (and this is often scarcely a hard division) there is a meeting involving different dimensions of God's spirit and the spirit of man. God's sustaining, creative Spirit is at the centre of every human life. It nurtures the human spirit, in the kind of self- giving which in turn creates autonomy, which only God can truly give. Within this dialogue of spirits in creation there is introduced the Christian spirit of the new creation. This is not a completely new beginning, but it is a decisive enrichment of the created order. The consequences of a renewed concentration on spirit for a new understanding of Church and society have recently been emphasised, again by Walter Hollenweger.

> It is my experience that many so-called unchurched people are prepared to offer their gifts, their charisms, if we ask them to share what they have. Is the denial of charisms in non- Christian or unchurched people one of the reasons for the uneasy relationship between churches and actors, writers and musicians? Many of them want to follow Christ in their vocation, with their gifts. As these do not fit our criteria, their gifts are ignored in the same way as we ignore the gifts of the indigenous Christians of the Third World. If we can recognise the Spirit in unusual places and in unexpected people, in all creatures great and small, we might win new friends.[5]

The secularisation of European society is not likely to go away, and it is probably preferable to the great new religious fundamentalisms which were a mark of the 80s. We need not deprecate modern civilisation. Equally, we need not conclude too soon that there is no transcendent God, creator and redeemer. We need not regard God as a name for human self-consciousness. God in Christian faith has always been the hidden, living presence who is always with his people, suffering, enduring, and sustaining. In every generation we need renewed imagery to relate this presence to human experience. It may be that reconsideration of God as Spirit, Spirit in the Church and in the world, can help us to think again about the unique spiritual reality whom faith knows as God.

[5]Hollenweger in Martin and Mullen, op. cit., 53.

4. The Historicality of the Spirit

God the Son was committed to our world in incarnation, crucifixion and resurrection, and remains committed to our world through the Spirit of the risen Christ. God the Spirit is committed to the created order from primal soup to nuclear winter and whatever comes after. In this section we want to think about the historicality of the Spirit. The historicality of the Spirit is related to the historicality of God in Christ, and to the notion of the cosmic Christ. In some religious thinking the manifestation of the Spirit is demonstrated by the occurrence of the extraordinary. However, in an understanding of the action of the Spirit in, with and under the history of the created order, rather different expectations are created. We should not be surprised when empirical observation yields little or no evidence of the activity of the Spirit, and we should certainly not deduce from the ordinariness of events the non-existence of God as Spirit. Such an argument can easily prove too much. Non-manifestation becomes proof of existence, malnutrition is a sign of well-being. Nevertheless if a cumulative case for Christian faith based on reason, revelation and experience adds up to nothing more, it is a continuing affirmation that out of the ordinary course of events there comes awareness of God's love as gift, as something making sense out of nonsense, enabling men and women to act as bearers of God's love to one another. This, in our view, is an important area of the historicality of the Spirit.

Here the historicality of the Spirit is related to the historicality of God in Christ. Human love, inspired by God the creator Spirit, is related to divine love, incarnate in God the redeemer. There is a basic reciprocity between God's saving love in Christ and human love wherever this is shown. Each may strengthen the other, not in any sort of co-operation but through God's self-giving which creates the condition of the possibility of self-giving in his creature, and nurtures self-giving as a reality through the Spirit. We must indeed overcome the plausibility criteria of a secular age in speaking of the living God. This is done, not by turning to the sensational, but by affirming the world of everyday experience as the theatre of the Spirit of God. It is precisely through the fellowship of Christian community in word and sacrament that we may affirm God's reality in experience outside this community of discipleship.

This reflection brings us, towards the end of this section, to the Old Testament. It is perhaps not without significance that the main Old Testament experience of God as Spirit is not in the special manifestations but in the everyday world of the politics and economics of the people of Israel. Here God moves in love among his chosen people, faithful to them even in their unfaithfulness. There are, indeed, occasional special manifestations. But these are only unusual indications highlighting the significance of the usual. They are also dangerous. For they are easily counterfeited, as men seek to rush things which move more slowly and in a more complex manner under the guidance of God's Spirit.

We have been thinking of the historicality of the Spirit, embedded not in the extraordinary but in the ordinary. This may have important implications for Christian dialogue with non-Christians throughout the world. Within Christianity, we observed, it is neither desirable to embrace fundamentalism, even if of a charismatic sort, nor to embrace secularism as being the new essence of the gospel, in the name of the Spirit. Similar considerations apply in relation to other religions and to militant atheism. It is no part of Christian duty to encourage fundamentalisms in other religions which would be unacceptable in Christianity, or to offer uncritical support for monolithic and potentially totalitarian ideologies. However, whenever the human spirit seeks for transcendence, in innumerable different ways, there is scope for dialogue through the bridge which the Spirit of God already provides. Such dialogue will have to take account of the distinctive character of the partners in discussion. The Spirit of the risen Christ is always intolerant of exploitation of some human beings by others, however exalted the aim of the exercise.

It is in reflection on transcendence, which may be the result not of conscious effort but of spontaneous response to human experience, that recognition of the Spirit of God comes. The sense of the presence of God is expressed in different theological traditions in different ways. In the recent European tradition it was expressed by Schleiermacher as God consciousness, awareness of absolute dependence, an awareness focused through Christ's gift of his own God consciousness to Christians. For Barth it was recognition of the sovereignty of the Word of God in judgement and forgiveness. For Rahner it was the movement of the Holy Spirit through the human search for self-transcendence. We may reflect that each of these approaches reflects in a different mode, the dialectical relationship between the Spirit as the Spirit of the risen Christ, and the Spirit as creator Spirit. It is a consequence of the historicality of the Spirit that it is apprehended in different ways at different times, but always as the Spirit of the love of God in history.

There may be occasions in history when the action of the Spirit is totally unseen. The historical witness to God in Christ has been in places, and may be more widely in the future, completely silenced or distorted into a lie. Yet since God's love precedes, accompanies and succeeds time, Christians believe that God's Spirit will always sustain mankind, whether in this life or in the future with God. The promise of fulfilment of life in the Spirit is a central dimension of the Christian hope. As such it has consequences for the present, encouraging us to seek a quality of relationship and of well being, physical as well as mental, which will increasingly reflect the future of God's Spirit into which it is destined to grow. This is a spirit of creative rather than destructive tension, and as such is as relevant to modern industrial disputes as it is to dialogue about the Filioque. It is hardly possible to over-emphasise the fundamental importance, in any discussion of the work of the Spirit, of William Temple's comment in the introduction to the 1938 Doctrine Report (23): 'If God is Love, it is only among people animated by mutual love that understanding of him can be advanced. To admit acrimony in theological discussion is in itself more fundamentally heretical than any erroneous opinions upheld or condemned in the course of the discussion.'[6]

---

[6]*Doctrine in the Church of England.*

5. The Spirit of Peace

The first and most important affirmation we make about the
Spirit must be that as the Spirit of Christ it is the Spirit of love
and peace. It comes from God, as a surprise undeserved, a
spontaneous divine gift. The fruits of the spirit are of joy, love
and peace, and these occur in a remarkable degree within the
Christian community.

Christians have to confess with shame that the Christian
community has often been, and still is, anything but a
community of the fruits of the Spirit. It would be entirely
hypocritical to commend peace, love and joy to others while
ourselves behaving with prejudice, jealousy, inhumanity and
plain indifference. Yet that is how Christians in community all
too often live in relation to the community and to people
outside that community. If we are unable ourselves to move
even gradually in the direction of a more visible manifestation
of reconciliation, we can scarcely complain either that non-
Christians are less than loving or that God is interminably slow
in working out his purposes for mankind. The crucifixion of
Jesus can scarcely have been a pleasant or edifying spectacle.
Yet his servants are often slow to identify with human suffering
where it hurts most. This applies as much to 'charismatic'
communities as to non-charismatic communities. When we
pray 'Come, Holy Ghost', we pray to be guided into a greater
personal openness, sensitivity and alertness to suffering, in its
social as well as in its personal dimensions in the world.
Anything less can only be a charade. The Spirit remains the
Spirit of the crucified and risen Christ.

It is important to be honest about Christian imperfection.
But equally, to conclude with ambiguity, hypocrisy and
indifference would itself be a kind of tribute to evil. For the
Spirit of God is and remains an effective Spirit, bringing love
and reconciliation in surprising ways into unexpected places.
As such, it is the source and inspiration of all that is good in the
created order.

10

Trinity

1. The Trinitarian Pattern

We come now to what is probably the most characteristic element of the Christian understanding of God, Trinity. The doctrine of the Trinity has long been the subject of impassioned debate. It is not explicitly biblical. But many theoretical and practical discoveries of crucial value to mankind have been made since biblical times. It was developed in the patristic period. The mere fact of the presence of trinitarian thought in the tradition need not in itself impress us, for even the Fathers recognised that antiquity of error is not itself a virtue. If we want to argue for trinitarian doctrine, we are not called upon to defend the clearly disadvantageous elements of patristic interpretation. However, though no particular interpretation or selection of tradition may be inerrant or infallible, the whole Judaeo-Christian tradition remains of central importance to theology. In this tradition the understanding of God as fully personal in himself has led people to trinitarian theology.

I want to look first at the Trinity in the work of Emil Brunner, a theologian in the middle distance of modern theology.[1] Brunner was traditional enough in his views to be highly sceptical of the 'assured results' of nineteenth-century scholarship, yet still aware of the real problems which the nineteenth century had raised for the theological task.

Brunner noted that, despite the importance usually attached to it by theologians, the doctrine as such formed no part of the

[1]Emil Brunner, *Dogmatics* I, 205f.

New Testament message. It was not even a focal point of the
theology of the Reformation. What then can be said for it? In
the first instance, it is not itself the kerugma, but it is a doctrine
which defends the kerugma, the central faith of the Church.

The starting point for Brunner is 'the simple testimony of
the New Testament'. God is called the 'Father in Heaven'. This
name was used and taught by Jesus Christ, whom the New
Testament calls the only son of the Father. The Father and the
Son are present in the Church through the Holy Spirit. If the
Father designates the origin and content of the revelation, the
name of the Son signifies the historic mediator, and the Holy
Spirit the present reality of the revelation.

The primitive Church lived on the fact that through the Son
it had the Father and that it was united with the Father and the
Son through the Holy Spirit. Belief in the Son means that God
has intervened in history, revealing and reconciling. Belief in
the Spirit means that this historical revelation of God is the
source of the inward personal presence of God, through which
we, as individual believers and as a community, participate in
the life-renewing power of God, and indeed only in this way
does the historical revelation become truth for us. In other
words, it is through the Holy Spirit that the past becomes
relevant in the present. Through the Spirit we, as individuals
and as community, may be touched by the love of God. The
Spirit in the New Testament is the giver as well as the gift. The
Spirit bears witness, touches, heals, works, imparts, prays and
wills.

Most Christians would agree with Brunner in affirming with
much of the tradition the faith that God makes himself known
in this threefold name of Father, Son and Spirit. God the
creator has given himself to mankind in love through the life
of Jesus, and wills to be with us as loving presence through the
Holy Spirit. From these three focal points of presence in the
biblical narrative and in Christian experience, the continuing
attempt to seek a better theoretical understanding produces
doctrines of the Trinity and alternatives to these doctrines,
some proposals being better than others.

The doctrine of the Trinity can be stated in a single sentence.
God who reveals himself to humankind is one God equally in

three distinct modes of existence, as Father, Son and Holy Spirit, and while three, yet remains one, through all eternity. By the time we reach the so-called Athanasian creed around AD 500, the basic formulation has this classical shape.

'We worship God in Trinity and Trinity in unity, neither confounding the persons nor dividing the substance. For the Person of the Father is one, of the Son another, and of the Holy Spirit another. But the divinity of the Father, and of the Son, and of the Holy Spirit, is one, the glory equal, the majesty equal. We are forbidden to say that there are three Gods, or three lords. The Father is made by none, not created nor begotten. The Son is from the Father alone, not made, nor created, but begotten. The Holy Spirit is not created by the Father and the Son, but proceeds. In this Trinity there is nothing prior nor posterior, nothing greater nor less, but all three persons are co-eternal and co-equal to themselves.'

Are there deep mysteries of the understanding of God waiting to be unfolded by patient re-examination of the patristic theology of the Trinity? Is the problem of God to be illumined rather by untying the knots into which the Fathers tied themselves? My own view is that the history of the doctrine, and indeed of patristic theology in general, was almost exhaustively explored by the great German Liberal Protestant historians of doctrine in the late nineteenth century. However when we move from history to interpretation – and there is no single dividing line – though there are clearly areas on one side or the other, the scope for deeper reflection remains wide open and at this point there is no reason to be bound by the limits of the nineteenth- or indeed the twentieth-century Liberal Protestant imagination.

The fruitful exploration of Trinity in much recent continental theology owes much to the positive legacy of Hegel, who taught scholars not to be afraid of ancient formulas where they could be used to give sophisticated articulation to modern problems. Kasper, Pannenberg and Moltmann and even Barth are much indebted to Hegel. It may be thought too that the scepticism with which the great historians of doctrine, Harnack and Loofs, viewed the doctrine is partly a product of their Neokantian dislike of Hegelian extravagance.

Like Hegel, Geoffrey Lampe was concerned with a radical exploration of God as Spirit, but unlike Hegel, he considered the trinitarian pattern less than fruitful for the Christian understanding of God. The main difficulties inherent in what came to be regarded as orthodox trinitarianism have often been pointed out, notably recently by James Mackey. The New Testament could be read as trinitarian by implication, but there are many equally possible interpretations of the implications of New Testament Christology. We are concerned primarily with the gospel of God's redemption of mankind through Jesus Christ. It may be however that trinitarian considerations can help us with this primary task through giving us models for the understanding of this self-giving, self-affirming, self-differentiating God. This is the basis of the affirmation of God as triune God throughout this study.

2. The Doctrinal Tradition

The term Trinity (*trias*) appears in extant literature for the first time in the writings of Theophilus of Antioch around AD 180. *Trinitas* was first used by Tertullian around AD 200. Much of the controversy in the early Church stems from the fact that the main words for nature and person had different meanings at different times and in different places. To this there were added further problems. Different words were used to express these or similar concepts in Greek and in Latin. Two main languages were used, Greek and Latin, and concepts were expressed sometimes first in Latin and sometimes first in Greek, with different sorts of translation from one to the other. Moreover, since meanings are conveyed as much by contexts as by single words, the process was not of mechanical substitution of words: new complications arose from the context. One controversial point would raise echoes of past controversies in philosophy and theology, which would in turn colour discussion. Discussion of *persona* and *hypostasis* in Trinity would evoke for example comparison, positive and negative, with Aristotle's logic on the one hand and Christological controversy on the other. Syriac and Coptic equivalents, not to speak of associations of words from secular literature, would add further complications.

The discussion, with the best will in the world, would not have been easy. There was manifestly not the best will in the world. Political and personal ambition often went hand in hand with the prayerful pursuit of spiritual truth. It was in this context that delicate rules of translation and development had to be worked out. How were men to speak of the one nature or essence of God, *mia physis, una substantia?* How is this to be related to the three persons, *tres personae, treis hypostaseis,* and how were each of these to be related to each other? Even these distinctions were the result of much work, for the earlier nature could be translated by *hypostasis,* a term now conventionally used only of the persons.

It is scarcely possible to discuss the Trinity without some reference to the historical development. How are Christians to speak of the unity, if not the numerical identity, of God, creator and reconciler, after the resurrection of Jesus? Already by the middle of the second century people were being baptised in the threefold name of Father, Son and Spirit. God was one God, but his unity was not necessarily simple. Soon Tertullian was to introduce the terminology of *trinitas,* and the concepts of *substantia* and *persona,* in an effort to clarify the meaning of the mystery. The next step was a conflict between subordinationist and modalist models. The former suggested that the Son was somehow inferior to the Father who was the core of the Godhead. The latter suggested that the deity had three changing aspects, as Father and Son and as Spirit, for different occasions. If the difficulty with the subordinationists was that the ultimate eternal God did not seem to be fully involved with human salvation, the difficulty with the modalists was that genuine personal differentiation in relation to God turned out to be no more than a pious fiction. If you decided not to speak in trinitarian terms at all, you appeared to deny either the revelation or the unity of God.

How then was it possible to affirm both that God was one and that it was really God himself who was revealed in the life, death and resurrection of Jesus and in the work of the Spirit? For an account of God as being in his essential nature love, this is of course a critical question. The task was given a new urgency by connection with the soteriological and Christological debate. If God did not take upon himself human nature, then we remain unredeemed. This is of course not necessarily the case, for God in his freedom may reveal his salvation through another if he chooses to do so. But not every possible religious option commended itself to Christians. It mattered that God the creator himself was somehow irrevocably involved in redemption and reconciliation. It mattered too, despite the problems involved in making beings out of functions, that God's spirit at work in the world was somehow more than just a picturesque expression for the action of the creator in the new creation. Here trinitarian formulation became a double-edged weapon in the armoury of Christian thought. On the one hand it led to the most arid and disastrous dogmatic conflicts, with omniscience self-evidently possessed on all sides. On the other hand, if not pushed to rationalistic extremes, it was a most valuable instrument for indicating a sense of the dynamic complexity inherent in the divine unity, for opening up rather than closing down the dimensions of the mystery of God.

What then can we say of God in himself, of the internal operations of the Trinity? As St. Thomas recognised, we can speak of the trinitarian God only through revelation. As Christians we may say that God in himself is as he is towards us. The essential and economic Trinity are one. Through the Judaeo-Christian tradition in the biblical narratives, through the events concerning Jesus and the apostolic experience of new creation, we may say that God is in his essential nature self-giving, self-affirming love, love expressed through maintaining and fulfilling relationships. We need not deny that we can say anything of God in himself. To say that God is in his essential nature love is to say a great deal, especially when we believe that through Jesus we have God's own parable for mankind of the divine love. But there are limits to the extent to which we may draw parallels and conclusions from the opera ad extra to the opera ad intra. To attempt to describe God on the basis of only one given clue, even if a trustworthy and definitive clue, is unwise. We are given enough light for the present, but we need not anticipate the eschatological promise.

It has naturally been the case that more conservatively minded theologians have opted for trinitarian theologies in recent times, and more radical ones for non-trinitarian concepts. As usual however some of the most imaginative treatments have included the unexpected. Process theology, in many ways critical of classical thought, has little difficulty in using the Trinity at the centre of its theology. Hendricus Berkhof, author of a moderate and well balanced recent Reformed systematic theology, declined to espouse a trinitarian framework with the enthusiasm of his great predecessor in that tradition, Karl Barth. Geoffrey Lampe, much more radical and critical, in the Anglican tradition, nevertheless combined critique of Trinity with a firm intention to maintain the divinity of Christ. My own position is that by no means every trinitarian proposal need be defended, but the doctrine can be used to illuminate the problems of theology today in an effective manner.[2]

Despite the pitfalls arising from oversimplification there is no need to be put off unduly by the terminology of persons, natures and substances. The main development can be lucidly set out, as was shown long ago by C.C.J. Webb in his *God and Personality*,[3] still a masterpiece of its kind. The Latin word *persona* was the mask worn by an actor, and by extension the actor himself, and the part he played. Beyond this, it might carry the implications, as Webb expressed it, that 'the being so designated had a part to play in some kind of social intercourse, and that of such intercourse only a human being is capable'.

The full theological history of the term develops in conjunction with the Greek term *hypostasis*. This word had a very wide range of meaning in different contexts, from drops of sediment to more abstractly a concrete existence, and then as a technical term of post-Aristotelian philosophy, the concrete individual element in which or whom some particular form is particularised.

---

[2]J. Cobb and D. Griffin, *Process Theology*; H. Berkhof, *The Christian Faith*; G.W. Lampe, *God as Spirit*.

[3]Cf. H.G. Kippenberg (ed.), *Concepts of Person in Religion and Thought*, Berlin, 1990.

In the trinitarian reference as parallel to *persona*, the term *hypostasis* needed to be distinguished from *ousia*, with which it could be and at first was often considered synonymous.[4] (*Ousia* itself could have a vast range of meaning, to add to the difficulty.) In making this distinction it was not to be allowed that the Godhead, the *ousia*, was any less substantial and concrete than the *hypostasis*.

From the purely etymological point of view the natural equivalent of *hypostasis* was *substantia*, but since this was paired early on with *ousia*, *hypostasis* came by convention to mean what in Latin was expressed by *persona*. There was yet another local difficulty, of embarrassing significance. It might well have been thought that the best translation of mask was *prosopon*, which after all did mean the actor's mask. But this tended to suggest the mask rather than the player himself, and so when used tended to suggest divine appearance rather than concrete reality, thus suggestive of Sabellian and Monarchian models. The final definition of person was given by Boethius. A person is the individual substance of a rational nature (*persona est rationalis naturae individua substantia*).

The outcome of this discussion was that *persona/hypostasis* became established as a technical term meaning a mode of existence in God, or a subsistence in the divine essence. Here again there was scope for significant variation in preference. We may think in the manner more characteristic of the eastern tradition of God as existing in three modes, as Father, as Son and as Holy Spirit. We may on the other hand think with the western tradition, of subsistence within the divine essence, of each mode subsisting in the Godhead, sharing in the fullness of the deity. Calvin preferred the latter, Barth the former. Each has its own advantages.

In either case we have a model which enables us to articulate a number of important theoretical considerations about the Christian God. The three persons are equal to each other in every way. The personal distinctions are more than logical abstractions, yet they have no distinct will or intelligence apart from the common essence of God, which possesses real

[4]Cf. G.C. Stead, *Divine Substance*; C. Arpe, *Hypostasis*.

personality. Among the persons there is no ontological priority, but a difference only in the order of subsistence. Though the persons are related yet they each have their own functions within the Trinity.

In relation to the world, the actions of the three *personae* are one, they tend towards God's common goal for creation. Within this common function the work of creation is regarded, especially the role of the Father, redemption of the Son, and sanctification of the Spirit. The nature of the distribution could have been otherwise; this order is suggested through revelation in the biblical tradition.

The distinction between the essence of deity and the modes of subsistence is summed up in the technical but succinct traditional aphorism: the modes are to be distinguished from the essence, not *realiter* nor yet *rationaliter* but *modaliter*. The modes are to be distinguished from each other not *essentialiter* nor *rationaliter* but *realiter*. The three persons are not then convenient pieces of theological shorthand, but are other than man. At the same time, their eternal ground of subsistence is the complex unity of the eternal God himself.

We cannot hope to resolve all the questions which arise about God in the modern world simply by reflection, even profound reflection, on the doctrine of the Trinity. But as a major component of the Christian tradition of talk of God, trinitarian reflection may still help us to forge new perspectives in the changing human encounter with the living God. As such, the doctrine is likely to remain a challenge of an existential as well as a theoretical nature to the question of God.

In *Mysterium Salutis* Karl Rahner stressed the identity between the economic and the immanent Trinity. T.F. Torrance has suggested that Rahner's approach provides a way of healing the breach on the Filioque between East and West. Walter Kasper offers a similar analysis in *The God of Jesus Christ*. As Torrance says, 'If God is not in himself as triune God what he is toward us in Jesus Christ and in the Spirit, if there is no relation of absolute fidelity between the act of God in his revelation and the being of God eternally in himself, then God in his own reality as God is not the object of our knowledge and devotion.'

God remains in important respects a mystery to us, but as an infinitely personal, trinitarian mystery rather than a cloud of Neoplatonic unknowing. In this way trinitarian reflection may lead to reconstruction of some of the basic concepts of God in the dogmatic tradition.

Rahner and Barth both replace 'person' in trinitarian discussion by 'distinct manner of subsisting' in order to get away from notions which may appear to suggest that God is three separate and independent people. Yet if God in relation to us is precisely personal, there is a danger of separation again between God in himself and in relation to us. The three persons are not merely links or relations, but some notion of consciousness is appropriate. They are not mere blank sounding-boards for each other, but in relating they achieve authentic individual integrity. This notion has of course been developed highly in Rahner's own work elsewhere, in Christology. I return at this point to Karl Barth's account of Trinity. As usual, it is unwise to judge the value of Barth's work simply in terms of the formal expositions in the first sections of *Church Dogmatics.* It is rather in the exposition of reconciliation in Volume Four that the account of God as a self-giving being, both in himself and in relation to mankind, brings out the relation between the persons of the Godhead as a relationship of grace and of mutual participation. This is the basic pattern of a trinitarian ontology of God.

This perspective on God as self-differentiated in himself in Christian perspective is shared, with variations in construction by most major modern continental theologians, and owes much to Hegel, Barth, Rahner, Jüngel, Moltmann, von Balthasar, Kasper. The tradition of Schleiermacher, on the other hand, has been critical of trinitarian theology, also with good reason: Ritschl, Harnack, Herrmann, in some respects, Troeltsch. In American and British theology there has been a greater negative reaction: Mackey, Lampe, Wiles. Trinity is an unnecessary complication. *Entia non sunt multiplicanda praeter necessitatem.*

For illumination of the problem of the Filioque we may begin from the excellent discussion of Walter Kasper. Kasper notes that in East and West there was a common ground of faith, but divergent theologies of the Holy Spirit. Both had advantages and disadvantages, and neither need be abandoned too lightly. Contrary to popular belief, the western tradition of the Filioque was framed independently of the eastern position, and not against this. Accordingly, 'East and West must reciprocally acknowledge the legitimacy of their divergent theological positions. Such a unity in multiplicity is, in my view, a far more appropriate ecumenical goal than a monolithic confessional unity would be' (*The God of Jesus Christ*, 221). This is really more important than the formal acceptance of a common formula, e.g. 'qui ex Patre per filium procedit' (who proceeds from the Father through the Son).

This ability to distinguish the heart of the matter shows throughout Kasper's reflection on Trinity. Trinity is seen not as an obscure item of overbelief but as a pointer to urgent contemporary problems. 'The way beyond theism and atheism, as travelled today by many influential protestant theologians, is safe from the dangers which threaten theism only if it does not throw out the baby with the bathwater; that is, if it does not hastily extend its criticism of theism into a criticism of monotheism. For monotheism is the answer to the question raised at the natural level about the unity and meaning of all reality. It is precisely this ambiguous and open question that is defined in a concrete way by the trinitarian self-revelation of God, so that the trinitarian confession is concrete monotheism and as such the Christian answer to the God-question of the human question' (*The God of Jesus Christ*, 315). Such an understanding of the interrelation between natural and revealed theology is precisely congruent with the approach to God taken in this study, and indeed in large areas of the Christian tradition.

I have written elsewhere of Geoffrey Lampe's carefully worked out case for abandoning Trinity, for historical as well as systematic reasons. It is often suggested that Trinity does not speak to experience. However, it may also be argued that God is sometimes experienced by Christians as a triune God, or at least that Trinity helps Christians to articulate their experience of God. The rational arguments of Wiles and Mackey against trinitarian thought point to the need for a conceptual analysis in a framework not to be found in continental theology. However, the lack of this framework in continental dogmatics may suggest not so much a task misconceived as a task still outstanding. Trinitarian theology is not easily produced in a framework of the sort demanded by the rigorous methodology of analytical philosophy. Some recent attempts have been singularly unsuccessful. Yet, as Michael Dummett and others have sometimes observed, it may take a long time for theology to take maximum advantage of recent developments in philosophy.

An impressive attempt to harness the resources of modern philosophy in the service of trinitarian study of God is represented in David Brown's *The Divine Trinity*. In the name of philosophical rigour the speculations of Maurice Wiles, James Mackey, Jürgen Moltmann and Geoffrey Lampe are demolished crisply and clearly. The claims of logic are satisfied by traditional dogmas of Incarnation and Trinity. These doctrinal formulations also correspond to the imagery of the tradition of Christian worship. Therefore they are true, and the only true formulations of Christian doctrine. There appear to be two main problems here. The first, less serious, is that a large variety of doctrinal formulations may be understood, with appropriate hermeneutical modification, to correspond to the worshipping tradition. The second is that the problems of historical contingency, which belongs to the nature of real incarnation, and of historical development in church history, may be too swiftly resolved in favour of the logically preferred positions. The attack on quasi-deist methodologies which preclude talk of Incarnation and Trinity is most impressive and convincing. But it may be that such theology, however intellectually weak, is trying to come to terms with real problems which are not simply to be vaporised with the magic wand of logic. The crux of Brown's position is an argument in favour of a 'Plurality Model' of the Trinity against a unity model. I think this is basically sound, though, as the work of Barth, Rahner and von Balthasar have shown, the issues are far from clear cut and the nature of our salvation remains in important respects residually mysterious.

I find illuminating the discussion of the Trinity in *We Believe in God* (C of E, 1987), Chapter 7, 'God as Trinity – an approach through prayer'. This section was largely the work of Sarah Coakley.

> We start with the recognition of a vital, though mysterious, divine dialogue within us, through which the meaning and implications of being 'in Christ' become gradually more vivid and extensive. Thus the Trinity ceases to appear as something abstract or merely propositional. It is not solely to do with the internal life of God but has also to do with us. The flow of trinitarian life is seen as extending into every aspect of our being, personal and social, and beyond that to the bounds of creation. (111)

There is also an excellent account in the final chapter of David Jenkins' *The Contradiction of Christianity* (1977), 'The Trinity symbolises the discovering of love which is both transcendent and committed to being at work in history and in human beings. The shape of the trinitarian symbol also indicates that in the end identity is not to be had at the cost of other identities but by being the fulfilment of them' (157, 158).

The relational dimension of God in Trinity is an important complement both to the substantial dimension discussed earlier and to the dimension of divine self-giving considered in the Christological chapter. Pannenberg has commented perceptively on the relational dimension of the reality of God in a number of his books.

Doctrines of the Trinity inevitably oscillate betwen modalism and tritheism, between a one-sided emphasis on the economic and a one-sided emphasis on the essential Trinity, beween unitary and pluralist models. Theories of correspondence or of unity between the immanent and the economic, theologies of perichoresis, debates between the ontological priority of the relational or the substantial, all serve to indicate the complexity of attempts to articulate the mystery of the Christian God, Father, Son and Holy Spirit.

Christians are monotheists. We believe in one God. At the same time it is clear that not all monotheistic concepts will do. God in Christian faith relates to the created order. God relates as Father, Son and Spirit, in the biblical narratives and in the experience of the Church. Faith reflects further that God does not have to relate to the world, in the sense of being dependent on the world for relationship. God is the creator. But God chooses to relate to the universe which he has made. It may be that there is a correspondence between the divine economy, the role of God in the world, and the divine essence in itself. It may be that only so could God relate to the world, if he were already self-relational. But even if this is so, this may be an indirect correspondence, far from the notion of a mirror image.

It may also be that there is a much closer connection, even as much as a strict identity, between the economic and the essential Trinity. This takes care of faith's affirmation that God takes up the cross in himself, and that the resurrection is also expressive of God's essential nature. But there remains the residual element of mystery. We have nothing like a blueprint of God. The problems raised by debates about the Filioque also reflect different but genuine insights into the nature of faith in God. Agreement here should reflect diversity rather than simply flatten out different insights.

Different understandings of God as Trinity have been worked out in the history of the Christian community, with varying emphases on reason, revelation and experience. The doctrine is certainly consonant with revelation, may be stated with logical coherence, and is not always divorced from experience. There may be too much stress on instant relevance in recent theology. Yet if doctrine is not perceived as relevant, it will do little to strengthen the faith of the community. In my view it will not do simply to proclaim trinitarian doctrine as a key to the problems of talk of God today.

It is this sense of the profoundly dynamic mystery of the living God, the God of Israel, the God of incarnation, crucifixion and resurrection, the God of the Spirit in the world, which Christians have sought to express through doctrines of the Trinity. These doctrines are always inadequate, but their various formulations have engaged with different dimensions of the Christian apprehension of God. They require an eschatological dimension, too, for they confess that the fulfilment of the economy of salvation is still outstanding. I do not take this to mean that God is somehow incomplete. Rather, the fullness of his self-expression is still to be completely expressed.

At different times and in different contexts, trinitarian reflection has been a vital chord of Christian devotion and inspiration. In other contexts it has not been explicit, and there has still been a depth of discipleship. It is precisely the dynamic mystery of the divine presence which evokes Christian response in different ways at different times, and it is not up to us to regulate this response. Trinitarian doctrines are products of the human imagination. God in Trinity remains the ground, the source, the inspiration of all reality. What we are seeking is a greater understanding, however faltering and incomplete, of the ground of our own being and the source of our faith.

It is through an understanding of kenosis, of God's self-emptying which is also self-affirmation, that we are given hints of self-differentiation. The Trinity of God as a self-focused presence, through the hidden activity of the Spirit, is a given clue to God's nature as love. The trinitarian formulae provide no blueprint. But they may still be a powerful aid to the theological imagination in pointing to the truth that in God being is sustained in being given away.

11

Creator of Heaven and Earth

1. God's Creation

Though the doctrine of the Trinity claims to say something about the nature of God in himself, it is also an affirmation that knowledge of God is not knowledge of a solitary being in himself. God is known as creator, redeemer and sanctifier. We can distinguish these activities and usefully discuss them in order. They are in God simultaneous activities. Here I want to think of God as creator of heaven and earth. As creator he is at the same time redeemer and sanctifier. This unique and peculiar dynamic which inhabits all talk of the Christian God makes the subject at once exciting and baffling. Again what we may hope to understand is only the tip of an iceberg. But awareness of what is underneath becomes all the more important.

God is the creator of heaven and earth. He is the source of all that is. God sustains and maintains the whole structure of the physical universe. He is the creator of all life, and especially of the human. How are we to try to understand God's relation to the universe, and his plans for its future? We know that the universe came into being several billion years ago. We know roughly how it has developed, and we can predict with reasonable certainty its physical development till it disintegrates in some billions of years in the future. It is reasonable to expect that a similar process takes place in all other universes. Such is the physical history of the cosmos.

The history of life on earth occupies a mere fraction of a second on the time scale of the life of the universe. It is a most

144

astonishing and fruitful development. At one level it involves the growth of community, joy and goodness. It also includes endless waste, disaster and evil. Against this background of risk, contingency and ambiguity on a cosmic as on a human level, faith affirms the active presence of God's love as the source and goal of creation.

The theological vision of creation as God's creation cannot offer an alternative cosmology to the cosmologies of scientific research.[1] We know roughly, and we may expect in time to know with much greater precision, how the universe will develop towards its end in masses of crushed and burnt out matter. But before that time arrives God may have countless fruitful developments in store for the human race. The doctrine of creation affirms that God has created the physical cosmos. It affirms that God has given mankind responsibility for its development towards the fulfilment of the abundance of life, centred on the New Testament understanding of agape, within the physical structures of creation. It also affirms that God's final fulfilment in love for mankind is eschatological as well as temporal. All men are mortal. The time may I suppose come when humanity, in whatever finally developed form, vanishes from the universe as the conditions for sustaining life disappear. Christianity affirms in the face of this future physical destruction, for us as individuals now and for humanity in the future, God's loving presence to mankind as a continuing spiritual relationship, in a dimension of reality more ultimate than that of the physical order.

---

[1] On the question of nature and theology, esp. J. Gustavson, *Theological Ethics*.
One of the best discussions of the relationship between science and theology known to me is the collection, *Physics, Philosophy and Theology: A Common Quest for Understanding*, ed. R.J. Russell, W.R. Stoeger, SJ, and G.V. Coyne, SJ. Particularly useful is Bill Stoeger's essay, 'Contemporary Cosmology and Science-Religion', on pp. 219-247. I note also Ian Barbour's comment, p. 45, that 'There are dangers if either scientific or religious ideas are distorted to fit a preconceived synthesis that claims to encompass all reality. A coherent vision of reality can still allow for the distinctiveness of differing types of experience.'
In this collection Frank Tipler makes the useful point, not often noted by theology, that 'Almost all of universal history, and possibly almost all of the history of life, lies in our future.'

To doubt all general theories appears to be a peculiar, and a most useful, attribute of human intelligence. New discoveries are made, new forms of community arise, through the questioning and development of existing patterns. Yet this questioning can also lead to lack of confidence and human failure. Against this attribute there is another. This is the creation of communities of belief, in which there is formed a sort of breathing space in which societies can consolidate and develop in a relaxed and fruitful manner.

For the last two hundred years there have been those who have been struck forcibly by the apparent absence of God from the modern world. The problem of theodicy has been a serious and often an insoluble issue. Some have abandoned belief in God, others have been left with a form of deism. Some may have thought it best to abandon the traditional imagery of God's personal involvement in history in particular events and occasions, not excluding the particular events relating to Jesus. Sometimes it is thought that the doctrine of creation is somewhat easier to affirm and understand than the doctrine of reconciliation. At least there we do not have the scandal of particularity and the paradox of incarnation and resurrection to cope with. A moment's reflection suggests that the truth of creation is by no means self-evident. We cannot read off the complexity of the universe the working of the hand of God, and it is far from clear that traditional argument from God as first cause ever gave an adequate understanding of God and creation.

What then is to be done? Where new explanations become necessary we cannot simply repeat old theories. If we abandon the traditional doctrine of creation much of central importance for faith disappears. It will not do, either, to strike a compromise and speak in moderate terms about the modest achievements of a partially ineffective God. If God is the living God, then Christian faith will inevitably maintain far-reaching claims about his activity. But the explanation of the claims demands critical reflection which will not be improved by minimising the scale of the difficulties which arise. Though faith may affirm God's unbounded love for all his creatures directly and without qualifications, yet the provision of critical explanation is anything but simple.

2. Creation Narrative

We come to the doctrine of creation in the second half of this study because creation is based directly on understanding of God the creator. This does not mean that creation is a part of God and that God is a part of his creation. But the created order is not self-interpreting. In speaking about creation we are speaking about the work of a personal God, who has created persons for a special role within that order. Creation helps belief in a personal God to avoid becoming narrowly personalist and anthropomorphic. At the same time, discussion of creation need not be conducted in a framework of almost quasi-physicalist concepts, as though material reality were somehow more ultimate than personal or spiritual reality. In creation we are involved with various sorts of ontology, of things, of persons and of the ultimate spiritual reality of God.

The doctrine of creation is not an attempt to explain the origin of the universe. There are of course conflicts between science and religion, but of a rather different sort. It is not a causal argument for the existence of God, being based on a particular understanding of the nature of God derived from the whole Christian tradition. The doctrine of creation cannot be a 'blown up' version of the Genesis creation narratives, though these have played an important role in the Judaeo-Christian tradition. The sources of creation are the Old Testament as well as the New. Within the Old Testament the whole story, from creation to covenant and eschatological expectation, is the framework of creation.

What is to be said about the Genesis creation narratives, which we can treat neither as history of an authoritative sort nor as 'mere' fiction of an inconsequential nature? Perhaps the most useful way of regarding them is as general religious myths, as stories which stimulate the imagination to communicate what cannot be rationally apprehended. The problem with myth is simply that in popular usage myth suggests something untrue. Karl Barth solves this problem to his satisfaction with the term saga, suggesting neither history nor myth, but a special sort of non-historical history, This too is difficult. Oscar Cullmann developed the notion of *Heilsgeschichte* or redemption history. But this too suggested a

continuous process of revelation, very different from the
stories of continuity and discontinuity in Israel's history. More
acceptable is the term parable, which has a biblical and positive
connotation. This has been used to bring out both the reality
of God's providential action and the reality of human response
to the creator in life. None of these categories need be used in
an exclusive sense. In these narratives we see the religious
response of the community to their experience of the presence
of God in every area of their lives.

3. Theology of Nature

The doctrine of creation is neither a purely philosophical
development nor is it an account given in authorised form in
the Bible. It is a way of articulating the Christian conviction of
God's active, originating and sustaining presence throughout
the cosmos. The cosmos is not chaotic and meaningless but
intelligible as the creation of God, though there remain dark
and unintelligible areas within it. It is not however part of God,
or indeed some sort of eternal structure, for God has created
it out of grace rather than necessity. It is contingent, it depends
on grace for its continuance. This dependence is emphasised
in the metaphor of creation *ex nihilo.*

Central to the Christian tradition about creation has been
development of the idea of *creatio ex nihilo,* creation from
nothing, which has played a quite decisive role in doctrine.
'*Creatio ex nihilo* is the mark of distinction between paganism
even in its refined form and Christianity even in its most
primitive form. The first task of theology is an interpretation of
these words' (Tillich, Systematic Theology, 1, 281f.).

Though attempts have been made to find it embedded in
the creation narratives in the Bible, the phrase seems first to
have come to prominence in the battle against Gnosticism.
'While men indeed cannot make anything out of nothing but
only out of matter already existing, yet God is at this point
preeminently superior to man in that he called into being the
substance of his creation precisely when it had no existence'
(Irenaeus, *Against Heresies,* 20,1). The phrase acted as a safeguard
against the twin errors of dualism and monism (in Gnostic

dualism the world often has the status of a recalcitrant uncreated entity coexisting eternally with God, out of which, despite which, God creates the cosmos including man). *Creatio ex nihilo* implies that the created order and men are an independent entity apart from God, but they owe their existence to God and there is nothing apart from God. In *creatio ex nihilo* creation does not become a part of the divine being. *Creatio ex nihilo* comes then to stress the absolute transcendence of God, his freedom and initiative in grace, and the utter dependence of creator upon creation.

Creation is *ex nihilo*. It is also, in Christian reflection, *creatio per verbum*, through the word. God spoke, and there was light. Bonhoeffer (*Creation and Fall*, 20) saw here the demonstration of the truth that with God imperative and indicative are one. God requires no intermediary but acts directly. Through the word a direct personal relationship between creator and creature is established, in such a way that the existence of the creature has its basis in God's word. Through creation God makes his will known and creates responsibility in his creature, at the same time making a commitment to creation.

Word in the Old Testament stories points forward to creation through the Word in the New. To be in Christ the Word is man's destiny from all eternity. Man is created to be in Christ, who is the perfect image of God. The gospel is not the reversal but the fulfilment of creation.

Creation is not only in the past but in the present and in the future. It is *creatio continua*. What God creates he protects, maintains and directs. Life itself is dependent at every present moment on God's creating activity. This area is often treated under the doctrine of providence. By his sustaining creativity God upholds and protects his creatures, and encourages us to commit ourselves in dependence and reliance to him. As in directing creativity, *creatio continua* refers to the permanent activity of God, directing everything towards fulfilment. In every situation, the freedom of God's grace keeps open a way to fulfilment. In St. Paul's words, nothing can separate us from the love of God.

It is not usually a good ideas to do theology by jumping straight from the biblical texts to the twentieth century without regard for what happened in the interval. More common in the English scene is a jump from the patristic period to the present. A grasp of the essential elements of the historical development should help us to understand talk of creation in the present. The early apologists and the Greek Fathers were deeply concerned about the relation of faith to contemporary culture. They faced the urgent problem of trying to reconcile their version of the biblical concept of the transcendence of God the creator with Greek notions of the immanence of the divine in the world. Creation implies for these writers the constantly operative relation of God to the world, which is motivated by his will: the will of God is at once superior to and turned towards the world. God is superior to the world. He is not the immanent, passive world principle but he is active. Theophilus derived the meaning of God from the Greek word *theein*, to run, harnessing etymology to theological use in a way not recommended today but characteristic of the Fathers. There is a clear difference between God and his world. God created the world out of nothing (*ouk ontas epoiiesin:* Justin, *Apology,* 1.10; *qui universa de nihilo produxerit:* Tertullian, *De Praescriptione Haereticorum,* 13). God is not a demiurge, as in Plato, dependent on the presence of the materials for building the world. He is the free creator of all things.

God is not part of his created order. But there is a definite relationship between creator and creation. There was to be no point in joining in the pessimism and dualism of the Gnostics and Marcion. There is nothing essentially bad or wicked about the created order. The creation of man in particular is grounded in God.

How is the link between creator and creation to be expressed properly? In order to safeguard the perfection of God Origen postulated the eternity of creation, including a world of pure spiritual perfection without temporal beginning which could only be spiritually perceived (the *kosmos noetos*). The fall of the angels then necessitated the creation of the material world. God responded to the rebellion through the inclusion of the fall in the process of creation. This notion of a double world (*kosmos diplous*) lived on and is echoed in all sorts of formulas, in the distinction between the seen and the unseen, for example, in the churchly hierarchy and the heavenly harmony of Dionysius the Areopagite. Throughout all this speculation the attempt to safeguard the biblical notion of the dependence of the creation on God for existence was being maintained.

The question of creation brought again into focus the old problem of the relation between the finite and the infinite in God, between his eternal being and his being for us, especially in his revelation in history. Augustine raised the issue in trying to relate being to time. Time is itself God's creation (*Confessions,* 11.12-31) and did not exist before creation. The world has a beginning. It is *ex nihilo,* that is to say, it was created not in time but along with time. For St. Thomas creation is the going out (*processio* or *emanatio*) of all that is from the universal first cause (*prima causa*), that is, from God, the *causa efficiens* or *agens.* Creation is the movement from possibility (*potentia*) to reality (*actus*). All things are united to God through participation in being, that is, participation in the primal being. In this (though this was not Thomas's intention) the biblical emphasis on the freedom of the living God is overshadowed. Duns Scotus, in stressing God's personal choosing of himself by an act of his will, tried to overcome this rather mechanistic pattern.

Martin Luther, taking a hint from his teachers in the Scotist tradition, took a short way with what he considered to be the logical abstractions of an abstract theory of causality by labelling it as a 'theology of glory'. To this he opposed the theology of the cross. God is not the object of formal logic but the creator who meets me in person. Creation is understood with the aid of the dialectic between the law and the gospel. The righteousness of God is active and passive, and the passive righteousness of God is God's primary action in creation (WA 44.186.3ff). The action through which God speaks the word of justification to the godless makes all his other works capable of interpretation to him who has faith. The scholastic rational thesis that God is the active force behind all things becomes the existential thesis that God alone is the motive force behind creation. *Creatio ex nihilo* is understood with the aid of the dialectic between the law and the gospel. The righteousness of God is active and passive, and the passive righteousness of God is God's primary action in creation. God speaks the word of justification to the godless and this action makes all his works capable of interpretation to him who has faith.

Creatio ex nihilo is understood soteriologically (WA 40,11) as making to live out of the opposite of life, through killing. This becomes the basic category of God's action. *Deus vivifacit occidendo* (cf. Gal. 2:19-21; Romans 6). That which happens in the Spirit in word and sacrament is part of God's creative act, and vice versa. The whole of creation is expression and realisation of his word. The creator who in Christ is identical with the creature leaves none of his creatures at rest, untouched by him. Both over against and identified with the world at the same time, he remains active in the whole life of the creature, under the disguise of his veiled glory. Taking up some of the themes, Calvin constructed a systematic doctrine of creation as part of his doctrine of God (*Institutes*, 1.1-15), seeing providence as a kind of applied creation. In God's hidden providence his creativity achieves a continuity tied to a definite goal, and so bears witness to and shows the truth of his claim to bring lost man back to his obedience in Christ.

The theologians of the early Reformation period tried to relate creation closely to redemption in Christ. The end of the sixteenth century brought a new Aristotle renaissance in which the medieval questions of theological cosmology were raised again. These were of course very real questions. Much use was made of the concept of *concursus divinus* in relating God's providence (*providentia*) to his rule (*gubernatio*) over the world, and the relation of these to the development of physical causes within the world. One difficulty was of course that the biblical creation concepts were never intended to perform this sort of function, and the development of natural science was soon able to demolish the theological speculation. The rationalising spirit of the day, trapped in the old metaphysical categories which were working openly in rationalism and secretly in orthodoxy, was unable to sustain any of the value of the ancient witness to God the creator against the sharp insights of the Enlightenment. Theology was ceasing to be intellectually respectable in many quarters, and for good reason.

It is in the light of this near bankruptcy of theology that the importance of Schleiermacher can be appreciated. Avoiding both deism on the one hand (God leaves the world to its own devices) and pantheism on the other (God is in all the world and is a part of it) Schleiermacher saw creation as 'a world determined by God alone, and set in the interdependence of nature' *(Christian Faith)*. From the observation that the proposition that 'the world is preserved in being' but not the proposition that 'the world has been created' is immediately obvious to us, he drew the conclusion that creation is an extension of the concept of preservation (36.1). Then referring to Quenstedt's seventeenth-century doctrine of the *concursus Dei* he explains that preservation and universal cause are the same thing seen from different points of view (46.2). There are problems. The human self-consciousness in 'representing the finitude of being', is rather overloaded in having to bear such a large part of the doctrine of creation. He was seriously concerned for the doctrine. 'How long will the doctrine still be able to hold out against the force of an informed way of looking at the world arising out of scientific combinations which no one can avoid?' (*Second letter to Dr Lücke*). Much of the theology which followed shared nothing of this concern, content to repeat the tradition without any new work, or to dissolve it into ethics or soteriology.

The coming of the dialectical theology brought a watershed in thinking about creation, as in all else in Christian doctrine. Emil Brunner has a long and careful chapter in his *Dogmatics*, on the creator and his creation. I shall concentrate here however on Karl Barth's doctrine of creation. For Barth the doctrine of creation is an article of faith (*Church Dogmatics*, 3.1,1). It is not self-evident that this world has its origin from God. We 'know' this only in Jesus Christ in whom we see by faith the union of God with man and the world, as his own creation and possession. Creation provides a basis for the covenant of grace. It is itself historical, in the sense of being a temporal event. Creation is also God's time in his primal turning towards the creature in eternity. We can comprehend this time and the event of creation when viewed in the light of the time of grace in Jesus Christ. But we cannot describe it in terms of creaturely, fallen history, and so we must use the language of saga. This saga is spelled out in the Genesis creation narratives.

The first saga description suggests that creation is 'the external basis of the covenant between God and man'. There is an intimate connection between creation as the external basis of the covenant and covenant as the internal basis of creation. The power behind the covenant fulfilled in Jesus Christ is God's creative activity, his affirmation of all that he has created. Creation is a benefit and a blessing, and means that the created order may be good, brought into being through him. The theological doctrine of the cosmos is first overshadowed through concentration on man as God's creature and then the wider context is brought back in the traditional order in discussion of God's providence and preservation. The doctrine of man is brought in at an early stage, through concentration on Christology as the basis of our understanding, and this has important consequences. The creation of man in God's image means that man lived in a way that is analogous to the eternal trinitarian life of God in relation to God and man. The second description (Genesis 2) suggests that the covenant is 'the internal basis of creation'. Creation already prefigures the covenant. What man is, is God's will, and his will is to have fellowship with his creatures. We know this only through faith in him in whom this bond of fellowship is fulfilled, in Jesus Christ.

Barth's rearrangement of the traditional elements did not meet with universal approval. Those who criticised the concentration on Christology have been able to watch the progress to anthropology in his pupils, the later Bonhoeffer, and Buren and Harvey Cox, and to feel that their doubts were justified. We can see a striking contrast, at once more conservative and more daring, in Paul Tillich (*Systematic Theology*, 1.280f.). 'The doctrine of creation describes no once for all event.' It points to the situation of creatureliness (in the case of man this means finitude) and to its distinction between essence and existence (283-4). To be a creature means both to be rooted in the creative ground of the divine life and to realise one's own selfhood in freedom. Preservation is continual creation, in which God creates from eternity things and time together. Preserving creation means the uninterrupted continuance of the structure of reality as a basis for being and activity. God's immanence in the world as a continuing creating ground and his transcendence of the world through his freedom are related. The transcendence of which we are aware in religious experience is the connection between finite and infinite freedom, which is realised in every personal encounter. In this way the different aspects of creation gain a new significance which is, however, dependent on the fine distinction made between act and being.

The concept of creation is a basic and indispensable component of a Christian understanding of God. Creation in the active sense signifies the act of divine creation of all things, and in the passive sense signifies the universe which God's creative act has brought into existence. The doctrine of creation is related to the world of empirical reality but cannot be deduced from it. It speaks of the goal as well as the origin of the world, speaking of God's word of promise and assurance to mankind. The subject of creation is the living God himself, who created life *de nihilo*. He is 'the God who makes the dead live and summons things which are not yet in existence'.

Everything exists through God's creative word. Likewise his creation is not limited to the past. As Luther put it, *creare est semper novum facere* (WA. 1.563.8). The whole structure of creation is the result of God's creating act. God relates by communication, and in so doing creates the possibility of disobedience and of commitment and responsibility.

4. Creation and Humanity

As creator God is the source of the whole physical cosmos. Within this, and importantly, he is the creator of man. We have considered the danger of undue anthropomorphism in theology. On the other hand, for Christian theology, man is not just one more aspect of molecular combination in the cosmos, or even just one more life form, which happens to be our own. There is for theology an integral connection between God and man, provided by God. Despite the dangers of anthropocentrism in modern times, awareness of this connection may help in the search for knowledge of God. God has related himself to man in creation, in history, and in new creation in taking humanity into himself as the trinitarian God. These connections have been fruitfully explored by a number of twentieth-century theologians. I mention here some recent work by Wolfhart Pannenberg and John Macquarrie.

In his most recent essays, Pannenberg lays stress on the bonds between God and the history of all humanity, bonds there from creation and renewed through God's participation in the history of Jesus. God chooses to bring himself to self-realisation through history. In all action in history God is involved. Yet precisely in this trinitarian self-realisation God makes possible human self-differentiation from God, authentic freedom. Here Pannenberg echoes Rahner and the whole tradition of intellectual reflection stemming ultimately from Hegel.

If we ask how this human self-differentiation is to be understood, then Macquarrie sums up the development of man in six propositions.

> The propositions are as follows. 1. Human life has brought to light more than anything else that we know the astonishing potentialities latent in the physical universe. 2. Some aspects of our humanity suggest a transhuman spiritual source. 3. The human being in certain respects transcends nature, in such a way as to provide an analogy of divine transcendence and to suggest that the goal of humanity is to participate in the life of God. 4. Human beings show a natural trust in the wider being within which their existence is set. 5. There are some negative factors in human existence which can be understood as limit situations, impressing on us our own finitude and at the same time evoking the idea of absolute being. 6. Finally, many of these strands come together in religion, in which men and women claim to experience in various ways the reality of God, and this claim has a prima facie case as one deeply rooted in the human condition and which has never been disproved and perhaps never could be. (*In Search of Humanity*, 257)

Though such an understanding of man falls far short of proof of the existence of God, it is eminently congruent with the picture of God, man and the universe built up in these pages, in reflection on the Christian tradition in the modern world. In this respect an anthropological argument is like a cosmological argument for the existence of God: it cannot prove, but it can show that God as creator of the cosmos and of man is not an inconceivable or irrational consideration. Kasper says of man that 'He is the being who lives in the presence of the infinite mystery and who waits and hopes for the free self-revelation of this mystery. He goes in search of signs and words in which God reveals himself to him' (*The God of Jesus Christ*, 115). He finds a sign supremely in the events concerning Jesus Christ.

5. God's Love in the Universe

The love of God is expressed as much in creation as in redemption. There is an important element in Gordon Kaufman's plea, notably in *Theology for a Nuclear Age*, for an understanding of the use of the word 'God' as a construct of the human imagination, with all the limitations of human relativity. Yet this awareness of the earth-bound nature of our language should not be allowed to obscure the basic affirmation of Christians that God is prior to our thoughts about him. In the beginning God made heaven and earth. Here in the language of myth is an assertion about the nature of God, as prior to his creation, temporally and ontologically. But this God is identical with the God who in the gospel is declared to be the reconciler of mankind through Jesus Christ. Creation is an act of the divine love. It is sustained, preserved and renewed through the same love. Because the character of creation is understood to be identical with the character of redemption, it is possible to understand God as a personal, suffering, reconciling creator throughout the universe. In this universe God suffers setbacks and disasters, through his having created freedom in the structure of matter, and on a personal plane having made himself vulnerable in incarnation. This personal dimension is a consequence not of human anthropomorphism but of divine contingency. What would be an anomaly in a deistic framework may be seen as the centre of creation in Christian theism.

A particularly perceptive account of creation is given in George Hendry's *Theology of Nature.* Hendry notes the comparative neglect of the doctrine of creation since the days of the philosophies of nature of Isaac Newton and Jonathan Edwards. True, Hegel produced an ambitious philosophy of nature, but this led to an even more general unease. The enormous strides made by modern science were not accompanied by parallel developments in the doctrine of creation. Among models of creation Hendry notes generation, fabrication, formation, conflict and expression. But all these models are fraught with difficulty.

> The question which both Schleiermacher and Barth point up is how the perception of nature on a cosmic scale can be affected by a faith that is articulated within a political or psychological framework. The cosmic process, assuming it is a process, is so incommensurate with human history and human existence that it is hard to see how it can come within the compass of human perception, any more than the procession of the seasons can come into the perception of a mayfly. If it cannot exactly be described, inasmuch as it is constructed by extrapolation from scientific observation, it is nevertheless so far beyond the limits of actual experience that it can hardly affect anyone's actual perception of nature. (181)

We turn to the question of relations between theological and scientific reflection on creation. Arthur Peacocke emphasises the great contrasts between the classical scientific world view of the nineteenth century and the present. Then, nature was regarded as simple in structure. Now we know that it is enormously complex. Then, the natural world was regarded as mechanically determined and predictable. Now we see indeterminacy at the micro-level and unpredictability at the macro-level. Then it was regarded as essentially complete. Now it is seen to be in process. Then it was thought to have accessible foundations. Now we are aware of infinite complexity (*Creation and the World of Science*, 62).

In the creation of life there is a complex interplay of chance and law, which is capable of many different sorts of interpretation. Christians see God as exploiting in continuing creation all these possibilities which he has made potentially available in the initial structure.

How God acts, especially in relation to human agents, must remain in many respects opaque to us. The nature of life and of human life itself is still largely obscure, even after discovery of the structure of the information carrier at molecular level, DNA. Even since the development of sociobiology there are more rather than less mysteries about the nature of biological evolution. When we consider the light that may be thrown on the question of man by theological appraisals we see that God makes possible a free response to himself, putting his own purpose at risk as a suffering, loving Creator (*Creation and the World of Science* 199, 213). The suffering in creation is resolved in the suffering of redemption. 'Jesus then is, as it were, a bearer of God's pain of the creative process' (ibid. 230).

In an illuminating essay on 'Profane and Sacramental views of nature' (in *The Sciences and Theology in the Twentieth Century*, ed. A.R. Peacocke), Sigurd Daeke has noted that for much German theology, kerugmatic, existential and political, nature is understood as profane, and as therefore outside the concern of theology. 'Reality here is divided like the house of Faraday, who locked his prayer-room when he went to his laboratory, and who locked the door of the laboratory when he returned to his prayer-room' (op. cit., 120). But though natural theology in the traditional sense may no longer be possible, the sacramental model for the understanding of God's relationship to nature remains an important dimension of the meaning of the Incarnation.

In his *God and the New Biology* (1986) Arthur Peacocke developed an illuminating interpretation of the relation between the natural sciences, the life sciences and theology.

> We now see nature as multi-levelled and hierarchical with new emergents developing in time which, significantly, are consciousness and reflective self-consciousness. the natural physical, biological, human and social worlds are the realm of God's immanent activity, indeed the manifestation of his creative presence — and sacraments are particular focused instances of what is happening all the time. (129)

Peacocke's account is in most respects congruent with that given in a series of small volumes by John Polkinghorne, looking at the issues as a mathematical physicist.

> God does not fussily intervene to deliver us from all discomfort but neither is he the impotent beholder of cosmic history. Patiently, subtly, with infinite respect for the creation with which he has to deal, he is at work within the flexibility of its process. (*Science and Providence*, 44)

In the continental tradition, one of the most remarkable recent attempts to relate the world of the natural sciences to the world of the human sciences in theological perspective is Helmut Peukert's *Science, Action and Fundamental Theology – Towards a Theology of Communicative Action*. He discusses the theory of science and the theory of action, in the tradition of Apel and Habermas, Rahner and Metz. The centre of modern philosophy of science, for Peukert, is not positivist observation of raw data, but the changing reflection of the scientific community on its own historical tradition. Typical for the new approach is Kuhn's famous theory of paradigm shifts. This connects with Habermas' theory of communicative action. But in fact human social interaction is brought up against the reality of human brutality, death and murder. Hence only a theological dimension allows the human to express itself in true humanity. God engages with death in the death of Jesus and brings a new reality out of the resurrection.

Here the theories of the nature of language developed by Chomsky and Wittgenstein are deployed to stress the essentially social nature of language as the basic vehicle of human interaction. Humanity must remember the unremembered, the oppressed in the past, in an act of 'anamnestic solidarity'. It is through such reflection that we can articulate the question of the reality of God in communicative action. God is remembered in this action of solidarity. 'The experience of the reality of God is mediated through others. A theory of human interaction in history becomes the hermeneutical basis for theology of the Trinity that, even as discourse on God himself, remains a theory of experience' (275). This is a most remarkable study, which we cannot enter into in detail here. It does however seem to me to leave out the important underlying issue of the relation of the cosmos itself as a reality, rather than our intellectual appropriation of its significance to God and to our human condition.

The vast question of the relationship between God and the physical cosmos is of central importance for theology. Christian faith has always maintained that God is not only involved in human history and society but in maintaining the whole created order. There is a very great deal which we do not understand about the cosmos. The confident assumptions of one generation are speedily overturned by the next, as a comparison of the works of, say, Sir James Jeans and Stephen Hawking will readily demonstrate. Revolutions in perspective take place. Sometimes it appears that hard won theories are indeed all in the mind, and there is no way of telling which is more true. Yet some theories last much longer than others, because they appear to more people to offer rational and coherent explanations.

John Polkinghorne has suggested that the physical world is characterised by ten qualities. It is elusive, intelligible, problematic, surprising, involved with chance and necessity, big, tightly knit, open to the question of futility, complete and incomplete. The list could of course describe other things, from television soap operas to soccer tournaments.

For most people the traditional conflicts between science and religion are no longer what they were. It is not insuperably difficult to think of God as working through the processes of development in nature. It is even possible to think of God acting, as we argued earlier, in highly unusual and specific ways at different times, in a somewhat similar way to the occurrence of surprising events, against expectation, in the cosmos. There remains on a human and personal level the problem of waste and disease, disaster and evil. But the possibility of various sorts of divine action, even if not in frameworks now conceivable to us, lies open.

It may seem improbable that a God who created the universe should be concerned for such an infinitesimal speck of it as the human race, even to the point of incarnation. Yet it is also the case that the fact that the universe can sustain human life at all requires a structured balance between finely drawn constraints. That it is such a universe, constructed, it has seemed to some, on an anthropic principle, counts more for than against the notion of a creator with a purpose for humanity.

Arthur Peacocke developed his argument further in *Theology For a Scientific Age*. Discussing causality in complex systems (in the light of a description of 'order through fluctuation' in the structure of dissipative energy systems), involving a two-way process of 'top-down' and 'bottom-up' interaction, he argues that God 'could be causatively effective in a "top-down" manner without abrogating the laws and regularities (and the unpredictabilities we have noted) that operate at the myriad sub-levels of existence that constitute that world' (159). 'But since God is personal, this flow of "information" is more appropriately described as a "communication" by God to the world of his purposes and intentions through those levels of the hierarchy of complexity capable of receiving it' (161).

We can no more see into the mystery of the mind of God than we can describe exhaustively the mind of man. But it is not unreasonable to believe that there is a connection between the mental and the material, such that the one is not dissolved into the other, in the purpose of God, who has created us as physical beings to respond in love to the divine love in a personal manner. In the contingency of this physical cosmos there is much that is bleak and incomprehensible. Christians believe that God has accompanied us into that bleakness, in the events recorded in the New Testament, and has produced light in the human condition out of the dark areas of the universe. This is the cosmological dimension of the resurrection. Such a highly particular engagement of God with the created order may be inconceivable, but it is not unthinkable.

12

Divine Action

1. Providence

God the creator maintains, directs and protects his creation. How does God come to act, and how is his presence expressed in the created order? Here we come to the areas of providence and theodicy, and to the greatest obstacle to any Christian doctrine of providence, the problem of evil. How are we to understand the protecting and sustaining love of God in the face of the stark reality of evil in our world? Faith in God the creator involves faith in providence, and such faith makes an empirical difference to people's lives. Faith in providence in the face of evil always has the character of 'nevertheless' and has to be related ultimately to the life, death and resurrection of Jesus Christ. Hence the position of this section after the Christological dimension of the doctrine of God.

In the biblical narratives God governs all things, and his character can be seen in his dealings with his creation, leading from creation to incarnation and anticipating eschatological fulfilment. Our lives are in the hands of God. Through Jesus' life, death and resurrection providence is certain. Nothing can separate us from the love of God. Structures of providence are to be found in most other religions. In traditional natural theology God's providence can be seen in all the basic structures of the natural world, in the animal kingdom and in all nature. For modern dialectical theology, on the contrary, providence is seen only in and through God's self-revelation in Jesus Christ. There is after all no generally apprehensible doctrine of providence, said Karl Barth (*Church Dogmatics*, 3.3, 1ff.).

'Providence' was a favourite word on the lips of Adolf Hitler. God preserves man from evil, accompanies man's activity in Jesus Christ, and rules in creation, signs of his rule being seen in the interpretation and transmission of scripture, in the history of the Church despite its own folly, and in the finitude of human life. God is sovereign. For Barth evil has no final reality. It may be that this approach underestimates both human freedom and the reality of evil. It does however give due weight to grace.

In Barth's picture God closely controls the natural order. This is in some respects parallel to the classical idea of the laws of nature, determined by God. Modern science has sometimes appeared to suggest a limited indeterminacy in nature, at least in random occurrences at the sub-atomic level. These can be used in order to introduces the idea of chance against a purposive creation, or to suggest that God may allow indeterminacy to work through this.

Different sorts of theory in natural science can be related to theology in different ways, and the conclusions reached appear not to enable us to decide between theistic and non-theistic options. The Christian God is not a substitute for still unformulated scientific hypotheses. It is possible for the Christian to see providence as belief in a sort of 'moral grain of the universe' in which the future is made out of decisions in the present in faith. God in the New Testament is weak in the world, but produces resurrection and effective action precisely out of weakness and crucifixion. Faith in providence is here *Fides quaerens intellectum.*

A good analysis of providence has been provided by Michael Langford. 'Providence is concerned with changes or effects in the world, with the influence of God (some would say with his interference) in the world of nature, in man and in history.'[1] God is creator, sustainer, final cause, active in general and in special providence, and in the miraculous. Appeal to providence is often grounded in experience, contrasting with concepts of God as timeless and passionless. Ideas of divine provision and government are implicit throughout the Old Testament. The New Testament picture is of an intensely active personal God

[1]Michael Langford, *Providence,* 3.

– this is the foundation for the Christian doctrine of special providence. Aristotle's God is the changeless, unmoved mover. For Aquinas, God can act in an infinite number of ways, always in accordance with his nature. The rise of scientific explanation of the world has led to a feeling that providence is redundant.

Accepting the claim that the tradition does give some initial meaning to the concept of providence, how are analogies for providential action to be found? The rays of the sun, the force of the wind, the movement of tide, spatial and temporal change, all provide analogies of limited value. Human action offers more help, if man is made in the image of God, even though God does not have a body. As man initiates movement through an act of will, God causes movement through his will. How God acts we cannot say, but we can distinguish different aspects of the affirmation that his will is effective.

God's providence is one of the factors which go towards the overall determining of every event. God's influence in the order of nature has been seen at sub-atomic level, through depth psychology, in evolution, etc. God is more like a creative artist than a mechanical engineer. Providence in the human order must be generally persuasive rather than coercive. God encourages personal change and development: this is grounded in atonement, in the incarnation as God's new initiative. What then of evil? Where there is free will there is also moral evil. We now come to the relation between providence and history. The Old Testament interpretation of the history of Israel is a study in special providence. But we cannot isolate single events in later history as God's specific acts. We can see only a long-term influence of God in history.

How then does God exercise his compassion in relation to individuals? It is possible to see providence as the activity of a personal God. Such a position requires faith. In Christian tradition any genuine personal response to love is already a response to God, even if the one who loves does not realise this. It is in respect of the treatment of evil and the relation of history to the biblical narratives that Langford's reconstruction seems most fragile, and he says little of his concept of God in all this, but the study shows that reflection on providence in the context of natural theology can still be worthwhile.

2. Evil

There remains in providence a strong element of mystery, which is related to the presence of evil in the world, and indeed of contradiction in so much of our motivation. We cannot deal fully with providence without facing squarely the problem of evil. Evil remains perhaps the greatest single objection to belief in God today, and so this issue is central to the Christian understanding of God.

The most significant modern treatment is probably that given by John Hick, in *Evil and the God of Love*. The problem of evil, says Hick, arises only for a religion like Christianity which insists that the object of its worship is at once both perfectly good and unlimitedly powerful. 'If God is perfectly good, he must want to abolish all evil: if he is unlimitedly powerful, he must be able to abolish all evil: but evil exists; therefore either God is not perfectly good or he is not unlimitedly powerful.' Hick traces the development of two types of theodicy, the Augustinian and the Irenaean. For Augustine, following the Platonic tradition and in opposition to Manichean dualism, evil is *privatio boni*, the absence or distortion of the good. The problem is that in our experience evil has a grim reality of its own. Augustine believed that, in the famous phrase of *Confessions* 7, 3, 5, 'Free will is the cause of our doing evil, and your just judgement the cause of our having to suffer from its consequences.' The primary sin is a turning away from the highest good, God, to a lesser good, his creatures. The angels fall, then man falls. The universe itself is beautiful (*pulchrum*) and perfect, and our awareness of death and decay is due only to our mortal frailty, which fails to perceive the larger harmony. This tradition has developed in the Catholic tradition, in the Reformers and in Karl Barth (*Church Dogmatics*, 3.3). Barth sought to distinguish evil in the strongest sense, the nihil, as he called it, from the shadow side or negative side of God's creation, which is part of creaturely existence. The nihil brought Christ to the cross and was there overcome. Here Hick criticises Barth's continuance of the old meontic philosophical tradition.

The other stream of tradition stems from Irenaeus' distinction between the image and the likeness of God. Man's basic nature (the image) is that of a personal being endowed with moral freedom and responsibility: he is made in the *eikon* of God. But as yet he is only potentially the perfect being whom God is seeking to produce (the likeness). He is at the beginning of a process of growth and development in God's continuing providence, which is to culminate in the finite 'likeness' of God. Our present life is pictured as a scene of gradual spiritual growth. Instead of the doctrine that man was created finitely perfect and then incomprehensibly destroyed his own perfection, Irenaeus suggests that man was created as an imperfect, immature creature who was to undergo moral growth and finally be brought to the perfection intended for him by his Maker. The fall is not something malignant but as it were an understandable lapse in the childhood of man. Life's trials then become not a punishment for Adam's sins but a divinely appointed environment for movement towards the perfection that represents the fulfilment of God's good purpose for him. This development is traced through to Schleiermacher.

John Hick himself set out on a remarkable contemporary theodicy in the Irenaean tradition. The trials of earthly life are seen as a 'vale of soul making' leading to the gradual perfection of the new creature in Christ. Evil remains evil, is demonic, but is not beyond the control of God. Even the presence of the mystery of suffering may contribute to the ethical character of the world as a place in which true human goodness can occur and in which there may be loving sympathy and compassionate self-sacrifice.

> If there is any eventual resolution of the interplay between good and evil, any decisive bringing of good out of evil, it must lie beyond this world and beyond the enigma of death. A Christian theodicy must be based on the hope that beyond death God will resurrect or recreate the human personality. Therefore in the present, in St. Paul's words, we rejoice in our suffering, knowing that suffering produces endurance, and endurance produces character, and character produces hope. (Ibid., 375)

Hick's solution is imaginative and illuminating. Evil has of course a complexity which completely denies analysis. The temptation to sin very often appears in the guise of the good: the last temptation is the greatest treason, to do the right thing for the wrong reason. Because we are still involved in the contradictions created by evil in the world, it retains an element of mystery for us. When we 'solve' the problem we may have lost the depth of the problem. It is part of the nature of evil to lead us to underestimate it. At the same time, to overestimate its effect is itself a final tribute to evil. In the events concerning Jesus, and especially in his death and resurrection, we see both the reality of and the overcoming of evil. Faith here points not so much to a solution but to a source of salvation. Here the force of the Christian contribution lies not in a single 'solution' to evil but in the whole cumulative case for God's love in creation and reconciliation.

No simple picture of the nature of God can provide us with anything like a satisfactory understanding of the presence and action of the living God, whose loving presence to his creatures is at the heart of the Christian tradition. How God is and how he acts remains mysterious to us, though the shape of the mystery is indicated in the sorts of things which our analogies lead us to consider appropriate to God. I have suggested elsewhere that these analogies include Christological analogies. What the Judaeo-Christian tradition tells us is that God is a personal God and that he is the creator and reconciler of the whole created order. We can recognise frankly that without this tradition we should be at a loss to continue to speak of a God who acts in love in the world. Given this parable of divine presence and action, we may turn our imagination to seeking to understand the divine process as far as we are able to do so.

How is the presence of the personal God made manifest in history? To ask this question is to come back to the problem of evil. In the case of evil, it is extremely difficult to go beyond the brute fact of the consistent and universal occurrence of evil in specific instances to produce anything remotely resembling a satisfactory general theory. God's signature is manifestly not written in indelible ink across the pages of history. It is a common step to move from such conclusions to assertion that talk of God is meaningless, or at least to revise the classical understanding of God in terms of deism, or a new understanding of Kant's moral law theory, or a package of strictly self-authenticating revelation. However, in all these options there is great difficulty in talking of God's personal presence in a satisfactory manner.

It emerged from our earlier discussion of hiddenness that belief in providence, in God's activity in the created order, is 'against the odds' and belief in God's victory over evil is focused on the death and resurrection of Jesus Christ. In human history there is much evidence of love and grace. It is far from being a picture of total blackness. Nevertheless the community of love is fragile and there is no guarantee that it may not be extinguished at any time. It is in God, in the God for whom to be is to love and to let others be in love, that faith in the ultimate triumph of love over evil is grounded.

It is in God himself that the understanding of providence and triumph over evil, and the effectiveness of divine presence and action may be understood. This is not to preclude various exercises in natural theology, but it is to indicate a framework. For Christians this framework is a gift of grace involving revelation and salvation though not excluding the powers of reasoning.

For God, to love is a mode of being, and it can involve a loving contemplation. But it also and essentially involves action. Human action involves intention, will, movement and change. Not all human actions are appropriate to God, and he is not a creature. But God is *par excellence* the one who loves, and since he does not deny the laws of thought, he is not strictly timeless, for a timeless God cannot act.

If we fail to see the differences between divine and human action then we may envisage a God who is so busily engaged in all sorts of contrary activities that all talk of his individuated action and response becomes inconceivable. In speaking of God's action we must invoke what the tradition knows as an analogy of extrinsic attribution, the ground for the analogy being the parable of God's presence given in the New Testament stories of salvation through Jesus Christ.

3. Action and Revelation

Because he is not an object in the world of objects God does not act exactly as created agents act. There has to be a complexity in the action of the loving God which rules out the perspectives of deism, pantheism, and interventionism. Because God is a personal God his action is not only general but also particular. Because he constantly sustains his creation in being, he is not bound by a closed system of natural causes. Because he has given freedom to his creation, he does not exercise direct control over its history. God is always present to his creation, loving, suffering, persuading towards goodness.

The obvious models are ruled out. It would be convenient if we could envisage God as intervening directly, as a child might operate a model railway. It would be convenient if we could regard the world as a causal nexus in which God can never be involved. Faith encourages us towards the former, for we believe in the reality of the guiding hand of God. Reason encourages towards the latter, for all our everyday activity is based on the assumption of a uniformity in the natural order, without which planes would always crash, cars would never start, food would never be digested, children would cease to breathe.

The obvious solution is to say that different models for God's activity serve the imagination of faith, in different ways, illustrating different aspects of the truth. This sounds fatally evasive. Yet it is of course the case that this is how the human imagination works, using combinations of imagery in different ways throughout our daily lives. The ground for claiming a basic unity of perception lies in the unity of the consciousness of the individual or society which shares this culture.

But the theological question goes deeper. What grounds are there for asserting the truth of the claim that God acts in certain ways in creation, beyond the observation that this is how life has sometimes been understood? Here in my view is the proper role of the appeal to revelation, not just in contradiction to reason but as a clue to the basic rationality of what natural reason, reflecting on the faith of Christians, suggests. God acts in love in the manner marked out in the way of the life, death and resurrection of Jesus. But the freedom built into the natural order creates the reality of havoc both in the external world of natural events and in human response to

God. Therefore the working of his love is often obscured from us, though it is not entirely unknown to the human race. It is indeed a light shining in darkness. It will not do to take the high ground and demand the stark alternative: either God acts directly as an object in the world of objects or else he is not involved in particular providence at all. The reality to which Christian life points is more complex. God does act in the created order, but his action is not usually perceived empirically, and its effectiveness is eschatological, appropriated by faith. This is not the death of a thousand qualifications but the acknowledgement that God is precisely God, no more and no less.

There is an even more fundamental issue underlying the question of God's action. That is the question of the meaning of ultimate reality. For Christians this is closely bound up with the question of the understanding of God's presence as grace.

In his Mendenhall Lectures of 1983, published as *Intimations of Reality, Critical Realism in Science and Religion,* Arthur Peacocke discussed our understanding of reality. He adopts a 'qualified scientific realism'. It is a realism about entities, whose existence is affirmed by discerning causal lines, rather than a realism about theories, which can be very different and certainly more cautious and agnostic than the other (28). Peacocke considers the creativity of J.S. Bach. 'So might the creator be imagined to unfold the potentialities of the universe which he himself has given it, selecting and shaping by his redemptive and providential action those that are to come to fruition' (73).

Peacocke's contribution, combining a positive attitude to scientific theory in the physical sciences and the life sciences with a sacramental understanding of the universe seems to me here, as elsewhere, to be particularly well balanced and constructive.

4. Acts and Events

God is the one who loves in freedom. Here is an excellent epitome of the nature of divine action. With Barth's position we may agree that there is no message 'God is Love' to be discerned in the Milky Way at night. But unlike Barth, we may not wish to reinterpret the meaning of divine action solely in terms of Christology. Having established the reference to God the creator, we shall want to think again about what it is for God to act within the created order. This is not to introduce groundless speculation but to avoid the constriction of Christological allegory. Though the mystery of the incarnation tells us about the basic nature of God it may not perhaps provide a key to the direct unfolding of God's action in history. Despite what Bultmann has said about the non-objectifiability of God and what Barth has said of a Christological key in history, we may say that the events concerning Jesus assure us of God's nature, a self-giving love through Jesus Christ, and leave us to work out the consequences in thought and action in the freedom of the children of God. We may have grounds for referring action to God, but not an intimate knowledge of the nature of such action. We may have some ontological confidence while retaining a measure of epistemological agnosticism.

God acts, in the manner appropriate to self-giving love in the created order. How he acts in different circumstances is left to the imagination of faith to work out, not in free speculation but in constant reference to the need of human beings for love in different ways, Commitment to love means endless different sorts of responses, not all identified by a simple direct association with loving as obvious motive.

Since God is creator *ex nihilo* and is not part of the created order, attempts to discern his hand in natural events in patterns of various sorts or in historical developments in men, are always likely to fail. He was not in the earthquake or the storm but in the still small voice. God is not to be found in the march of history or on the side of the victors, his prophetic word often cuts across history and finds its 'lessons' fatuous. Yet it is still important for us to try to think through the implications of what it is for God to act in history and for his action to be effective. This should illuminate our appreciation of the dimensions of God's love, even if it does not provide primary grounds for affirmation of that love. Secondly, God's love is grounded in historical contingency in Jesus Christ. This is not a 'key' to a Christian doctrine of history. But it is a ground for thinking that what happens in human history is not irrelevant to God. He is committed to history to love though not to furnishing us with history books. The primary ground for God's action in love we find in the gospel. The interrelation of acts and events, in God and man, we have to continue to work at.

Our talk of God's action involves the characteristic features of human personal action. There are however important qualifications, since God is a disembodied self, and he is complex in himself, persons in relation, and above all, since he is not part of the created order.

Because we cannot think of God's personal presence as ultimately less personal than the presence of the human persons whom he has created in his image, we must think of God's love as involving thought, intention, will, memory, and the other components of his activity. We may think of God's actions, like the actions of persons within the created order, as composed of millions of individual and overlapping sub-acts and sub-events which go to constitute larger movements, which we then recognise as acts and events on the level of human encounter. We find it very difficult to individuate God's actions. This is scarcely surprising. It is not always easy to individuate human acts and events, e.g. those leading up to a murder (cf. Donald Davidson's essay on 'The Individuation of Events').[3]

For God time and eternity are linked in a way which it is virtually impossible for us to conceive. He has created and sustains the structures of created existence. Within these structures God may act in particular ways, where human history is concerned, through individuals, eliciting a response in love to his love.

Here the continuing value of the distinction between his active and his permissive will can be upheld. God is ultimately responsible for all that happens in the natural order yet without this environment human life as we know it could not

[2] John Hick, *Evil and the God of Love.*
[3] Donald Davidson, *Essays on Actions and Events,* 177.

flourish. We may feel that one who acts in love would surely have constructed a less harsh and unequal human environment, without the sickening random catastrophes which blight so much human existence. Here perhaps is process on a time scale beyond our comprehension.

Because of freedom there is always the possibility that we shall destroy ourselves. Because as creator God grants a real and not merely relative independence to the created order, he is not specifically responsible for natural disasters as they happen in creation. Even more so, when evil is of human creation, this is squarely the responsibility of man, who must learn, and painstakingly relearn in each generation, to turn to good rather than evil.

Beyond a general sustaining activity in creation Christians have always understood God to act in particular ways in specific circumstances. They have understood themselves to be upheld by God's love, often in the most difficult of circumstances. Though it is not possible to produce empirical evidence of such action, yet this faith certainly makes an empirical difference to people's lives. This love is usually related to the preservation of human life, but may also be exhibited where life is lost.

Here the eschatological dimension of divine action is crucial. God's love is not a failure but its triumph may not be in this world. Categories of understanding God's power as based on models of human power must here be resolutely disregarded. The effective love of God in cross and resurrection is often weak and powerless in the world. This proposition is central not only to Christology and devotion but to the philosophical development of a Christian concept of God. Without such a perspective an entirely proper moral outrage at the presence of endless evil in a world created by a God of love may become a self-torture which is a barrier to faith. The freedom which allows the development of love is part of the persuasive rather than coercive nature of God's action. God does not permit suffering to provide opportunities for moral virtue. Rather God's love is categorically expressed in cross and resurrection, in the eschatological effectiveness of a purely loving witness, and it is to discipleship to such a love that we are called.

5. Divine Compassion

The whole question of God's activity was thoroughly explored by Keith Ward in his monograph, *Divine Action* . Though I am not persuaded by his initial argument for the necessity of God's existence, it seems to me that the following account of divine creativity, with due attention to correlation with the natural sciences, is illuminating.. He suggests that there are a number of distinct types of divine action in the created order – at least five. Quantum physics helps us to understand the nature of our universe, and indeed gives us some clue to the delicate balance between chaos and order which is a necessary condition of human existence in the universe, the so-called anthropic principle. Physics in no sense demonstrates the existence of God, but neither does it rule God out. 'God may work within the probabilistic structure of physical laws to select a set of paths which would not necessarily have eventuated by physical laws alone, though the possibility of such a path exists in the natural world' (120).

God's action is not fixed from the beginning of creation. 'This is the heart of the theistic contention: that God changes his particular purposes in response to what happens in the world, and therefore that there are divine causal influences not already set up in the act of creation, which govern how the world goes' (130). For Christians, the focus of divine action is incarnation, atonement and the fulfilment of creation in new creation.

There is another full discussion of our theme in the collection *Divine Action*, edited by Hebblethwaite and Henderson (1990). The focus of this collection, arising from the work of Austin Farrer, is the coherence of the notion of Double Agency. Here God acts within nature, rather than directly upon nature. I am reminded of John Baillie's famous insistence on God's action being in, with and under human action. How can God both act autonomously in himself and act through other agents, especially through human agency? Most of the writers decide that he can do so, and may do so in different ways, though it is not easy to find good analogies for such action. It is difficult to identify the acts and intentions of the two agents. Particularly interesting is David Brown's idea that divine-human interchange

takes place through natural symbols, sometimes at a sub-
conscious level. These are then appropriated in changing ways
through history, enabling God to carry on a dialogue in history
without violating human autonomy.

I should want here to return to the central link between
God's action and God's being. God acts in the manner
appropriate to his own being. This is the personal being of the
hidden, self-giving God. Therefore divine action will always for
us be referred back to the pattern of the events concerning
Jesus, and their prelude and sequel in history. The actions of
Jesus himself are the only actions we know directly as the acts
of God in history. It is as prior and consequent actions are
characterised as the actions of self-giving love that they are seen
as the actions of God.

Experience, revelation and reason have led people to
understand God's action in self-giving love. We do not have,
and in the nature of the case are never likely to have, a
blueprint for the mechanism of divine action. We cannot by
reasoning deduce the mode of action of one for whom creation
is *ex nihilo.* We are not provided with such an account by
revelation. We do not need such an account in order to enter
fully into Christian life, devotion and appreciation of God's
love.

The nature of divine action remains closed to us. Even
though the high road of critical knowledge of the springs of
God's action is reserved for the eschatological future, it makes
eminent good sense to seek the best account of such action
within the limits of our imagination. Kant here is both right
and wrong. We do not have the capacity to attain critical
knowledge of the transcendent God. But God has granted a
clue at least to knowledge of himself through his salvation.
Because there is this double focus of knowledge of God and
man we may explore different sorts of analogy in our talk of
God.

The accounts of divine action in Thomist, patristic, process
and other frameworks, will not operate in the ways which their
creators imagined, for the highway is more securely barred
than they realised. But critical reflection on such approaches
is not a waste of time, for the development and clash of

concepts may help us to appreciate more fully the depth and complexity of God's action. At the same time, we may take up theologies of analogy of grace and dialectical encounter in the continental kerugmatic tradition, making use of their insights into God's grace without necessarily taking up their understanding of the self-authenticating word. We may even make sympathetic but critical use of the mystical theologies advocated by von Balthasar and others. In all such study, we shall not want to lose sight of the priority of God's love or of the limitations of our critical reflection.

The hidden presence of the transcendent and immanent God is the ultimate spiritual reality for human existence. As God's loving presence it has been a source of inspiration, comfort and encouragement to millions of human beings. But God's love is often weak and powerless in this world. There are millions who live and die without, it seems, any awareness whatever of God's loving presence, without hope or consolation in a bleak universe. Since the Christian God is not only compassionate in terms of human experience of him but compassionate in himself, this must be a source of continuing sorrow in God. We may recognise too that for all of us the sense of the presence of God may be inhibited, either by particular individual circumstances or by the development of a secular consciousness, in a reductionist direction, due to plausibility criteria about the uniform operation of the laws of nature and the consequent inconceivability of divine action.

13

Grace and History

1. Act and History

Consideration of act and presence leads to reappraisal of the question of the identification of God's actions in history. Since Christianity is both uniquely related to the revelation of God's salvation in history and the continuing historical development of mankind, it will always be interested in the interpretation of history and the philosophy of history. It is unlikely to support theories of the one correct interpretation of history. There are innumerable secular interpretations and philosphies of history, and their contrast and comparison provides a useful clue to understanding. So it is with Christian understanding of history.

There are often common elements in Christian philosophies, even if not all Christian interpretations may be mutually acceptable. On my understanding of act and presence, theologies of *Heilsgeschichte* will be likely to be less than appropriate. Such uniformity takes away from the risk, contingency and vulnerability of God's commitment in incarnation to historical particularity. We cannot even extrapolate from this particularity to some general principle of contingency. The nature of the hiddenness of God's grace in history does not lead to formal patterns and particular manifestations of divine providence in empirically documented events.

To this general rule exceptions have sometimes been seen, in the growth and continuing presence in history of the Christian community, in the formation of the canon of scripture, in the preaching of the word and the administration of the

178

sacraments. Provided that such an interpretation is not tied too closely and exclusively to particular manifestations of Christian life in community, this is eminently reasonable, for without a continuing tradition of Christian life and thought there would, humanly speaking, be no Christian faith.

As far as general theories of the philosophy of history are concerned, these can only be judged, and have been judged, on their historical and philosophical merits. Christians are no more called upon to adjudicate between them than they are to adjudicate between different interpretations in the philosophy of science, or of law. Certain sorts of theory, e.g. cyclic theories of history or theories involving thoroughgoing determinism of various sorts, will not commend themselves to a Christian understanding of God's purpose for mankind. Theories which are too optimistic will run counter to the Christian sense of the tragedy of moral evil, a theme spelled out brilliantly in the work of Reinhold Niebuhr. At the opposite end of the spectrum, theories which encourage cynicism, based on a negative evaluation of human life, individual and collective, will equally be unacceptable. Though no human quest after understanding of providence can be dismissed as a complete waste of time, it will always be subject to the limitation of the hiddenness of God's action. Faith in the constancy of God's love is based on continuity of ultimate reality in God himself, rather than in any evidence for personal continuities in the created order.

God is involved in history, and his work can be seen in acts and events. This basically valid affirmation can be taken too far, when all God-talk is seen in terms of act and history, or in an historicist perspective. When all is explained in terms of history, explanation fails. In any case, philosophy of history is a live subject, characterised by continuing debate on all fronts, and especially in the understanding of historical objectivity. After the work of Hegel and Troeltsch in particular, there has been a new awareness of the importance of history and its complexity.

Intensive discussion in theology of the acts of God has brought out the difficulties inherent even in the most attractive theories. Some of the problems may be limited by reference to

God in the first instance in incarnation, and then only to God's general action in all history. Modern theology tends to be more at ease with the notion of God's particularity in the totality of human history rather than in particular providence in the traditional sense. But this wider totality is itself a mere fragment of the life span of the universe and a mere speck on its scale.

The acts of God in history take place in, with and under the experience of communities and societies. They remain the action of the hidden God, to be appropriated by faith. There is one important new dimension in which thought on God's involvement in history has been developed in recent writing, and that is in the area of process philosophy. Here all depends on the detail of the process argument. In particular, process thought has been able to make the concept of the loving God central in ways which have eluded much traditional theology in this century.

The Christian God is then irrevocably related by his own choice to historical process. But as in the incarnation of God, all of this engagement takes place through grace. In subjecting himself to historical contingency God remains sovereign over this process. Grace is triumphant through self-giving. Where the dimension of grace is played down, a theology of history tends to collapse into agnosticism or banality. Grace misunderstood gives way to ecclesiastical triumphalism. Grace is the grace of the loving, self-giving God, and is received as the substance of the gift of faith. God acts in history on a personal level, as hidden presence.

Talk of grace in history must bring us back to what is in a sense the test of all talk of God as the loving God, evil, not least of the expressions of which has been within the Christian community itself: *corruptio optimi pessima*. Christians want to say that on the cross and in the resurrection God died out on the evil in this world and so overcame it. Once again the minimum requirements of the Christian claim are breathtaking.

It is sometimes rather readily assumed that demythologising the Fall narratives automatically solves the problem of evil. Banishing concepts unfortunately does nothing to remove or neutralise the unpleasant and often overwhelming consequences of evil. It is sometimes suggested that on the cross God identified with evil and so overcame it. But identification is not enough, at least it scarcely provides an explanation of success in tackling this problem. Though incarnation denies claims of divine impassibility, it need not be thought that God ceases to be the sustaining creator of the universe. Faith in God's love is faith in his effective and unfailing love. The origin of evil remains mysterious to us and its practical scope unbounded. Yet we need not regard it as ruling out the effectual character of divine love. To do so would itself be a real tribute to the power of evil.

2. What is History ?

What is history? We have suggested that it is whatever historians of different sorts and scholars working in cognate fields make of it. Theologians can prescribe to historians neither their techniques, their interpretations, nor their conclusions. In this sense there is no more a 'Christian understanding of history' than there is of an orange, a tin of sardines or a Lego train set. Beyond this level however there are at least four senses in which it is possible and indeed important to speak of a Christian understanding of history.

Firstly, not all historians' interpretations of history are equally consonant with Christian faith. Faith maintains at its heart, with all due qualifications, an interpretation of freedom which permits neither of thoroughgoing determinism nor exaggerated individualism in the understanding of human life. What we do is always open to the freedom of God's grace, and at the same time it affects others in society. Secondly, since Christians understand God as the sustainer of the natural order and of mankind, they understand him to be working out his purposes within the created order and within the development of human life, in what is sometimes known as general providence. Thirdly, they understand God to be involved as a hidden God in actions of particular providence within this general framework. It is always possible to see life as within the hand of God, in prayer and in answer to prayer. Fourthly, the mystery of the incarnation, however further understood, means that God is understood as committed to history and to particularity at a particular time in human development. This time is a focus between the whole history of Israel and the history of the Christian community since the coming of Christ.

There is a fifth and central consideration. What does it mean to say, as is often said, that God is a God for whom historicality is part of his very being? This is in the first instance a reference to the incarnation. This means that God is in himself contingent, vulnerable. God makes himself vulnerable for us. For him self-consciousness includes a dimension of historical consciousness. Process theologians have gone further here in seeing God as essentially involved in the processes of world history.

Focus on the timelessness of God in the tradition, suspect though it was in many ways, had the advantage of pointing to transcendence. God is not bound by the limitations, including temporality, of the created order. However, through his involvement in the history of Israel as a whole and in incarnation through Jesus he has participated in the processed temporal change while remaining the creator God. He is neither strictly temporal nor strictly eternal. He is, in a unique and mysterious way, both. Because God has participated in this way in past history his relation to present history is unique. He is both able to experience human emotions and response and yet not to be overwhelmed by their number and variety. Further, since to him all times are one, this historically defined period of participation affects, through his choice, God's relationship to temporality throughout the duration of the created order, as it were, prospectively and retrospectively. Here is the value of the stress in modern theology, in Barth and Bultmann, and in Pannenberg, of *die Geschichtlichkeit Gottes,* the historicality of God.

The presence and action of God occurs, I would want to suggest, in, with and under the tradition of experience of communities and societies. It is the presence and action of the hidden God, to be apprehended in faith. Through his involvement in different ways in history, in the events concerning Jesus and the entire cosmic process, we may speak of the historicality of the divine presence, mediated through history but not to be 'read off' the course of events. For it is the presence, precisely, of God, the divine presence.

3. Grace and Particular Events

We may now begin to see further dimensions to the relationships between God and history, and particularly to the history of the human race. We have seen that an understanding of God as Trinity underlines God's commitment to history in vulnerability. Historicality is in that sense vulnerability. It is also a pointer to the understanding of the human, understood as God's creature, and to the nature of the creator.

Philosophers have long debated the meaning of history, the nature of historical judgement and of historical explanations, and the results of these debates may throw light on aspects of the explanation of God's relationship with history. Since God in Christian tradition has always been understood as the God of Jesus Christ, it is usually in the context of the doctrinal significance of the events relating to Jesus, the context of incarnation and atonement, that history has been discussed. But this commitment of God to history has also been central to Jewish theology, even if the Bible may not be a 'history book', but a prophetic witness in which history is involved.

Theories of historical explanation may be divided broadly into objectivist theories, stressing the intrinsic significance of the events themselves, and relativist theories, stressing the importance of the context in which events take place, and the importance of the context in which they are subsequently interpreted, for the development of a 'meaning'. Some versions of these theories are more exclusive, some more inclusive: some see overlapping between objectivist and relative aspects of events. Theorists often speak of soft and hard perspectives of objectivism and relativism.

Discussion of events and their interpretation has been influenced by wider philosophical debate about realism and idealism. Central to all this discussion in recent years has been the debate about R.G. Collingwood's philosophy of history, with its distinction between the inner and the outer aspects of events, and discussed by e.g. William Dray, W.H. Walsh, and A.C. Danto. It is clear that historical explanation must have both subjective and objective aspects, and may include many facets or levels of significance for different purposes, whether existential, metaphysical, sociological or whatever.

We have noticed already that the notion of events is far from straightforward. Acts and events may always be broken down into further sub-acts and sub-events in an indefinite regress. What counts as events depends on the scale on which you decide to work. Phenomena which may be significant at the level of microphysics may not impinge on the personal relationships of human beings, and vice versa. Which particular clusters of data we choose to regard as 'facts' will depend on our purpose on a particular occasion. This does not mean of course that the reality of the external world is entirely dependent on our preferred interpretation. If we step out of an aeroplane without a parachute at 30,000 feet we are likely to find the landing inconveniently hard whether we like it or not.

Facts of course gain their significance within a particular interpretational context. This is why the fact of Julius Caesar's crossing of the Rubicon, precipitating major change in the Roman Empire, was of much greater significance than Bloggs' crossing of the English Channel by Hovercraft for a summer holiday. It is indeed conceivable that the mere rumour of Caesar's crossing of the Rubicon might have precipitated revolutionary change or even that the fictitious legend could have profoundly affected politics hundreds of years later. But as it happens, we know that it was the physical threat of the imminent presence of Caesar's legions which precipitated war on that occasion.

Much theological discussion of history has revolved around the process of critical study, especially historico-critical study, of the Bible. The historicity of the gospel narratives, the miracles of Jesus and especially his resurrection have given rise to a vast specialist literature. Fashions in depicting the Bible as a history book, stress on the history of salvation or revelation through the acts of God in history, have all contributed to the way in which we look at the issue of God's relationship with history. The intensive modern debate about the nature of faith, raised in rather different but overlapping ways in the interpretation of the Reformation's *sola fide*, the Kantian turn to the priority of moral categories, and existential philosophy, Rudolf Bultmann's distinction between *Historie* and *Geschichte*, stressing that facts without existential response were of little value in understanding Christian faith, in itself an unexceptionable suggestion, all these provoked renewed debate. The reaction, in ruling out fideism and often faith of any sort, despite the manifold grounds of faith, has been equally influential in theology.

God the creator has brought into being the physical cosmos, and within this, in some improbable manner, by creating precise conditions within an extremely narrow range of biochemical tolerances, has brought into being life as we know it, and humanity as we know it. I do not think that it follows logically that God needs the human race in order to evolve in himself as God. But it is part of the human experience, reflected notably in the biblical narratives, that God has become involved in relationship with humanity. Awareness of God is awakening of faith. This historical consciousness was connected in Israel with the development of an emergent nation, and Christians have seen the culmination of this development, an irregular but providential development, in the incarnation of God in Jesus Christ.

God's relation to history is relation to human history and is the medium of his relation to man. It is intimately connected with the nature of theological anthropology. This must of course be an inclusive rather than an exclusive affirmation. It does not rule out responsibility for the animal kingdom and for the natural environment as a Christian and human responsibility. It says nothing of the exclusion of questions of substance and physical nature from discussions of being.

God's originating, directing and sustaining creativity is involved throughout the cosmos, and is put as a power at the disposal of human beings in ever increasing degree. Human use of this power must be to God a source of delight and of sorrow, delight at its use for good, sorrow at its use for evil purposes, delight at its use for the benefit and flourishing of man, sorrow at its use for the exploitation and diminution of humanity.

That God is himself involved in a particular way in history, being neither a remote controller nor an interfering manager, is expressed in Christian tradition especially in the perception of God as a trinitarian God. God the creator has always related to mankind personally through his presence as gracious presence. Through the incarnation he became self-involved in a new way, in vulnerability to the plane of temporal events in public history. Through the resurrection of Christ God consolidated that presence as the presence of the Holy Spirit. Hence God is present as loving, suffering, effectively peace-bringing Spirit throughout human history and beyond, through and despite human shortcomings. That, in a sense, is the essence of faith, faith in the permanent and universal presence and activity of the love of God.

In this sense it is possible for us to understand God for us through the affirmation of the sense of the presence of God in the history of the experience of the human race, and to understand this presence to humanity as trinitarian presence.

Reflection upon God and history may serve to bring into focus for us several major themes of this study. As human beings, we come to know God and to think of God through human concepts. God has created man and produced a reciprocal divine-human relationship through grace. God is concerned with the whole human experience through time, and not simply with ecclesiastical existence. Through participation in the created order at different levels God invites mankind to response, encouraging response through his trinitarian engagement with the human, giving freedom to creation in order to encourage a creative development.

In speaking of God's unique involvement with the human we are not emphasising an exclusive involvement which would be an anthropocentric narrowing. God is committed to the human, not against but along with the development of the physical order beyond the human.

Such reflection on the nature of God enables us to say this about history. God lets history be. He uses history as the vehicle of a prophetic witness to himself in different ways at different times, but he does not automatically control history directly. Since he is himself committed to history this involved for him risk, vulnerability, seen at its most disastrous in the condemnation of Christ. God has created the cosmos *per verbum*. Through grace he persuades it, effective through powerlessness. This in human terms though intelligible is impossible: God is alone the condition of such a possibility, and alone is its fulfilment.

4. God and Religious Pluralism

We have spoken of God's grace in creation and reconciliation, in creation and new creation. It is clear that God is there, for human beings *qua* human beings as much as for human beings who are through baptism engrafted into the Body of Christ. We must face here again the question of the relation of Christianity, not only to humanity in general, but to human beings who embrace other religious faiths. What of the relationship of Christ to Hinduism, Buddhism and the major world religions?

The alternative possibilities here may be set out in a number of different ways. A useful framework is the threefold division into exclusive, inclusive and pluralist. If we regard Christ as the Way, the Truth and the Life, then the obvious conclusion is that all other religions are simply wrong. Quite apart from being an uncharitable attitude and scarcely likely to contribute to good relations between different races in community, this is clearly not the only possibility. After all, Christians have moved over the centuries from the position of regarding all denominations but their own as wrong, schismatic, heretical or satanic.

Another possibility is to say that though for the present it may be appropriate for there to be a number of religions, yet Christianity is the superior religion, and all other religions are destined to flow into Christianity in the fullness of time. This, in essence, was the position of the Schleiermacher of the *Speeches*. A development of this line would be to suggest that the uniqueness and finality of Christ is an eschatological affirmation. Though men and women may live and die in different faiths, yet they will come after this life on earth to see that in eternity Christ is the fullness of the peace of God. This is the position which I myself would favour.

There are, however, more open positions available in the more radically pluralist options. The great theological pioneer here must still be Ernst Troeltsch. For Troeltsch in his famous reflection on the absoluteness of Christianity, Christianity is the highest and best form of religion now for Western Europeans. Through Christianity we experience God most profoundly. But in other cultures and at other times, God may be most profoundly experienced through other faiths. Such a position may be supported by a Hegelian reflection on incarnation as not confined to a single instance, but rather God's commitment to all creation at all times, the identity of the one and the many, in which incarnation and inspiration mesh and overlap.

On rational and religious grounds such a position has much to commend it, and it has been memorably expressed in recent years by John Hick. However, at this point there are historical and theological judgements to be made. How do we judge the historical claim of the classical Christian tradition that God's relation to Christ was a unique, *sui generis,* unrepeatable relationship? How do we judge the theological claim that God's relation to Jesus though in some ways like his relationship to other human beings, was unique in respect of his ontological commitment to this single, short human life? It is perfectly reasonable to regard this as a once-for-all commitment. In this case, there are clear limits to the allowable pluralism. What is in the nature of the case is a control upon what may be logically or philosophically pleasing. This remains the scandal of particularity, and is related to the particularity of God's involvement with the Jewish people. How odd of God to choose the Jews. But that is how it was and is.

Christians understand God as at once hidden in the process of natural order and intimately involved in the lives of all individuals in history. God is not aloof from but deeply and personally involved in his creation. He is not present exactly as one human being may be present to another, so that each may be familiar with the other's sphere of work and daily engagements' diary. God's presence is a hidden presence, not at our disposal for our particular and often self-centred convenience. This is a presence reflected in the numerous

.world religions, and for Christianity centred in the presence of the Spirit of the risen Christ.'[1]

---

[1]Cf. J. McIntyre, *The Christian Doctrine of History*; V. Harvey, *The Historian and the Believer;* and D.M. MacKinnon, *Borderlands of Theology.*

14

The Presence of God

1. Hidden Transcendence

The God of Christian faith is radically transcendent to the world. In his essential nature, love, he is the hidden divine external referent. On God, we believe, the created order depends for its continuing existence. He is present to his creation. He works in, with and under the structures of creation, immanent in its structures as their sustaining force.

Transcendence can of course mean very different things. The classical Christian understanding of God is that he is more transcendent than the God of Neoplatonism because he has created the physical structure of the universe from nothing, *ex nihilo*, and is not linked by any chain or order or degrees of being to the created order. At the same time he is more intimately involved in the created order than pantheist conceptions of deity allow, for he is the sole sustaining power of all that exists, directly and immediately.

God's transcendence is at once the clue to his unique nature as God, and the source of many of the difficulties facing the human quest for understanding. Because of the peculiar nature of divine transcendence our theories are always underdetermined by the available empirical facts. There may be other sorts of facts, of a transcendent and spiritual nature. There remains the central quality of transcendence, not reducible to other components. Transcendence is interpreted in relation to particular cultural dimensions within the theological traditions themselves. In this way a multiplicity of often conflicting perspectives arises at the heart of faith's reflection on God. Differences are not necessarily the reflection of obtuseness, insincerity, or defective logic, but constitute the variety of experience. Faith is driven to deeper understanding among these various perspectives.

Understanding transcendence includes awareness of the various roles of transcendence in non-theological reflection. Between the radical divine transcendence of neoplatonic mysticism and a deeply pragmatic empiricism there lie numerous levels. There is an important area of what is sometimes called this-worldly transcendence, in all sorts of aesthetic experience in music, art and literature, in the appreciation of moral and cultural values, perhaps especially in experience of and reflection upon personal relationships.

God's transcendence is by definition unique. There is then no possibility of moving from human to divine transcendence by an easy analogical step. Christians understand themselves to be given some clues to God's nature through grace. Though God's transcendence is unique, our language about it is not. Here is a central paradox about talk of God.

Not all experience of transcendence may be understood in a religious context, even by religious people. Some often is, however, and this may help our imaginative appreciation of divine transcendence operating in human life. Such transcendence may be directly linked to the understanding of God, or, in a non- theistic religion such as Buddhism, to the essence of the numinous.

In the Judaeo-Christian tradition the prime source of understanding of divine transcendence is the Bible, and the experience of God in society, worship and individual imagination which this reflects. Creation from nothing suggests at once the complete independence of God from his creation and the utter dependence of creation on God. The Old Testament offers accounts of experience of God as the transcendent God who acted through a covenant relation with his chosen people Israel. Christians have come to trust in this transcendent God through seeing the subjects of the New Testament narrative as the providential culmination of this tradition. They understood God as the transcendent, self-giving God, whose nature is characterised through the life, death and resurrection of Jesus Christ.

God's transcendence may be understood by individuals through reflection upon personal experience of God's grace. It may be related to the experience of others. It may involve theoretical reflection on the manifold logic of fact and interpretation which is the basis of description in most subjects. For some people, thought of God's transcendence may be a source of joy, gratitude and peace. For others, there may be more a sense of meaninglessness and disaster at the root of human society. A general theory of divine transcendence ought to take account of both ends of the spectrum, of quiet confidence in divine blessing and of weary despair in the face perhaps of mass deprivation.

Awareness of divine transcendence is sometimes seen as a state of blessed serenity, characterised by a natural sovereignty over the natural order. Exceptions may be seen in the mystical experience of the blank wall, the concept of dread in Kierkegaard and the existentialist tradition, and notably in Martin Luther's relation of transcendence to the death and resurrection of Jesus. Recent Jewish theologies of the Holocaust have explored the transcendence of the suffering God. God's transcendence overcomes the barrier of death, the Achilles' heel of most conceptions of inner-worldly transcendence. God who is self-giving love brings life out of death in the mystery of his eternal goodness. This is difficult territory, but is not on that account to be neglected. God's transcendence is mysterious. The modern world seems to belie talk of mystery. The obvious solution is a compromise, talk of the semi-transcendence of a reasonably comprehensible deity. But of course we can be content neither with a restatement of the verities of the past nor with vacuous reinterpretation.

Understanding transcendence is closely bound up with understanding God as creator. God is the maker of heaven and earth. God is in no sense an object in the world of objects. He is independent of space and time except as he chooses to be involved in space and time. Modern cosmological study can make no difference to central affirmations about God as creator, we may say. Yet it is difficult to conceptualise notions of God's providential care in a universe which appears to be infinite, but in which each galaxy has a fixed and finite term of existence.

Awareness of this vastness of scale may help us to form a renewed conception of the divine transcendence. The cosy familiarities of a local dignitary with his clients are not the appropriate model for such a God. God's love works on a scale in which the span of human life on earth, indeed of the existence of our planet, is a mere fragment. On such a scale particular providence may seem unthinkable. But precisely here we may perhaps grasp some heightened awareness of God's grace, so that in St. Paul's words nothing can separate us from the love of God through Jesus Christ.

God's transcendence is a hidden transcendence. On grounds of revelation we may be justified in speaking of positive characteristics of God's nature. Yet the fact that God is not an object in the world of objects renders our analogies from the natural world, including of course personal analogies, seriously inadequate.

Luther's God is *Deus revelatus* as *Deus absconditus*. God is revealed in Jesus Christ though hidden except to the eyes of faith. In the modern reinterpretation of that tradition by Rudolf Bultmann, the hiddenness of God in creation is recognised in the refusal to develop a speculative theology of creation. Only in the realm of personal, existential encounter around the pivot of the Christ event is the experience of the presence of the hidden God possible.

God's hiddenness is the hiddenness of presence. It is the medium of the 'love that will not let us go'. The appropriate response to God's hidden love is prayer, which involves talking to the hidden God. That the presence of the hidden God should be grasped through faith alone should come as no surprise in a tradition which includes Augustine's *Confessions* and Aquinas' hymns of adoration of the hidden saviour in the eucharistic elements. But it was precisely in the doubtly secularised society of the twentieth century, secularised by widespread abandonment of belief in God and by human savagery on an unprecedented scale, that Dietrich Bonhoeffer came to understand God's presence in his hiddenness.

God's hiddennness is manifested as the transcendence of the hidden God in his inconceivability. This becomes especially clear in God's engagement with the events concerning Jesus. Christology points to this metaphysical opacity of God in creation and redemption. It is not then from a particular abstract concept of transcendence that we may hope to understand God, but from Christian faith in the God who is trusted as the transcendent God.

God in Christian faith is not only transcendent but deeply immanent in his creation. Reflection upon experience of God's presence is at once the most basic and the most ambivalent of criteria. If we have no experience of God then God is at best peripheral to our lives. But experience is often deceptive, and the history of mankind is full of discovery that the certainties of past experience are no longer the certainties that they were, in the light of developing knowledge.

Immanence without transcendence is problematic. But the scope of God, not as the absolute dialectic between immanence and transcendence but as the God of all grace, is all-embracing. Creation without reconciliation is nothing. Through God's hidden presence in Christ the created order – Bonhoeffer's secular world – may become again the intrument of God's gracious love to men. To live *etsi deus non daretur*, as if there were no God, is easy, and is indeed part of our contemporary condition of alienation. To live *coram deo*, before God, *etsi deus non daretur* may be part of a particular form of Christian commitment. No one has emphasised this more eloquently in English than the late Ronald Gregor Smith. To speak of the action of God in Christ is to recall not an exclusive but an inclusive act, and should lead not to a weakening but to a strengthening of awareness of the significance of God as creator.

2. Divine Presence

How can we conceive of the divine presence? The sense of the presence of God is filled out for us in its objective pole through reflection back upon the biblical understanding of God as creator and redeemer. The subjective pole of Christian experience is in the sphere of forgiveness and reconciliation. As Luther knew, the experience of God is the experience of a gracious God, whose presence is a forgiving and reconciling presence.

God is experienced in various religions. How to distinguish such forms of religious experience from modern concepts of inner-worldly transcendence remains a central question. For Christians the core element remains the experience, however frequent or infrequent, intense or less intense, of the reconciling grace of God in Christ, understood further as the presence of the Holy Spirit, the gift of God's peace.

The sense of the presence of God is a natural consequence of the sustaining grace of the loving God. But, all too often, men and women have lived and died in human history with at best a gravely fragmented or at worst, but most commonly, an entirely non-existent sense of God as a sustaining presence, especially in times of dire need. What about the love that does let us go? We saw that the problem of the absence of God was classically explored in the ancient world already in the plays of Aeschylus. Against the notion that the gods were amoral in their dealings with men Aeschylus developed his own concept of the divine justice. Through the cycle of his tragedies he works out the reconciliation of the claims of the Furies with the judgement of Zeus the High God.

If we believe in the ultimate unity of creation and reconciliation we must assert the presence of the divine love to men who had perhaps no belief in God, no sense of divine presence and consolation, even in the most desperate of circumstances. God must be able to rejoice with those who rejoice. A God who cannot do this is scarcely worthy of disbelief, not to speak of belief.

The presence of God is mediated to men and women, and the action of God towards man occurs, in an historical environment. But God's presence is not directly accessible historically. Involved everywhere in countless acts, God cannot be conceived by us as aware of and conscious of each action exactly as a human personal agent might be. God acts in different ways at different times, but all his actions are equally *his* actions, and they have eschatological dimensions. God is concerned for people in this life and beyond. As self-giving, self-affirming love, God abhors all evil and suffers under evil when his creatures suffer. The existence of evil under God is part of the condition of the possibility of finite freedom. It is overcome eschatologically and is always opposed now by God, in suffering and in persuasion.

God's hiddennness is not ineffable inaccessibility – not all mysticism is Christian. God may be experienced as hidden presence in Christian community. But even in the absence of experience he may be affirmed as one who is there, as a compassionate and hidden presence, on the basis of historical events in the past and our own reflections about the nature of God from these.

We shall want to say then that men and women have faith in God's presence as a loving God, even in the absence of particular direct experience of loving presence in extreme situations. We may be wrong. But the reasonable ground for such faith will lie in appeal to God's grace in history through historical experience, though not just revelation of experience.

3. Suffering Presence

To speak of God's involvement in the depths of all human experience, in immanence within the created order, is to make a statement of very far-reaching consequence. I have suggested that the argument from the apparent absence of the presence of God in the evils of the world to the non-involvement of God is not adequate. It could indeed be that God is not involved, but this cannot be readily demonstrated.

Sometimes people *have* affirmed a sense of God's presence as loving presence in times of apparent desolation. Where this has been absent, Christians believe that this presence will be affirmed to them eschatologically after death. The grounds for this hope lie in the present, in reflection through faith on the nature of God as creator.

Wherever there is human suffering God is involved, even if his presence does not prevent the physical or mental consequences of such suffering. Here God is indeed powerless by his own choice, not intervening in the structures of his creation though present to and through them. This powerlessness is emphasised in the parable, which is not just our parable but God's substantially enacted parable, of the experience of the creator with death in the cross of Jesus. God's power is emphasised in the resurrection of Jesus. Through suffering as through rejoicing, God brings eschatological reconciliation.

The problem of evil is then closely associated with the mystery of the hiddenness of divine presence in the depths of the created order. The theological response is to point to the cross, where love is crushed and at the same time released through human hatred. But, it may be argued, it is one thing to suffer oneself and quite another to permit others to be tortured. God however is God. God is there in suffering, silent identification, wherever such suffering occurs. God both lets us be, by making possible authentic human loving response, and yet will not let us go, in constant total concern.

God is immanent in the created order in a manner which is in important respects unique and inexplicable. He remains the hidden sustaining presence, quite independent of any sort of created presence. Because he has created men and women within this order, he has made it possible for us to have a human understanding of this presence. This is the basis and medium of human relationship with him. Christians find the central clue to this relationship and to God as the loving God, in the historical events relating to Jesus Christ. This specific presence in love provides a means of discernment for testing our human visions.

4. Resurrection Presence

What sort of concepts of person do we regard as helpful for understanding the creator and reconciler of all mankind? There are all sorts of people. God does not partake of humanity in biological terms. Perhaps we ought rather to think of the personal presence of the crucified Christ? This is clearly important. I have myself suggested though that the essence of Christianity, if there be such a thing, is not the cross of Christ, but the love of God in Christ. God's self-giving, self-affirming love is decisively expressed on the cross because of the nature of man rather than the nature of God. God expresses himself primarily in resurrection and joy, the fullness of life. God's love is not a beautiful solidarity in suffering but an identification which is utterly intolerant of the evil which is the opposite of love. Death is indeed the last enemy.

The nature of the hidden, mysterious presence of God is disclosed through death, but also through resurrection. The presence of God is the presence of the Spirit of the risen Christ. God is the creator of heaven and earth. He is the creator of the physical universe, of all life, of man. No simple model can provide us with anything like a satisfactory model of the living God. It follows from our reflection on God's hiddenness that belief in God's providential activity within the created order is 'against the odds' and belief in God's victory over evil is focused on the events concerning Jesus. God acts, in the manner appropriate to self-giving love. *How* he acts is left to the imagination of faith to work out. In human life commitment to love means endless different sorts of responses, not all identifiable by simple association with 'love' as the obvious motive.

Because we cannot think of God's personal presence as ultimately less personal than the presence of his creatures, we may think of God's love as involving thought, will, memory, intention and the other components of our activity. We may think of God's actions, like the actions of persons, as composed of millions of individual and overlapping sub-acts and sub-events which go to constitute larger movements which *we* then recognise as acts and events on the level of human encounter. We find it very difficult to individuate God's actions. This is scarcely surprising. It is not always easy to individuate human acts. Nothing can separate us from the love of God. This love is usually related to the preservation of human life, but may be exhibited also where life is lost.

Experience, revelation and reason have led Christians to understand God's action in self-giving love in this way. The hidden presence of God is the ultimate spiritual reality for human existence. It has been a source of inspiration, comfort and encouragement to millions of human beings. But God's love is not always effective in this world. It is often weak and powerless and its triumph is eschatological. Since God is not only compassionate in terms of human experience of him but also in himself, this must be a source of continuing sorrow in God. We have to recognise too that for all of us, the sense of God's presence may be inhibited, by individual circumstances or by the development of a secular consciousness, in a reductionist direction, due to plausibility criteria about the uniform operation of the laws of nature and the subsequent inconceivability of divine action.

The acts of God take place in, with and under the tradition of experience of communities and societies. They remain the actions of the hidden God, to be apprehended in faith. What would it mean to say that God is a God for whom historicality is part of his very being? This is in the first instance a reference to the incarnation. The historicality is at the same time intimately related to the spirituality of God. It is as a self-focused presence, as one who has acted decisively in history in the events concerning Jesus and now is present to humankind through the Spirit that God sustains mankind with his grace. That presence is the presence to faith of the Spirit of God.

God is involved in the history of the created order, and in all human history, in general and in special providence. God is engaged in all human life, in its religious and in its secular strivings. *Fecisti enim nos ad te, et cor nostrum est inquietum donec requiescat in te.* God is involved especially in the Judaeo-Christian tradition, in the history of the Christian community, the Church, and in the influence on human life and thought of Christianity across the ages. In this process God uses men and women as the instruments of his love, wherever they are ready to be open to his service. As such God is not simply a matter of academic interest. God is the God who loves, and who continues to invite us to response, to discipleship.

II. GOD IN RECONCILIATION

3. GOD IN RECONCILIATION

15

Introduction

The name of Jesus Christ is still perhaps the best known name in human history. For millions of human beings, Christ has been experienced in faith as a reality at the centre of their lives. This reality has always been both a decisive reality and a mystery, perceived differently in different circumstances. Faith understands the presence of Christ as the presence of God. God was in Christ reconciling the world to himself.

But this process of reconciliation took place, the Apostles' Creed reminds us, 'under Pontius Pilate'. It was a drama played out in the world of public events, in a world of totalitarian oppression, a world notably lacking in such virtues as liberty, equality and fraternity, a world of compromise and collaboration. It is this struggle and its consequences for our history, for humanity and inhumanity, with which we are concerned here.

The centre of Christianity is Jesus Christ. In the history of Christian thought and Christian life thousands of books have been written about the place of Jesus Christ in the Christian understanding of man. It has, in one sense, all been said, but, in another sense, of course the mystery of Christ has to be reflected upon, thought out carefully again and again, in every generation. It is, after all, possible to define and to analyse the nature of man in many different ways in brief compass and this is easily done. The mystery of human existence continues to be a question until the end of the human race. It is possible to speak of deity, of theism in many different religions, yet the mystery of the nature of God remains a continual question and challenge to mankind.

In speaking of Jesus Christ we are speaking of both God and man centred upon this one figure. This is the perplexing nature and at the same time the whole point of Christology. We shall be concerned with Jesus Christ in relation to God, Jesus Christ in relation to man. This is of course an impossible task. I have attempted elsewhere to spell out the implications for various branches of theology of the fundamental Christian affirmation that God is love. Here I propose to draw some of these reflections together in considering further the central issues of Christology and the understanding of God as love in relation to the events concerning Jesus Christ.

Christology has consequences for the understanding of the sources of theology, scripture, tradition, and human creative thought. It involves consideration of the understanding of the nature and the action of God. It brings in dimensions of ethics and of ecclesiology, all of which have been the subject of these earlier studies. It involves consideration of the long history of Christian thought, the Christian tradition concerning Christ and the enormous industry relating to Christological research which has characterised the last hundred years of academic theology.

The centre of Christology is the self-giving love of God through Jesus Christ. Christology is part of the Christian doctrine of God. It is also part of Christian doctrine of man. It is concerned with the life of God and with the life of man. It is concerned with a particular man in whom Christians believe God was present in a unique, final and decisive manner. The story of the Church's attempt to understand the mystery of God is the story of centuries of technical theological discussion. It is also the story of the attempt through the centuries to understand Christ in relation to the life of the people who seek to be faithful to Christ. In every age it is a story with a technical component, a reflection with all the scholarly resources available upon the Christian mystery. It is also a non-technical story, the attempt to understand the meaning of the salvation which Christians believe to have come to us through Christ. Christians have reflected upon the meaning of the Christ event in innumerable different ways. Theologians have approached the problem of Christological method in an enormous variety of ways also. It is clear too, despite the claims of rival methodologists that in fact many different theologies have led to the illumination of different aspects of the Christological problem. *Solvitur ambulando*: what matters is that an account should be given in which each project creates some new illumination however small of the Christian mystery. Much has been learned in the centuries of reflection, much has been assumed which can be shown today to be based on cultural conditioning which applies only to a particular situation and which needs to be redefined in every new situation. Much has also been forgotten for this reason. It is not inappropriate to reconsider the wisdom of the past in general and in particular detail in order then to concentrate on the essentials.

In the patristic period, there is a rich stream of Christian reflection upon the mystery of Christ. The more the different contributions are analysed in detail, the more the complexity of the stream can be appreciated. But still this tradition took place and developed within a fairly narrow context, that of the Christian community around the Mediterranean Sea around the first six centuries. In the interval there has been an enormous development. But somewhat as the population of the world has increased enormously in the last hundred years so the pace of change in reflection from different cultural perspectives has also increased tremendously. It is not surprising that the consequence has been often an impression of complete disintegration, of completely different and conflicting meanings in the Christian understanding of Christology. Anything becomes possible, given a sufficiently sophisticated approach to theological method. Any kind of new hermeneutic makes possible a new Christology. In response to this there has been a not unnatural desire to go back to fixed norms, to produce once again objective standards. It seems to me that we can be content neither with extreme relativism and the notion that there is no fixed substance to the Christological belief, nor can we be content with stemming the tide of research by recourse to some convention however venerable from the past.

We live in a situation in which there must be a system of

checks and balances in which we may have confidence in the tradition, the worshipping, reflecting living, thinking tradition of the Church and yet be open to fresh reflection upon this in each generation, fresh reflection upon the central strands of belief. In this study we shall consider most of the main traditions of Christological thought. We shall aim at a constructive free statement rather than simply a placing of the traditions on a kind of taxonomy of Christological forms. Ours is a generation which is as near to God and as far from God as any previous generation. It is a generation however in which theologies which are unable to face the harshest realities of life collapse. Ours is a generation in which it is often said all the words have been over-used, issues overhauled until it is impossible to say anything at all. Yet if we are concerned Christians and believe we are concerned with the living reality of God, we may hope to find ways of fresh articulation of the truth of God despite the difficulties of the limitations of imagery and language which have been so used in the past.

This is a Christology of the love of God. It will really not be sufficient simply to speak of God's love, God's self-giving, self-affirming kenotic love without relating this to the various problems of a technical, imaginative, cultural nature which this raises for the reader who is not abstractable from the context in which he or she reads.

On the other hand, it is always possible for a philosopher to read theology and philosophy of a somewhat abstract nature without particular reference to the context in which he works. It is possible for the physicist and even for the poet to understand his dialogue with a particular conditioned slice of reality. It is then unnecessary for the theologian to imagine that, because he or she is writing and thinking in the complex, pluralistic world, the reflection is totally meaningless if it does not take up explicitly all aspects of this complexity. In other words, we need not think that the assimilation of a straightforward theological argument has now become impossible in this generation.

Much Christological formulation has been hammered out through controversy. In some ways this has been a good thing because it has forced us to seek deeper explanations and to take account of objections raised to particular lines of argument. In other ways it has been counter productive. Ritual arguments often bring tedious animosities into play. We shall attempt to analyse these arguments in such a way as to produce more light than heat.

The Christian understanding of Jesus Christ is an integral part of the Christian understanding of God. God in Christian faith is creator and redeemer. The events concerning Jesus are not simply an appendage to the Christian message concerning God. They are an integral part of Christian understanding of God. This has been acknowledged in various ways throughout the main Christological discussion of the Church even in such undoubtedly opposed figures as, let us say, Harnack and Barth. All the intellectual considerations referring to the nature of God and divine action are directly relevant to all the problems of Christology and vice versa. That is one of the reasons why simplified Christologies based on an understanding of the man Jesus of Nazareth, for example, alone, if the understanding of any human being can ever be described as simple, are less than helpful as comprehensive statements of the nature of the mystery. Of course they may be helpful in eliminating one aspect of the mystery and this contribution is not to be underestimated. But in talking of Christology we are talking of the whole Christian understanding of God. This is not to invite such spectres as Christomonism where everything is based on Christ to the exclusion of all other considerations of God. It is not to invite neglect of the Holy Spirit, it is not to invite neglect of all other dimensions of Christian doctrine. Nevertheless, in Christology we are concerned with the centre of Christian faith by definition.

Christ is not, and has never been, intended as a private possession of a single group or community. It may be through historical accident that this is how the ministry of Christ manifests itself in the world in visible form in particular cultures through persecution of various kinds, fluctuations of cultural paradigm, plausibility criteria and the like, but it is central to the faith that Christ lived, died, rose again for all humankind and not simply one privileged group. Even a Christology which is particularly concerned with the understanding of the Church, and precisely such a Christology, is always at the same time a Christology for all humankind. It may be necessary on occasion to concentrate on the spiritual practice of small communities in their worship, in their eucharistic practice, in devotional context, but all of this is always to be understood as the Church as a servant of God in the service of all humanity.

16

The Tradition of the Gospel

1. The Question of Christ

The pages of the New Testament cover a wide variety of topics, but nothing like as wide a range as appears in the Old Testament.[1] There is a tremendous concentration on one man, Jesus of Nazareth. If there had been no such concentration, or if the texts had been uniform in the nature of their descriptions, there might perhaps have been no need for Christology, for critical enquiry into the significance of Jesus Christ for Christian faith. But there is this concentration, and the terms in which the subject is expressed are extremely varied.

The centre of the synoptic gospels is the story of a man's life. There were shepherds in the fields with their flocks. They were afraid, but the angel said, 'Do not be afraid. Today in the city of David a deliverer has been born to you, the Messiah, the Lord' (Luke 2:10). An age-old expectation has been fulfilled. For the Pauline community the child of Bethlehem has become the Lord. 'It is not ourselves that we proclaim: we proclaim Christ Jesus as Lord, and ourselves as your servants, for Jesus' sake. For the same Lord who has said, "out of the darkness let light shine" has caused his light to shine within us to give the light of revelation, the revelation of the glory of God in the face of Jesus Christ' (2 Cor. 4:5f.). The Johannine Christ is himself

---

[1]This section is based on my articles on 'Christology' and 'Soteriology' in *A New Dictionary of Christian Theology*, ed. Alan Richardson and John Bowden. I am most grateful for permission to use this material.

209

the incarnate Word. 'So the word became flesh: he came to dwell among us and we saw his glory, such glory as befits the Father's only Son, full of grace and truth' (John 1:1-14).

The man Jesus and the Christ of faith are understood and portrayed in the New Testament in a large number of different ways. Throughout the history of the Church hundreds, if not thousands, of answers have been given to the central question: What think ye of Christ? We in turn will inevitably be influenced by the fact that the question is not asked in our day for the first time. Christology, the doctrine of Christ, is enquiry into the significance of Jesus for Christian faith. In the classical Christian tradition, faith is understood as faith in the person of Jesus Christ. Where the symbol, principle or idea of the gospel is differentiated from the man, one can speak of faith like Jesus's faith, or faith because of Jesus, but not of faith in Jesus, in the sense that in his person and history he does not simply bring or represent the truth of salvation, but *is* the truth, the ground of salvation. It is this stronger claim that is at once the glory and the problem of classical Christology.

What are the grounds for faith in Jesus Christ? Basic questions arise. How can faith, which involves trust without reservation, be based on anything so complex and so relative as a cluster of events in history, on the ever shifting sand of what is known as the quest of the historical Jesus? It will not do simply to say that what matters is not Jesus the specific historical individual but the kerugma or proclamation of the early Church. The New Testament writers were not preoccupied with modern notions of historicity. But they were reporting things which they believed to have happened. It would hardly be true to say that only the professional historian can have any knowledge of the person and history of Jesus. Christians usually work from the understanding – which constantly needs to be tested – that a basic outline at least of the life and activity of Jesus is available to us. This information is an important part of the data from which faith arises.

Christology involves the reflection of faith on its own grounds. We cannot begin, it may seem, by presupposing the validity of a doctrine of Christ and then trying to understand it, moving as it were from above to below, from the trinitarian God above to the man Jesus below. Rather we must begin from the man Jesus and try to spell out the meaning of the Christ from below, where we ourselves are. Though God may be before us in the order of being, we are concerned with the order of our knowing. Yet things are not so clear cut. When we speak of God in relation to Jesus and to all humanity there is an element of 'from above' wherever we choose to begin. In most critical investigations we begin from what we take to be 'the facts'. Christian faith involves the claim that through Jesus human beings are brought into a deepened relation with God their creator. Faith arises from the life and worship of the community as a gift of grace, and God does not offer us empirically verifiable proofs of his activity and presence. But without supporting evidence faith would be no more than blind credulity.

2. The Christology of the New Testament

In the New Testament, Jesus is portrayed as a witness to God. He speaks with authority, as the Old Testament prophets had spoken. This authority is more than that of a prophet. 'You have heard that it was said but I say to you.' He proclaims the breaking in of God's kingdom, which has come in his presence. He calls for repentance, and God's forgiveness is granted to those who will follow him. He speaks strikingly of God as his father.[2] His friends and followers were to go further, calling him the Messiah, the Lord. But his life has never been the sole ground for belief in him, for the disaster of his execution put all that he was into question. Whatever may have happened after his death, around what the tradition called the resurrection, this was part of the ground for belief in Jesus in the apostolic communities. We are invited to believe not in the dead Jesus but in the living Christ.

Paul can speak of seeing the glory of God in the face of Jesus Christ (2 Cor. 4:6). For the author of the Fourth Gospel, 'When

---

[2]Pannenberg, for example, stresses in *The Apostles' Creed* and in *Jesus God and Man* that the most significant piece of information we have about the life of the man Jesus is his complete devotion to God his Father.

a man believes in me, he believes in him who sent me rather than me, seeing me he sees him who sent me.' This belief in God is directed towards the man Jesus. The man is not the same as God: he speaks of his Father in heaven. He is not good but only his Father is perfectly good. He is and remains a man, and still participates in the life, action and thought of his Father. He is at the same time the glory of God and the glory of man.

This unique relationship of Jesus to God was expressed by the New Testament communities in a number of titles of honour – the Messiah, the Lord, the Word of God, the Son of God. As Messiah Jesus completes and fulfils the expectations of Israel, yet in completing transforms them. Christ is the end of the Messiah, it has been said. As the Johannine Word of God Jesus is not only the messenger but is himself the source of true life. The most striking claim of all is that Jesus is God's only son: 'God so loved the world that he gave his only son, that everyone who has faith in him should not die but have eternal life. It was not to judge the world that God sent his son into the world, but that through him the world might be saved' (Jn. 3:16-17). God has come into humanity in the person of his son. But how can Jesus be a man and at the same time the only Son of God? We are led straight into the central problems of Christology.

It is natural that Christians in the modern world should wish to understand the essence of the gospel in terms which they can recognise and relate to the world in which they live. This search has brought drastic reinterpretation. The notion of God sending his son into the world suggests that God is from eternity Father, Son and Spirit, and this ties up with the Pauline idea of the pre-existent Son of God. An obvious move has been to regard the concept of an eternal Son who comes into humanity as mythological in character. Christology then turns on the significance of Jesus for human existence; the relation of Jesus to God the creator of the universe remains unexplored. Critics have made the point that, at least in the New Testament, the coming of Jesus brings more than a new understanding of the world: something has happened in the history of creation.

A Christology which attempts to preserve the breadth of its traditional scope would seem then to be faced with two tasks. The first is to express and explain the presence of the full divinity of God in the man Jesus, showing how he is both truly God and truly man. The second is to bring out the full differentiation between God and man in Jesus, avoiding the sort of confusion in which Jesus would be neither fully divine nor really human.

The classic solution was on the following lines. The full presence of the divine and so the unity of the divine and human in Christ takes place through a continuous giving on God's part and a continued human receiving by Jesus. Jesus is the person he is only through his constant receiving of God's gift, and even his devotion to God from whom he receives is a gift of God. In so far as the traditional doctrine that the man Jesus has no independent human nature intends to make the point that Jesus to be himself is always totally dependent on God, then this must be right. But the expression remains problematic. For this dedication to God involves an individual, who gives himself to God and receives God's gifts in a truly human way, in faith, prayer and obedience.

In this interpretation God, without ceasing to be God, comes into human existence, into vulnerability to temptation. openness to suffering, actual suffering. God does this precisely through his power as God, for the infinite is capable of assuming finitude, abandoning himself for humankind. This self-giving, of which only God is perfectly capable, is seen on the cross. Self-giving is brought to self-fulfilment in the resurrection.

For Jesus of Nazareth the meaning of the incarnation is that God gives him participation in his divine nature, within the limitations of the human. He participates in God's power to heal the sick, to forgive and to renew. In devoting himself to his Father he receives the power to act in the way he does for the salvation of mankind. The full divinity of God is united with the man Jesus, but in such a way that the divinity is not changed into humanity, and man is not in any way divinised. Jesus is at once the bearer of the presence of God and the medium of its hiddenness. God does not force himself upon us; we become aware of his presence through faith. This mystery of union is beyond our comprehension, but we must continue to seek the best available explanations. In such an approach we come to understand who Jesus was by looking at his whole life and activity. Through life, death and resurrection there takes place a costly reconciliation, in which the relationship between God and man is renewed, to await the perfection of the eschatological peace of God.

3. Doctrinal Development

Who was this Jesus Christ, the subject of the Church's confession? Was he human or divine or both? Partly the one and partly the other? From the earliest times to the present there have been those who have seen Christ as a divine being walking the earth in human disguise. The Docetists, as they were called, understood Jesus' historical existence as appearance (*dokein*, to appear) rather than reality. In much Hellenistic thinking the world of the flesh is inferior to the world of the spirit. Ebionitism, on the other hand (a word possibly derived from a Hebrew word meaning 'poor') reflected the central problem facing Christians of Jewish background, of how to reconcile their Christian faith with the strict monotheism of Israel. Jesus' humanity was not in question, but divinity was played down: some suggested this was a special dignity which descended on Christ at his baptism. Both in Hellenistic and in late Jewish thought – and it is artificial to see these as either distinct or uniform, for both overlapped and were pluriform in themselves – there was an important distinction between the earthly and the heavenly realm, between creator and creation.

One important answer to the central question had roots in the Palestinian background. Jesus was God's messenger, his word, his logos.[3] The word became flesh and dwelt among us. But the logos was also the all-pervasive rational principle of the universe in Stoic philosophy. So Justin Martyr, writing in Rome in the middle of the second century, when accused of blasphemy for worshipping not God but the man Jesus, could say that Jesus Christ was not merely a man, but the eternal and universal

---

[3]In my view the best guide to the logos tradition remains Grillmeier's *Christ in Christian Tradition* I and II, despite my reservations about it in *Theology of the Love of God.*

logos of God from which all order and rationality were derived. His birth and conception were unique. He had indeed a body, soul and spirit, yet it was right to call him Lord and to worship him, for this man was the logos of God. Here was logos Christology.

Still, within this conceptual framework the logos was secondary, in some ways inferior to God. Faith and worship seemed to involve that God was in Christ in such a way that there was no inequality. The problem was how to express this state of affairs, which arose in the realm of worship and commitment, in a conceptual framework. All kinds of variations on logos Christology arose. Paul of Samosata thought that the man Jesus united with the logos by willing the same things — one in will with God. His opponents argued that the very essence, and not just the will, of the logos is incarnate. But where in a human being do you locate essence? How could you combine the essence of God, who did not change, with the nature of a man, who was crucified, dead and buried?

One important approach was that of Arius, which has been put like this. Christ was the incarnate logos: Christ was subject to change. Therefore, the logos was subject to change. But, granting that God the creator was impassible, that he did not change, the logos could not be identified with God. The logos suffered in Jesus, while God remained unchanged. The main advantage of this approach was that it preserved the emphasis of the school of Antioch on the solidarity of Jesus with authentic human nature. The disadvantage, pressed by the school at Alexandria, was that what was seen in Jesus was something less than God. This destroyed the defence against the charge of worshipping a man rather than God. It left Jesus as neither God nor man but something in the middle. Arius' theology was indeed a theology of the incarnation, but the incarnation of the logos rather than of the creator in the created order.[4] The Council of Nicaea (325) insisted that the Logos or Son was of one essence (homoousios) with the Father. This was not a final solution, for it could lead to a

---

[4] The work of Greg and Groh has thrown much new light on this development. On all this area see G.C. Stead, *Divine Substance.*

minimising of Christ's humanity and a confusion of divine and human natures.

Apart from putting Jesus in a somewhat ambiguous position, the Arian solution raised difficulties concerning the nature of salvation. A central point of patristic Christology was that God became man, took flesh, in order to redeem humanity to a new human nature in Christ. In Gregory of Nazianzus' famous phrase, what is not assumed is not redeemed. If God did not himself come right into human life, then we remain imprisoned in our sins, in Pauline terms. The incarnation did not work. Fully aware of this difficulty, Apollinarius of Laodicea proposed that in the incarnate Christ the place of the human *nous* was occupied by the divine logos. It is indeed perfectly possible to hold that the incarnation of God did not involve any sort of quasi-mechanical replication of creator in creation. But within the anthropology proposed, of body, soul and spirit, Apollinarius' solution inevitably looked like a diluted Christology at two-thirds strength, and was accordingly rejected. Without solving the problem, Nicaea made it clear that Christ was in no sense a part of the creation, subordinate to God, but that he was equal to God, of one substance with the Father. The discussion of the next century was concerned with understanding the relation, given this equality of the divine and the human in Jesus. The upshot of this discussion was the Chalcedonian discussion of 451, which said among other things that

> We confess one and the same our Lord Jesus Christ, the same perfect in Godhead, the same perfect in manhood, truly God and truly man, the same of a rational soul and body, acknowledged in two natures, without confusion, without change, without division, without separation; the difference of the two natures being by no means taken away because of the union but rather the distinctive character of each nature being preserved and combining in one person (*prosopon*) or entity (*hypostasis*): no universals without particulars.

This led on the one hand to Nestorianism (dualism in Christ's person) or (if only one and one) to Monophysitism, which made all divine and left no room for Jesus' human nature.

Chalcedon broke the rules and is on the face of it a bad compromise: two natures in one person. Some modern scholars would say that this simply indicates the logical impossibility of the project. Yet within the terms available it was the best option. Two natures are affirmed, so stressing the full humanity of Jesus at a time of pressure to lose everything in divinity. At the same time Christ is only one person — there is no duality, he is one. The oneness is described in terms of *prosopon* and *hypostasis*, another diplomatic compromise because the terms could have slightly different meanings, but the main points which faith seemed to require were made.

There is then in the Christ of Chalcedon a human nature, but no separate human *hypostasis* (a solution echoed in recent times, e.g. by Barth, *Church Dogmatics*, 4.2, 49ff.). Some went on to say that the human nature of Christ had no *hypostasis* at all — it was a *physis anhypostatos*.

One important further suggestion was made by Leontius of Byzantium at the beginning of the sixth century. Though the human nature of Christ has no *hypostasis* of its own it is not on that account completely *anhypostatos*. It is rather a *physis enhypostatos* — it finds its *hypostasis* in the *hypostasis* of the logos. The distinguishing features of the particular man who Jesus was are then attributed to the divine *hypostasis* as well as the essential qualities of the species (mankind) to which he belongs. These ideas were to be further refined in a distinguished line of Orthodox theologians in the East.[5] In the West Chalcedon was transmitted through the theology of Augustine. The Reformation and the Enlightenment were to produce pressure for other perspectives, first as alternatives and then as replacements. Chalcedon marks out as it were the limits of useful discussion within the classical framework of reference. It shows how the Christian tradition, out of which to some extent at least we must work, has arisen, enabling us to relate the biblical narratives and present circumstances to past Christian experience.

Christology did not stop with Leontius. Broadly speaking the medieval Christologies of the West, following Augustine,

[5] Cf. J. Pelikan, and J. Meyendorff.

tended to be interested not so much in the nature and person of Christ as in the salvation brought by Christ to men (see section on Soteriology). Luther's classic question at the Reformation was 'How can I find a gracious God?', and the Reformers concentrated on the nature of the gift of the divine presence, especially in the understanding of the eucharist. Luther supported his doctrine of the real presence with the patristic theory of *communicatio idiomatum* (exchange of divine and human attributes): Calvin stressed the divine transcendence, in his famous *extra Calvinisticum*. The Lutheran tradition developed a new Christology of the two states of Christ's humiliation and exaltation in cross and resurrection, in accounting for the biblical stress on historical contingency in incarnation. Humiliation and condescension led to further reflection on kenosis, self-emptying, in Jesus and in God. Though the great watershed of the Enlightenment was to put Christological discussion, for many Christians at least, in a quite new light, the previous tradition remained deeply influential, at times inhibiting and at other times enriching the discussion.[6]

4. Salvation

The Christian tradition has long held that we can understand who Jesus was only by looking at his whole life and activity. Recent theology has stressed this inseparability of the person and work of Christ. Here we come to the other side of Christology, to the work of salvation through Christ, in the New Testament and in the history of the Church.[7]

There has never been an 'authorised' version of soteriology. The understanding of salvation has been and probably always will be as diverse as the humanity to which it comes. People have thought of salvation as rescue and restoration, as revelation and reconciliation, as representation and substitution, judgement and making righteous, liberation and the establishment of specific forms of social and political order. Salvation is from God himself and it comes through Christ.

---

[6]Cf. B.A. Gerrish on *The Old Protestantism and the New.*

[7]Cf. Colin Gunton, *The Actuality of Atonement.*, and John McIntyre, *The Shape of Soteriology.*

Sometimes the work of Christ is seen primarily in the rescue of mankind from some great evil, corresponding to a generally pessimistic doctrine of man, in the tradition of Augustine. Sometimes the image centres upon the positive fulfilment of the goal to which man is naturally inclined by his creator, in the tradition of Irenaeus, Origen and the Renaissance. Modern theology usually attempts to take account of the advantages of each line, stressing on the one hand the reality of the gulf between human frailty and the goodness of the transcendent God, and the assurance of grace to all.

Soteriology has sometimes been seen as Christ's cosmic victory over an evil force, sometimes as the healing of a disease. However, just as it is not necessary for the case-worker to become identified completely with his or her charge, it is not necessary to argue that God had to come into our world and take human flesh in order to redeem us. A transcendent God does not need to act in order to be able to save. Yet Christians still want to affirm that God is always involved with us in the constancy of his love.

On the other hand, salvation may be seen as the goal to which men have been directed from the beginning of creation. Jesus of Nazareth brings God's message to his fellow men, transforming the law of Israel and inviting us to live as free men and women. The problem here is that the will to action is sometimes precisely what we lack in times of disaster. Still, we may hope for grace in creation and redemption to lead us on, however hesitantly.

We can see again perhaps how the understanding of soteriology depends on our understanding of the nature of God as the author of salvation. Many Christians would affirm that to be God is to be able among other things to give oneself away in such a way as to enable mankind to give itself without restraint, to destroy alienation from within. The God of the New Testament narratives freely chooses to involve himself in human life and death, and overcomes death in the raising of Jesus. God is involved in creation and providence, and in salvation through the life, death and resurrection of Jesus.

The work of Christ is then a work of God's love from beginning to end. It is also a work of man, of the man Jesus, a person sustained in thought and action by devotion to God. Soteriology depends on Jesus' humanity, and on God as the source of his unique freedom as a human being. Here the lasting value of 'exemplarist' theories of the work of Christ can be appreciated. Atonement must evidently include both subjective and objective elements. Simply because we may not be in a position to respond to a moral example, this does not take away its intrinsic value as a deed done. The human cost of soteriology in the struggle of Jesus through love with evil can hardly be overestimated.

Soteriology in the Early Church developed along the two main lines indicated above, in parallel with Christology. The dictum that what is unassumed is unredeemed had a powerful effect on doctrines of Christ's person. The medieval Christologies of the West, following Augustine, stressed the gulf between God and man, and tended to be interested not so much in the nature and person of Christ, the fact of incarnation, as in the salvation he brought. The forgiveness of sins, the ransom paid on the cross, coupled with the development of a theory of penance, was the main theme. Atonement dominated the discussion. So St. Anselm's brilliant *Cur Deus Homo* centred on the satisfaction made by Christ for the sins of men. The medieval emphasis on the penalty paid by Christ in his death – the wages of sin – to atone for man's treason against God was continued at the Reformation.

Since the time of Calvin doctrine in the churches of the Reformation has traditionally represented the work of Christ in terms of his three offices (*triplex munus*) of prophet, priest and king. This has the advantage of bringing together three important strands of the biblical tradition. It does however tend to break up the unity of soteriology, choosing three categories at the expense of others (e.g. shepherd, saviour and servant), and scarcely takes adequate account of the extent to which Old Testament categories are transformed through Christ – their fulfilment is also in an important respect their abolition.

Soteriology examines the means by which, Christians believe, God wills to bring the created order into a perfected relationship with himself in the eschatological future. It includes a personal relationship to the creator for all human beings, of any faith or none. Somehow, this relationship has been worked out in God's involvement with the created order, in his engagement with a single human life through Jesus. God is involved, in a way which remains largely mysterious to us, in Jesus' life. Jesus lives a completely human life in devotion to God and man. He dies, an example of integrity and a witness to a particular understanding of God, exposing the contrasts between the divine love and lesser loves.

But when the creator becomes directly involved in creation more takes place. The resurrection, however partial our understanding of it, indicates the significance of the life and death which have preceded it. A new way has opened up for a new humanity. We can see here that the traditional imagery of soteriology was not unperceptive, There is a great gap between God's love and ours. God's personal involvement in human life and death has bridged the gap and has done what we could not do for ourselves. How can we see Christology as effective? It is because Jesus was involved with God that he is involved with us, and because God was related in a particular way to Jesus that he is related to us in a new way. God has related himself decisively to contingent historical experience within his own created order.

This historical order is in turn taken up into God's being, providing the eschatological dimension of soteriology. Death will not separate us from the constancy of God's love, for this love is effective not through sentimental benevolence but through agonising decision and infinite cost.

17

Our Contemporary Christ

1. Modern Christology

Modern Christology may be said to begin in the European Enlightenment, at a time when all sorts of new questions had arisen concerning the nature of man and his world, in relation to God, questions to which the classical categories seemed to provide no relevant answer. To meet this challenge a new Christology was produced, notably in the work of Schleiermacher and Ritschl. It attempted, following a suggestion from Herder, to look for the divinity of Jesus in the unique quality of his life on earth. The focus is a picture of a man of pure compassion and kindness, who set a moral example in all that he did. He began the work of the kingdom of God, which we may carry on by acting in love towards our fellow men. Usually there was much more to this Christology than twentieth-century critics have allowed. Though we may laugh at Victorian pictures of gentle Jesus meek and mild, after the manner of Sir John Seeley's *Ecce Homo*, at least here there was a genuine attempt at communication in contemporary terms. In part at least, the impression that later Christologies were better may be due to the fact that we have had less time to find out the difficulties involved in them.

Still, there could be no going back. By 1910 it seemed clear that the Jesus of much nineteenth-century piety, the leader of a moral kingdom of God in which we might co-operate, was not to be found in the gospels. As rediscovered by Johannes Weiss and Albert Schweitzer, the Jesus of the New Testament preached an eschatological message, warning of the imminent end of the world. God will bring in his kingdom, and human moral effort has nothing to do with it. Critics argue that though the example of Jesus could easily be related to the private moral duties of the individual and his family and friends, the old classical understanding of the Christ who makes a radical difference to the way the world is – however unintelligibly described – had largely gone. It was left to Marx and Engels to provide an account of alienation, of sin, of the gulf between the actual and the desirable state of the population of the nineteenth-century world, which was much less shallow than many Christian assessments.

It was in reaction to this scene that the so-called dialectical theology arose, the foremost exponents of which were to be Barth, Brunner and Bultmann. For Karl Barth, the Swiss pastor, it was the German theologians' glorification of the First World War (British scholars, it must be said, were no better!) that sparked off rebellion.[1] For Bultmann it was the collapse of the liberal picture of Jesus when compared with the latest New Testament scholarship. Barth's God at this time is the wholly other, who in Christ reveals himself as and when he wishes. For Bultmann Jesus is the one who confronts man with the eschatological message, demanding response in existential commitment. For Barth there is a return to the high Christology, for Bultmann a renewal of the attack on 'metaphysics' and concentration on obedience to God's will as revealed through Jesus' message. Barth's thought, perfected in the symphony of the *Church Dogmatics*, is perhaps most easily caught in *Dogmatics in Outline*. Jesus Christ is a unity, a single word of revelation. Therefore we cannot move from the historical Jesus to the Christ of faith, nor from the man Jesus to the divine Christ. In Jesus the old covenant promise, that God wills to be with his people, is fulfilled. The Jewish background is essential. But Jesus is not just the hope of Israel. He is God's only son. 'Either in Jesus we have to do with God or a creature, and if with God, we have to affirm what Nicaea affirmed.'

Jesus Christ is *the* man, the measure of all human being. This truth does not depend on our acknowledging it as such.

[1]Sir George Adam Smith and Bishop Winnington Ingram were classic examples.

Incarnate by the Holy Ghost of the Virgin Mary, he lived a life of obedience as the Son of God and the son of man. Humiliated, murdered by the judiciary, dead, he is exalted by the empty tomb to be the eternal source of salvation. Barth's grand symphony is clearly not the only music in theology, but its intrinsic merit already makes it a classic.

In principle Barth accepted the modern critical approach to the Bible.[2] In practice he often ignored its implications. More recent scholars, aware that we might have only a dozen or so of the *ipsissima verba* of Jesus, have produced rather different Christologies, building upon what are to be taken to be the reflections and liturgies of the early communities. Where Barth saw lineaments of the classical Christology of Chalcedon in the Bible, others have drawn very different conclusions. Partly through the influence of the philosopher Heidegger, Rudolf Bultmann developed an existential understanding of the New Testament, interpreting the message of Jesus for the modern world in order to produce a contemporary invitation to commitment. Before the message can be accepted it must be understood, through demythologising, by discarding the wrappings of ancient culture and expressing the gospel in truly contemporary terms. Faith for Bultmann has its origins in the kerugma or event of proclamation, rather than in value judgements concerning an historical portrait.[3] Some of his pupils, notably Käsemann, Ebeling and Fuchs, developed a 'new Quest' of the historical Jesus, accepting the importance of kerugma but seeking to relate it again to history.

Bultmann and his disciples have been criticised for adopting solutions which are just as 'abstract' and 'metaphysical' as those which they rejected. There is then scope either for a reaffirmation of metaphysics, of a more or less traditional sort, or else for a more determined attempt to get beyond metaphysics. Yet Bultmann, along with Barth, and perhaps Troeltsch and Rahner, must count as a major contributor to

---

[2]On Barth's approach see Ingolf Dalferth's *Theology and Philosophy*, and David Ford, *Barth and God's Story*.

[3]See esp. Roger A. Johnson, *Rudolf Bultmann.*, and D.A.S. Fergusson, *Rudolf Bultmann.*

Christology in the modern world. In the work of Barth and Bultmann it is possible to see most of the elements of post-Enlightenment Christology in interaction. Tens of thousands of volumes on Christology have appeared since 1800. Here only one or two of the most significant thinkers can be considered.

British Christology in the twentieth century has been centred in large measure on the classical doctrine of the incarnation and attempts to reinterpret it. Theories of kenosis, of the self-emptying of Christ, were an important vehicle for the understanding of Christ's human nature in the work of Gore, Weston, Forsyth and others. Kenosis in turn has been much criticised, then used again successfully by Barth and Rahner. In Scotland Donald Baillie's paradox Christology provided an important holding perspective between classical Christology and concern for the humanity of Jesus, though the details could not be pressed without dissolving the paradox.[4] In Anglican theology the continuing debate with the Fathers was pursued especially in discussion arising from the Modern Churchman's Conference of 1922, on the relation between the humanity and the divinity of Christ. The divinity of Christ was explored by Eric Mascall, the humanity by John A.T. Robinson. A more traditional Christology of the incarnation was worked out by Creed, Mozley, Quick, Hodgson and Ramsey, and attacked by the authors of the *Myth of God Incarnate* symposium, notably John Hick and Maurice Wiles. In Scotland significant and contrasting contributions were made by John McIntyre and T.F. Torrance.

On the Continent as in Britain all the elements of Christology are subject to continuing reappraisal. In the tradition of Barth, Jürgen Moltmann and Eberhard Jüngel see the cross of Christ as the key not just to Christology but to all legitimate Christian talk of God. On the cross God suffers. There is death in God, though not the death of God. From this suffering relationship between Father and Son we may understand the Trinity. Through the cross

---

[4] See 'A Tale of Two Exchanges: The Christology of D.M. Baillie', by John McIntyre, in *In Divers Manners, A St. Mary's Miscellany*, ed. D.W.D. Shaw, St. Andrews 1990.

we may share in God's identity with men and women crushed by evil. 'Even Auschwitz is taken up into the grief of the Father, the surrender of the Son and the power of the Spirit' (*The Crucified God*, 278). Such a theology of solidarity with suffering has powerful echoes in Liberation Theology.

Where the cross is absent, strange things happen. On the other hand, it can be argued that the centre of Christianity is not the cross but the love of God. Evil is to be opposed firmly rather than accepted *sub specie crucis*, through the gift of the grace of resurrection. It is interesting that British and continental theology have taken such opposing paths in meeting the same challenge of the complexity and often the tragedy of the modern world, the one in abandoning and the other in reaffirming the classical doctrines of Incarnation and Trinity. God's hidden presence is not easily to be read off our theological measuring devices.

Wolfhart Pannenberg has produced the most comprehensive of modern Christologies after Barth. He is radical in rejecting the theology of the Word of Barth and Bultmann, in deciding that the incarnation is definitely not the correct starting point, and in stressing the need to do Christology from below, or in a sense from before, through eschatology. Yet he takes a fairly traditional view of resurrection. Pannenberg stresses a need both for rationality and for an apocalyptic framework. It is hard to see how these criteria can coincide. But his work is of major significance, taking up, almost alone among the writers mentioned so far, the concern for the correlation of theology and history, and the problem of historical relativity, pioneered by Ernst Troeltsch.

2. Beyond Rahner and Schillebeeckx

Catholic theology has been extraordinarily fertile in the field of modern Christology, especially in the work of Rahner and Schillebeeckx, Küng and von Balthasar. Karl Rahner displays an almost unique versatility in criticising the ancient formulas, reinterpreting them radically in line with a Post-Enlightenment anthropology, and then still using them to interpret the centre of Christology. The doctrine of man which is his genius is also, it is sometimes thought, his Achilles heel. Why should we accept a general anthropology any more than a particular apocalyptic framework as definitive?

But Rahner's insights are many and varied. For Karl Rahner, God alone can become something. He who is unchangeable in himself can become subject to change in something else. Giving himself away, God posits the other as his own reality. Humanity is the medium of God's kenotic presence in the world: the word becomes flesh. The nearer one comes to God, the more real one becomes. As men and women open themselves to one another, and so to God, they may become 'anonymous Christians'. There is reciprocity between selfhood and dependence in man and God. 'The only way in which Christ's concrete humanity may be conceived of as diverse from the logos is by thinking of it in so far as it is united with the logos. The unity of the logos must constitute it in its diversity from Him, that is, precisely as a human nature: the unity must itself be the ground of the diversity' (*Theological Investigations* I, 5.181). Such a solution may be thought, like Chalcedon, to mark out the parameters of a problem rather than to offer an explanation. This level of explanation may be all that the theological mystery allows, and is certainly valuable. But we shall no doubt always look for other levels of clarification, at least in part. Such an other level may be seen in the exegetical struggles with historical evidence which characterise the work of that other major Catholic Christological interpreter, Edward Schillebeeckx.

Like Rahner, Schillebeeckx is concerned to take account of the whole of the Church's tradition. But unlike Rahner he settles firmly for a decisive shift away from incarnation and Chalcedon to stress on Jesus, the Mosaic-messianic 'eschatological prophet', as the basic New Testament model from which all others are derived. This '*maranatha*' Christology is the centre, a centre of experience by man of God and the world, then and now.

Christology is to be done by reflection on experience of life in modern society, and the impact of the Christian tradition on this reflection. We may not simply 'apply' biblical models to the modern world in the hope of illumination. We look to Jesus' own experience, the experience of his followers and the experience of God in community ever since. The appeal to experience is characteristic of modern Christologies, producing different results in different traditions.

For the Q community in the New Testament there is experience of Jesus as present now and soon to come. Resurrection is important, centred not on the person of Jesus but on the experience of his presence in community. Repetition of this saving experience leads to transformation of human life, and to a challenge, not about formulas but about our social structures. Christology is 'concentrated creation'. Christology can only be understood as a specific way of making belief in creation more precise. It is not yet entirely clear, perhaps, on Schillebeeckx' account, what difference it makes to God the creator that he is involved in incarnation in human life. But real progress is made in filling out further our understanding of the human significance of Jesus and his relationship to us.

Process Christology looks back in the tradition to Irenaeus, and attempts to achieve a better understanding of the relation between creation and an ongoing process. A.N. Whitehead's *Philosophy of Process*, and C.L. Morgan's *Philosophy of Emergent Evolution*, provided a theoretical framework, first explored by L.S. Thornton in *The Incarnate Lord* (1928) and more recently, especially in America, by Norman Pittenger, D.D. Williams, John Cobb, David Griffin and others. Pittenger understands the logos as the self-expressive principle of God at work in the whole creation. The incarnation of God is the culmination of the process. Christ is not a 'divine intruder', but one who emerges from humanity. He is the fulfilment of man's capacity for God and of God's purpose for man. It may well be possible for those who find it hard to accept general theories of dipolar theism to learn from the imaginative insights into the relation between creator and creation which process thought provides. Again it is notable that logos and incarnation, suspect in some avenues of recent thought, are quite acceptable in others.

Nothing has been said so far of the increasing amount of theology being produced in the so-called Third World, by such scholars as Cheng Song in Asia, John Mbiti in Africa, James Cone in Black Theology in the United States, and by Liberation theologians, mainly in Latin America. In its commitment to love for the poor and the dispossessed Liberation Theology relates incarnation to salvation in the most direct possible way.

In L. Boff's Christology we are concerned supremely not with a heavenly Christ who lives in and belongs to another world, but with the Jesus of history who is engaged in all the continuing conflicts of history. God's humanity in Jesus Christ is a fact which we are urged to consider with renewed urgency.[5]

It has been suggested by George Hendry that 'Christological thought is fluid at the present time, and no one can predict what course it will take in the future' (*Dictionary of Christian Theology*, SCM 1st Edition, art: 'Christology'). With this we may safely agree. Not all however is complete confusion. Let us imagine an account along these lines. The parables of Jesus, his life and his teaching are *the* examples for Christians of self-giving love. God's kenotic self-giving is incarnation and service is the way of the cross. Through the suffering humanity of Jesus Christ in humiliation comes resurrection. God is compassionate and creates compassion in us. Jesus Christ is God for us, answering God's self-emptying in his own life of sacrificial love, a love eschatologically effective through resurrection. Such an account says more than a little about Jesus, about God and man, and the way of discipleship in the world today, and most Christians would agree on it. The task of constantly improving construction and design in detail is left to the professional skill of theologians to work out in creative tension and discussion. This may be no bad thing. Complete unanimity often indicates the death of a subject, or of freedom of thought.

In concluding this survey, it will be recalled that we have already considered Gerhard Ebeling's understanding of God. There is much to be learned from him also in the area of Christology, in volume two of his *Dogmatik* (1979), 'Belief in God the Reconciler of the World'. As in volume one, God and humanity are always understood in relation to each other. The first of four main sections is entitled 'God in Christ'. He considers three areas, the incarnation, the death of God and the life of God – the latter a meditation on resurrection. Jesus'

---

[5]This list is far from exhaustive, e.g. there is now an impressive literature of Minjung theology in Korea , cf. e.g. *Minjung Theology, People as Subjects of History*, ed. Commission on Theological Concerns of the Christian Conference of Asia, Maryknoll, New York: Orbis 1983.

incarnation, death and resurrection tell us both about the nature of the human and about the nature of God. This setting of the scene leads to a long second section on 'The Human Jesus', which involves a detailed search for the historical Jesus. Interest in the historical data is focused on the importance of Jesus for faith. Central to Jesus' character is his *exousia*, his indirect authoritative power, expressed in his word and his actions. This word, in language and conduct, is an invitation to response in faith, and it is itself self-authenticating, creating the response for which it calls. Jesus enables us to ask for and receive forgiveness, and so to dedicate ourselves to God. Here as elsewhere Christology and soteriology are interconnected. The greatest sign of his power is not his miracles but his acceptance of powerlessness, at the end in crucifixion. Christology is neither a repetition of the tradition nor a report on the latest results of critical method. It is reflection of the contemporary response of the believer to Jesus' *exousia*.

The brief penultimate section, on 'The World Loved by God', deals with three problems which arise in human relation to God, nostalgia, hate and conflict, and are resolved by Jesus. The Christology is then completed in a section on 'Faith in Jesus Christ'. Jesus is the word of God, the brother of humanity, and the Lord of the world. He is the key to communication, to relationship, and to the exercise of power in the world. Faith in Jesus is the giving of one's life to God, the cost of discipleship. Jesus is the hidden ruler of all reality.

3. Christological Structures

'And in Jesus Christ, His only Son, our Lord.' So the Apostles' Creed affirms faith in Jesus Christ. Other creeds speak of 'the only Son of the Father', and 'Son of God'. Hold to Christ, said Butterfield, and for the rest be uncommitted. Affirmed in confidence or in trepidation, the divinity of Christ is the cornerstone of Christian faith. To return to the playground of the theologians, does it matter *how* Christology is expressed? Does discussion inevitably lead to consensus ?[6]

---

[6]'When the Pandora's box is opened, such consensus as is won may disappear' (G.M .Newlands, review of Harvey, *God Incarnate, Story and Belief*, *Theology*,1982, 137-9).

I think we might agree that the first word of Christians is of the importance of the subject of common affirmation. 'In him the broken is mended, divisions are healed and creation begins anew. He gives us real, ultimate grounds for confidence and hope.'[7] The second word, too, might be the agreement that a Christology which we might regard as seriously intellectually deficient might produce a transparent discipleship.

We might go further and agree, thirdly, that there may well be important areas of overlapping in doctrinal affirmation, reached by different routes and concepts, which produce new illumination. On the other hand, fundamentally sound theological concepts do not always result in fundamentally sound theology. Recall the car sticker: designed by a computer, built by a robot, driven by a moron. For example, as Christians we need a focus of unity, but not every sort of principle of leadership will do. Fourthly, both as Christians who believe that Christ is the truth, and as academics who are paid to pursue truth, we have to make theoretical choices, which neither the claims of koinonia nor the literary imagination should be allowed to soften.

Son of God. What does this mean? Jesus is not in the physical sense a son. It is hard to think that he inherits God's genes, that his hair is God's colour of hair. God does not have that sort of relationship with people, any more than he discusses theology with them. There is then a metaphorical element in the title. But it does take up, in the language of the ancient world, the idea of expressing the closest possible ties. God the Son was incarnate. I am happy to reaffirm this. This does not prevent errors but it does reaffirm a vital point.

God was intimately involved indeed in inspiring humankind elsewhere, but here was the incarnation, a mystery in principle unique. There are of course references to incarnations in other religions, but in the Judaeo-Christian religion incarnation is understood, at least up to recent times, as implying uniqueness. All presence may of course be regarded as unique, as all individuals are unique. But this is something more.

---

[7]P. Baelz in   A.E. Harvey, *God Incarnate, Story and Belief,* 100.

The uniqueness of incarnation means that God the creator has himself come into the particularity and contingency of human life, in such a way that God is immediately and directly affected in himself as creator by the events of that contingent life. Jesus is a man, fully human, particular, limited. Jesus Christ is also fully God, *autotheos*. God participates in humanity. How is this possible? We can never know fully, but we have to keep thinking.[8]

There are, let it be said at once, certain limitations on accounts of truth in Christology. Because God is a hidden presence we cannot give any sort of precise account of the nature either of God's being or of his action – whether we be of the school of Dummett, of Davidson or whoever, and however close we grind the wheels of analysis. We have to appeal additionally to experience and imagination, but not to the exclusion of analytical procedures and metaphysical implications of the tradition of Christian life and thought in history and in the present.

What precisely, in so far as it possible to be precise, do I mean by affirming that Jesus Christ is the Son of God, the only son of the Father? In Jesus we see the self-giving love of God, Father, Son andSspirit. Christology is kenotic. Here is the full involvement of God the creator in redemption. Still, there are many possible patterns, incarnation and not incarnation. To affirm incarnation is not necessarily to solve the problem, because everything else can be, and often is, wrong. To deny incarnation in principle, though eliminating some errors and raising some possibilities of new insight, is in the end to miss something central too. History is important, but a Christology of the historical Jesus alone is inadequate. The doctrine of God is important in Christology, but neither Aquinas nor Cupitt alone will do. Metaphysics is important, but there are also metaphorical elements. Logos has advantages and disadvantages – compare Lampe and Pittenger.

I have suggested that 'A new interpretation of the activity of God's love in the humiliation and exaltation of Christ, in the

---

[8]There is an excellent symposium on incarnation in *Lux Mundi, Essays on the Incarnation*, ed. Robert Morgan.

resurrection of the crucified Jesus, may begin to provide new pointers in response to our critical questions.'[9] There is an excellent analysis of self-giving, self-affirming love in L. Richard's *A Kenotic Christology*, based largely on Rahner. But still, this is not enough. It is not enough, either, to produce a philosophical analysis of love (*pace* Brunner). Love is the clue to the understanding of historical events and the metaphysical implications of these events concerning God in history, including all human experience. The resurrection is the clue to the constancy of God's love, in time and eternity. What must a Christology involve?

I want to look now at Sobrino's *Christology at the Crossroads* to see how well Liberation Theology copes with the classic claims of Christology.[10] For Sobrino, the starting point for Christology is the historical Jesus, Jesus the man acting on the plan of public history. He compares the approaches to Christology of Rahner, Pannenberg and Moltmann. Discussing 'Jesus in the Service of God's Kingdom' he emphasises the importance of the Kingdom of God for Christology. We then come to 'The Faith of Jesus and Liberation History'. A chapter on resurrection and the hermeneutics of hope leads to the theological problems of the resurrection, the tension between the historical Jesus and the Christology of faith, and the Christological dogmas. The last chapter is entitled 'Theses for a Historical Christology'.

Sobrino considers the theological milieu of recent theology, the attitude to the Enlightenment, the understanding of the relationship between God and the world, the density of the Christological concentration. Rahner is aware of the challenge of the Enlightenment, but not that of Marx. He offers a transcendental Christology. Pannenberg is interested in history and hermeneutics, but 'Pannenberg's own hermeneutics is basically explicative, not transformational' (27).

Moltmann has a theology of hope which is closer to Liberation Theology. For Liberation Theology as in Boff, hermeneutics becomes a hermeneutics of praxis. Liberation Theology is

---

[9]G.M. Newlands, *Theology of the Love of God*, 198.
[10]Cf. the discussion of Sobrino in part 1, p. 58f.

concerned in Christology in so far as it reflects on Jesus himself as the way to liberation. Sobrino explores the relation between Jesus and the Kingdom. There is an integral connection between orthodoxy and orthopraxis.

We come to the faith of Jesus. As Boff puts it 'Jesus was an extraordinary believer and had faith. Faith was his very mode of existence. The history of Jesus is the history of Jesus' faith' (Ibid., 79). Jesus' prayer is always related to his historical experience. Hence, without the praxis of love people cannot experience the God of Jesus, and hence they cannot pray to the God of Jesus. The death of Jesus related theology to the cross. The cross calls into question all knowledge of God based on natural theology. Knowing God means abiding with God in the passion. The question of knowing God must be posed in terms of theodicy, in terms of our experience of evil in the world.

Sobrino then turns to resurrection and hermeneutics. History should be seen in terms of promise. The rest is still an unfinished reality. It is still in the process of fulfilment in so far as its saving efficacy is concerned. The hermeneutics designed to comprehend the resurrection must be political. The consequences of the resurrection are developed. There is a tension between faith and religion. 'To the extent that Christians tend to overlook or forget the historical Jesus, they tend to structure Christian life more and more as a religion in the pejorative sense' (305).

We come back to reconsider the classical Christological dogmas. The truth of Chalcedon is best verified through the course of the history of Christian discipleship . This leads to a final constructive chapter on 'Theses for a Historical Christology'. He asks this of the Enlightenment Christology: 'Is it trying to show that the truth of Christ can be justified before the bar of reason or is it trying to show that it can be justified before the demands and yearnings for a transforming praxis?' (348). The access route to God is the concrete praxis of love. Here is a dimension of theology which raises new and valuable critical questions. We must now look for answers in detail.

18

Jesus of Nazareth

1. Unity and Diversity in the Gospels

In this section we shall be concerned with the life of Jesus. We have seen in that it is impossible to make theology out of history by some simple process. The 'Jesus of History' of decades of New Testament scholarship can scarcely function alone as the subject of Christian devotion. Equally we have to rule out an exclusive concentration on the Word, whether in the form of Barth's or Bultmann's understanding of revelation. A remarkable development of the kerugmatic tradition was made by Eberhard Jüngel in treating the parables of Jesus as God's parable for self-communication to humankind. Jüngel was right, I have suggested, to attempt to draw together concern for the historical Jesus and the concern of Barth and Bultmann for the event of the self-revelation of the living God in the presence of Christ in Christian life. But the medium of the presence of Christ is best seen not in a one particular literary genre but in the significant events themselves which constitute the life and message of Jesus.[1]

It might then be thought that the solution to the problem of perspective is to be seen in the work of Pannenberg, for whom revelation as history was a major methodological principle. There is a sense in which this may be true. But revelation is not,

---

[1] E. Jüngel, *Paulus und Jesus*; G.M. Newlands, *Hilary of Poitiers*. See now J.B. Webster, 'Introduction to E. Jüngel', *Theological Essays*, 1990, and my review in *Theology*, July 1990, 309f.

I believe, to be seen as offering something like Luther's external clarity of history. To see the events themselves as constitutive of revelation, as disclosures of the character of God, is itself an act of faith. For the events can be construed in different ways. They do not automatically evoke faith.

What constitutes *the* authoritative events will always include an element of individual choice on the part of the believer. What matters is that through these clusters of events human beings continue to come to faith which expresses itself in love, after the pattern of God's self-giving love in Jesus of Nazareth. *Nunc dimittis*. For mine eyes have seen thy salvation. Indeed we see this salvation differently through different eyes. Yet the Christian community has always regarded certain dimensions as central features of salvation, though viewed differently in the different strands. The strands have added up to a characteristic pattern of understanding of the meaning of the Christ, even though different aspects have been prominent at different times. Despite the multiplicity, it is possible and even essential to seek to work out integrated and coherent accounts of this salvation.

The principal way in which we have access to the life of Jesus is through the fourfold cord of the gospels. Rich in mythical and symbolic meaning, a remarkable combination of report and interpretation, endlessly analysed through the ages, they remain the standard Christian way into understanding Jesus of Nazareth. We shall follow their structure in making our critical analysis.

It is striking that St. Mark's Gospel, the earliest in basic form, neglects the introductory material of the other three gospels and plunges almost at once into a consideration of the work and activity of Jesus. What is uppermost here is not Jesus' pedigree or eternal status, but his action and the content of his teaching. We may imagine that modern preferences for orthopraxis rather than orthodoxy, for function rather than metaphysical status, might have found an echo with Mark. Jesus comes into Galilee announcing the coming of the Kingdom of God and calling for repentance and faith.

The power of the Kingdom does not come into a power vacuum. From the beginning there are other powers in the world. There is confrontation and conflict. In the face of sin there is repentance and faith. Jesus himself is baptised. He identifies with his fellow men, and *so* is identified as God's beloved son. Jesus begins his ministry in Galilee, a provincial preacher among unsophisticated rural Northerners.[2] This of course does not mean that his message, or indeed the Kingdom, is more appropriate to the unsophisticated than to the sophisticated, more suitable to Middle Eastern men than to Polynesian women, or anything of the sort. This is simply part of the random nature of the circumstances in life of one individual among millions. But equally it does nothing to indicate that the events concerning Jesus are somehow best appropriated by a privileged élite.

Jesus' early teaching is represented as being in the open air, and also in the local synagogue. His first group of disciples were fishermen, a group not of course at that time hallowed by the association of sacred memory, but often seen as a rather motley crew of dubious provenance. There is throughout Mark's Gospel a consistent mix of the sacred and the secular, appropriate perhaps in any typical section of Ancient Near Eastern society. Jesus is clearly on familiar terms with ordinary members of society. He is certainly not part of a religious order, or anything of the sort. But the basic characteristic of his work is his concern with God, God in the power of forgiveness at his baptism, God in his synagogue instruction.

The gospel records that his hearers were astonished at his doctrine, for he taught them as one who had authority. Here the well-known Marcan note of astonishment focuses on his 'authority', a characteristic of Jesus' distinctiveness throughout the New Testament. We shall consider this '*exousia*' in later sections. Here it may simply be noted.

Mark's Jesus is particularly concerned for the sick. He turns instinctively to those from whom society instinctively turns away, the sick, the mad and the victims of contagious and

---

[2]Throughout this section I attempt to reflect the consensus of current biblical interpretation, without pretending to expertise in that field.

On the Galilean background, see G. Theissen, *Lokalkolorit und Zeitgeschichte in den Evangelien.*

disfiguring disease. He casts out demons, bringing about a transition from mental instability to faith. These passages, which are concerned with Jesus' physical activity, of course pose as many problems in the late twentieth century as metaphysical issues. In the nineteenth century physical cures of the sick by Jesus were regularly interpreted as referring to the cure of mental illness. Today the ascription of the alleviation of mental illness to faith has become almost itself an indicator of dangerous mental instability. Between a dangerously anthropomorphic conception of faith as an instant remedy for all natural calamities and a sceptical refusal to allow faith any kind of tangible content or effectiveness there is clearly a careful line to be drawn. Faith confused with knowledge is not faith. Faith evacuated of any distinctive content is meaningless.

In the opening chapter of the gospel Jesus' intention is to act effectively but without courting public debate. This purpose is from the first frustrated by the enthusiasm of faith and the hostility of opposition. Personal pastoral concern is drawn inexorably into the forum of public events on the political stage. Jesus sets out on a ministry of welcome, healing, teaching, openness. The reaction of humankind is, with some significant exceptions, hostility and rejection. This rejection gradually builds up into a climax of confrontation and disaster.

Jesus gathers groups of fellow workers, and they help him in his campaign. His teaching largely, though not exclusively, is given in the form of parables. Characteristic of Mark's conception is the parable of the seed growing secretly. The mystery of the Kingdom is open only to those who have faith. Jesus works on quietly and patiently, teaching, feeding, healing, preaching, acting always with a distinctive authority. When asked about the source of his authority, or about possible exalted claims, Jesus deflects questions and is not prepared to give public demonstrations of miracles. Despite his avoidance of external demonstrations his disciples and others become aware that here is someone extraordinary. This is represented as reaching a climax in Peter's confession that Jesus is the Christ, and is immediately followed by Jesus' preparation of the disciples for his own death. Life comes out of death.

What shall it profit a man if he gain the whole world and lose his own soul? The last shall be first. The little ones and the poor have the prior claim. The perspective from which Jesus' ministry takes place is summed up in the kerugmatic sentence at Mark 10:45, 'For the Son of Man also came not to be served but to serve and to give his life as a ransom for many.'

St. Mark's Gospel is a passion narrative. This accent is strengthened after chapter ten. Jesus enters Jerusalem. He challenges those who question his authority. Israel is again confronted with judgement. The conflict intensifies. The authorities resolve on Jesus' execution. Jesus, anticipating death, founds a new covenant in the community meal of the Last Supper. But the strength of the community is immediately put into question by the events in Gethsemane, the disciples' neglect and terror, Jesus' agony of doubt and despair. Jesus is betrayed and arrested, condemned and crucified. He does not deny the charge of making a messianic claim, yet he dies haunted by being forsaken by God. Death is real. But it is followed by the reality of resurrection.

For the other strands of the narrative I shall note only some key elements. St. Matthew's strand of the narrative differs in details and emphasis from Mark, but not in its assessment of the central strands of the Christian story. Through Jesus the destiny of Israel is fulfilled, and the old covenant is transformed in the new. Matthew stresses that the Son of God is killed by the people of God. The faith is now open to the Gentiles. From his birth he receives the homage of the gentiles, the Magi. Matthew narrates his baptism, temptation, the sending of his disciples. He focuses upon John the Baptist, pointing to the Messiah. He centres the first section of his narrative on the Sermon on the Mount. Jesus does not act in silence, does not engage in generalities. His action includes as an integral element his teaching, and he has highly specific things to say. He is concerned with the Kingdom of God, the quality of conduct appropriate to the Kingdom and with a reciprocity of love and justice. He is concerned with the disadvantaged and the outcast in society. The life of discipleship is set out, and is epitomised in the Lord's Prayer: trust in God as Father in all things.

Even more than Matthew, St. Luke lays stress on the importance of Jesus for *all* humankind. Jesus is the saviour, not just of Israel but of the world, and he is committed above all to the poor. God puts down the mighty from their seats, and exalts the humble and meek.

The Fourth Gospel strand in the narrative is superficially very different from the others, but comes from the same Palestinian background. The meditation on the Word with which it begins has had a colossal impact on Christian thinking about Jesus. This gospel too is a gospel, not of serene progress but of terrible tension and tragic conflict. The light shines in the darkness. The people to whom Jesus seeks to minister are the people who try to kill him. Jesus is the way, the truth, and the life, the good shepherd, the true vine, the source of life itself. In his death and resurrection the salvation of the world is achieved.

In our model the fifth and final strand of the narrative thread we may take to be the rest of the New Testament. This makes our final strand multiplex in itself. The centre of the Acts of the Apostles is not Jesus himself but the Church as the community of martyrdom and persecution. In St. Paul's letters the centre is faith, as the Christian response to and through the risen Christ. We are reminded that in the New Testament, Christology arises out of the death and resurrection, as well as from the life of Jesus. Characteristic is the famous hymn of Philippians 2 in which Paul, probably quoting a very early hymn, reflects on Jesus' self-giving, sacrificial life and death. Trust in God through Jesus Christ is the centre of justification by faith. Justification is connected with life in union with Christ, with faith that Christians are sustained by God's presence in Christ.

The ramifications of justification through Christ are explored classically in Paul's letter to the Romans. Through Jesus' death and resurrection, life in the Spirit, the life of the new creation, has begun. Death and sin, guilt and alienation are overcome. Through Christ traditional religious conventions are revised and a new freedom of the children of God is inaugurated. The reality of the new age is the basic significance of Paul's reflection on Jesus' resurrection in his first letter to the Corinthians, and is reflected in the imagery of being dead to the law in Galatians. Though the theme of justification is absent, the emphases on cosmic salvation in Colossians and on the Church as the Body in Ephesians reflect in the deutero-Pauline writing the cosmological and sociological dimensions of the historical and political events concerning Christ of the Apostle's own letters.

From the remainder of the New Testament writings, the sacrifice of Christ in Hebrews and the love of Christ in 1 John, together with the climactic concentration on eschatology of Revelation remind us that a Christocentric theology is not simply an invention of nineteenth- and twentieth-century post-Kantian European theology but has been of the essence of the gospel from the beginning. We shall return to the fifth strand in considering the death and resurrection of Christ.

In the above sketch of a fivefold strand of testimony to Jesus Christ I have stressed the considerable amount of unity of theme in the narratives. There is also of course diversity, conflict, difference of perspective and interpretation. To say that there is both unity and diversity will not help us. What is crucial is an assessment of the nature of the unity and the nature of the diversity, and then an analysis of the consequences for Christology. We may of course reflect that this unity is itself the criterion for the collection and preservation of this particular set of documents. Anything incongruous or dissenting from the authorised picture was left out and soon disappeared. To accept this picture as central rather than, say, the various pictures reflected in the apocryphal gospels is to accept a basic reliability in the New Testament narratives as a guide to the events concerning Jesus, as reflected on in the earliest Christian communities.

The unity of perspective in the narratives comes firstly from the emphasis on Jesus' mission to all humankind, a mission of preaching and teaching, call to repentance, proclamation of the Kingdom of God. The second main strand is the rejection of that mission of love and self-giving. There is real darkness, and it is in darkness that the light shines. The third main strand as I see it is Jesus' teaching about the nature of that Kingdom. The Sermon on the Mount is not accidental to the gospel of the passion narrative but integral. What is wanted, and promised, is a completely new quality in human relationship. Finally there is the paradox of life and death. The narratives of the gospels are passion narratives. Death is certain, terrible and real. But it is emphatically not the last word. Jesus has come to bring newness of life.

Beyond this there are important negative strands of accord. None of the gospels has much to say about Jesus' private life, thoughts and intentions. This is all the more striking when we consider the wealth of information available on major figures in the modern world, from their memoirs and those of their colleagues, from diaries and recollections of every sort. The impact of the historical Jesus as such depends on the theological reflection of the community on his actions and his teaching, and their public consequences. That is all.

I turn now to the differences between the narratives. There is difference in assessment of the role of the Jews and the Romans in bringing about Jesus' crucifixion. There is difference between the gospels and Paul in the extent to which the law is fulfilled or abolished through Christ. There is significant difference in the range of reflection on the relationship between Jesus and God, between the synoptic gospels and the Fourth Gospel. There are differences between the gospels and Paul, in the use of important concepts – Son of Man, Kingdom of God, and Coming Aeon. There is the famous sharp contradiction in the conflict between the law and the gospel in Paul's letters to the Galatians and the Romans, and the later New Testament letters, notably James. There are important differences in the conception of the community, notably between Ephesians and the letters of Paul, reflecting different existing community structures. All of these features have been the subject of debate and the basis of endless disputes in the history of the Church and of theology.

2. Jesus in History

The question we must now ask is this. Given these specific sorts of unities and diversities, what sort of assessment can we make of Jesus' life? I have not spoken here of a life of the historical Jesus. More is involved, for we have to sift among a pile of data including at least a diversity of historical, theological, liturgical, and sociological observations. It seems to me that one useful way of approach will be to retain the fivefold strand as we have previously described it, noting both the range of diversities it encompasses and the range of unities. It should then be possible to move forward to consider the evidence in coherent detail, while enabling modification and revision of the whole material as we proceed.

Jesus was born in Palestine almost two thousand years ago. We are not in a position to shed light on the historical circumstances of his birth. The various infancy narratives appear to have arisen out of the preaching of the resurrection, and do not allow of many historical conclusions about his birth. The tradition states that he was born in Bethlehem. His parents appear to have been neither from the poorest nor the wealthiest sections of society. The story that Joseph was a carpenter fits the general scene of Jesus' social background which comes through the gospels. The gospels are not interested in exact sociological reflection on this background. What mattered was that God the creator was uniquely involved in one particular contingent life. Had Jesus been born at another time and place, this would not in itself have changed the nature of the gospel. But to this statement we have to make one significant qualification. It was as a Jew, as the culmination and climax of the tradition of Israel, that Jesus came into the world. That at least limits the absolute theoretical contingency of God's action in Jesus.

The New Testament, we recalled, is significant in its silences as well as in its affirmations. It is important to realise that the gospel does not require information about the first thirty years of Jesus' life in order to be the effective gospel. This is quite extraordinary, when we consider how central the humanity of Jesus is to the Christian understanding of salvation.

It is true that there is reference to the twelve-year-old child in the temple in the narratives. But we can scarcely regard this as solid evidence for historical reconstruction. When we reflect on the cruciality of this long period for the formation of a human character, we may see how very far we are from any sort of life of the historical Jesus. We have no data for 90% of Jesus' life, and what we have for the remainder accounts for only a very few days in his three years of ministry.

The historical Jesus acts and teaches within the framework of the history of Israel, though he clashes with and modifies numerous elements of that framework. It is Israel's God whom he worships and to whom he is devoted. It is through his devotion to the God of Israel that his entire ministry comes to take place. It is then a peculiar irony that the Christian Church has engaged in relentless persecution of the Jews over the centuries. It is an extraordinary indictment of European Christianity that it contributed, even if indirectly, to the massacre of six million Jews in the middle of the twentieth century for no other reason than that they were Jewish. This was not of course intended by Christians. Yet there was an astonishing lack of resolution to prevent the holocaust, no attempts to stop it, no warnings even broadcast to those ignorant of their fate. If, as is sometimes thought, the history of the Church is part of the history of Christ, then in our day this unprecedented suffering is part of the suffering of Christ.

The earliest indication of Jesus' forthcoming ministry mentioned in the narratives is his baptism by John. Jesus grew up in a milieu of natural acceptance of the rituals of the law. It is suggested that he was circumcised as an infant. It would have been strange if this had been omitted. His baptism, which may very well reflect an historical occurrence, suggests that he decided to undertake an unusual form of purification in addition to the customary requirements. There is a stage, perhaps not the only stage, of deliberate dedication to a task of ministry.

Jesus' preaching ministry was by no means unique in the local culture. From time to time men would engage in itinerant preaching, throughout the Jewish tradition, in a manner parallel to the official teaching of the local rabbis. The style of his ministry and the composition of his followers are likely to have been very similar to that of other contemporary groups. The New Testament narratives stress his *exousia*, as authoritative for their communities, and it would be inappropriate to see this characteristic as itself constitutive of his messianic status, as has sometimes been thought. It is particularly in the context of his death and the resurrection that the characteristics of this particular life are seen to be of cosmic importance. But in this framework, the *exousia* of this man becomes especially central: it gains a retrospective centrality. Pannenberg was right to insist that it is in the light of the resurrection that the full theological significance of the life of Jesus becomes clear.

Jesus' ministry consisted both in action and teaching., according to the narratives. This again is entirely commensurate with the practice of the times. What is striking here is the insistence of the narratives on Jesus' particular attention to the disadvantaged and outcast in society, to the lepers, the mentally unstable, those engaged in unpopular and little esteemed occupations. For the narratives these people are often, though not exclusively, the subject of his power to produce miraculous healing, and to perform other miracles. The whole question of the miracle narratives became in modern times the focus of intense debate. Some denied the miracles or explained them away in psychological terms. Others followed Schleiermacher in universalising the events. 'To me everything is miracle': the world as a whole seen through the eyes of faith. Different theological perspectives dictated different approaches to miracle approved of as objective, reinterpreted as subjective, considered primary or secondary according to taste.

I prefer to see the whole sequence of events of the gospel of the incarnation as the basic miracle. Among these events the resurrection of Jesus is central. I regard the healing miracles as a reflection of Jesus' extraordinary pastoral impact on those who came in contact with him. The miracles associated with the physical environment I would regard as illustrations making a theological stress on Jesus' centrality rather than reporting of natural events in the empirical world. I do not think however that one should categorically rule out any kind of unique occurrences where Jesus was concerned. We may think that Jesus probably acted in every way as any other human being did. But God's freedom to be God makes anything possible, and we must beware of importing uncritically the compulsions of our own perspectives.

In the narratives Jesus' work is characterised by personal pastoral concern for those with whom he comes in contact, in teaching and in healing. The initial response is of enthusiasm. But then, as often in public life, all sorts of tensions arise in the community and enthusiasm turns into ambivalence and open hostility. Jesus' appeal generates jealousy and provokes bitter rejection, notably among the traditional guardians of the divine teaching. Religious intolerance is a universal phenomenon in societies, a reminder that religion, like all things human, can be an instrument of evil as well as of good.

Jesus does not work alone. He gathers a group of followers. From the beginning there is a communal aspect to his impact, which is not of accidental significance. The service of the Kingdom involves a sharing of insight and concern and a growing together in faith in God. It is part of the consequence of the power of evil in the world that the group is dispersed and overcome by fear at the time of Jesus' death. This separation and division is removed as part of the meaning and consequence of the resurrection.

3. Teaching and Action

Jesus' ministry is characterised in the New Testament narratives particularly by his teaching, both to his disciples and to larger groups. His private conversations with individuals over these years, like his private thoughts on the issues he confronted, have gone unrecorded. Most important for the narratives is his stress on the coming Kingdom of God, which is already inaugurated in his presence but which is yet to be fulfilled. This kingdom of the reign of God, the fulfilment of messianic expectation, is foreshadowed especially in the amazing variety of apocalyptic and eschatological vision of the intertestamental period. Most of his preaching, though not indeed all of it, used the form of parables, and the parables were parables of the Kingdom.

The Kingdom is a sphere in which the world's priorities are reversed. The poor and the underprivileged are the subject of God's special concern. This emphasis is stressed too in the enigmatic figure of the Son of Man, whose coming is associated in the narratives with the kingdom. The Son of Man has no place to lay his head. The role of the son, and the authenticity of the various sayings relating to the earthly son and the coming son, has been endlessly debated, and indeed the facts are equally capable of sustaining various explanations. It may be that Jesus combined reference to the Son of Man, the coming age and the Kingdom in ways that had not been done before, and certainly that were not prominent in earlier communities, whether in Qumran or in other Jewish communities.

The triumph of the Kingdom of the Son is through death. For the Son of Man also came not to serve but to be served, and to give his life in a ransom for many. Support for Jesus turns into hostility, hatred, determination to bring about his death, crucifixion. Jesus is perceived as a threat to a large number of vested interests in the society in which he lives. This hostility can scarcely be viewed as an unfortunate result of a series of misunderstandings. There is here the response of power, privilege and authority to a profound challenge. The traditional sources of authority join in closing ranks against this outsider, and they murder him. Whatever the technical details of the charges and the trial may have been, this is the unpleasant reality. Resentment, anger, jealousy, calculated malice, communal conspiracy, murder — this is a sequence endlessly repeated in human society, the dark side of history.

The wave of hostility which arose was a phenomenon to which Jesus remained entirely vulnerable, and he may very well have been aware of this. There is some indication in the narratives that he did not seek martyrdom.[3] The healed are told to be quiet and say nothing. When there is controversy Jesus withdraws from active preaching for a period, presumably to let things calm down. Nevertheless, when Jesus went up to Jerusalem he must have realised that, humanly speaking, his prospects for survival would be bleak. Why then did he decide on this action? Here again the major clue is likely to be the complete devotion to God which throughout the narratives is a central feature of his human life.

Here I want to return to the question of the nature of Jesus' teaching. It is dominated by the expectation of the imminent

---

[3]See the portrayal of this atmosphere of terror and counter-terror, in Gerd Theissen's *The Shadow of the Galilean.*

coming of God's Kingdom. The Kingdom provides continuity with the past, suggests a heightened significance for the present, and heralds a new future for humankind. This is emphatically the Kingdom of the God of Israel. Though Jesus often taught in the open air rather than in the synagogue, it was still Israel's God who was the centre of his life. The present also has a new significance. However Jesus may have imagined the future to be, it seems clear that he understood his own mission to play a pivotal role in connection with the coming of the Kingdom. It seems likely that Jesus imagined the end of the world, perhaps of the existence of mankind as he knew it, in the totally new event of the establishment of the Kingdom. His activity was part of the preparation for this new era.

Though we are unable to discern the precise strands which emanate directly from Jesus, we know that there is continuity with the ethical and religious ideals of the Old Testament.[4] There is stress on the need to create conditions of justice and peace, of compassion for the poor, of concern for each individual as precious in the sight of God, to be valued as a child of God. Jesus calls for obedience to the law of Israel, not simply in the letter but in the spirit. Here compassion for the unique individual case may temper observance of the strict general principle. This compassion is linked with a call to repentance, to a renewed commitment to God.

There is a new element in the proclamation of forgiveness in the present. God's forgiveness of sins is not simply a future possibility but a present reality. This factor creates the possibility of a new life now. This act of forgiveness corresponds to the reality of healing through miracle, to which we shall have to return. Finally there is the future dimension. The fact that God's future is a future of the Kingdom, of love, peace and justice, has consequences for the ways in which the present may be viewed. The present sufferings are not to last for ever. Evil is seen for what it is, and at the same time put in a perspective against the victory of love.

[4]Cf. A.E. Harvey, *Jesus and the Constraints of History*; Ben Meyer, *The Aims of Jesus.*

God's Kingdom is preceded by the activity and by the authority of Jesus. It is clear from the narratives that Jesus was in some way conscious of an authority to act as he did. Others in history have been conscious of divine authority, often with disastrous results. The test of Jesus' authority is faith in his resurrection and in the character of this authority as the character of God's love. This authority is both striking and indirect. It is striking in that Jesus clearly makes an impact, either positive or negative, on those with whom he comes in contact. It is indirect because Jesus avoids situations of dramatic demonstration of power in conventional terms. This is precisely not the nature of the Kingdom.

This authority is comprehensive. Jesus does not hesitate to commend obedience to the law in all its force, or to commend disobedience, for the sake of the Kingdom. Indirectly this amounts to a claim that here too is the law of God, calling for unconditional discipleship. There is a close connection between the nature of this authority and the nature of Jesus' whole life and teaching. This is the authority of self-giving love. Such an attitude does not rule out indignation and anger. But it informs all thought, speech and action.

Action is coupled with teaching, notably in the sphere of the miracles. It seems clear that Jesus offered help to people in a way which produced the healing of illnesses. Today we are aware of the numerous psychosomatic roots of many aspects of illness. Jesus doubtless understood his activities in the concepts of his time, as works of wonders, confirmatory of his divine mission.

How did Jesus himself understand his healing miracles? Here again we face the perennial question of evidence with which scholars have wrestled for decades. Edward Schweitzer stressed (*Jesus*, 4) that Jesus appears to have cared little for the recording of any of his acts or words for posterity. He appears to have taken absolutely no trouble to ensure the transmission of a tradition. This is one of the reasons why we find it hard to pronounce on *ipsissima verba* or specific authentic acts. On the other hand, Anthony Harvey has pointed out in *Jesus and the Constraints of History* that we may well have a great deal of information about Jesus' life and action even if we cannot be specific about which data are most authentic and original. Neither the extreme scepticism nor the extreme credulity of succeeding theological fashions can be justified on rational or logical grounds. At the same time, as Ben Meyer has shown in his sharp critique of the nineteenth-century scholar Karl von Hase (*The Aims of Jesus*, 98), a blanket liberalism which encompasses every possible viewpoint in each individual case provides no escape either. Each historical and theological issue has to be assessed afresh on its own merits, as far as humanly possible.

The age in which Jesus worked was, like all ages, perplexed by sickness and suffering, disaster and evil. Much of this was attributed to the existence of demonic powers. In the Kingdom, all such pain would vanish, and Jesus' activity was here as in all else a foretaste of the Kingdom.

Jesus' teaching was largely in parables. This corresponds to the indirect nature of his authority, and was also a common mode of instruction in the Judaism of his time. The exact nature of the parable as a means of communication in the New Testament has been endlessly debated. Usually a parable seems to have one basic religious meaning, though it may have other implications as well. In one of the most striking of modern interpretations, Jüngel has traced a correlation between the synoptic parables and the Pauline understanding of justification, and has gone on to suggest that all theological discourse ought to be essentially parabolic, reflecting the givenness of parable as the vehicle of the gospel. This is an attractive and forceful way of bringing out the undoubted importance of the parable in the substance and the style of Jesus' teaching.

No one concept seems to be sufficient to describe Jesus' life and action. There were the parables. But that most important narrative, the Sermon on the Mount, was manifestly not in parable form. It is worthwhile to go through this passage in some detail, for it epitomises much of the concern of Jesus of the gospels.

'How blest are those who know their need of God: the kingdom of heaven is theirs.' Jesus' teaching is a religious teaching. It is about devotion to God. The Kingdom is the presence of God, and the path to the Kingdom is the path of devotion.

'How blest are the sorrowful: they shall find consolation.' Those who find trouble in this life will find happiness in the Kingdom. God's promise is an effectual promise.

'How blest are those of a gentle spirit: they shall have the earth for their possession.' Jesus was capable of anger, if the episode of the clash with the money-changers in the temple is to be regarded as reflecting a particular incident. His concern for righteousness made for impatience with the unrighteous. But his basic message was for love of God and neighbour. It is the compassionate, and not the belligerent, to whom the world as God's world belongs.

'How blest are those who hunger and thirst to see right prevail; they shall be satisfied.' Fundamental to Jesus' message is mercy, so that even those who are less than just are shown compassion. Once again, self-giving love is central to the message.

'How blest are those whose hearts are pure. They shall see God.' In the Old Testament there is a concern for the purity of heart, for a straightforward openness to God and man. This is the attitude which leads to the vision of God.

'How blest are the peacemakers: God shall call them his sons.' Peace is the normal, conflict the abnormal, condition in God's view of human affairs. There can be no question of attacking others for God's sake. This is a contradiction in terms.

'How blest are those who have suffered persecution for the cause of right: the kingdom of heaven is theirs.' The way of the Kingdom is liable to bring persecution. The right is not always popular, not always the popular choice. But the followers have a duty to say what is the right, and to expose wrong. This is repeated in the next phrases. 'How blest are you, when you suffer insults.' 'You are salt to the world.' 'You are light for all the world.'

Right, devotion, consideration for others, are universalised. 'There must be no limit to your goodness, as your heavenly Father's goodness knows no bounds.'

Closely tied to the ethical teaching in the Sermon is the teaching on prayer. Prayer is not to be an act of public ostentation nor of vain repetition, but a personal act of devotion. The Lord's Prayer again underlines the priorities of the Kingdom which are found in the Beatitudes.

'Our Father in heaven.' Again there is the stress on the fatherhood of God, with the implication that God is not simply to be contemplated but to be trusted. God is the heavenly Father, who is not limited by the created order but who is the creator and sustainer of the universe. 'Thy name be hallowed.' God is central and literally vital to human existence, and should be respected as such.

'Thy Kingdom come.' The disciples of Jesus are asked to remember the perspective of the Kingdom in their prayers as in all their actions, and to ask for the speedy establishment of the Kingdom, which Jesus appears to have regarded as imminent. 'Thy will be done, on earth as in heaven.' Throughout the history of Israel there is the affirmation that God's will is what is best for his creatures, and there is the prayer, notably in the Psalms, that we should seek his will and seek to do it, to understand it, to accept it. Here as often elsewhere Jesus stands in the direct tradition of the religious teaching of Israel.

'Give us today our daily bread.' Though the precise meaning of the allusion to bread is uncertain, the basic significance is clear. We owe all that we have to God. We may trust in him to be concerned for our welfare, and we should be thankful to him for what he gives us.

'Forgive us the wrong we have done, as we forgive those who have wronged us.' The disciples are not perfect, and should be aware of this. They constantly stand in need of God's forgiveness, and should not be afraid to admit this and ask forgiveness. They should also be forgiving to those who wrong them. As Jesus pointed out, to love those who love us and whom we like is not a special virtue. It is much harder to love those who have wronged us, and whom we may have very good reasons for disliking.

'And do not bring us to the test but save us from the evil one.' Jesus knows that the disciples are not infallible, that they are subject like all human beings to various sorts of temptation. The disciples are invited to pray to be delivered from sources of temptation. They are also to pray to be spared the assaults of the powers of evil. In New Testament times there was almost universal belief in the presence of a cosmic evil power, whose presence was manifest as a kind of personal presence. Jesus shares in these beliefs of his time. He too is tempted and wrestles with the temptation to avoid the Father's will, and to follow the advice of Satan. For Jesus, as for his disciples, these are real temptations. They are not to be avoided by outward conformity, but by the obedience of the heart. 'Not everyone who calls me "Lord, Lord" will enter the kingdom of Heaven, but only those who do the will of my heavenly Father.'

What then are we to make of Jesus' use of the Son of Man imagery? It seems to me that Toedt was right to point to Jesus as 'the self-expressive activity of God' and to understand his personal note of authority as a pointer to awareness of being in a soteriological continuity with the agent of God's final redemption.[5] There is a pervasive New Testament picture of Jesus asserting the will of God as if he in some sense stood in the place of God, performing acts of healing of body and mind, addressing God as father, prefacing his words with 'Amen'.

It may well be that Jesus' baptism marked the beginning of a deepened understanding of his mission. He now preaches the imminence of the Kingdom which is both present and future. He gathers disciples. Decision for himself implies decision for the Kingdom. He begins to understand that he will suffer, and this is gradually explained to some of his followers.

It may be then that Jesus took the phrase 'Son of Man', which was known to him from the scriptures and known to be current in apocalyptic, and used it in different ways. He may have used it in his public preaching to emphasise the importance of decision for himself. Here he perhaps made a distinction between himself and the eschatological Son of Man. This would avoid making himself the object of political pressure and expectation of a political messiahship. The ultimate source of final judgement and power was rather his Father, whom he obeyed. If this reconstruction is along the right lines, then there is a high probability that the 'eschatological' sayings are reasonably accurate.

It is possible that Jesus may on occasion have used the Son of Man sayings with a more direct reference to himself, perhaps to his closest disciples. He could have spoken of the need for

---

[5]H.E. Toedt, *The Kingdom of God and the Son of Man*.

humiliation before exaltation. If so, this usage could be reflected in the frequent references to the suffering Son of Man in Mark. But there is a considerable contamination of these phrases by a late apocalyptic colouring, making it very difficult to reach a definite conclusion about any particular saying.

Thirdly, it is not impossible that Jesus used Son of Man in speaking to the High Priest (Mk.14:62) with reference to himself, and meaning what the high priest would have taken it to mean – a vindication at a future coming of the Son of Man. It may also be the case that Mark 25 points to a usage of Son of Man in reference to a future consummation by an exaltation of the Son.

How did the tradition arise in the way that it did? Perhaps rather on these lines. Within their chosen frameworks, the makers of the gospel tradition probably attempted to pass on as much as they had of an authentic tradition stemming from Jesus, even where they might not have understood this themselves. Some members of the early communities may have interpreted the apparent differentiation between Jesus and the Son to mean that Jesus had a messianic secret. Elsewhere the Son of Man was readily interpreted in terms of the exaltation of the suffering righteous. In the Johannine tradition the eschatological sayings probably represent the same authentic tradition as we find in the synoptics.

What are the present-day implications of the phrase 'Son of Man'? The Son of Man is to be vindicated by God in the final consummation. But first of all the role of the Son of Man, and of all the righteous, is to suffer. Jesus' service manifests itself in a complete surrender of his will to God. This enables him to exercise a unique freedom in his approach to others, a freedom which was infectious and which was made decisive through his resurrection. On that basis Christians are called to exercise the same sort of freedom which the Son of Man exemplified. This may involve suffering, but it is effective as redemptive suffering, on the basis of the reality of reconciliation through Christ.

Jesus preached and taught. He healed the sick. He moved around the country, living in different places. Little is said in the narrative of the details of his daily life, in the short period of his ministry which is all we have recorded.

We don't know if he ever had a holiday in that period, if he was ever ill, if he commented regularly on the political issues of his day. We do know that like all other human beings he had meals, and that, rather unusually, he was accustomed to eat together with all sorts and conditions of men, with tax gatherers and others of uncertain reputation. Precisely because this was unusual it is reasonable to suppose the social mix to be of symbolic significance, expressing the catholicity of his mission. There are no limits to his concern. He is not looking for the salvation of an élite, but of all humankind. The same concern is evident in the choice of the disciples. Fishermen were people of dubious reputation in the period, rough and bordering on the undesirable. As for inviting a tax gatherer, a collaborator with the oppressor, to join the group, that was indeed very odd. Here, as often, Jesus' choices defy any conventional stereotype.

It would appear that these meals expressed, as meals often do, the cohesion of the community. Whether or not Jesus held a final supper with his disciples of specially solemn significance cannot be demonstrated, but is perfectly probable. Whether he instituted a symbolic meal to be carried on in the future is even more shrouded in mystery. As an occasion for celebrating Christ as the sacrament of the world the eucharist remains at the centre of Christian devotion.

19

Jesus and Historical Explanation

1. Text and Interpretation

The question of what can be known about the Jesus of History has been and continues to be the subject of intense debate. The development of historical scholarship in the nineteenth century sought to clear away the layers of doctrinal and religious accretion in order to get back to a basic picture of the man Jesus and his message. His words, shorn of later addition, were to be the basis of a new vision of the historical Jesus, who was himself the ground for faith. This was not of course the whole picture. The most radical of the critics, David Friedrich Strauss, soon recognised that a purely historical analysis could not be an adequate basis of faith, and proposed his own concept of the Christ. But this was not to be the majority view, and the course of historical positivism largely prevailed.

The end of the century brought a radical shift in conviction. Perhaps Jesus had proclaimed the immanent end of the world. His remaining moral and religious teaching and action were entirely secondary for him. Perhaps too we could recover almost nothing of the original words and message of Jesus. In any case, what mattered was the existential appropriation of the eschatological message of the Kingdom. Historicism turned faith into works.

The middle of the twentieth century saw a new quest for the historical Jesus. The message of the Christ of faith was in continuity with the historical Jesus. The existential response was to the historical Jesus as much as to the kerugmatic Christ event. More recently attention has been focused once again on the historical Jesus, notably in America, where the existentialist and often Lutheran categories of faith and works, response and justification, have found no automatic resonance. Indeed the concerns of traditional Christian doctrine have usually not been at the centre of this work, often undertaken in a context of modern study in comparative religious practice, and in the sociological and anthropological study of religion. Here again a decisive shift in approach has shed much new light on the issues, though as we shall see, the new perspectives are no more 'definitive ' than the old.

One significant change brought about by the new approach was a radical questioning of the conviction, created by the Schweitzer/Weiss era, that Jesus was an apocalyptic figure who preached the imminent end of the world. Perhaps the coming of the Kingdom did not mean the end of the world, but rather a new order of priorities. The notion of the end was historically a reflection upon the resurrection. In this perspective Jesus comes across as a teacher, a teacher with a radical message about the state of society and the appropriate response to it. The world of conventional wisdom is sharply put in question. Established values and social hierarchies are not to be taken for granted. Security is not in social position but in God.

Jesus' place within the society in which he worked begins to take on a new importance. Here sociological study is brought to bear on the New Testament. When the rituals associated with the Jewish Law and with social custom are challenged, this causes profound social dislocation. But the society in which Jesus lived was already a volatile society, charged with political and religious tensions. In such a tense situation, any new movement will immediately be perceived as a serious threat by the established vested interests, who may then combine to destroy the newcomer. (It is not hard to see parallels, e.g. in Protestant and Catholic attitudes to Anabaptists at the Reformation, or in the histories of modern party politics in several continents.)

Scholars have approached the social world of Jesus in different ways. Gerd Theissen has used sociological and psychological research, along with secular sources for the history of New Testament times, to produce a fresh appreciation of Jesus as an opponent of most of the conventional powers, the Romans, the religious authorities , even the Zealots, in a new devotion to God and man. This is strikingly epitomised in *The Shadow of the Galilean*. Theissen has combined New Testament research in a theory of religion, as a replacement for the previous existentialist framework common in German New Testament scholarship.[1]

Marcus Borg has concentrated, again, not on an attempt to recover the words of Jesus, but on a typology of religious figures – the charismatic holy man, the sage, the prophet and the founder of a religious movement.[2] As someone who embodied elements of each of these types, Jesus was much concerned with changing his social world. Though not shedding light on traditional doctrinal and ecclesiological issues, this portrait is directly relevant to the question of the gospel in the world. Discipleship may mean a more direct call to change in our social structures than we are accustomed to contemplate, a sharpening of the evangelical challenge.

There are of course other studies in this area, too numerous to list here, but to which reference will be made in the succeeding pages. Again we may note the single-minded approach which lends depth and urgency to the most recent research. But we may also reflect that previous questions and proposals are not thereby rendered irrelevant. The basic doctrinal issues raised by the challenge of incarnation as the focus of creation and reconciliation remain, as part of the task of faith seeking understanding of the mystery of God.

2. The Unknown Son of Man

Christians affirm that in incarnation God has committed himself to participation in the contingency of a single human life at a particular time and place. Evidence for the life of this individual, his teaching and action, partakes of the risks involved in the assessment of all historical material. The circumstances of the life determine how much of the appropriate evidential

[1] G. Theissen, *On Having a Critical Faith*, and subsequent studies.
[2] M. Borg, *Jesus, A New Vision*.

material is likely to be preserved. We have much more material for a twentieth-century American President than for a Babylonian slave in the third millenium BC! We do not have much material for the life of Jesus.

Theologians lay stress on the Bible as an important norm for Christian theology. On this they are united, whether their central criteria have a mainly intratextual or mainly extratextual reference. They are usually able to cite areas of the biblical narratives which they regard as basic to their theology, and to develop these themes further in systematic reflection. Very often however there is little detailed exegesis of particular texts. This is partly because systematic theology is not simply biblical theology. It arises also because even in some important exegetical issues it remains quite unclear what the best solutions are. There remain unanswered questions.

Exceptions to this general reluctance to wrestle with particular texts in systematic theology may be seen recently in the work of Karl Barth, Gerhard Ebeling and Edward Schillebeeckx, where there is a huge volume of exegetical material. I believe that there is justification for the procedure taken in this study, in which central biblical texts on which there is a broad exegetical consensus are developed in a systematic analysis. However, this analysis would be incomplete without some significant reference to the difficulties for historical interpretation posed in crucial areas. I therefore intend to develop the issue with reference to a problem basic to the synoptic narratives, namely the question of Jesus' relation to sayings about the Son of Man.

Each decade appears to bring something of a new scholarly consensus on the matter. We have already referred to leading conclusions of the 80s. But the enormous extant literature on the subject shows the real complexity of the underlying issues, and the uncertainty yet to be resolved.

By 1954 R.H. Fuller felt able to say of this issue that 'The term Son of Man, it is now generally agreed, was used as a title by Jesus himself' (*The Missional Achievement of Term*, 96). Almost ten years later Philip Vielhauer was equally sure that 'None of the sayings is authentic. Jesus did not proclaim the Son of Man, either in the sense that he identified himself with him, or in the sense that he awaited another as the Son of Man.' (*Autsätze*, I,

133) Why the discrepancy ? H.E. Toedt spoke of 'the singular authority of Jesus, which cannot be captured through titles and attributes' (*The Son of Man in the Synoptic Tradition*, 202).

Part of the difficulty clearly arose from the large variety of possible sources for the New Testament usage. Forms of the phrase 'Son of Man' are found in the Psalms and in Job, and are generally considered to be a circumlocution meaning 'man', probably in festival contexts connected originally with a cyclical idea of creation, and showing (Ps. 80:17) traces of a characteristic oscillation between the singular and the corporate. In Ezekiel the prophet is addressed by the phrase over 100 times, both as a mere man before God and also as raised to a divinely inspired manhood, a man 'set for a sign' (12:6) with a message for Israel and all mankind. I think that the resemblances to the gospels long noted here, especially by Curtis and the American 'Prophet School' may indicate the use of Ezekiel by the writers and possibly even by Jesus, Jesus appears to have understood himself to be more than a prophet in the manner of Ezekiel, more than 'the last and greatest herald'.

Daniel 7 has been the favourite background source. But the text of the book is complex, possibly influenced by a couple of redactors. The figure 'like a son of man' who appears after the vision of the beasts, represents one who, after a period of evil and suffering, will come to the throne of the Ancient with the clouds. A judgement will take place, and the kingdom will be divided among 'the saints of the most high', who are originally the angels who form the entourage of Yahweh.

The son is a heavenly figure with a human appearance. If there was a first redactor, he may well have applied the vision to his own times, expecting the son to establish his kingdom for the benefit of the remnant of Israel. The second then gives the passage a nationalistic colouring, so that there will be an earthly kingdom obtained by a victory over Antiochus by God's grace – a significant demonstration of the tendency to turn apocalyptic into the politico-nationalistic. Some have then concluded that Jesus used the phrase himself, aware of the connection in Daniel of the Kingdom of God and the Son of Man and of the combination of glory and suffering, individualising the figure. Coppens' stress on a corporate/

individual oscillation in Daniel was a useful corrective to arguments for a purely corporate (T.W. Manson, H.H. Rowley) or purely individualistic explanation of Jesus' usage.

There are other, much less plausible candidates for origins. The question of a direct relationship between the New Testament Son of Man and the Anthropos, the syncretistic form of either the Iranian gayomaritan figure or the Greek Sophia who brings forth the seven planets, seems to me to have been decisively answered in the negative many years ago by Kraeling. But this is a further indication of the complexity of possible associations. The heavenly man, identified with the first man at the beginning of time, of Philo and the Pseudo-Clementines and now of Nag Hammadi, is, as Van Unnik has remarked, very different from the Son of Man of the synoptic gospels. This figure in another form, a heavenly king who will appear at the end of time, appearing in Enoch, Daniel and the post-Christian 1V Esdras, was probably a current conception in various sections of the Jewish community at the time of Christ.

Within a continuing controversy over the precise nature of 'current conceptions at the time of Christ' there remains a fertile field for the adduction of dubious evidence in support of arguments based on other presuppositions. The following would appear to be fairly clear. The entire absence of the peculiar colouring of the complex known as 1 Enoch from the New Testament and the fact that probably only chapter 70 is of the time of Christ make it very difficult to believe that Jesus, if he used 'Son of Man', took the phrase from 'Enoch'. On the other hand, the notion of a righteous suffering servant of God probably represents a current general conception of the vindication by God of the suffering righteous which is found in Qumran. 1 Enoch 70 does not however speak of the vicarious and redemptive function of the Son of Man. Likewise the Hasmonean suffering Teacher of righteousness (cf. 1 Zd.1:4; 9:34b) is the prophet like unto Moses of Deut 18:15, but no more.

Attempts were made, notably by Mowinkel, to distinguish an origin for 'Messiah' in oriental kingship and for 'Son of Man' in Primal Man myths . But there is evidence of interchange of attributes and titles. While there are references in apocalyptic literature to the Kingdom of God which do not mention Son of Man and vice versa, the evidence is against a rigid distinction between the two of the sort once posited by Vielhauer.

We may consider, too, the linguistic background to the phrase 'Son of Man'. It seems clear that *bar nasha* was most commonly used in Palestine and the surrounding areas to mean simply 'man'. It might conceivably, despite Vielhaue, be used to denote 'I'. It was also present in 1 Enoch 70, Daniel, and so possible elsewhere, as a title. The position is complicated by the existence of a known fluctuation in the strength of the demonstrative pronoun/definite article at this period.

I come now to the New Testament background, use of the phrase, and questions of authenticity. I should like to invite the reader to reflect here again on the complexity which lies behind phrases which we all use about the clarity of scripture. intratextual reference, narrative theology and the like, with reference to what is after all a source of major interest for the evangelists, the events concerning the Son of Man. The issues raised are particularly important for theologies which lay great stress on the history of Jesus as a basic centre of reference.

In an earlier chapter we summarised the course of St Mark's Gospel, 'a passion narrative with a long introduction' around Jesus the Son of Man and the suffering servant. Though it is not clear that Jesus was directly influenced by Isaiah 40 or 53, the continued emphasis in Mark on 'for many' may reflect some understanding of suffering service stemming from Jesus. T.W. Manson thought long ago (*Studies in the Gospels and Epistles*) that Son of Man was the final term in a series remnant, servant, I (in the Psalms) and the Son in Daniel, so that Jesus defines 'Son of Man' in these terms, perhaps envisaged as consisting of himself and his disciples, then embodied alone, unto death, from which arises the body of Christ in continued expansion from the focus in Christ. This is highly convenient for the theologian, but not on that ground alone to be ruled out as impossible.

A different theological explanation was provided by J.A.T. Robinson (*Jesus and his coming*). He saw that any explanation must be an interpretation of an interpretation. The kingdom is already announced as being present in Jesus. There is little 'authentic' reference to a future consummation.Now the Church, incredulous at the suggestion that the Kingdom was already present in the troubled days after the crucifixion, influenced by apocalyptic and expecting a further fulfilment on earth of things mentioned in Jesus' teaching, attributed to Jesus the sayings referring to the parousia of the Son of Man. Rudolf Bultmann noted the apparent differentiation between Jesus and the Son of Man (esp. in Mk. 8:38 and Lk. 12:8f.), and concluded that Jesus never thought of himself as the Son of Man (i.e. as messianic) but expected another, the identification being made by the post-resurrection community.

At this point we may indeed appear to have arrived at the 'methodological impasse' of which 'perhaps the classical instance has to do with the title "son of man".' Here I turn again to Toedt's contribution, in my judgement one of the better efforts. From a study in redaction criticism he felt able to confirm Bultmann's conclusion that some of the sayings referring to the coming Son of Man and not identifying Jesus with the Son are authentic. The grounds were lack of reference to scripture for authentication, lack of apocalyptic colouring, challenge in the message of the imminence of the kingdom, with characteristic warning and promise, demand for allegiance to himself (and not the Son of Man) and lack of 'Christological content', i.e. of direct claim to be the Son. Present response to Jesus determines future confirmation in the fellowship of the son of man in the presence of God. The community made the continuity between Jesus and the coming son into an identification, completing the process which Jesus had begun in relating concepts connected with the kingdom and the Son respectively.

If Jesus himself used Son of Man as a title, not predicating it of himself, then it would be very difficult to think that he could use it to mean simply 'man', for it was probably not his purpose to speak in riddles, though the *Urgemeinde* may at times have thought so. Consequently all the Son of Man titles making the identification are inauthentic, according to Toedt. Edward Schweitzer claimed that in contemporary Jewish eschatological thought there was a pervasive picture of the righteous man who was to suffer death, and be exalted by God to confront his accusers in a final judgement

– the chief sources being Jubilees 4:23; 10:17; Wisdom 2:5 and especially 1 Enoch 71. At Wisdom 2:13, as M. Black confirmed, the suffering righteous is defined in language from the remnant prophecies of 2 Isaiah. In Paul and John the tradition roots in a view of Jesus as the new Patriarch. The meaning of Son of Man, present only in 1 Enoch and not in Wisdom, was then changed by the Church into 1) a title of Christ with parousia connections and 2) the conception of the Church as the true Israel, the body of Christ. Schweitzer accepted e.g. Mt. 11:19 and Mt. 8:20 as genuine references by Jesus to his humiliation and Luke 12:8 and Mark 14:62 to the exaltation, in which Jesus originally referred to himself as the exalted witness at the eschaton, rather than as coming to earth again, a connotation applied later with distortion of the sayings. Black adduced Phil. 2:5-11 and Jn. 3:14, and the central motif of Hebrews, in support of the persuasiveness of this conception, noting too its corporate implications.

We may note that in John's Gospel too the emphasis is on exaltation. The stress on 'He that descended hath ascended' is probably due to the conception of Son of Man as 'Man' the image of God, rather than Mandaic influence (cf. the comments above on this similar genre at Nag Hammadi). The crowd can actually be represented (Jn.12:34) as identifying the Christ with the Son of Man of whom Jesus spoke, the bystanders being represented as understanding the Johannine idiom.

What then can we say of the use of the term Son of Man in the gospels? There are many who find Jesus' use of it as a personal term impossible. Bornkamm sees no connection between the coming suffering for Jesus and the resurrection appointed for the Son of Man: he says of Mk. 8:31; 9:31;10:34 'there is nothing here of parousia and judgement' (*Jesus of Nazareth*, 175f.). It might be asked whether this was to be expected. Conzelmann explained that even in the early church 'Jesus was not addressed, but expected, as Son of Man' (RGG, *Jesus Christus*). Therefore the non-identifying sayings were created. He emphasises 'the indirectness, which characterises his whole appearance' following Vielhauer. The questions were raised in their most acute form in Vielhauer's comprehensive reply to Toedt and Schweitzer (*Aufsätze*, I, 92ff.).

Considering the background in the history of religions Vielhauer reiterated constantly that where the eschatological kingdom was expected and hailed as God's future, neither the Son of Man nor the Messiah nor any other judge and saviour are present in apocalyptic literature. He noted the rarity of Son of Man in 'coming aeon' contexts and concluded that the reign of God of the preaching of Jesus was something 'qualitatively different' from the new aeon or its equivalents, that the Kingdom for Jesus must have meant something different from the new aeon. But this is far from conclusive in my view, bearing in mind the oscillation of attribution already mentioned, the dubiety concerning the direct influence of Enoch, and the lateness of 4 Esdras. In any case we have noted the parallelism between the saints of the new age and the Son in Daniel and in Enoch. Likewise his note on the coming aeon is not conclusive.

We turn to the question of authenticity in the sayings. I want to look first at the sayings which were accepted by Toedt. Considering Mk. 8:38/Lk.12:8 he remarks, correctly I think, on the disunity in the Marcan version and the diversity in the text. He regarded the theme of confession and acknowledgement as unique and so suspect, and even forensic and so suspect. But this might be thought to disregard the main tenor of the teaching, that decision for Jesus now determined status before God in the coming Kingdom. Vielhauer rejected the idea of the apparent non-identification of Jesus and the Son of Man on the basis of Iber's theory, holding that the community created the distinction to differentiate between the same person's operations in two separate ages, made manifest by the appearances after the resurrection, but yet a concept which came easily only later (as in Mt. 2:10). Against Lk.12:39f./Mt. 24:25, the appearance of the intruder by night, it is argued that the reflection of the parousia fits in well with the reflection of the community and of early preaching, and so is to be rejected. This does not of course follow. Rather, there is no clear indication of authenticity. The day of the Son of Man (Lk.7:27/Mt. 24:26) is rejected on the question of the Kingdom and the Son, and the same basic reason disallows Lk.11:30/ Mt.12:40, the sign of Jonah, and the same theme is then reiterated with variations.

Since however we have already noted the weakness of his argument from history of religions grounds, and we appear to have a direct connection of Son of Man and Kingdom of God at Lk. 21:24 and 31, and perhaps at Mk. 8:39 and 9:1, apart from the connection at Lk. 11:29f., Vielhauer's case is very far from conclusive.

Against Schweitzer, Vielhauer argued that the fact that the exaltation motif occurs in the New Testament only in John and in no other Son of Man context (rejecting Mt. 14:62), clearly shows its secondary nature. He noted the diversity of tradition regarding Lk.17:24 and 24:27, and, for the suffering servant, the unusual connection of Elijah and the Son of Man in Mk. 9:12 and the doubtful nature of Mk.14:21. He insisted that 'the Son of Man' could never mean 'I' (which as we have seen is not strictly accurate) and regards Mk. 2:10 as the work of the community.

For Vielhauer the obvious difficulties of Mk. 2:28 and Acts 8:20 suggest only the later introduction of Son of Man as a title (though in fact Mk. 2:28 and Mk. 8:20 might be explained by the possibility that some other word for 'man' was used, and then changed to Son of Man). Mk. 11:19 is out, along with Lk.7:34 and the sign of Jonah. On the background question he noted correctly that the suffering servant is never called the Son of Man in apocalyptic literature (except perhaps in Daniel) and stresses, as might be expected, a likely place for 1 Enoch 70 in Jesus' background. He concluded that none of the Son of Man sayings are 'authentic'. The disciples applied the traditional expectation of the Son of Man to Jesus after the post-resurrection appearances, creating the 'non-identifying' eschatological sayings first, using Son of Man in the third person in the tradition of prophecy and apocalyptic. For Vielhauer there can be no 'soteriological continuity' between the life of Jesus and that of the community. The sole link is death and resurrection. However, we have to note again that the crucial case for an absolute incompatibility between the Kingdom of God and the Son of Man is not proven.

Can one ever hope to make progress in this problem? The answer must be, yes. Bultmann's absolute division between the world of the earthly Jesus and that of the resurrection period, though important theologically, could clearly distort historical assessment. If Jesus could in principle have had no messianic self-understanding, then the interpretation that Jesus distinguished himself from another who was to come as the Son of Man is very plausible. If we go a little further and recognise Jesus' consciousness of authority, of a place in the fulfilling of the Kingdom, then the 'soteriological continuity' is attractive. It is possible that Jesus even went further than this, as 'the self-expressive activity of God', performing acts of healing of body and mind as if he in some sense stood in the place of his Father.

I am inclined to the view that Jesus' baptism may well have had a crucial place in his self-understanding. From that point he may had been conscious of being something more than simply another in a prophetic line. He now preaches the immanence of the Kingdom of God, which is both present and future and is present where and when he is present. He gathers disciples. Decision for himself means decision for the Kingdom. He sees that his mission involves Jerusalem, and suffering.

3. Life, Death and the Future

Jesus' teaching concerning the nature of the Kingdom was worked out against the background of powerful strands of apocalyptic tradition, on which much new light has been shed in recent years, notably by Christopher Rowland.[3]

It is in an apocalyptic context that the solution to the puzzling New Testament references to the Son of Man is to be looked for. The evidence here leads the experts in various directions. It seems to me to be most probably that Jesus did indeed speak of the Son of Man. He did not identify himself, even implicitly, with this figure. But he connected his own mission with the messianic expectation of the coming of a figure who features in a number of strands of Ancient Near Eastern literature. The references to the earthly Son of Man who is working now, and who is sometimes in the New Testament identified with Jesus, may arise from reflection after Jesus' death.

We have said that Jesus very probably anticipated his death,

[3]See esp. C.C. Rowland, *The Open Heaven*.

as a very likely consequence of his mission, a mission undertaken at a time of considerable tension and political instability in the province of Judaea. It is by no means inappropriate that the gospels are written as passion narratives. When we consider the historical sequences of events in the final weeks it is extremely hard to be sure of the detail. As elsewhere we are likely to have a fair measure of authentic factual material, but we are not in a position to say which pieces are closer to the historical sequence than others. Jesus decided at some point that it was necessary to go to Jerusalem. The mission to all Israel had to come to a focus in the centre of Israel.

The narrative of the agony in the garden, underlining the gravity of the anguish which Jesus experienced, appropriately reflects the daunting nature of that final journey. How plans for his arrest were made and how they originated we simply don't know. The consequences of his unpopularity, of his being perceived as a threat by a number of vested interests, themselves under pressure from each other, were speedily apparent.

The details of Jesus' trial remain a matter of debate. It is not particularly profitable to speculate on whether the charges on which he was condemned were religious or political. Religious matters had political consequences and political issues had religious overtones. We cannot reconstruct the proceedings in court. We may note one striking feature of the accounts. On trial for his life, Jesus says very little. He leaves the procedures and hypotheses almost entirely to his opponents. He is condemned. He is executed.

'Became incarnate.' The life of Jesus can be noted in a single phrase and almost glossed over in a concentration upon the cross, the resurrection or a technical formulation of dogmatic Christology. But of course the life of Jesus has always been of central importance for Christian faith. However it has been understood theologically, God has been understood to have been involved here decisively in a single contingent human life. This identification with creation by the creator is central to the mystery of God's nature. Jesus' struggle against the opposition which led to his death is part of the human cost of salvation as Christians understand it, a cost which would be hard to overstate. The long theological tradition which spoke of Jesus' identification, not simply with human nature but with fallen human nature, humanity of the sort that we all share, is central to the interpretation of the gospel. We shall return to an evaluation of this humanity. But first we must bring to bear on our quest the dimensions of the death and the resurrection of Jesus.

The fact of God's involvement in Jesus' life has the greatest consequences for all human life. God's involvement in Jesus' death has consequences for all human death. God's involvement in resurrection takes all human life into new relationship with God, the consequences of which will only be known eschatologically.

As a matter of report we know that only fragments of these events concerning Jesus are available to us in historical perspective. It requires the commitment of faith to bring the data into theological perspective. Faith cannot supplement, far less be a substitute for history. But for Christians it puts narrative into the context of the presence of God.

20

Death and Resurrection

1. The Passion Narratives

We noted earlier that the gospels are interested not only in the life but in the death of Jesus, which forms an integral part of the gospel structure. Christology arises from the life, death and resurrection of Jesus, as a manifestation of the action of God in human life.

In the Fourth Gospel Jesus is the good shepherd who gives his life for his flock and gathers them into the fold. He is the saviour of the world, as the Father draws men to his Son. He is the new vine, in whom his disciples abide through faith. He is the source of new life. He promises to come to the Church in the person of the Spirit. There is to be a close interrelationship between God, Jesus and the Christian community through the Spirit. There is a continuity between Jesus' life, death and resurrection, and the results of his ministry will be seen as the fruits of the Spirit. God's love overcomes the barrier of death. In the remainder of the Johannine literature the fruits of the Spirit of Jesus Christ are seen in the practice of love. Jesus Christ is the embodiment of the divine love, drawing a response in love from those who follow in the way of discipleship.

The Pauline corpus draws an equally close connection between Jesus' life, his death and his resurrection. The significance of the one element depends heavily on the other two. Modern scholars are understandably suspicious of attempts to turn the biblical writers into systematic theologians, turning out balanced and consistent theologies. Paul has suffered more than most from this practice, and here it is perhaps least appropriate. We are faced rather with a collection of occasional pieces, involving contrasts and contradictions, written for particular situations. However, there are certain central themes which run through the letters of Paul and those influenced by him, and these are highly relevant to Christology.

Through his death and his resurrection Jesus Christ defeated all that is opposed to God, evil, sin and death. Christians have been enabled to enter into a new age of redemption, into a union with Christ. The old life, of bondage to the law, of self-reliance and moral failure, is transformed through the Spirit (esp. Galatians 2, Romans 6, 8). Traditional prejudices based on local cultural norms are to be overcome (Galatians, Corinthians). Through baptism there is incorporation into Christ (Romans). Through his sacrificial death Christ has made atonement for sin, creating righteousness through grace (Romans). Sinners are justified by faith through grace. There is still a participation in suffering, but Christ is present through the Spirit, and in the form of a slave, so that there is no separation from God's love (Romans 8, 1 Cor. 13, Phil. 2, 3). There remains a promise of conformation to Christ in life with Christ after death (1 Cor. 15). Salvation in Christ is for the Gentiles as much as for the Jews (Romans). This eschatological peace of God has both individual and corporate dimensions, for it is achieved in the body of Christ. Christ died in order to destroy death (Hebrews, 1 Corinthians, Revelation). Those who were buried with Christ in baptism are risen with him in resurrection (Colossians). And in all of this the presence and action of Christ is the presence and action of God. God was in Christ reconciling the world to himself (2 Corinthians).

2. Crucifixion

Jesus died. The crucifixion of Jesus is one of the most well attested facts of Christian faith.[1] For many Christians through the ages the cross has been the centre of the faith. For Martin Luther theology was the theology of the cross. For Moltmann

---

[1] Cf. the work of Martin Hengel.

God is the crucified God, and this emphasis has been stressed in much twentieth-century theology, Catholic and Protestant. Some of the world's greatest art has been evoked by Christ on the cross. Crucifixion was one of the most unpleasant ways to die invented in the ancient world. The reality of the torture in detail and the extent of the humiliation and degradation which it included has become clear in recent research.

It has been said that the New Testament does not assert that the purpose of Jesus' death was to show God's love, but that such a connection between the depth of Jesus' commitment and the depth of God's love would be fully justified theologically. The significance of Jesus' death is part of the significance of Jesus' life. His self-giving resulted directly in his death. He did not draw back at the point of impending disaster. His commitment led inexorably to his death, long before the age at which most theologians write their studies in Christology.

In trying to understand the place of this disaster Christians were naturally inclined to try to find a meaning in the traditions of Israel. There, as in most religions, there were complex traditions of sacrifice, with the aim of propitiation and of restoring or enhancing the favour of God. This is the tradition in which Jesus grew up, and in which, Christians believe, God chose to become involved in a single contingent human life. These traditions were and perhaps still may be helpful in understanding problems of loss, alienation and restoration. Yet we must always remember that the ancient world is the world of Aeschylus as well as of St. Paul, and that this is not a divinely authorised medium for a definitive disclosure of the significance of this dying.

In the light of God in Jesus Christ all imagery is transformed. That was the abiding significance of John McLeod Campbell's stress on 'seeing the atonement in its own light'. Having said this however we may notice that the atonement in its own light might include a number of different dimensions, sometimes obscured in the theological tradition by the strident claims of one set of positions over against other sets.

I do not at this point intend to explore all the associations of the word 'atonement' in Christian theology. That must await a consideration of the Christian affirmation of the resurrection of Christ. We are concerned with the crucifixion of the one who was raised, and with the resurrection of the crucified one. There is for faith an integral connection between crucifixion and resurrection, humiliation and exaltation.

We may note here however a number of significant features of the death of Christ already. In the terms in which we judge all human enterprises, we must judge Jesus' mission to have been a failure. True, he had limited success in preaching his message of the coming of the Kingdom. But this success in the initial stages was finally and disastrously counter-productive. It led to his death, to what was, as is common in many periods of history, a kind of judicial murder supported by the religious and political authorities of the state, by all that was authoritative and respected. His death was not an accident, an unfortunate consequence of a trivial oversight or casual mischance. It arose out of that which constituted the central characteristic of his humanity as we see this in the narratives, namely his unswerving devotion to God as his Father, and to the actions which this devotion entailed. In this his death was not unique. Indeed, it becomes intelligible to us as something which occasionally occurs in human history. We may think of the death of Socrates, and of the deaths of many Christian martyrs, sometimes known only to God.

It had, as such deaths often have, both private and public dimensions. Not least because of its particular brutality, its private face included the contemplation and endurance of the utmost physical and mental stress. Its public dimensions included a full measure of the ritual humiliation and degradation which societies regularly reserve for those who appear to threaten their values and objectives, particularly in times of insecurity. These private and public faces of death constitute central parts of the cosmic, historical and personal dimensions of the soteriological significance of Jesus' death.

In traditional discussion of the death of Christ there has been much consideration of Jesus' accepting the punishment of God due to mankind for their sins. We shall have to consider the whole question of penal substitution further. Here we may note that there is little indication in the narratives to suggest that Jesus understood himself as accepting a punishment due to the sins of Israel, or even of substituting himself in some way as the victim for an execution, as for example happened in the modern Holocaust.

It is equally implausible to suggest that Jesus committed suicide. At the same time, he appears to have been well aware of the serious danger of arrest and execution which the focusing of his mission on Jerusalem would entail. In this respect his death is entirely of a piece with the rest of his life, in reflecting his total commitment to the task which he understood himself to have been given.

3. Risen from the Dead

The life of Jesus, leading to his sacrificial death for his cause, is significant as a human life lived, and as a human life seen in the light of the history of God's messengers in Israel. It is however in the retrospective light of the resurrection that the life and death of Jesus gain their full significance. Life, death and resurrection are mutually illuminating. Here we must consider in the first instance the events surrounding belief in the resurrection of Jesus.

Despite frequent reference in theological literature to 'the resurrection event', it is clear that discussion of resurrection involves a number of clusters of events. The historical circumstances can be reviewed in a number of ways.[2] This is how I view the sequence.

Jesus died. The narratives stated that he was buried, and we have no reason to doubt this. It is said that he was buried in a rock tomb originally intended for Joseph of Arimathea. This may also be the case. We then have to consider the narratives referring to the discovery of the empty tomb. These, like all the New Testament narratives, have a theological purpose and are in that sense 'kerugmatic' narratives. This need not in principle mean, as we have seen, that they are devoid of historical facts. Sometimes it has been possible to affirm precise historical

<hr/>

[2]Cf. H. von Campenhausen on the resurrection narratives in *Tradition and Life*, 42ff.

information with some confidence. At other times we shall consider that there may be facts here but we cannot discern which individual elements are most historically reliable. In other cases we may conclude that there are probably no direct historical antecedents.

In the empty tomb narrative it is said that women came to the tomb early in the morning and found that the tombstone had been rolled away. There is the detail of the empty tomb and the folded graveclothes. There is no body. Then there is the appearance to the women of a figure like an angel. Here is Jesus in disguise, an appearance of the risen Christ by the tomb.

What are we to make of this appearance? We note that there is a whole cluster of appearances of the risen Lord; by the Sea of Galilee, to Thomas and the other disciples, on the road to Emmaus. In modern times it has been customary to describe these visions as a kind of hallucination symbolising a new confidence that somehow disaster had been turned into victory. It is not at all clear however how this confidence had been generated, in order to stimulate the symbolic expression.

The narratives note, and Christians have always drawn comfort from, the remarkable and apparently swift transition from the scene at the crucifixion, of the disciples in panic and flight, and the inexplicable new mood of confidence which followed. Such a change, it has been noted, does not in itself create a cast iron case for the fact of resurrection in the interval. But if Jesus were indeed risen from the dead, this would be an entirely appropriate reaction, and it would explain the transition.

What is the truth behind the claim that Jesus rose from the dead and is alive? In Christian tradition this has been interpreted in many ways. For most of church history the main line of interpretation has been a literal one, in the sense that the dead man rose out of the tomb, walked around Galilee in a spiritual body which was like an earthly body but with additional properties, such as the ability to walk through doors, and finally ascended to heaven. Such imagery is to be found in rich detail in medieval and renaissance art. Further reflection has always suggested however that there is here a mystery, to which normal earthly circumstances can at best only approximate. It is of course possible that God could have raised Jesus from the dead, reconstituting him as he was and that he then through a miracle was able to act in a remarkable way for a period, before undergoing a further development and vanishing from earth to be with his Father. God can by definition do anything. But brief reflection suggests enormous further problems. If Jesus visibly rose from the dead and was publicly observable in this way, where did he physically go to at the end of the forty day period? The problem of the transformation arises again, at the forty day interval.

At the opposite end of the spectrum it is often held that the resurrection refers to no particular event directly connected with Jesus' body, but that the accounts are a symbol for the appearance of the phenomenon of faith. Through the mystery of divine providence people began to realise that Jesus had not died in vain, that somehow his death had been a victory. A modification of this approach, rather less frequent, is the proposal that because the promised Kingdom had not visibly arrived on earth, belief in the resurrection of Jesus' body was invented as a substitute for this. This is not of course inconceivable, and it is hard to refute negative propositions. But there is no real positive evidence to support the hypothesis.

How then are we to approach the question? I want to go through a step by step investigation. Jesus died, and was buried. We can deal with some ancient theories fairly quickly. It has sometimes been thought that at that point the disciples, or Jesus' enemies stole the body, and the disciples then invented the resurrection belief when the tomb was empty. But clearly this could have been easily refuted if Jesus' enemies had taken the body. There exists no evidence pointing to a removal by a group of disciples.

Jesus died. In the tradition of Judaism there were strong strands of expectation of a resurrection of the dead, whether of a righteous remnant, or of all the dead. There were stories in the Old Testament of raising from the dead, which may be thought to be repeated in the story of the raising of Lazarus. Jesus' resurrection gains some intelligibility and context from this background, pointing towards the fulfilment of God's Kingdom. There are in the case of Jesus' resurrection very significant differences. Jesus is not raised, only to die a natural death later. His resurrection is not accompanied by a general resurrection. His body is not exactly the same as before, and he does not resume his previous activities.

4. The Meaning of Resurrection

How are we to seek to begin to reach an understanding of resurrection? However we begin, this will influence our picture. Let us ask the question of what happened to the body of Jesus. We do not know. We can scarcely regard the accounts of the visions as the equivalent of historical reporting. St. Paul's encounter on the Damascus road was a seeing in faith, not quite equivalent to seeing another human being. Paul does not give us a description of the resurrection body of Jesus. His notion of the resurrection of Christians is of a spiritual body, like our bodies in some respects and unlike them in others. It is sometimes suggested that the resurrection, or the Christ event, has nothing to do with the body of Jesus, but refers only, and precisely, to the decisive encounter with God's Word in which a person is grasped by the power of the gospel and transformed. This is clearly an important perception of a major consequence for Christians of the resurrection. God is personal and he acts personally for persons. But this may by no means exhaust the significance of the resurrection.

The theological significance of the personal does not entail that the resurrection was purely on the plane of personal spiritual encounter. An equally important theological motif, which would be eminently appropriate, though it cannot for that reason be deduced to have been inevitably present, is consideration of the renewal of creation in new creation. It might very reasonably be held that the restoration and redemption of the material cosmos in a spiritual renewal, though not the bodily reconstitution, of Christ's body, is a powerful and decisive breakthrough in the history of the created order. Jesus died. It has sometimes been thought that he may have been unconscious, and then recovered a few hours later from a deep coma. That however would not account for his later disappearance from his disciples. In any case, there is no evidence to support this. Modern knowledge of the mechanics of crucifixion would appear to rule out anything less than death, after painful and prolonged torture. We know that after a few seconds the memory traces in the human brain disappear, making it impossible for there to be any continuity between the previous and the succeeding brain states. There could therefore be no physical continuity between Jesus who was and the body which remained, if it were resurrected after a considerable interval.

If there was indeed a special continuity between the dead Jesus and the risen Christ, as classical Christian faith asserts, then this was a continuity in God, created by God, rather than arising within the natural order. In that sense faith in the resurrection is faith in a miracle, perhaps the original Christian miracle.

It becomes increasingly clear that we cannot construct historical data out of theological propositions. This neither rules in nor rules out particular reconstructions. In the present state of discussion we have the advantage that we need feel neither obliged to follow tradition nor obliged to take an opposite view in being liberated from tradition. A whole range of views has become equally respectable. We may choose whatever seems best to fit the case.

My own choice is for a theology of the resurrection which is closer to the classical theology of the resurrection than to, say, a modern paradigm like Schillebeeckx's *maranatha* Christology. Christian theology asserts a decisive link between the Jesus who died and all humankind, those who have no faith as much as those who have faith, today, and indeed between Jesus and those who have lived and died since the beginning of the human race. It also asserts a continuity between creation and redemption in the material order. All of these central affirmations of faith would be entirely consonant with an affirmation of the resurrection of Jesus as a spiritual body to be one with God his Father. Nothing in the evidence available or the stock of accumulated theory rules this out. It therefore seems to me to be the most sensible available option. This is not a position that can be proved over against other positions. It simply commends itself as the most preferable option. Having taken up a classical position on the fact of the resurrection, I would not however think it necessary or desirable to accept all that has generally followed this choice.

At the end of his comprehensive study of concepts of resurrection Peter Carnley argues that resurrection faith may be understood as a kind of knowing by acquaintance of the presence of the risen Christ as Spirit.[3] This kind of perception 'involves an identity judgement in which the spirit of the Christian fellowship is identified as the gracious presence of Jesus' (266). It is by virtue of the memory of the historical Jesus that the judgement of faith is made possible. Jesus is remembered as the person who exhibited agape. 'Thus, to remember Jesus, is to remember a disposition, not an episode.' It also includes the memory of his death. This memory is brought to the believer within the tradition of the Church. Knowing and remembering come together. The particularity of Jesus, to which faith's memory refers, is the particularity of love, of the distinctive self-giving of Jesus. Through the diversity of the Church's tradition of memory the unity of the risen Christ is mediated to us, as through faith we recognise the pattern of the *Christus praesens* (368). This is a careful study, similar in its approach in many ways to Dietrich Ritschl's *Memory and Hope.*

We may agree that encounter with the risen Christ brings us back to the pattern of the historical Jesus, and that this happens in the context of word and sacrament in the Church. That this meeting takes place is sometimes despite the Church rather than through it, for the Church is not always faithful. Wherever the presence of God is felt in the world this is understood by Christians to be at the same time the presence of the Spirit of the risen Christ, creating Christlikeness. The divine presence is not dependent on the Church, but is there wherever the Church allows itself to be the open channel of God's love.

Christian belief in the resurrection is based on a cumulative case, on different aspects of the tradition of the events concerning Jesus, as they filter through from the past, from the

---

[3] Cf Peter Carnley, *The Structure of Resurrection Belief.*

biblical narratives and the appropriation of these narratives through word and sacrament in the history of the community. This appropriation is a living reality in the present, taking different forms in different ecclesial cultures. Past and present affirmation provides grounds for hope of future consequences of the resurrection.

It must be emphasised here that the events concerning Jesus include importantly Jesus' belief in God. The resurrection has to be seen, not only in the light of the whole of Jesus' life, but also in the light of the Christian understanding of God. There is here a hermeneutical circle, because the resurrection informs that understanding. But equally, it is in the framework of transcendent personal being, active in the created order, that the diverse streams of resurrection data begin to take on a minimally comprehensible shape. It is part of the Christian hope that the shape of resurrection as new life will be made entirely clear to us in God's future.

It is not surprising that Christians have interpreted the shape of the new in different ways. John Macquarrie (1990) ended his Christology by offering the reader a choice of two endings, a happy and an austere ending, and leaving them to decide. Thomas Sheenan, more radically, has asked us to return from Christianity to the Kingdom of God. Tensions among theological perspectives may be fruitful, provided that we try to ensure that these are constructive rather than destructive tensions. Classical models are not infallible – the dangers were memorably highlighted by Tom Driver in his *Christ in a Changing World*. My own view is that the main traditional view of resurrection, restated through a continuing process of reform, is more likely than the alternatives to be able to support and inform the faith of most Christians in the future.

The significance of the resurrection of Jesus Christ may be expressed in different dimensions. As far as the person of Jesus is concerned, we have affirmed that he died, and that faith understands him to have been raised by God from death, in a spiritual body which was and is related in a spiritual identity to God his Father. For the Christian community, there is the continuing human experience of the presence of the Spirit of the risen Christ as a further ground of affirmation of resurrection. Beyond this, faith reflects that here is the inauguration of cosmic new creation within the structures of creation. Here is the consequence of atonement, the effective victory of God's love over evil in all its dimensions. The fruits of this victory are still to be manifested to all humankind in God's eschatological peace. But here is the future which affects the present, and encourages us to view creation, and to act in creation, in the light of God's future peace. The consequences of resurrection are central to all Christology, both in helping to shape the perspective in which we may assess the person and work of Christ, and in the understanding of the role of Christian people within God's ongoing relationship with humanity, the sphere of the action of the Spirit of the risen Christ.

21

Divine Humanity: Human Divinity

1. Truly Human

The Christian gospel is about God. It is also about man, about humankind. The good news is that in the events concerning Jesus, God recreates all humanity in a new relationship to himself. The importance of the humanity of Christ has been appreciated in fresh ways this century, notably in the work of Barth, Pannenberg and Rahner.

In his profound restatement of doctrine Karl Barth has described Jesus as the basic form of humanity. There is some deep bond between the character of God and the character of man as new humanity in the life of Jesus. This could, and easily did, give rise to misunderstanding. There was the danger that the notion of Jesus as God incarnate could, paradoxically, detract from the significance of incarnation as commitment to all the historical contingency involved in a single human life. Barth did not intend such an interpretation. He spoke of the Holy Spirit, and the spirit of Christ, as the most intimate friend of a proper understanding of man. But his mistrust of the conclusions of New Testament scholars, whom he saw as hopelessly entangled in subjectivism, did not help him in tackling this problem.

What escaped Karl Barth was partially rescued in John Robinson's *The Human Face of God*, in which the psychological implications of particular humanity are explored. Here is a sensitive study of the questions of the sort of feelings, emotions and inner conflicts which Jesus must have experienced in his life.[1] It will not do to say that such questions are rendered absurd or redundant by lack of empirical evidence. It requires the imagination of faith to seek to envisage, however falteringly, something of the human cost of our salvation.

Particular humanity involves particular personal and private feelings. It also involves particular cultural, social and perhaps political commitments. Private and public perceptions cannot of course be completely separated. But they can be distinguished. The public human face of Jesus has been emphasised in recent Liberation Theologies, in reaction to what they have perceived as an enslavement to intellectual conceptualism in ancient classical and in modern European Christologies. This public face has also been emphasised, with different ideological connotations, by the social theologies of the late nineteenth and early twentieth centuries, and by concentration on Jesus as 'the man for others', notably as part of the theological legacy of Dietrich Bonhoeffer.

Jesus was indeed the man for others.[2] It would have been hard to express adequately his human concern for other people in every direction. But we must note too that as the man for others he was at the same time the man for God. His love for his fellow men and women was intimately connected with his love for God, and vice versa. There are distinctions, but there is no ultimate separation, between Jesus' religious, social, private, public and political concerns. All Jesus' relationships, with God and man, are closely identified with his mission, to announce and to facilitate the coming of God's Kingdom.

In assessing this role of Jesus as the man for others we have to beware of different sorts of historical anachronism. Jesus lived in a culture in which religious practices had a high profile in practically every area of social life, unlike the case in modern Europe. It was not quite like a modern Islamic state, in which

[1] One of the difficulties about this important area, humanity, remains of course that we have no record of Jesus' private thoughts and feelings as he faced the various stages of his ministry. Cf. J.A.T. Robinson *The Human Face of God*.

[2] Jesus is the man for others as the representative of humanity, not of maleness or masculinity. That he was male rather than female, and lived in the Mediterranean rather the Pacific basin, is part of the contingency of the gospel: cf. the discussion in part 1 on God and gender, p. 60f.

religious practices may be understood, by some at least, as in conscious reaction to a modern secular culture. It was a world in which numerous religious practices were perceived as self evidently embedded in the fabric of human existence. This was the world in which Jesus lived and moved and had his being. Though we may well be justified in maintaining that Jesus signified much more than the whole of the parts of the cultural amalgam in which he lived, we must be careful not to modernise him in our reconstructions. We may note too that Christian discipleship in the very different world of today may involve rather different levels of engagement with explicitly religious and non-religious concerns. We are invited not to replicate first-century conditions but to act on the basis of the freedom which Jesus has won for humankind.

This was indeed a particular single struggle in a particular single life. Here we recall all that was said earlier about the life of Jesus. This is part of the truth of the theological scandal of particularity, *eph hapax*. But this human battle has its universal aspect too. Here the man Jesus is identified with all human struggle, for God and man, for love and justice, for health and integrity in the human race. Here is a life lived with which all human beings can identify, through all history, with the aid of all the concepts, pictures, reasons of the mind and reasons of the heart. We shall return to the important role of myths in Christology. Here we may just mention that we are not simply concerned to relate the myth or myths concerning Jesus to the reality which is our perception. All reality is God's reality. The source of reality is God in Christ, in whom alone, as Aquinas put it, essence and existence are one. Our myths of autonomous humanity help us to understand our myths of God incarnate, and to appropriate the salvation which God has provided for us, at the cost of the dismemberment of the humanity of Jesus.

2. Truly God

The gospel assures us that Jesus is the man for God and for others. It also affirms that God is with us. In classical Christology this affirmation has often appeared to be synonymous with the affirmation that the logos became incarnate, and that Jesus is one person in two natures, very God and very man. There is no need in rethinking these matters today to deny the magnitude of the intellectual achievements of past generations of Christian thinkers. It is through the scholarship of the past that we are enabled to make progress in the present. Nevertheless, there are well-known reasons why we cannot be content to repeat ancient verities. Though many Christians may still find the ancient formulas illuminating and persuasive, very many others seem to find them less than helpful, because they naturally could not address the sorts of questions about the nature of God and man which have arisen through the development of society and of thought in the last five hundred years, and not least in this century. There do not seem to me to be many good reasons for thinking that Christians in previous ages were mistaken in their perception of the fundamentals of the faith. But there are always pressing needs to give fresh reason for the faith that is in us, to use the biblical phrase, in every generation.

God with us. Sometimes it is thought that the Godward side as it were of the question of Christ is confined to the death, or even more frequently, the resurrection of Christ, while the manward side is manifested in his human life. This distinction has clear disadvantages. It seems much more helpful to think of God as with us, as he is with Jesus, in life, death and resurrection equally in different ways.[3]

In ancient and in modern theologies, in Bultmann and in Athanasius, it is reaffirmed that the resurrection, understood in different ways, is the point at which God's identification with humanity takes on its decisive shape. In some senses all Christians have been unanimous here, in agreeing with St. Paul. If Christ was not raised, our faith is in vain.

Twentieth-century theology has seen a new emphasis on the death of Christ, not as the sphere of an act of penal substitution, as for example in St. Anselm, but as the crucial point, where God participated in human death, in a movement which had central significance for creator and creation alike. Moltmann's

---

[3]Cf. part 1 on God's presence. It belongs to the centre of the gospel that at times when we are not with God, as it were, God is with us.

volume, *The Crucified God*, may stand here for a large number of studies, diverse in approach but unanimous in their focus. I have argued above that Christ's death and resurrection have to be taken together in order to begin to see their significance, as the crucifixion of the Christ who then rose, and the resurrection of the crucified one. I shall come back to this theme in reconsideration of the classical motif of humiliation and exaltation.

But what of the life of Jesus, in consideration of God with us? Christians have from the first been aware of the danger of adoptionism, of the thought that Jesus only became one with God at a particular point. They have stressed that the incarnation encompassed every point of Jesus' life. They have stressed the Virgin Birth. They have stressed the fundamental miracle of Christmas. *Natus est*: God was born in a cradle, made small for us, as Luther said. God is with us in the fact of particular humanity. That is indeed an astonishing assertion, especially in contrast with the frequently expressed view that talk of God as person is incoherent. But the reality of God with us in the human life of Jesus offers us resources for Christian life and reflection far beyond the bare fact of his having lived. In his mission, in his teaching, in his pastoral concern, in his temptation, suffering, dying, God was constantly there, identified in a mysterious way, which Christians since New Testament times have struggled to comprehend. This engagement, faith believes, has momentous consequences, not only for us but for God.

God is with us. We explored already in part one the Christological consequence of the doctrine of God. God participates in human life. It is indeed almost inconceivable for God as person to relate personally to every human being who ever was, is or shall be, when we conceive of God as always over against the world. If we conceive of God as always immanent within the cosmic process, there is an opposite difficulty. It is hard to imagine his mind as distinct from the process of the created order, moving from one state to another, to end in final cosmic burn-out. But if we may somehow begin to think of God as participating in this single life in such a way that this experience, as a divine experience, is always there, we may begin to imagine that here there is an indication of the personal relatedness within God, in which God's commitment to historicality is expressed. Here God shares in, but does not become a component part of, the historical development of humankind within the created order.

God shares in historicality. We have already begun to explore this theme. Now we must take it further. God's sharing in historicality was traditionally expressed in the language of the incarnation. Sometimes it is thought that the language of incarnation is a denial of historicality, and in particular usages this may be so. However, the concept of incarnation as God's unique engagement with the human life of Jesus has always been central to Christian faith and there do not appear ever to have been good grounds for denying this.

What the recent debates about concepts of incarnation appear to me to have shown is that the concept, like all theological concepts, is capable of obscuring as well as illuminating understanding of God's presence in Jesus.

The Word became flesh. Historical study has shown how the seminal Johannine symbolism became the centre of a classical line of Christological theory, which drove out alternative theories and became established, as the normative Christian Christological category.[4] Sometimes the Word was thought of as identified with flesh, sometimes with humanity. Both the subject and the object of incarnation were to be understood in different ways. With regard to God, how was the Word related to the Godhead? God was totally committed to incarnation, but perhaps not all of God was incarnate. But it was difficult to think of part of God being involved without affecting all of God. Judaism suggested a gulf fixed between creator and creature. Platonism suggested that God's perfection included an inability to suffer change. How to affirm incarnation without breaking these limits was a problem, and led to a limitation on commitment to the affirmation that the fullness of God was involved in the fullness of historicality.

---

[4]Effective communication involves listening, silence and supportive action as well as speech. This is part of the wider significance of the Word.

With regard to the man Jesus, it was not easy to say how the divine consciousness of the Word was related to the human consciousness of the man Jesus, without reducing the reality of the one or the other, or describing a curious confusion.

The classical solution affirmed on the one hand the full divinity of the logos and on the other the full humanity of the man Jesus. It spoke of a differentiation, but not a subordination, between God the creator and God the logos within the Godhead. It spoke too of the humanity of the Word as a *logos enhypostatos,* a single centre of consciousness in which the humanity of Jesus had his consciousness in the consciousness of the logos. This was as far as that particular terminology could lead.

God with us. A further way of exploring the relationship between God and Jesus was found through using the biblical imagery of humiliation and exaltation. This was done notably in the Christologies of Martin Luther and Karl Barth. This had the great merit of commitment to theological realism without buying in heavily to the particular conceptual frameworks of the ancient classical ontologies. God commits himself to suffering in the suffering of Jesus, and resolves this suffering in the exaltation of Jesus. This is a Christology of the resurrection of the crucified one. It has the merit of safeguarding the normative nature of the centre of the biblical narrative, without extending the same normative role to the classical ontologies.

There is a particularly good discussion of incarnation in *The Logic of God Incarnate* by Thomas V. Morris. Morris defends the traditional doctrine of the incarnation from the charge of incoherence. In his model,

> The divine mind of God the Son contained, but was not contained by, his earthly mind, or range of consciousness. The divine mind had full and direct access to the earthly, human consciousness resulting from the Incarnation, but the earthly consciousness did not have such full and direct access to the content of the overarching omniscience proper to the Logos, but only such access, on occasion, as the divine mind allowed it to have. (103)

It can then be said of Jesus that 'he is fully human, but not merely human. He is also fully divine.' One person with two minds, Jesus is completely aware of the reality of temptation, but does not succumb to it. As in the tradition, Christological discussion has trinitarian implications. 'Recognising three distinct persons or centers of consciousness as divine will not clearly involve either an abrogation of duty or a flouting of logic' (218).

Morris's argument does not seek engage with all the factors adduced by supporters of the 'Myth of God Incarnate' debate, such as the important social and cultural issues. But it does remind us that sentiment and fashion are not an infallible guide to what may or may not be logical.

Pertinent comments on Morris have been made by a number of writers, notably Swinburne and Ward. Swinburne (*The Philosophy in Christianity*) offers a similar defence of incarnation, using the term 'essential nature'. A human being cannot lose its essential nature and continue to exist (54). But there is plenty of scope for different explications of what it is to be human. Indeed, 'God could have become man in a rather fuller sense than the traditional interpretation allowed' (68).

Keith Ward comments, 'The trend in much modern theology is to make Jesus merely human, on the ground that only so can he be sufficiently like us. If what I have said is correct, this is a fundamental error; since, while Jesus must be fully human, he must be very unlike us indeed if he alone is to be the Saviour of the world' (220). There is a complementarity between incarnation and atonement. 'One way to bring out the plausibility of one unique incarnation of God in history is to recall the centrality of the idea of atonement for the Christian notion of incarnation' (221).

I welcome these suggestions, though I do not myself believe that the strength of the logical case for incarnation is theologically decisive. Incarnation may be logical, but it may not be a logical necessity. What is decisive is the interpretation of the sequence of cross-resurrection events, of what Luther saw in terms of humiliation and exaltation, and Barth as God's parable of the prodigal son. Incarnation, appropriately defined, is an important means of affirming that reality, somewhat as Trinity is a central means of affirming the same reality as the actuality of the self-giving, relational God.

Jesus Christ is present to humankind as word and as sacrament. These are central dimensions of the life of faith, and as such are focal points for appropriation of the myriad imagery and conceptuality of the Christological tradition.

Jesus Christ is word. In the introduction to this section we looked briefly at the development in the early Church of the logos Christology. The strengths and limitations of this imagery became clear in the development of the tradition in all its branches, in the *logos sarx* tradition of Alexandria, in the *logos anthropos* tradition of Antioch, and in later patristic and medieval development. It is often thought that this is an area now completely explored and exhausted. But this is far from clear, as recent imaginative reinterpretations, notably by Karl Rahner and Bernard Lonergan, make clear. Dietrich Bonhoeffer took up this development towards the end of his 1933 lectures in Christology.[5]

The logos Christology led to the Chalcedonian definition of the person of Christ with its two natures in one person. From this the Lutheran tradition developed its characteristic doctrine of *communicatio idiomatum*. In incarnation there is a personal union of God with individual humanity. The communion of nature means that the particular characteristics of each individual nature can also be predicated of the particular characteristics of the other. Jesus is God and Jesus is man, though Godhead is not manhood. The unity is in the persons, while the integrity of natures remains. From this thought there follows the mutual participation and exchange of individual properties of the nature, the *communicatio idiomatum*.

First there is the *genus idiomaticum*. What is true of one or the other nature can be predicated of the whole Godhead. As Jesus suffers, God suffers. Second there is the *genus majestaticum*. Now the predicates of the eternal Godhead can be expressed of the human nature. Jesus can be seen as omnipotent. Third is the *genus apotelesmaticum* (the productive, effective, inclusive mode). The saving action of the person of Jesus Christ can also be affirmed of the individual natures.

[5]D. Bonhoeffer, *Christology*, pp. 92-103.

Against this the Reformed tradition protested that in the *genus majestaticum* the real humanity of Christ is overwhelmed. The logos enters into flesh, but remains also outside the flesh. The humanity remains humanity. *Finitum incapax infiniti.* In turn the Lutherans replied, *finitum capax infiniti; non per se sed per infinitum.* Christ experienced two states, of humiliation (*exinanitio*) and exaltation (*exaltatio*). The humiliation is that of the incarnate one, not of the logos itself. The incarnate one, Jesus in his human nature, renounced the use of his divine powers during his lifetime, either through concealment (*krypsis*) or through renunciation (*kenosis*).

In the nineteenth century the kenosis was taken up again, but now referred to the logos himself (as in the earlier Reformed tradition). The difficulty with some of these theories was that Christ appeared to be neither truly God nor truly man, but some kind of demi-god. Bonhoeffer thought that here was an ultimate result of turning a Who? question into a How? question, which could never be answered positively but only negatively. It is not clear that there can be a neat distinction between these questions in the way Bonhoeffer then imagined. What does emerge is that the notion of logos leads on to notions of the content of incarnation and vice versa. There is not a dichotomy but a complementarity between the divine and human natures and the concepts of humiliation and exaltation. This was noted by Barth in his reinterpretation of classical Christology with the aid of the parable of the prodigal son.

Christ is Word. This word is expressed through the life, death and resurrection of Jesus. The word is a word of incarnation, of contingency, of the self-giving and self-emptying of God into the random events of a single human life. The word in Jesus Christ is the decisive word for the ultimate meaning and truth of all human language and all human activity.

An extension of this theme, again anticipated in the Lutheran tradition, is the use of concepts of kenosis. Taken at face value this metaphor is at once open to the objection of being at best paradox and at worst nonsense. If God gave up some of his attributes in self-emptying, in order to participate fully in contingency, who was looking after the universe when God was suffering in the weakness of the cross? In answer it might be said that God can act in different ways at the same time, but this is scarcely illuminating. It might further be thought that the passive self-emptying of God scarcely takes account of the positive self-dedication of Jesus. It could also be objected that self-emptying does not really constitute an explanation, beyond affirming the self-giving nature of God's love.

This difficulty in speaking of the nature of the relationship between God and Jesus brings us straight back into discussion of the entire trinitarian problem. It is as a self-differentiating God, differentiated in a dynamic unity which includes different patterns of interaction, that we may begin to think of kenosis. The character of kenosis must be the character of the economic Trinity, that is, the character of self-giving, self-affirming love shown in the life of Jesus, sealed in his death and affirmed in his resurrection.

Taking up the concern of the Reformed Christology of the seventeenth century, we see that Jesus Christ is seen here as especially the mediator of salvation. When the logos becomes incarnate, the humanity of Christ is the perfect instrument of reconciliation. The divinity of the logos remains however in some sense existent apart from the incarnation. The divinity of Christ is involved concretely in the suffering of the man Jesus, but not abstractly so.

The man Jesus may have concretely a divine authority, but he does not have the abstract attributes of majesty and omniscience, for the finite is not capable of infinitude.

The Lutheran Christology of the same period stressed the reality of incarnation in a rather different way, emphasising the presence of God himself in and through the man Jesus Christ. One line of interpretation was followed in Helmstaedt along lines developed by Martin Chemnitz. A more logical but in some ways more extreme position was developed from positions worked out by Johann Brenz, in Tübingen, Wittenberg, Giessen and Jena. *Infinitum capax finiti*. There is an exchange of attributes, not only between the divine and human persons, but between the divine and human natures. It is then proper to say that the humanity of Christ is omnipotent , and that the divinity of Christ died. There is a perichoresis or circulation of attributes, but in one direction only, so that the divine attributes of majesty are conferred on the incarnate Christ.

Later, attempts were made to consider the perichoresis in the opposite direction, to stress the suffering of God, while the possession of the attributes of divinity by the humanity was qualified by distinctions between possession and use of the attributes, and between states of humiliation or self-emptying and exaltation. Continuing debate brought further degrees of fine tuning, especially concerning the precise nature of the divine presence. Attempts at reaching an agreed solution, e.g. the *Decisio Saxonica* of 1624, led to further debate, involving what has been described as an anatomical approach to Christology.

In the continuing debate there was much discussion of whether Christ voluntarily gave up the attributes of majesty (*kenosis* or self-emptying) or whether he simply concealed them (*krypsis*). There was an argument as to whether he had the potential still to use the attributes if he wished to do so, or if he did not. There was debate as to whether he deliberately concealed the attributes of majesty throughout his time on earth, or whether he occasionally manifested them as signs of his divinity.

But even if the humanity of Jesus had, in whatever form, the attributes of the divine nature, then the divine nature should also participate through perichoresis in the attributes of humiliation. So to the *genus majestaticum* in the human nature there was held to correspond a *genus tapeinotikum*, state of humiliation in the divine nature. There were then the consequences of *communicatio idiomatum* to work out. But these had to be related to the consecutive states of the life of Jesus before and after the crucifixion. Was the relationship of the divine and the human attributes the same before and after Easter? It was a point of honour with some Lutheran theologians to stress that Jesus manifested the divine majesty precisely in spending the three days in hell between crucifixion and resurrection. There came conventionally to be held to be two states of before and after the resurrection, the *status exinanitionis* (humiliation) and the *status exaltationis* (exaltation) in a temporal sequence, as well as the two natures in one person throughout the period. Some insisted however, rather parallel to the case of the natures, that the two states were also bound in a seamless dialectic.

In all this the orthodox Lutheran Christology, though stressing *theologia crucis*, God's participation in death, was at the same time paradoxically inclined to emphasise the involvement of the human rather than the divine nature of Christ in suffering. For the divine nature, incarnation, taking flesh, is itself a humiliation, which has to be counterbalanced by the continuity of majesty in the human nature.

For the Reformed Christology, incarnation is not in itself humiliation. It is rather the chosen self-expression of the divine love. For both, there is a further consequence, endurance of love through suffering and death. It is extremely important to bear in mind however that the crucifixion is in no sense the object or goal of incarnation. God is not suicidal. Crucifixion is the result of human sin in encounter with love incarnate.

A further step in this sphere was taken in kenotic theory, developing the hymn writer's paradox that, in the death of Jesus, God is dead. Here kenosis is the complete self-abandonment of God, followed by a sort of reconstitution of God in resurrection. Again the bounds of conceivability were being exceeded. It seemed obvious that beyond a certain point classical Christologies were no longer productive. But there are still lessons to be learned from combining contemporary and classical arguments in the continuing quest for perspective.

3. He Came Down from Heaven

Kenosis remains a fruitful concept. Lucien Richard's *A Kenotic Christology* is a remarkable tribute to the influence and power of the theology of Karl Rahner. 'True dialogue is the key to all relationship. God, in and by the fact that he empties himself, gives away himself, poses the other as his own reality. The basic element to begin with is not the concept of an assumption. God himself goes out of himself, God in his quality of the fullness which gives itself away.'[6] Change is possible through the

---

[6]Cf. L. Richard, *A Kenotic Christology*, 172.

becoming of the Son within the immanent Trinity . Creation and incarnation become possible through the Trinity. Richard does not develop the relation between kenotic Christology and creation. But it may suggest to us a way of linking the human dimension, which is central to Rahner's philosophy, to the cosmic dimension in God.

Kenosis opens a Christology which begins from the human person of Jesus, where we are, yet is grounded in God. This meets, for Richard, the need to find new ways of expressing transcendence in a technological age. Jesus' life and teaching was the enaction of the form of a servant. All the later titles of honour have to be understood in this framework. Jesus' self-giving, grounded in God's self-giving, is the condition of the possibility of human freedom. Kenosis, far from being a dilution of classical claims about God's power, is rather an affirmation about the nature of that power. It provides a basic clue to God's presence in human suffering, in solidarity with the human.

The Christian God defines himself as the God who is with us and for us, as personal agent in history. This relationship is as much from the side of man as of God, as Jesus has universal human significance. The invitation of faith is to self-giving on the basis of Jesus' self- giving, to compassion and solidarity on the basis of Jesus' solidarity.

In considering the person of Jesus Christ we are reflecting on a unity in faith's understanding. We cannot see the divinity or the humanity in isolation. In the same way the person and work of Christ, who he is and what he does for human salvation, are also a unity. Nevertheless, for the purpose of reflection we may have to consider these aspects separately, in order to understand the unity more clearly. But we must remember that in the nature of the case we may sometimes understand the divinity particularly in terms of the humanity and the humanity in terms of the divinity. We may understand the person sometimes best in terms of the work, and vice versa.

With these necessary qualifications, we may then go back to the question of the humanity of Christ. At one level, which we need consider neither as the highest or the lowest, but simply as an integral part of the picture, we understand Jesus the

Christ in the story, which is also the history, however incomplete
to us, of Jesus of Nazareth, his life and his death.

We have already explored the life of Jesus in the New
Testament narratives. This was the nature of the life in which
God was uniquely involved. This was the particularity of human
existing and striving. This was also, faith reflects, a pattern for
our reflection, a pattern of the character of true humanity,
before God. In the character of Jesus we see the divine
compassion in human terms, in his teaching and his action, his
temptations and his doubts, his suffering and his obedience.
Here we see the human side of the many dimensions of
Christology, the human face of God. In reflection on this man,
in Christologies from the side of man, Christian faith has
discovered much of the riches of Christ. It need not be
ashamed to own its real and lasting debt to such men as Adolf
Harnack.

Here there is a human and a moral struggle, a concrete
struggle between love and justice in human terms, an agony
which was too costly to be ignored by Christian minds. This too
is part of the truth of incarnation into particular humanity.
Here is endurance and dedication, faith and hope in the face
of despair, a holding on to God in the moment of disaster.
Here is a human life centred on devotion to God, and in the
service of his fellow human beings.

Jesus experienced, it would seem, temptation to sin. But he
did not sin. In this way he participated in our condition but not
in our blindness. It is true that he did not explicitly call for
social justice and political reappraisal. Yet in his gospel of
repentance, forgiveness and unconditional commitment to
neighbour, there is an entailment of all that love and justice
required. It is however part of this mystery that in the human
life of Jesus we may also see his divinity. It is this human being
who is also completely devoted to his Father in prayer and in
service. It is this human person who is inextricably mixed up in
the culture of his time, and yet does not actually sin. That is to
say, he is free of the pressures which all other human beings
exert on the others. He is uniquely committed to other people.
He offers forgiveness in the place of God. He heals diseases. He
is brought through death into resurrection. Divinity is expressed

in the created order precisely through complete humanity. In the person of Jesus we see humanity, and at the same time more than empirical humanity as we know it. It is part of the miracle of incarnation that divinity does not take away from humanity but perfects it.

Now I want to look at the divinity of Christ notionally from the side of God. Here we cannot see the divine in its appropriate empirical reality in the way in which we can see the empirically human. The mystery of the divine nature is signalled perhaps most recognisably by seeing Jesus in the sequence of before and after, as the point of fulfilment of the expectation of Israel and the point of inauguration of the coming Kingdom, between creation and new creation. This continuity of God's self-articulation is reflected in the tradition by talk of Jesus' pre-existence, and by the language of descent – he came down from heaven. Talk of pre-existence can create more confusion than illumination, when it is taken to mean that the man Jesus of Nazareth somehow existed before his birth, or that the logos or divine Son was somehow at work in creation from the beginning. The point of such language is rather to emphasise that God the creator is both beyond time as its creator, and involved in time as its redeemer. God is self-differentiated in himself. He is also the creator of time. But pre-existence ought not to suggest a kind of pre-incarnational temporality of Jesus Christ.

Further pointers to the divinity of Christ are sometimes seen in the mysteries of the Virgin Birth and the empty tomb. The essential theological point of these pointers is their reference to the manifestation of *the* miracle of incarnation, namely the resurrection of Christ. It is in the framework of the fulfilment of Israel's expectation of the birth of the Messiah, and the breakthrough of the Kingdom in resurrection from the dead, that the divinity of Christ is revealed to faith. This remains a revelation to faith, but it is nevertheless revelation. The resurrection has consequence in all the dimensions of Christology.

The mystery of the divinity of Christ is expressed to faith in the resurrection of Christ. But it is located at its deepest level in the fact of incarnation, in the engagement of God with human particularity in the contingency of history. For this reason, I regard Karl Rahner's emphasis that the divinity is most profoundly manifested in the humanity of Christ (and the humanity of Christ most profoundly present in his divinity) as especially illuminating. This is consonant with the emphasis which we found in the old Reformed Christology that the incarnation into human flesh was not in itself a humiliation but a self-fulfilment. In this way the categories of the classical Christology may be restructured to emphasise the profoundly personal nature of God's engagement with the human. At the same time the humanity of Christ, explored with new urgency since the Enlightenment, may be understood as a humanity not diminished but profoundly reaffirmed in the new creation.

I have said that the person of Christ may not be understood without consideration of the work of Christ, and vice versa. This work is what we must consider. But mention may appropriately be made here of the soteriological dimension of the person of Christ. Jesus Christ is not a figure to be understood with the aid of a set of Gnostic diagrams. His human life is itself, in action, the substantiation *in concreto* of what he is. This life has saving significance in the events which constitute it. Jesus' divinity is itself, in action, the act of incarnation and the reality of resurrection; this also has central saving significance for the human race. Therefore in being who he is Jesus acts for the redemption of humankind. In reconciling God and man, Jesus is who he is, as the one person, truly human and truly divine.

22

Reconciliation and Atonement

1. The Work of Christ

How are we to focus our understanding of the work of Christ, of reconciliation? We saw at the beginning of the section on Christology that discussion of the work of Christ tended traditionally to focus upon two directions, rescue from a great evil and entry into a great good. It is probably true to say that in any adequate appraisal of the work of Christ both these elements are involved, and Christians come to appreciate the one in the light of the other, in a reciprocal process.

Through Jesus Christ humankind is brought into God's peace, his salvation, his Kingdom. In the light of this new situation they turn in gratitude to God, and realise in a fresh way the poverty of their previous position. That is a fundamental fact of Christian experience through the ages. The Christian gospel is good news. It is the gospel of the incarnation, of the resurrection, of God with us, of his constant love upholding humankind.

The effect of the work of Christ may be to produce an escape from evil. But it is emphatically not an escape from this world. The world is reaffirmed as the sphere of God's gracious action in new creation. There is also however a reaffirmation of the connection between this world and God's eschatological consummation. The Kingdom is inaugurated now and continues for ever. Human death cannot separate us from God's love.

There is a vital truth in the affirmation that the incarnation was no accident or emergency measure. God's being is expressed in self-differentiation. It is part of the fulfilment of God's action to relate to his creation in new creation through the incarnation. To that extent, Christianity distinguishes itself from religions which view salvation in terms of escape from this world for the individual soul. Christianity brings us back to the continuing task of the humanisation of mankind. This too is part of the universal scope of salvation in every sphere of human activity, and beyond this throughout the physical cosmos. In committing himself to the fragility and complexity of a single human life, in its psychological and molecular complexity and contingency, and in raising Jesus from the dead, God signals and brings about a transfiguration in the order of the cosmos, a fundamental reordering in the structure of the universe. Here is a dimension complex beyond all human imagining.

The work of Christ is always at the same time the work of God. Reconciliation, we have stressed, is the fulfilment of the perfecting of relationship which began in creation. The goal of human salvation is the bringing of human life now into a deeper loving relationship with God, which is to be perfected in the eschaton. God's love is both the instrument and the reality of salvation. It is persuasive but not coercive, inclusive rather than exclusive.

The working out in human terms of this love takes place within the life and indeed the career of Jesus of Nazareth. Here the struggle between divine love and evil is worked out in innumerable small and costly conflicts, leading up to crucifixion. The physical struggles of Jesus' existence and the moral struggles which must have accompanied them, together with the faithfulness to God which went with them, constitute the human cost of salvation within the confines of a single life.

Through God the Father's love, the gulf between creator and creation is overcome from the side of humanity. The nature of this gulf is not simply the difference between creator and creature. That is part of the divine order from the outset. The gulf is rather between creator and sin, alienation of the creature from God. Jesus preaches and offers the forgiveness of sins. Human sin, individual and corporate lack of love, active hostility and intolerance, bring him to the cross. God's forgiveness is universalised in the victory over evil in the resurrection. This is the nature of atonement, the forgiveness of love without limit.

The whole question of the nature of the atonement remains a mystery which we shall never completely resolve. For the Judaeo-Christian tradition is linked inextricably to the fulfilment of God's law. That law, however interpreted, is broken by human failing in love, and there arises a cry for justice, against individual and corporate misdeeds. How is justice to be done? Between the fulfilment of justice and of love there is a conflict. If justice demands a due penalty, love offers mercy, but includes justice as fairness. Anselm is often thought to be the author of the notion that God sacrificed Christ to make satisfaction, as a penalty for the sins of man. But for him this is only a theoretical scenario. In fact God's self-giving love overcomes the position which a consideration of strict justice alone would require. The doctrine of penal substitution is a later development, on both sides of the Reformation.

Reflection on the Old Testament tradition of sacrifice, with the liturgical echoes in the eucharist and its ritual and sociological dimensions, has had a powerful influence on soteriology. The notion of Abraham's near-sacrifice of Isaac has been seen as an echo of God's sacrifice of his son – though we may reflect that this was precisely what God in the event did not require. The concept of Jesus' self-sacrifice on our behalf seems to sum up ultimate human concern for others. The completeness of Jesus' dedication, expressed in sympathy and empathy, has been a necessary counterpoise to the objective emphasis on the fact of his death as a condemned criminal. Central to the work of Christ is his resurrection, alongside his life and his death. There is sympathetic commitment. There is costly atonement. There is effective reconciliation in new life. Something has happened in the order of creation which makes possible a new order. This reality includes a transcendence of the barrier between life and death. This does not take away the tragedy of death. But it emphatically opens an eschatological future which has nothing to do with human triumphalism but which is the peace of God.

The peace of God has consequences for this world now. It

sets up the parameters of the divine kingdom, and invites us to live individually and socially within these pointers. Individual salvation is a reality, but it is not perfectly completed till all enjoy God's peace equally. Inequality before God and man is part of the corporate reality of sin, overcome but still to be eliminated. In opposition to centuries of tradition we may have to say today that as salvation is perfected corporately, so sin is largely corporate, though it also has individual dimensions. It is our corporate failure to love all our neighbours on this planet that is the greatest barrier we ourselves set up to full enjoyment of God's salvation. But the decisive step has been taken for us. Whatever our shortcomings, the light shone on in the darkness and will continue to shine.

2. The Atoning Narrative

The Christian tradition has long held that we can understand who Jesus was only by looking at his whole life and activity. Recent theology has stressed this inseparability of the person and work of Christ. Here we come to the other side of Christology, to the work of salvation through Christ, in the New Testament and in the history of the Church. There is a sense in which this section may be thought to be superfluous. I have argued that the whole Christian understanding of God, creator and redeemer, is about reconciliation. We have considered Christology at length, noting the indissolubility of the person and work of Christ. The theology of the love of God is in itself soteriology. Yet there remains at least one important ground for a separate discussion of the theme of atonement.

Atonement is an Old Testament concept which remains at the heart of Judaism. The treatment of the Jews in the Christian world in this century raises fundamental questions about the love of God, as the love of God in Christ. It is therefore appropriate to reflect further on the work of Christ under the rubric of that rather old-fashioned but central word, atonement.

In all areas of theology we are concerned with God and man, with subjective and objective, with invitation and response. Christology means that God has committed himself in a unique way to human persons. In this section I want to explore further some of the ways in which Christians have understood the consequences for their lives of God's reconciling presence, and to develop these ideas in the light of what has already been said.

The need for improvement, and the consequences of God's presence for this fulfilment, have been the object of reflection since the earliest days of humankind. Improvement in relations with God loomed large, with the need to propitiate divine displeasure. Prayer and sacrifice, the designation of sacred places, ascetic practices and a proliferation of religious rituals were common. Mediatorial figures, whether on the side of man, like sacred priests, or on the side of God, like lesser divine messengers, were introduced to facilitate communication and commerce.

Most of these features might be noted in the narratives of the Old Testament. God has created a chosen people, and has given them his law. The people have broken the law. Acts of atonement are necessary, in order to restore the flawed relationships. Where sacred rituals and rites of purification have been neglected, cleansing is required, and this may take place through offerings made by the priesthood, or by private individuals. It was possible that an animal could come to represent the alienated people, and be sacrificed to restore the people's relationship with God. But there is an increasing sense of a gulf between the people and their God, which only a messiah sent by God himself can heal. Humanity is incapable of its own redemption. This messiah remains the goal of the hope of the Jewish people. The prophets and wise men, among whom Jesus may be reckoned, anticipate this coming, but are not themselves its fulfilment.

Centrally important in the Old Testament, the word atonement does not feature widely in the New Testament, being used only by St. Paul. We cannot atone for our sins. Only God does this, not taking account of our shortcomings (Rom. 5; 10:2; 2 Cor. 5:18f.). We may therefore praise God, who has reconciled us to himself through Jesus Christ. Colossians speaks of the reconciliation of enemies (1:20), St. Mark (5:24) of the need to be reconciled with one's brother before being reconciled with God. Atonement is linked to propitiation and the forgiveness of sins. It is Christ who has brought atonement by dying 'outside the camp' in expiation of the sins of humanity (Hebrews).

The broken relationship between God and his people is to be healed by the coming of the Messiah, still expected by Judaism and fulfilled for Christians in Christ. That there will be a fulfilment is guaranteed by the covenant between God and his people in the Old Testament, and for Christians through word and sacrament, through baptism and eucharist.

The recognition that relationships between human beings, and between God and his people, were not always all that they might be appears to be a universal human conviction. A working towards better relationships, at least among the members of the chosen community and their God, seems an equally omnipresent priority. It was the conviction of the people of Israel, at least of important elements of the people at significant times, that reconciliation was to be sought from God himself. Christians have seen the decisive step in the events concerning Jesus.

3. The Eternal Sacrifice

When we ask ourselves how this conviction has shaped the memory of the Christian communities, we find in the period immediately after the New Testament writers a sense of thanksgiving for the reconciliation made at the cost of the blood of Christ. We have noted that despite its prominence in the New Testament the doctrine of the atonement received comparatively little emphasis in the earliest classical theology. Stress was laid on the recreation of mankind through the incarnation. Irenaeus' doctrine of recapitulation expressed the retrieval of the disaster brought by the first Adam in Christ, the second Adam. Origen can speak of Christ paying a ransom to the devil.

For Athanasius the Word became flesh to snatch mankind from destruction. Traces of a doctrine of satisfaction are first found in the West, in Tertullian and Cyprian. Augustine introduced a distinction between reconciliation and redemption as ransom from the devil. Anselm develops the classical doctrine of satisfaction. Satisfaction can only be made by the death of the God-man, because only God is capable of this complete obedience. This teaching was in essence repeated by St. Thomas. Luther stressed God's initiative in making possible the satisfaction. Calvin likewise saw the centre in God's grace, poured out through the threefold office of Christ as prophet, priest and king.

In the seventeenth century the doctrine came under increasing critical scrutiny, notably from the Socinians, who felt acutely the tension between satisfaction and forgiveness, and the difficulty in the idea that one man could bear the guilt of another. In modern theology the question has been approached in many different ways. Kant looked for salvation in the fulfilment of an ethical ideal, Hegel in the reconciliation of nature and spirit. For nineteenth-century German Protestant theologians we are reconciled to God, rather than God to us, and so the old theory has little to say to us. For others, in a tradition stemming from the Pietists, the sovereign love of God implies a critique of the doctrine of satisfaction. On the cross the love of God in Jesus destroys sin, and in the resurrection the new creation is inaugurated. Others saw the satisfaction as a self-sacrifice of Christ after the fashion of the Old Testament sacrifice, while yet others, e.g. the dialectical theologians, stressed the role of God himself in Christ as the judge judged in our place.

In this study we stressed the close connection between the understanding of God as creator and the understanding of God as reconciler. It is stressed that the doctrine of salvation encompasses equally the life, death and the resurrection of Christ. Nevertheless the gospels, after all, were passion narratives and it is from the death of Christ that Christians often continue to reflect on the meaning of salvation. This emphasis is not limited to one section of the Christian community. It is to be found equally in authors of liberal or conservative, of more modern or more traditional sympathies. The modern American writer, John Knox, says 'It must be recognised first that the death of Jesus was the actual centre of the event to which the Church looks back in memory and in which lay the beginnings of its own life.'[1]

---

[1] J. Knox, *The Death of Christ*, 133, 164, 174

It was also, however, the death of Jesus Christ, as John Knox also reminds us. The significance of the death is closely related to the significance of the life which preceded it. Faith, but also love and devotion to Jesus, would have accentuated the impact of his death. Equally the Church's own openness to persecution would have helped to cement the bond in identification with Jesus' persecution. Knox says:

> One can do three things with the Cross, and only three. One can deny that it happened because if acknowledged it would make nonsense of life. One can acknowledge it and decide in consequence that life is meaningless. Or one can find in it a clue to a deeper meaning in life than otherwise appears. There are no other possibilities. (164, see footnote 1)

He stresses the continuing significance of the death of Christ in the Church's sacramental life. From time to time Christians celebrate together the Church's deep remembrance of the death of Christ. It is best seen by the symbolic action of their participation in the body of his crucifixion and in the blood of his perfect sacrifice.

> God knows we are not worthy. We have let Christ die alone. But though we have failed to bear our Cross, He did not fail to bear His. And for all our sins, past, present and future, we do not profane the body of our Lord but only each time we fall beneath our Cross we grasp at the foot of His and take the love God offers us in Him. (174)

Remarkably similar sentiments to those of John Knox can be found in the writings of the Glasgow theologian James Denney, almost seventy years before, coming from a very different theological tradition. Denney put it thus, 'The simplest truth of the gospel and the profoundest truth of theology must be put in the same words "He bore our sins".'[2] Denney then goes so far as to say this:

> It is the doctrine of the Atonement which secures for Christ his place in the gospel and which makes it inevitable that we

[2] J. Denney, *The Death of Christ* 283, 318.

should have a Christology or a doctrine of his person. Reduced to the simplest religious expression the doctrine of the Atonement signifies that we owe to Christ and to His finished work our whole being as Christians.

In noting these comments from Knox and Denney, however, we may reflect that the death of Jesus is the central link in a set of events which gains in significance from what precedes and what follows it. It is first in Israel that the hope and promise of God's salvation is expressed. It is in Jesus' preaching of the coming of the Kingdom that the good news of salvation, now a freedom from bondage, peace with God is announced. In the death of Jesus which is the outcome of his mission in the service of the Kingdom that mission is brought to a climax. It is in resurrection from the dead that God's victory is achieved in the face of all that is evil in the world. Kasper in *Jesus the Christ* speaks of the soteriological significance of Jesus' death in these terms, 'Jesus was among his disciples as one who served' (p. 22-3). Following Jesus meant following him in this service. If anyone would be first, he must be last of all and servant of all (Mark 11:22).

Against this background the idea of the sacrifice of his life as a service to his followers, just as all his activities had been, must have forced itself upon Jesus. The fact that Jesus did not directly claim the title Servant of God, any more than that of Messiah, Son of God, does not show that he did not know himself to be the Servant of God who served and suffered for men. In this way, in his life and in his death, Jesus is a man for others, existing for others. In his very essence, it is that which makes him the personified love of God.[3] Kasper stresses Jesus' complete aloneness at the end. Even Jesus' immediate disciples misunderstood him at the end and he was forced to make his last journey in anonymity. He was on his own. He made it like all his others, in obedience to his Father and for the service of others. That obedience and service became the only point at which the promised coming of the Kingdom of God could become a reality, became reality in a way which made all

[3]W. Kasper, *Jesus the Christ*, 120.

previous models useless. Finally, in the ultimate loneliness and complete darkness of blind obedience all Jesus could do was leave to the Father the manner of its coming.

The depths of human atrocity are well brought out in *Atonement: From Holocaust to Paradise,* by Ulrich Simon. This is a remarkable study of the theology of atonement, which draws on depictions of crime and punishment in literary traditions. Ulrich Simon, formerly Professor of Christian Literature in London, survivor of a family decimated by the Holocaust, is eminently qualified to tackle this theme.

How can we justify the ways of God to man when we stand in the midst of violence? Overwhelmed by atrocity, how can we comprehend guilt and the possibilities of reconciliation? In the natural world there is a sphere without guilt. In human life all guilt is often denied, in the name of *realpolitik*. Healing of guilt is strictly limited to men of good will. Institutional violence fosters lies, fraud and cruelty.

How can we conceive all this? Dante and Marlowe, Goethe and Thomas Mann record the consequences of pacts with the devil. Most relevant to our time is Dostoevsky's *The Devils*, in which individual crime and cosmic evil combine. How can the murderer come to repentance? Kafka's *The Trial* epitomises the torment of the contemporary damned.

It is not so much death as atrocity which is the final evil. Only God can produce final redemption, in the future of his Kingdom. Has atonement been achieved? Nothing can separate us from God's love in Jesus Christ. Here is the cosmic redemption of cosmic evil, union through the Holy Spirit, echoed in great sacred music. Against the continuance of torture, the only hope is that 'out there' the truth will prevail, the right will be vindicated. This is a powerful cry, which needs to be heard.

4. Love and Judgement

Jesus' mission of loving concern led to his death. 'In the case of Jesus the wonder is not so much that he was struck down so quickly as that he lasted as long as he did.'[4] As saviour he

---

[4]G. O'Collins, *Interpreting Jesus*

brought liberation, redemption and transforming love. He liberated humankind from ultimate bondage to the powers of evil which have wrought such havoc on the earth in every generation of life, and not least in our own time. This was a costly and painful victory. He brought redemption by expiating the guilt of humankind, not in some narrow calculation but by the overflow of his compassion for his fellow men, in such a way that mercy is identified with judgement. His self-giving love produced a new situation, beyond self-righteousness and self-justification, in which a cosmic breakthrough occurred. The created order cannot be ultimately as bleak as it often seems.

It is true that atonement is concerned with justice as well as with mercy, with judgement as well as forgiveness. But the justice which Jesus creates, the just unjustly judged, is not fundamentally a justice tied to our individual selfhood. It is a justice in which cosmic injustice is unmasked, in which the gates of hell are torn down. Here the collective madness of many human power structures, the inner dynamic of institutional violence, is exposed. That is why Christians can speak of Good Friday, because out of real disaster faith believes that real reconciliation has come.

This concern for cosmic justice, rather than a purely forensic understanding of individual righteousness, can be seen to underlie the imaginative treatment of the relation of incarnation to atonement found in the theology of Karl Barth. The reference back to incarnation, precisely in trying to spell out the significance of atonement, is of course not unique to Barth. Walter Kasper says 'Jesus is the mode in which the self-communicating, self-outpouring love of God exists on the human scene; he is this for us.'[5]

5. Forgiveness

God's costly self-giving in Jesus Christ is incarnation. God's costly self-giving in Jesus Christ is atonement. Richard Swinburne has spoken of the central words in a Christian

---

[5]Karl Barth, *Church Dogmatics* 4.1, 4.2.6; W. Kasper, *The God of Jesus Christ,* 171

understanding of salvation being guilt, atonement and forgiveness. Salvation is both positive and negative. It is positive in the inauguration of the Kingdom, and of the joy of new creation, through the events concerning Jesus. It is negative in the pain and suffering through which Jesus overcame evil and death, evil which reflected and actualised the human condition of frequent inhumanity to God and man, in the life, death and resurrection of Jesus.

There is a frequent paradox in human understanding of guilt. Often we feel guilt about things for which we should not feel guilty, and we don't feel guilt about things for which we ought to feel guilty. Sociologists have made distinctions between cultures centred on concepts of guilt and cultures centred on concepts of shame. Some people are more conscious of guilt than others. There is a flood of literature on guilt in the modern behavioural sciences. For some people it is part of their human pathology that they never feel guilt, in any circumstances. Modern technology makes it possible to treat soldiers with drugs so that they will commit any atrocity and be almost unaware of their actions afterwards.

In the light of the love of God, there is much of which humanity has been and is guilty. Only God can break this circle of wrong done and guilt acquired. Christians believe that he has done this in the atonement made for all this wrong through the life, death and resurrection of Jesus. The judicial imagery of the classical theologies paints a grim picture of the raw realities of much human life which is more recognisable in our century of totalitarianism than it appeared to be to the more optimistic thinkers of the nineteenth century. Purifying the assessment of our human predicament of barbarity does not actually clarify the situation. The problem however was that in some classical theology God was himself pictured as a mirror image, and so in some sense as an accessory to barbarity. God did not punish, torture, murder his son to produce moral improvement of however great value. In such a view the end is subverted by the means.

Atonement is made by the opposite of evil, by self-giving, unconditional love. God is not the torturer but the victim. God the Son is the judge judged in our place. Because the cross is followed by the resurrection, atonement is effective. The landscape is transformed by being flooded with God's creative love. Atonement creates forgiveness. However bitter, entrenched and hardened human divisions may be, God has provided a way which overcomes them. Human nature being what it is, we do not always find it possible to begin again. National memories are easily inflamed. Racial tensions are easily fanned. In families deep rooted conflicts do not vanish overnight. It is difficult to see a single root meaning in God's forgiveness. It is rather the creation of a framework in which different values prevail, in which God's love is overwhelming. Forgiveness produces reconciliation. Not automatically, or as a matter of course, but often through long pain and endurance, God's love through Jesus Christ has been seen to transform human relations, between individuals and groups, between peoples and nations.

It is perhaps useful here to summarise briefly the main classical theories of atonement.

1. The *incarnational* theory. This is expressed negatively in Gregory of Nazianus' phrase 'the unassumed is the unredeemed'. Positively stated, it affirms that the Word took flesh and redeemed flesh. By identification with the totality of the human, the logos of God redeemed humanity. Since the logos is equal to and identified with God the Father, the Godhead participates in fallen humanity, yet without change, to redeem fallen humanity. Later identification was extended to include the self-emptying participation of the Trinity in humanity.

2. The *satisfaction* theory. God's honour has been stained by man's sin. Man owes reparation, but cannot make it. Christ has given God satisfaction, on behalf of man, and this has brought divine forgiveness. Christ has to share human nature in order to atone in man's place, he has to share fallen human nature. Yet he cannot himself sin, for this would render him too incapable of making satisfaction.

3. The satisfaction theory may be developed further, in a theory of *penal substitution*. If the justice of God is to be upheld, sinful man

must be punished. Christ bore the full punishment on behalf of man. The merit of this theory is that it recognises the gravity of sin and the absolute need for God's justice to be upheld. It has always been difficult to conceive of Christ's bearing the sin of the whole world. Christ's identification with all the human, especially his fallen nature, may begin to be understood. But his identification is precisely the identification of God, participation in the human by the divine, and not an alienation from the human by the divine. The contradiction is felt in all its sharpness by God himself, and justice is served through the passion of God. If this is the intention of penal substitution, there are clearly less misleading ways of expressing it.

4. *Christ as victor.* Here the defeat of evil in love is envisaged as a battle between cosmic powers of good and evil, in which God in Christ is victor, destroying the devil and all the powers of evil. Such a metaphysical battle may seem very far from human life. Yet the imagery has perhaps received new meaning in our century, in the destruction of millions in the technology of totalitarian liquidation, in the kingdoms of the night.

5. *Moral influence* or exemplarist theories. Here the example of Jesus' suffering love is seen as evoking an answering love in mankind. As it stands such a simple statement would appear to be belied by the selfishness which often leads to the destruction of the weak by the powerful in society. It is however modified by reflection on the fact that Jesus' human example is the more effective because it is sustained by the power of the creator himself. It is validated by the fact of the resurrection, and as such represents a cosmic triumph of God's justice over evil. As such the theory develops into a cumulative case.

We may reflect that an adequate theory of atonement is likely to include a number of strands developed as a cumulative case, though a mere rehearsal of a number of unrelated alternative theories will not provide explanation.

We have seen that the whole study of theology requires us to take careful account of issues and questions which simply never arose for classical doctrinal statements of the past. The articulation of the consequences of particular humanity in Jesus, the problems in speaking clearly about divine action, and the need for the political and social dimensions of the gospel to be spelled out, are areas which come readily to mind. Yet the need for precision here need not make us blind to the poetic quality of much classical theology, which may still stimulate the theological imagination to reflect again on the wonder of the gospel.

Nowhere is this more evident than in reflection on the relation of atonement and incarnation. *O felix culpa, quae tantam potuit mereri redemptionem.* Christians have always been clear that the relationship between the two is ultimately a mystery, God's mystery. Here is an identification which is indeed beyond comprehension. The biblical story is simple but its simplicity conceals complexity. God created man in his own image, in perfect freedom for fellowship with himself. Somehow man fell, disrupting relations both with God and his environment. God in his love did not allow man to go into annihilation. Choosing and creating Israel as a people for himself, he revealed himself in a word of promise, of covenant. Providing a means of covenant response, of restoring the fellowship, Israel remained unmoved, rejecting God's messengers and breaking the covenant. At last God sent his son, whom they also killed. In the face of rejection he mysteriously broke down the impasse. In his death he overcame death and being for ever alive has created a new human fellowship with God. In humiliation and exaltation, through faith and loyalty, through judgement, justice and forgiveness a new reality has been moulded.

Where man refused to recognise creaturely limitations and pretension, Jesus lived a life of costly devotion to God, being able to be completely selfless through complete dedication. In the language of the classical Christology, in the assumption of complete humanity by the Son of God, Christ's human nature has its subsistence not in itself but in the being of God, and is given truly authentic existence in the divine existence. In Jesus' life there is both unconditional obedience to God and uninhibited commitment to man. His life of trust, of prayer, of mission, is the ground of ours. He is God's witness, present with an indefinable authority, meeting dark with light, force with humility. This compassionate humility is not without its own power. Jesus speaks God's word of reconciliation, bringing healing of mind and body, inaugurating the Kingdom of peace which is confirmed in his resurrection.

This classical story is meaningfully reconceived in the work of Barth and Rahner, Kasper and Schillebeeckx. I want to look here at Barth's version. Following Martin Luther, Karl Barth sees the humiliation of the Son of God and the exaltation of the Son of Man as two forms of the one reconciling action of Jesus Christ. Humiliation demonstrates the glory of his deity and exaltation restores his true humanity.

'That Jesus Christ is very God is shown in his way into the far country in which he the Lord became a servant. *Tua res agitur* made sin for us, he stands in our place' (*Church Dogmatics*, 4.1, 241). The very heart of the atonement is the overcoming of sin: sin in its character as the rebellion of man against God, and in its character as the ground of man's hopeless destiny in death. It was to fulfil this judgement on sin that the Son of God took our place as sinners (253). He took our place as judge. He took our place as judged. He was judged in our place. And he acted justly in our place.'

But the real significance of the *pro nobis* is consummated in the resurrection. Here is new creation. 'In him man is made the new man, reconciled with God' (4.2, 4). This is tied in eternity to election. 'The true humanity of Jesus Christ was and is and will be the primary context of God's eternal election.' His power is weakness, 'a defiance of the power of destruction which enslaves man, of *phthora* in all its forms' (232) Yet it is the cross which controls and penetrates and determines this whole (242).

This fulfilment of covenant in new creation has been expressed in reflection on a wide variety of Old Testament redemption imagery, notably in John Calvin's elegant exposition of the threefold office of Christ as prophet, priest and king. It reflects also of course the image in Hebrews of Christ as the perfect high priest, setting human life on a new basis by the seal of his blood, and Paul's reflection on righteousness. God's own faithfulness and righteousness create new righteousness. Through the 'wondrous exchange' disrupted existence is restored and peace with God is achieved, for all through Christ, by individuals appropriated through the Holy Spirit.

The cross is the cross of the resurrected one, and the resurrection is the resurrection of the crucified. Beyond this is the peace of the divine Kingdom, the presence of the king who is the lamb that was slain, ruling by reconciliation, the realm of the triune blessedness. This goal is the result of the struggle of the divine love with the forces of evil, the fruit of the cry of absolute dereliction on the scaffold.

When in the face of injustice in the world we ask where God is, we may always say that God is and was in Christ, at the sharp end of oppression. Faith in the face of evil is participation in good, in union with this God. As the community of the faithful, the Church is brought into participation in the mystery of God in Christ, through word and sacrament, through service as the servant Church in the world. Because this world, our world, has already been taken up into the new creation, a world with an eschatological dimension, it is possible to be the Church in the world, with a faith grounded firmly in God as the ultimate reality for humankind.

6. The Scope of Atonement

One of the best modern studies of atonement is F.W. Dillistone's *The Christian Understanding of Atonement*. Dillistone began with a study of the human condition under the heading 'Alienation and Atonement', and went on to analyse theories of atonement under eight different themes. These were, in order, the eternal sacrifice, the unique redemption, the supreme tragedy, the decisive judgement, the all-embracing compassion, the all-inclusive forgiveness, the image of perfect integration, and the word of final reconciliation.

What Dillistone described as the 'First Analogue to the Atonement' was the theme of the eternal sacrifice. Disaster faces the universe. One alone can effect a rescue, at the cost of his own life. Christ is that one. Through him recapitulation to perfection is achieved. This is a theme repeated in numerous world religions. In its ancient Greek versions it has become fused with versions of Christian soteriology. In Plato and Aristotle there are sophisticated versions of the myth in the expectation of a future eternal perfection, while the whole scheme of things in Neoplatonism is based on a scheme of emanation and return, of *exitus* and *reditus*.

In the early Church the most impressive statement of the theme was that of Irenaeus. Creation, fallen through man's sin, could only be restored through man. Adam was saved in Christ and creation was saved through the redeemed Adam. In modern times the theme of restoration to life through death, as a coincidence of opposites, was powerfully developed by Hegel. Jesus' death is the death of God. This death produces resurrection, mirroring the process at the heart of all that happens in the universe. A further development of the notion of God in process was provided in the work of L.S. Thornton, the first of many examples of Process Christology.

Dillistone's next major category is that of the unique redemption. In the Ancient Near East there were numerous redemption myths, taken up and developed in the Old Testament. In the New Testament the cosmic powers of evil crucify Christ. But his resurrection is cosmic victory, notably in the Johannine theology. The death of Jesus becomes a trap for the devil. Christ defeats evil by preaching to the dead in hell after his death. No one has explored this imagery more fully perhaps than Gustav Aulén in *Christus Victor*, though the radical nature of evil in all human society has also been much stressed in theology after each of the world wars, e.g. by Reinhold Niebuhr in America.

The supreme tragedy is the next analogue. There is tragedy, pain, suffering and purifications, in much of the drama of the ancient world, notably in Greek Tragedy. In the Old Testament there is the central ritual of the Day of Atonement. The gospels' narratives, and especially Mark's Gospel, are passion narratives, and to that extent are tragedies. Yet the gospel is not a tragedy, for there is ultimate victory over death. The medieval miracle plays were of course important precursors of modern drama. But there remains between the times an important element of the tragic, in all the disasters which are caused by human inhumanity to man, and in natural havoc and disaster.

Dillistone's second parable is that of the decisive judgement. The themes of law, judgement, punishment and atonement run through the history of Israel. Judgement on the sins of Christians was a constant issue in the early Church. Anselm's *Cur Deus Homo* was a profound reflection on sin and satisfaction, in which God allows Christ to suffer the punishment for the sins of humankind. Calvin stressed Christ's fulfilment and reinforcement of the Old Testament law. In legal theory, developed in different ways, it was axiomatic that where there is crime there must also be appropriate punishment. Law is clearly fundamental to society. No one can be made to depend on his neighbour's moral qualities and inward perfection. Yet the God of Christians is a God of forgiveness and reconciliation. whose grace goes beyond the varieties of legal theory in its manifold forms.

This thought may serve as an appropriate introduction to the third analogue, that of the all-embracing compassion. Compassion, says Dillistone, is characteristic in the Old Testament of private rather than public life, of the family. The passionate relationship between Jesus and God on the one hand and Jesus and his fellow men on the other is brought out in the agony in the garden of Gethsemane. Compassion is a keynote of the development of Marian devotion, and of much medieval painting, e.g. the great Isenheim altarpiece. Compassion has been differently interpreted in interpretation of the relationships between men and women through the ages. Compassion raises too the issue of the passibility or impassability of God, reflected for example by F.D. Maurice and R.C. Moberly in their interpretation of the divine sacrifice.

Dillistone's projection receives light from a new angle in the third parable of the all-inclusive forgiveness. Reconciliation was taken up in humanism and in the development of the understanding of friendship. Reconciliation was a central theme for John McLeod Campbell. Jesus makes a perfect response to God in sorrow for human transgression, entering into the mind of God and into the mind of the sinner. Christ's identification with the holiness of God was to be emphasised by

P.T. Forsyth, by H.R. Mackintosh, and, as the revelation in personal terms of suffering love, by H.R. Farmer.

From forgiveness, Dillistone moves to the image of perfect integration. Mystical union with Christ was central to Johannine symbolism, and continued not only in the Neoplatonic strain of classical Christianity, but also in Schleiermacher's concept of redemption, and in Jung's psychotherapy. The fourth parable is the word of final reconciliation. The God of the psalmist is the answer to the cry of deepest despair. The words of the last supper, of Gethsemane and of the cross are words of a turning to God from the depths. For Martin Luther, for Pascal and Kierkegaard, for Dietrich Bonhoeffer, life comes out of disaster. The freedom of God overcomes the shadow of death.

The events of the life, death and resurrection of Jesus, and the divine movement from creation to reconciliation, are reflected in human thought in innumerable ways. God was in Christ reconciling the world to himself. As humanity has developed so Christians have responded with further meditation on their faith. Reconciliation was seen to have cosmic, personal and social elements, different aspects were stressed at different times in prose and also in poetry, art and music. Those who have shared in this journey have experienced the peace of God, 'a peace which passeth all understanding for it is in very truth the peace of God'.

I have devoted considerable space to Dillistone because in my view his book was a major achievement, which deserves much wider recognition than it has received. It is indeed a work of synthesis and description rather than a single integrated conception from the mind of its author. But its great strength lies in bringing before the mind of the reader in well-organised form the riches of the Christian tradition on atonement, to stimulate further the imagination concerning the centre of the faith.

We shall now sum up this section on the substance of Christology, the being and action of God in redemption. God was in Christ reconciling the world to himself. In the events concerning Jesus the nature of God as a self-differentiated, self-giving God is brought to expression in the world. Jesus of Nazareth lives a life of complete devotion to God and to man.

He proclaims and inaugurates the coming of the Kingdom of God. He summons to repentance. He brings forgiveness and the peace of God. He is tried and crucified. God raises him from the dead. Through God's identification with Jesus, human salvation is achieved, in all dimensions. These include personal, cosmic, historical, social and political dimensions.

The person of Jesus remains in many respects mysterious to us. We have to use all our powers of imagination to try to comprehend the many strands and levels of his challenge to our lives. He is there, completely devoted to God, a pattern for prayer, worship and service of God. He is also a pattern for service to humankind, in all his action, of concern and pastoral care, of identification, solidarity, anger, judgement, protest, calm and serenity, anguish and despair. Jesus' life of commitment to God and man is part of the drama of redemption. It is linked to the redemptive significance of his death and resurrection. Here God takes his chosen path of participation in the contingency of a single human life. Here is created a new freedom for human relationship with God, a new possibility for human flourishing.

I have said that the person of Christ may not be understood without consideration of the work of Christ, and vice versa. This work is what we must now consider. But mention may be made appropriately here of the soteriological dimension of the person of Christ. Jesus Christ is not a figure to be understood with the aid of a set of Gnostic diagrams. His human life is itself, in action, the substantiation *in concreto* of what he is. This life has saving significance in the events which constitute it. Jesus' divinity is in itself, in action, the act of incarnation and the reality of resurrection; this also has central saving significance for the human race. Therefore in being who he is Jesus acts for the redemption of humankind. In reconciling God and man, Jesus is who he is, as the one person, human and divine.

23

Christ the Bread of Life

1. Christ, Word and Sacrament

Christology involves the events concerning Jesus, his life, death and resurrection. It involves the history of Israel and of Israel's God. It also involves the Spirit, the spirit of the crucified and risen Christ. We have already spoken of the Spirit as the bearer of the divine presence to humankind and we shall later explore the consequences of the presence of the Spirit in the created order. Here we consider further the reality of Jesus Christ as the reality of the presence of God after the resurrection.

God is with us. Traditionally this identification and its consequences have been expressed in terms of incarnation and atonement. Increasingly these have come to be seen as a single integrated movement from creation to recreation in reconciliation. We must now try to understand further the continuing consequences of reconciliation, first from the perspective of understanding Christ as the bread of life, the results of the presence of the risen Christ in the world, and then from an understanding of the Spirit in the world.

Christ in the Johannine metaphor is the bread of life. He is the basic source of human nourishment, the spring of living water, the true vine. Some time after his book on *The Nature of the Atonement* John McLeod Campbell wrote a short study of the sacraments, under the title *Christ the Bread of Life*. This was an excellent choice. The bread of life combines the role of word and sacrament, pointing to a specific message and a vital gift of salvation.

Christ is both word and sacrament. All that has been said of the word incarnate applies to Christ, along with the tradition of Christ as the basic sacrament. The consequences in the ecclesiastical traditions, in the churches of the word and the churches of the sacrament, equally follow from Christ himself.

Christ is the word. As such he comes with a specific message, pointing us back to his teaching, pointing to the consequences of his resurrection. He is also on occasion a silent word, a word expressed not in articulated expression but in action. Sometimes too he is a passive word, suffering and grieving with the suffering of his people, enduring till the full realisation of his Kingdom.

This state of affairs is also reflected in the complementary Christian tradition of the affirmation of Christ as sacrament. We shall not consider here in detail the significance of the individual sacramental signs of baptism and eucharist. But it is worth taking careful note of the Christian understanding that the personal presence of Christ is made manifest as a recognisable reality to believers through the preaching of the word and the celebration of the sacraments in the worshipping life of the community. The presence of Christ as a reality in his world does not cease at the resurrection though its form of manifestation changes. On the contrary, the present of Christ becomes the ground which sustains the life of humanity as a new creature in Christ.

The understanding of Jesus Christ as God's sacrament for the world has echoes in various branches of the Christian tradition. A sacrament has classically been defined as an outward and visible sign of an inward and spiritual grace. God is the ultimate source, ground and sustainer of all grace. Jesus Christ is the incarnate reality generated by God's turning in love towards his created order. Jesus is God's being for us. As such he is *the* sacrament of God. In him are united all the various dimensions of reality, spiritual and temporal. That is why Christology always has many dimensions, historical, political, social, moral, existential, metaphysical and cosmological. The imagery of Christ as sacrament may be a powerful reminder that the gospel is not simply a matter of word or words, of theory or language. It is concerned directly with the entire sphere of physical reality in the universe, and with the spiritual dimensions of that physical reality. The gospel is concerned with the consequences of geophysics as much as with the consequences of literary criticism. It is also concerned with sacramental reality in the Christian community, with the prayers and devotion of Christians over the ages as well as with their written works and articulated theories. It is not without significance that the imagery of Christ as the bread of life has evoked a striking resonance in the human mind over many centuries in widely differing cultures. The further development of the consequences of sacrament in the sacramental signs of the community will concern us again.

2. The Way, the Truth and the Life

This Johannine phrase provides us with a particularly appropriate avenue for approaching questions of the ultimate significance of Christ. Jesus Christ is the way. Human life involves a restless striving, individual and corporate, for improvement in the quality of life. It involves a search for moral values, for standards of goodness to be articulated and to be achieved. It involves a search for corporate concern to be exercised in society. The Christian understanding of Christ is that he is the way. He is God's guide to the nature of goodness and love. The life, death and resurrection of Christ have a moral value. That is why there is a constant struggle between love and justice in a world in which there is evil, in which there is opposition to God's love. Jesus' struggle had a central moral dimension, highlighted in the narrative of the agony in the garden and in the lonely decision to go on to almost certain destruction. Christ is the way for Christians. He is also the way for all humankind, a way related to other ways. We shall return to the relation of Christ's way to other moral and religious ways.

Christ in Christian tradition and faith is also the truth. The assertion that a person is the truth is a strange assertion. It has however been central to classical Christianity in its strongest sense. The Christian gospel asserts that Christ is the reality which embodies the ultimate truth about the nature of all reality. Such truth has many dimensions, as in the case of the way, and may be articulated in different ways in relation to these dimensions. Different philosophical traditions offer different theories of truth, none of which would be irrelevant to reflection on Christ as the truth. Christ, in classical Christianity, is true God and true man. The nature of this truth needs to be spelt out in relation to the various dimensions of reality. These projections in turn may help to illuminate our understanding of the true relationship of Christ to God and man. Our understanding of this truth will never be complete. But it may nevertheless be substantial, the more substantial the more we renew the effort.

Christ is the way, the truth and also the life. God is not simply the embodiment of a moral or metaphysical principle, he is a living God. Christ is a living presence, creating and sustaining new life, in and beyond the bounds of the physical order. It is worth remarking that for the Christian Christology has affinities not only with the humanities and the natural science, but also with the life sciences. Christ is the sustainer of life. This does not necessarily lead however to support for theories of 'reverence for life' of any sort. For we are concerned with life in Christ, life which places emphasis on our temporal life, but also on an eschatological dimension of eternal life. This is a fruit of the resurrection, for all who have lived and died in the history of humanity. This reflection again leads on to the eschatological dimension of reconciliation, which we shall reconsider in the chapters on the Spirit.

I want to return to appraisal of the claim that Christ is the truth. The primary aspect of Christ as the truth is indicated by what has already been said of Christ as word and sacrament. Christ is God's self-manifestation in the created order. Christ is the basic clue to the understanding of God. This is a fundamental and also a highly controversial claim, in the context of the urgent contemporary search for a theology of the world religions, a search to which we shall return in speaking of Christ and culture.

The truth of Christ has different implications in the various different spheres of Christology. Truth in Christ has an historical dimension. Jesus of Nazareth was a figure in the course of human history, whose life was led in particular historical circumstances, whose death took place under Pontius Pilate.

This historical dimension has economic, social and political implications. It affects all the life of humankind in the light of public history. Truth in Christ has anthropological and existential dimensions. Here are standards and norms for a Christian understanding of the human, for individuals as selves and in their relationships with other selves. Truth in Christ has a cosmological dimension. Through the life, death and resurrection of Jesus Christ there is inaugurated a new creation for the whole physical order. This may be focused in man, but it has implications for all life and for the cosmos as itself to be fulfilled in God's creative and redemptive purpose. Truth in Christ has a metaphysical dimension. As such it is a clue, though not necessarily a key, to the continuing human quest for meaning and order in human existence and in human understanding of the universe.

There need not be thought to be a single divinely authorised interpretation either of history, or anthropology, or cosmology, or metaphysics. The claim is, rather, that consideration of Christ provides for Christians a necessary dimension of the understanding of the ultimate meaning of these spheres. Consideration of truth in Christ will not always provide a clearer, or even a more integrated picture. But it will point for Christians to the heart of the matter, to the ultimate truth of being and existence.

3. Christ and Culture

Jesus of Nazareth lived at a particular time as a member of a particular nation in a particular place. He shared in the cultural norms, aspirations and limitations of that people. Yet his message was not specifically limited to any one group. It was concerned with the new people of God, which was to spread, following the fulfilment of the Old Testament promise, as God's salvation through all lands.

It was decided fairly early in the life of the apostolic communities that the gospel was intended for all humankind. God's concern for humanity was unlimited. The Jewish people remains historically unique as being the historical source of redemption in Christ. But beyond this, no nation or group is privileged before God above any other nation or group. Jesus stresses his mission to the oppressed, the poor, the marginalised in society, because they are often furthest from the peace and justice which are the hallmarks of the Kingdom. But God loves all human beings equally.

It follows from this equality of God's love in Christ that all racism or prejudice on similar grounds is contrary to the love of God. But is often held that stress on the uniqueness, decisiveness and centrality of Christ, or of the doctrine of the incarnation, inevitably leads to a negative judgement on all other religions and their adherents, even to the point that those who are not committed Christians are reckoned to be damned. Such an argument has been forcefully put in recent years by John Hick, Paul Knitter and others. We have suggested already that this however is not a necessary conclusion.[1]

Theologians who have traditionally taken an exclusive view of salvation in Christ have not always drawn the negative inference that those who do not become Christians during their lives are damned. Even Karl Barth, whose encounters with Nazism led him to emphasise the inherent ambiguity of religion, held that the Holy Spirit operated in the world, among the religious and the non-religious, in ways entirely mysterious to us.

Many scholars have in recent years adhered to an inclusive understanding of Christ. They have wished to retain an understanding of Christ as the decisive, final clue to God's salvation and to the nature of God. But this decisiveness may well remain hidden to many, perhaps to most human beings on earth. The centrality of Christ will first be made clear to all humankind eschatologically. Then God will be seen as the self-giving God whose self-giving is characterised definitely through his history, including the history of his one incarnation in

[1]See P. Knitter (ed.) *The Myth of Christian Uniqueness*. In this collection Raymond Pannikar stresses the importance of the kenotic Christ, in writing of 'the christic principle'. 'The Christian point of insertion is the kenotic experience of Christ, which entails acceptance of and openness to the Spirit'(112). Paul Knitter lays emphasis on right practice, a soteriological liberation theology of religions, with a preferential option for the poor and non-persons (192).

Christ. A third approach would be basically pluralist.[2] In such a perspective the central figures of the major world religions could be seen as guides to the character of God and of his salvation. All would have equal validity for the culture with which they were primarily associated. Jesus Christ would be one such major guide. It might be possible to draw parallels and find similarities and overlaps between these paths, so that there would be a unity in diversity, or reconciled diversity, somewhat as in Christian ecumenical dialogues.

It seems to me that the inclusive approach is by far the best for a Christian understanding of God. Both the exclusive and the pluralist approaches limit salvation through Christ to a particular sections of humankind. It is absolutely basic to the Christian understanding of Christ that he is not partisan. He is not concerned for one particular group, but for all, regardless of nation, creed or race. The basic objection to my perspective is that such a position is often held to be arrogant and imperialistic.

If the approach to other faiths were to be insensitive, condescending or manipulative, then it would indeed be entirely objectionable. However, it is possible to consider an inclusive position in a quite different manner. God's power, as the power of new creation, is not diminished by his historical involvement in the life, death and resurrection of Jesus. But his power manifests itself in the world through the medium of powerlessness, of service and total self-giving to all his creatures. This Christological determination of God is in no sense a threat, implicit or explicit, to the autonomy or well-being of his creatures. It is, rather, an invitation to which they may or may not respond within the accidents of culture and particularity. Human invitations may often carry an element of pressure or persuasion which infringes, at least notionally, human autonomy. But since God is pure, self-giving love, God's invitation stands purely on its own credentials. It commends itself on the basis of itself, as the goal of all human striving, religious and non-religious alike.

[2]See Alan Race, *Christianity and Religious Pluralism.*

Christianity is about love and respect for all human beings. One of the most moving and illuminating guides to this respect in the context of the relation between Christianity and other religions is provided in Klaus Klostermaier's *Hindu and Christian in Vrindaban*, a narrative of a two-year stay in an Indian village, completely immersed in the local culture. Klostermaier's approach was to listen, to respect, and to seek to understand Hindu culture in the light of his faith as a Catholic priest.[3]

It is always easy to caricature faiths which one does not share, does not understand, and in the presence of which one may feel somewhat apprehensive. Klostermaier sought to read Hindu customs, culture and devotion in the best possible light. 'The theologian at 70 degrees F in a good position presumes God to be happy and contented, well-fed and rested, without needs of any kind. The theologian at 120 degrees F tries to imagine a God who is hungry and thirsty, who suffers and is sad, who sheds perspiration and knows despair.' What is needed is genuine dialogue. 'Dialogue in depth shatters the self-confidence of those who regard themselves as the guardians of the whole and only truth. Truth has to be searched for in order to be had; the kingdom of God is arriving, and only those who are on their way will reach it' (103). 'Christ does not come to India as a stranger, he comes into his own. Christ comes to India not from Europe, but directly from the Father' (112). The Christian way is the way of Christ, who came to give his life, on behalf of the many.

It is then as much in the framework of social reality as in that of physical reality or of metaphysical reality that the truth of Christ may be apprehended. Within this eschatological perspective we may see that the mystery of the divine spirit is none other than the mystery revealed in the man Jesus of Nazareth, but it is not given to all God's creatures to make the connection in this life.

In Jesus Christ word and sacrament, nature and history are united. God is involved in human life, death and resurrection.

---

[3] K. Klostermaier *Hindu and Christian in Vrindaban*, 40, 103, 112. Cf. too Keith Ward's exciting study, *A Vision to Pursue*.

God is involved in life, in perishability, in new life. God's incarnation is his self-fulfilment as well as his self-giving. God's *kenosis*, in participation in fallen humanity and in an unreconciled cosmos, becomes in the resurrection his *plerosis*. God participates in powerlessness without being completely defenceless. Contingency involves accident, tragedy and betrayal, as well as restoration and new creation. Incarnation is a word easily misunderstood. It does not refer to a magical mode of presence which escapes empirical reality. It refers to empirical reality with all the hazards which this brings. Incarnation in a human being relates Christ to the changing drift and caprice of social reality. It also relates Christ to the cosmos in all its arbitrary and chance development. Through this life, its destruction and its resurrection God the creator brings reconciliation to the social and the physical order. This reconciliation has social and physical dimensions. But these will be finally fulfilled eschatologically. This reconciliation, importantly, is transformed through its spiritual dimensions. For God is ultimate spiritual reality. This is not a contradiction but a fulfilment and a deepening of social and physical reality. Through the Spirit of the living Christ, who is who he is because he has been the incarnate, crucified and risen Christ, God is and will be all in all.

4. Christus Consummator

In his fine study of Christology, *Christus Consummator*, B.F. Westcott stressed reconciliation in Christ as the consummation of all things.[4] There is an eschatological aspect to this concept, in the final fulfilment of all truth in Christ. I want to use the concept however to focus upon the many dimensions of Christology, and their interrelation. We have already touched on these dimensions. Christology has, at least, historical, personal, political, anthropological, social, cosmological, pneumatological and theological dimensions, all of which are central to the basic enterprise. I now want to look at each of these in turn.

[4]Cf. F. Olofsson, *Christus Consummator.*

1. Christology has a central *historical* dimension. It is concerned with Jesus of Nazareth, a man who lived and died in particular circumstances in Palestine, and whom Christians believe to have been raised by God from the dead. In its basic meaning, incarnation involves God's commitment to the random, chance, contingent reality of particular events and a particular time. There may not be one authorised Christian doctrine or interpretation of history. But without its historical matrix Christology would be fatally impoverished. It would be divorced from its original and vital ground. It would also be bereft of a central feature of its soteriological function, as a statement about the perennial human predicament, caught between pressures for good and evil.

2. Christology has a *personal* dimension. God relates to human beings. This is basic to the Christian understanding of creation and reconciliation, to the story of the Old Testament and the New. God is in himself definitively understood through a human being, through the person of Jesus Christ. God is personal. Most Christians also wish to say that God is a person, in some ways like and in other ways unlike human persons. Knowledge of God as person is knowledge in faith, of the hidden personal presence of God. Theologians have approached the question of God's personhood in many different ways. Origen thought of God as a spiritual person. The Cappadocians stressed the interrelatedness of the persons in the Trinity. Luther spoke of God as personal rather than as Aristotelian substance. The Enlightenment spoke of God as an individual personal spirit, binding finite and infinite, material and spiritual. Existentialist theologians have spoken of God as personal, reinterpreting the whole tradition in personalist terms. Harnack spoke of the freedom of the children of God, as persons to be respected in their individual freedom. Twentieth-century theologians have explored the personhood of God in innumerable ways.

3. Christology has a *political* dimension. Jesus was heavily involved in the politics of his day. He probably played no overtly political role, and he sought no political involvement.

He was certainly no party politician. Yet he came up against the political realities of the day with increasing frequency. His missions could easily be construed as having political significance. Neither then nor now is it possible to make public pronouncements on serious issues without getting caught up in all sorts of political and social pressures. The public arena is not neutral. It is not static or inert. It produces reactions and ripples as soon as its surface is stirred and the directions of these reactions cannot always be predicted in advance. It is not clear that Christology must always be a political Christology, far less a particular sort of political Christology. But Christology is always relevant to political issues. Certain political programmes are always contrary to the character of Christ. Others are more likely to be more consonant with that character. All may be seen in the light of Christ, and stand under the judgement of self-giving love. Connected with politics are of course issues of authority, or power and powerlessness. Absolute power may corrupt. Absolute powerlessness may be equally corrupting. All the major problems of politics, notably the relation of justice for the individual to justice for society, may be involved here.

4. Christology has an *anthropological* dimension. This is closely related to, but not identical with, the personal dimension. In the Christian gospel God is especially related to humankind. God is the creator of man. In Jesus Christ we see, in an important sense, the basic form of humanity. It is not for nothing that incarnation means God's engagement with human nature. All the dimensions of the human may illuminate and in turn be illuminated by the Christological enterprise. It is also the case that Christology may benefit from the skills of the disciplines of social and cultural anthropology. It is not necessary to espouse an exclusive approach to these disciplines, such as the adherence to a 'cultural linguistic' model for theological discourse, in order to benefit from the anthropological sciences.

5. In this field we touch on the areas of the social sciences, which are equally relevant but equally not prescriptive. Christology has a *social* dimension. The life of Jesus Christ was

lived in society, and its consequences are worked out in society. Its structure and its meaning may be worked out in relation to the whole range of the social sciences. We have already considered politics. Here we might also consider economics. The economic dimensions of self-giving love are as appropriate as the political or philosophical dimensions. This is a corollary of incarnation, of God's engagement with all that is germane to human welfare.

In reflecting on the life of Jesus, New Testament scholars have recently used sociological analysis with considerable effect. Analyses of power and its use, of group behaviour, of individual and social psychology, of ritual and of communication, have all a role to play in spelling out consequences of the mystery of Christ. Used in an unimaginative way, these topics may produce flat and reductionist understandings of Christology, but they may also be immensely useful.

6. Christology has then a number of dimensions, some of which may be summed up in the umbrella term of anthropological dimensions. But Christology has another, rather larger, dimension, the *cosmological* dimension, within which the anthropological is itself subsumed. God is creator and reconciler of the entire physical universe. God is the creator of man, and the redeemer of man. In the person of Jesus the resurrection is classically understood as a sign and seal of the redemption of the realm of the physical cosmos, of matter as well as of spirit. This does not entail the resuscitation of a corpse, for death is the end of all perishable matter. But still, in God there is continuity, symbolised in the spiritual body of the Pauline understanding of resurrection. Through Jesus Christ comes new creation, the redemption of the physical cosmos and the reconciliation of the physical and the spiritual in Christ.

7. Christology has also a *pneumatological* dimension. After the resurrection Christ is one with the Spirit of God, and the Spirit is the Spirit of the crucified and risen Christ, the Spirit which creates Christlikeness. We shall come on to speak of pneumatology in its own right. Here I want simply to recall the important connection. This dimension is important for

understanding both the Church and the world, as the spheres of the action of God as Spirit, working both through the promised presence in the work and worship of the Church and mysteriously in the world, in and out of the various competing creeds and religions. Linked with pneumatology is *eschatology*, to which we shall return.

8. Finally, mention should be made of the *theological* dimension of Christology. The most humanly significant aspect of Jesus is his total devotion to God his father. The most theologically significant aspect of Christology is that it is the revelation of the nature of God, creator and reconciler. Granted that knowledge of God is still to faith alone, and that God in his revelation in Christ is still a mysterious hidden presence to his Church, nevertheless this is at the centre of Christology. The fact of Christ means reconciliation, present and eschatological, for all the human beings who have ever lived, and for the whole created order. Such is the God whom Christians worship, the Father revealed through Jesus Christ, and manifested to them by the Spirit.

These are the dimensions – and the list is not exhaustive – of Christology, of the faithfulness of God's self-giving love in incarnation and atonement, in reconciliation.

It is interesting to see how three of these perspectives, the cosmological, the anthropological and the eschatological, are picked out as basic by Moltmann in his *The Way of Jesus Christ*, as arising from a messianic perspective, which looks forward to the parousia of the resurrected one and reinforces relations with Judaism. From the time of his baptism in the Spirit, Christ preaches the Kingdom of God to the poor, healing the sick, accepting the outcasts, expressing in his activity the messianic way of life and being the messianic person.

Beyond the actualisation of the messianic person comes the reality of the apocalyptic sufferings of Christ. God's child dies as a Jew and a slave, and in his dying God participates in death, creating righteousness. Contemporary martyrs remind us of Christ's suffering, and of God, who knows the cry from the depths. From suffering comes the eschatological resurrection of

Christ, producing from historical contingency the new creation, a potential unity between human civilisation and nature. The cosmic Christ is the ground of creation, the foundation of a unity of human beings, plants and animals, based on law. This restructuring will be complete in the parousia of Christ, when the coming one will complete the righteousness of heaven and affirm embodiment in God's presence.

This Christology is pro-Judaistic, not anti-Judaistic, appreciates feminist insights, and emphasises the need for a fully developed Christology of nature, of the lordship of Christ over all areas of modern life on our planet. Righteousness, as the basis for lasting peace, is a key concept. The all-embracing consequences of Christology are again underlined.

We have seen that the Christian understanding of Christ involves a long tradition of searching through various cultures and with the aid of various sorts of philosophical and other models. It involves the life of Jesus, his death and his resurrection, and the Christian response through the ages. There is an integral connection between the person and the work of Christ. Christ is understood through the thought, the life and the worship of Christians, and as an integral part of the whole understanding of God.

5. The Promise of the Spirit

The events concerning Jesus reinforce the understanding of God as the one who loves, who is in his essential nature self-giving love, who is a personal God. We have seen that there are many difficulties in the concept of a personal God, and that the development of a Christian understanding of God involves a high level of complexity, if justice is to be done to what faith believes. It is through reflecting on God in the light of Jesus Christ that the basic understanding of the God who loves is reaffirmed. God is God. God is not any sort of conceivable God. God is at once creator and reconciler, reconciler and creator, self-defined through the manner of his engagement with the created order.

The Christian understanding of God includes faith. There remain elements of mystery in our vision of God, partly because we are thinking of the ground of creation, and partly because our response to God is often an affirmation against the appearance of things, a commitment to love as basic reality in the face of waste, suffering and indifference. We soon become aware that our attempts to analyse and map out the divine love are no more infallible than any other intellectual enterprise. We hope to learn to persevere, believing that out of the debris of many projects in the history of the Christian tradition a deeper knowledge of God is achieved. God is neither entirely inscrutable nor entirely unavailable to us. The sense of the presence of God, the shadow of the Galilean, is also part of the Christian view of the way things are.

On the cross God delivered himself into our hands, God has also delivered himself into human minds to understand him as humanity's God. In the Bible God has made available in human conditions a record of his reconciling presence. This is a human record, which can be used and abused with all the sensitivity and intelligence, duplicity and fanaticism, of which the human mind is capable. The various academic disciplines can be employed to throw light on different aspects of the Bible. But the individual Christian in community has to decide how best to utilise the available data.

The Bible, the Christian Church, and the understanding of the gospel in the world, all are subject to restatement and reappropriation in every generation of faith. This reappropriation may be assisted by reflection on developments in the whole range of the human and the natural sciences, Though we understand through faith, different combinations of approaches have led to a deepening of faith at different times. Philosophy and physics, sociology and politics, all may assist faith's imagination, provided they are not allowed to become myopic perspectives. The God who is love may be understood in many different ways. Excluded only are ways of intolerance, evil and exploitation, of the mind, body or soul.

We have explored the understanding of the Christian God as personal being, as the creator, hidden in his presence, yet active throughout the created order. God is there in the complexities of the cosmos, in the complexities of the life sciences, in the complexities of the human condition from cavemen to a computerised culture.

God's nearness to his creation is permanently stabilised in his incarnation in Jesus Christ. The incarnation may be understood on many levels. It is an event, or series of events, both eloquently simple to grasp and endlessly complex to conceive. Historically many Christians have understood their lives as focused on Jesus without taking account, by accident or design, of a classical view of incarnation, and this continues to be a most powerful source of inspiration to them. But if the classical view or a variation of it, points to the mysterious truth of the matter, then of course it has immense implications. It validates the virtually inconceivable omnipresence of the self-giving God in reconciliation throughout the created order.

Incarnation I find easiest to conceive as an indicating rather than a defining concept. It points to a reality which is the presence of God in the life, death and resurrection of Jesus Christ. This man, rather than the idea, is incarnation. As such it remains in many ways mysterious to us, and embraces many dimensions of the human. As we discover more and more about the human, perhaps over millions of years to come, so we may hope to understand more about the incarnation. Theology as a discipline may be older than say microbiology, yet in terms of the potential human future, we may do well to reflect that all our thinking is still perhaps in its most primitive stages.

Incarnation points to the life of Jesus as uniquely part of the life of God. Does God understand from a human perspective thoughts, desires, fears and aspirations? It is to the life of Jesus, however inadequately understood, that we look for an answer. Does God's presence include presence with us in our dying as well as in our living? Does God notice or care about the deaths of the innocent? We look to the cross for answers, or at least clues. Does God's love make any difference to the way things are, or shall be? We look to the resurrection as the ground of hope in God's future.

Incarnation is the incarnation of the creator as reconciler. The purpose and centre of the incarnation is salvation. There is something odd about much modern debate, in which theories of incarnation and salvation are opposed to one another. Incarnation is the mode of the historical presence of the creator in the created order. Luther was right in an important sense in stressing that the God of the gospel is God for us, *pro nobis*. Any other God is irrelevant to us. But it is the God who is in himself *extra nos,* his own self-focused presence, who is God for us. It is through God's own reality, and not simply as a mirror of ourselves, that he encompasses us with his salvation.

We have seen that salvation has many dimensions, corresponding to the complexity of the cosmos and the humanity which participates in salvation, We shall explore the human dimensions of salvation further in the next chapter. Here we recall that the saviour is the incarnate one, Jesus Christ. It is his human life, his struggles, his pain, his sacrifice, that is the source of the reality of salvation for us. This is the ground for faith in the peace of God in the future. Whatever God may have in store for us out of his love in the future, here in Jesus we see the determining characteristics of his love.

Out of this love comes Christlikeness in the created order. The gift of salvation is the gift of the Spirit, of the new creation. God uses the Church as an instrument of his love, as a channel of the Spirit. But faith believes that the Spirit is present throughout creation, transforming it into new creation, the new heaven and new earth of the coming eschatological reign of God. As such the activity of the Spirit is a clear judgement on all that is unloving in the world, and a power of transformation in every place – a light both in darkness and in daylight.

24

Spirit and Church

1. Spirit, Word and Sacrament

God was in Christ reconciling the world to himself. The significance of the life, death and resurrection of Jesus did not stop at the resurrection. God's involvement in human contingency is taken up into his own self-identity, and has consequences for his engagement with the created order. The New Testament reflects upon this development in various ways, in speaking of the action of the Spirit of the risen Christ in the world, working throughout the created order, and working also in the particularity of the Church, the community of the disciples of Jesus Christ.

In this section we come to the fruits of reconciliation. Here the tradition speaks of the work of the Holy Spirit. The Spirit works both in the Church and in the world, in relation to humankind and indeed to the whole cosmic order. But of course, as the tradition also reflected, the Spirit does not work in isolation from the Father and the Son. God the creator is simultaneously God the reconciler. The Spirit is the Spirit of the crucified and risen Christ. In the Spirit the way of discipleship of Jesus of Nazareth is carried forward in succeeding generations.

Here is the inauguration of new creation, the dawn of a new era, the beginning of a new reality of the fruits of the Spirit within the old reality of the human predicament. Though evil is still tragically real in the world, there are signs of the results of Jesus' victory over evil. The light shines in the darkness, and will not be overcome. Within the Church and the world, the

Spirit creates Christlikeness. Precisely in the face of the reality of suffering, there is also a reality of forgiveness and reconciliation, peace, love and joy. The shape of the reality of the presence of God as Spirit within the reality of the created order as it is, rather than as we might like it to be, will be the subject of our next chapter.

Through God the Father heaven and earth were created. Through Jesus Christ something new happened in the created order. Creation was recreated as new creation. Through the Spirit, the Spirit of the Father and the Spirit of Christ, the freedom of the children of God is inaugurated and begins to be more fully realised. Twentieth-century theologians have spoken of freedom under the word. They have spoken of encounter with the Christ event. They have spoken of liberation. They have spoken of the freedom which comes from Jesus as the man for others. All of this reflection upon the Christian life, the life of faith, may be understood as the dimension of the Holy Spirit.

All that we know of God is of grace. There is an element of hiddenness about this. In New Testament language, the life of Christians is hidden with Christ in God. Talk of the Spirit of God is quite fundamental to Christian faith. Whether or not the role of the Spirit is seen in the framework of a classical doctrine of the Trinity, yet the Holy Spirit is the source of life for all that comes from the drama of creation and reconciliation.

The Church is the Church of the Spirit. The life of Christians in the wider human community is the fruit of the Spirit. The work of God in our world is the result of the mission of the Spirit, opening up new possibilities of love in situations where nothing, no movement of any sort, seemed possible. Far from being a rather obscure area of doctrine, the understanding of the Spirit should be perhaps the most exciting area of Christian exploration. The letter kills, but the Spirit gives life.

Reflection on the Spirit immediately puts into perspective the doctrine of the Church. The Spirit blows where it wills. The Spirit of God is active, as the Spirit of the risen Christ, throughout the created order. The Spirit is active in all human society. Jesus Christ brought salvation to all humankind, to those who have been, who are and who will be. The Church of Jesus Christ is the Church of the Spirit of the crucified and risen Christ. As such it is there to serve all humankind. In order to be of service it may have to concentrate its resources, to build up its strength and to focus its energy. But it remains the Church of the servant. Grace is given to be given away, and enjoyed in being shared.

A church which is for all humankind must clearly seek to go beyond cultural barriers. But it should not seek to build a multinational institution for its own sake, as a kind of alternative community to the whole human community. It does not mean that the Church must be militant in the sense of seeking to make converts in a triumphant manner. It does mean that no human concerns are alien to the church of the spirit.

The Bible uses many areas of the human imagination to evoke imagery concerning the Church. The idea of the people of God is a powerful theme throughout the New Testament. This is the stream of thought into which Jesus enters, taking it up and developing it in his own way. The imagery of the people is reinforced with the imagery of the Kingdom, the explosive force which is to transform human life in the future.

The Church in the New Testament is also the bride of Christ, the body of Christ, and the temple of the Holy Spirit. There is indeed a whole series of models for the Church. The Church is called out of the world. It is also called into the world. The Church is a worshipping community, in which the Spirit of Christ is present and active, through word and sacrament. The Church waits for a more perfect community with God when the Kingdom is fully realised. The Church anticipates the new creation. Therefore the Church may be a medium of God's love now to all humankind. This is the ministry of all Christian people, the priesthood of all believers.

Any virtues which the Church may manifest are gifts of the Spirit, and are exercised only when the Church is truly obedient to the leading of the Spirit. The Church, according to the creeds, is one, holy, catholic and apostolic. These are gifts of the Spirit. Peace and harmony are anticipations of the eschatological peace of God. The holiness of God is the goal to which the children of God are led. The catholicity which sees all human beings as equally children of God in every way is the product of grace. Grace is always related to Jesus Christ, and so is apostolic. All of these features participate now in provisionality, but are nevertheless signs to faith of the consummation of God's Kingdom.

The Church is the Church of the Spirit. It is also a human institution, and as such participates in the social structures of the world, their power and powerlessness. God's power is the power of self-giving love. The Church has to evolve a responsible use of the power which its place as a large social organisation gives it. Here again it is constantly under the judgement of the Spirit.

As an institution the Church has its officials and its members. These officials are subject to all the constraints and temptations to which officials in any organisation are subject. Once again, they must seek to act as the servants of God rather than as ecclesiastical functionaries. But they will be aware that their judgements and aspirations cannot be regarded automatically as the will of God. For they too are human beings, and to err is human.

As the Church of the Spirit, the Church is one. The oneness is that of its obedience to the Spirit. There are however the numerous different organisations, each with its different structures, especially of ministry. This diversity, born of different cultural developments, need not in itself be a problem. The difficulties arise from the fact that each denomination in practice tends to regard its own claims as exclusively correct, over against other forms of ministry. Each group tends to regard assimilation to its own pattern and power structure as the ideal and often the only appropriate ecumenical structure. In this way a diversity of worship, of work in the wider community and of internal organisation which ought to be creative becomes instead a source of destructive tension at every level. Instead of witnessing to the manifold nature of the work of the Spirit it becomes a monument to human capacity for alienation. This is nowhere more clear than in dissension concerning the ministry of women in the Church.

God's creative and reconciling action takes place in the Church and in the world, as people are enabled to become instruments of God's love to their fellow men. The tradition understands God's presence in the Church to be focused through word and sacrament, strengthening the members of the community for their service.

The Church is the Church of word and sacrament. Sometimes too great an emphasis on word or on sacrament can be made. There can be a narrow sacramental view of the Church. There can be a verbalisation of the gospel, when all is reduced to word. But we need not be overcautious. Both word and sacrament belong to the centre of Christian faith. Both express God's love.

The word was the vehicle of the communication of God's relationship with humankind in the Old Testament and the New. Through the reading of the biblical word and through action in reflection upon that reading, the life of the Christian community is sustained. Through preaching people are brought to God and sustained in faith. Here they appropriate the forgiveness and reconciliation of Jesus Christ, and they become aware of the Spirit of God as a living presence. Through the word they are guided in their pilgrimage towards a life of discipleship. Through the word they are encouraged towards a relationship with God in the sphere of prayer.

Sacraments are understood in the Articles of the Church of England as 'effective signs of grace', that is to say, manifestations of God's grace which bring about that which they promise.

Jesus Christ is the sacrament of God for the world. Jesus was born in Israel and called for faith. To this corresponds the act of God and the human response in the sacrament of baptism. God acts in the world through the Spirit of the risen Christ. In the sacrament of the eucharist a new awareness of this living presence becomes possible, and men and women respond in thanksgiving for the continuation of his presence in the world.

In the gospels people repent of their sins, and receive forgiveness through baptism by water. After Pentecost comes baptism through the Spirit, which marks both repentance and the placing of the baptised in the household of God, the Christian community. In the New Testament the eucharist is seen as a fulfilment of the paschal meal in the Old Testament. It also points forward to an anticipated eschatological community.

The eucharist is more than a memorial of the death of

Christ and an anticipation of the eschatological peace of God.
It is the means by which we may receive through faith a
heightened awareness of the presence of Christ in the world
and in our own lives as Christians. As such it is an occasion for
prayers of thanksgiving to God.

The Church of the sacrament is always and also the Church
of the word. In its life of prayer and worship the Church both
attends to the word and gives thanks for its base in God's grace.
As a community of the grace of God the Church is a community
too of reconciliation, living on the basis of God's reconciliation,
In relation to society it emphasizes forgiveness and
reconciliation first.

In the last volume of his *Dogmatics* Gerhard Ebeling considers
God as the completer of the world. God is creator, reconciler
and completer. We begin with the human person as a person
in Christ, and then move to faith, world and God. God is God
and man is man. But the Holy Spirit is in the human person in
Christ, and creates the new person from the old in humanity.
The new person is constituted by the freedom which is the gift
of the Spirit.

Faith accomplishes righteousness. This comes through the
word, and establishes the community of faith, in Church and
sacraments. Through the justifying word comes the
development of the personal life in election, repentance and
salvation, leading on to social engagement. The word comes as
law and gospel, and also as sacrament. The Church is understood
as the community of faith. In engagement with the world, it
must work out the meaning of unity, apostolicity, holiness and
universality.

Ebeling turns to eschatology. Already in the Christian
conscience there is a dimension of eschatological judgement.
Christian hope is there in the face of death. Christ's resurrection
leads towards the peace of God. Through judgement the
power of sin is destroyed, and the vision of God is no longer
hidden. Now God is all in all, and is understood as the triune
God, the living God who is the ground and content of our faith.

The Church of the Spirit is an instrument of reconciliation.
In this work it lives from the fact that it works within the whole
economy of the divine spirit in history. It is important to

recollect this wider framework for the task of the church.[1]

2. Spirit and History

We have already discussed God's historicity.[2] How are we to imagine the role of the Spirit in history? Valuable hints in a similar direction may be gained from Peter Hodgson's excellent *God in History: Shapes of Freedom*. Hodgson examines traditional theologies of history such as salvation history, and then considers a postmodern reconstruction. He looks at traditional doctrines of God as Trinity, and at theories of divine action. He proposes a new theology of transfigurative praxis, creating shapes of freedom. 'God is present in history as a divine gestalt. A gestalt is not a person. A gestalt, rather, is both transpersonal and interpersonal: it is a complex, doubled, plural unity' (206). How does this relate to Jesus ? 'God was incarnate, not in the physical nature of Jesus as such, but in the gestalt that coalesced both in and around his person – with which his person did in some sense become identical, and by which, after his death, he took on a new, communal identity' (209). The three images of the Kingdom, the cross and the resurrection are the paradigm of transfigurative practice. They generate shapes of freedom in history, in the face of evil, as the divine Spirit inspires the human spirit, as an antidote to despair. 'Maintaining anamnestic solidarity with the victims of history, refusing to forget them, insisting on telling and re-telling their story, can have a transformative effect within history, even if the final redemption of their suffering is in the hands of God alone' (227). God as the consummation of all things is the perfection of communicative freedom.

---

[1]A lively recent discussion of ecclesiology may be found in *On Being the Church: Essays on the Christian Community*, edited by Colin Gunton and Daniel Hardy. Among other things, the importance of the ecclesiology of the Reformers is discussed by Christoph Schwoebel, the continuing importance of kenosis by Richard Roberts, and the themes of *Faith in the City* by David Ford. Discussing authority in the light of Paul, Ford comments that 'Incarnating the glory of God is the face of Christ, the ultimate embodiment of a persuasive, vulnerable authority, freely distributed through his Spirit' (253).

[2]Cf. part 1, chs. 9 and 10.

This is a powerful study of the presence of God in history which does not minimise the intellectual difficulties, and is genuinely creative. Its stress on the unity of God, and on the Spirit as the Spirit of the risen and crucified Christ, is similar in many ways to the work of Geoffrey Lampe which we considered earlier. We may note that one of the main objections to traditional doctrines of incarnation has been that they tended towards impersonality. Here the role is reversed and the personal is moved towards the interpersonal and the suprapersonal. Hodgson is very careful to retain the force of the personal. But it may be that the notion of gestalt suffers from some of the difficulties encountered in the concept of incarnation, which it seeks to balance. The person whom God is is clearly not the same as a human person. But it may be that the Spirit remains the Spirit of the mysterious person of the risen Christ, who is one with the creator in a complexity which yet retains a fully personal moment. To borrow a hint here from Karl Rahner, to be fully interpersonal and suprapersonal it may be also necessary to be fully personal.

However that may be, as a study of the presence of the one who loves in freedom, as Hodgson's paraphrase of Barth has it, this is a seminal and ground-breaking study. It reinforces the basic theme of this study that God is not an abstract logical hypothesis but one who defines himself in the events concerning Jesus and in the experience of the Spirit in the Church and in the world.

We may say that the understanding of the dimension of the Spirit is an integral part of the Christian understanding of God. The problems involved for Christian theology in relying too much on particular philosophical frameworks without regard for the tradition of the gospel are strikingly pinpointed, with reference to the development of modern atheism, by Michael J. Buckley in *At the Origins of Modern Atheism*.

> The Christian God cannot have a more fundamental witness than Jesus Christ, even antecedent to the commitments of faith: Christian theology cannot abstract from Christology in order to shift the challenge for this foundational warrant on to philosophy. Within the context of a Christology and a

Pneumatology of both communal and personal religious experience, one can locate and give its own philosophical integrity to metaphysics, but Christology and Pneumatology are fundamental. If one abrogates this evidence, one abrogates this God. For the Christian, Jesus belongs to the intelligibility and to the truth of God. (361)

Christian theology is not simply about esoteric doctrinal arguments. It is also about the reality of faith, hope and love as fruits of the Spirit in the lives of individual people. Faith is a reality which keeps men and women turned to God, often in the most unpromising of circumstances. Love to God and to neighbour is often a kind of touchstone of the reality of the gospel in the most unlikely of circumstances. Hope in God is there, often hope against hope, when there appear to be no other grounds for hope in a bleak world. These are basic realities of the life of the Christian individual, millions of ordinary people, in a complex society. It is not always obvious that faith, hope and love have any great empirical impact on the communities in which they are expressed. Yet for Christian life they point forward, and indeed they lead forward, towards the eschatological consummation of faith, hope and love after death.

The gospel is concerned about individuals. It is also concerned with society as a whole. Sometimes the Church has to separate its message clearly from the values of prevailing culture, to stand against the world, even to the point of martyrdom. Such a stance calls for, and has often evoked, heroic sacrifice on the part of Christians.

At other times the need is to build bridges between the gospel and society, to engage in dialogue, to seek to enrich social and cultural environments through the gospel. This can be in some ways an even more difficult task. For here the boundaries are blurred. When does identification with the world for the sake of the gospel turn into assimilation with the world's values at the cost of the Christian message? This is a constant and serious temptation. Assimilation with prevailing social values and current trends is all too easy. Maintaining a balance is important, especially in the highly complex structures of a modern industrial society. Such a balance cannot always be a simple middle way. For wherever people are exploited, where human rights are infringed, the Church is called to speak out in the name of Jesus Christ.

3. Spirit and Tradition

Here I should like to draw attention again to the manifold and multifaceted nature of the biblical traditions concerning the Church. There is no single pattern, no dominating or authorised image. At different times and in different places there were different emphases. The service of the gospel to humanity requires flexibility in order to be the consistent service of the same gospel.

The Church is about the expression of the gospel, as it came to be made known within the Judaeo-Christian tradition. The Bible is primarily concerned with that story, and only with the Church as an instrument of the articulation of the gospel. The Church is about God, about the expression of God's love in the events concerning the life, death and resurrection, about the consequences of this love for humanity.

In the book of Acts there are already Christian congregations working in society, through them the Spirit is at work. The Spirit within the Church is emphasized in Paul's early letter to the Galatians; gradually the idea of a continuity with the synagogue or assembly of the people of God in the Old Testament develops. In the later Pauline corpus, in Ephesians and Colossians, the Church is already the people of God, the body of Christ. Paul brought in other striking metaphors, the bride of Christ, the head of the body. The Johannine writings stressed the mystical headship of Christ in the community. Already, perhaps within fifty years of the crucifixion, there is a powerful sense of the specific role of the Spirit within the community, and of the community as a special instrument of salvation, of the service of the gospel.

The messianic imagery of the Old Testament becomes increasingly related to the New Testament communities. The apocalyptic and eschatological imagery of Israel finds a resonance in the self-understanding of the Church. Jesus' teaching about the Kingdom is linked to the Church. In the *ecclesia* the continuing awareness of God's grace is linked to the resurrection of the crucified Christ.

St. Paul stresses the impact on the individual of the presence of the resurrected lord, creating a new life in Christ. 'I, yet not I.' Individual groups are part of the greater Church, the one body whose head is Christ. Jesus Christ is present in the worship of the Church, in word and sacrament. In the Church the promises of the Old Testament are transformed and fulfilled. In this way the Church becomes the basis of the new creation. As in Adam all die, so in Christ new life is brought to all men and women. The Church is the centre of the new Israel. In its participation in the sufferings of Christ, in solidarity with human suffering, the Church becomes an instrument of the Spirit, a place of growth for the fruits of salvation.

The total dependence of the Church on Jesus Christ for its life is brought to a new emphasis in the Fourth Gospel, not least in the great 'I am' sayings. Christ is the true shepherd, the bread of life, the true vine, the fountain of living water. The unity of the Church is grounded on its unity with Christ.

By the time we reach the letter to the Ephesians, this unity has been extended crucially and explicitly to involve a reconciliation of Jews and Gentiles, through the peace of God. There is a more assured Christian self-understanding. 'You are built upon the foundation laid by the prophets and the apostles, and Jesus Christ himself is the chief foundation stone' (Eph. 2:20). Conduct must be related to faith. Those who have been forgiven should exercise forgiveness, and should pray for all men. There is then a process of gradual consolidation. But within that consolidation there is always a challenge to renewal, an awareness of the Church as the pilgrim people of God, ever open to the Spirit. Classic is the imagery of the 'wandering people of God' in Hebrews. The Church is a people always ready through faith to move out in new directions.

Recollection of the Christian tradition calls for both thanksgiving and repentance. The modern world owes an inestimable amount to the Christian Church. The Church also has much for which it must ask to be forgiven. This is part of the paradox of human response to the gospel. God's self-giving

love is unambiguously there for all humankind. The human
religious response involves strong emotions which may be
channels of God's love or which may be vehicles of self-
righteous intolerance or even blind hatred.

By the early second century there was great stress on the
quality of the lives of Christians. They were the salt of the earth,
patterns of morality and purity. Already there was a danger of
moralism and a false sense of superiority. But in a society
renowned for brutality and corruption at all levels this was a
valuable witness. The liturgical rites of the communities began
to be seen as anticipations and then as copies of the order of
things in heaven. Here was a natural expression of the mystical
dimension of worship. There was here too a danger, of
magnifying the authority of the rituals and of the celebrants till
they threatened to overshadow the authority of the gospel in
the service of which everything was done. Structures and
institutions were clearly necessary for the functioning of the
Church in society. Gradually the church authorities developed
increasingly absolute authority within and outside the Christian
communities.

Reformations and reconstructions tended to change the
form rather than the scope and breadth of authority. The
decisive authority of the churches was to be a prevailing feature
of Christendom right into the modern era, with all the
advantages and disadvantages that this brought with it.
Theologians developed complex theories of the subordination
of church structure to divine authority. The Church was only
a pale shadow of the Kingdom of God. It stood in a dialectical
relationship to the gospel. There were divisions between the
visible and the invisible Church. Yet those officers of the
churches who controlled the various ecclesiastical bureaucracies
continued to wield considerable power. It was necessary that
authority should exist, and that the implications of power
should be faced responsibly. The problem lay, and continues
to lie, in the maintenance of an appropriate correspondence
between power in the Church and the power of the self-giving
love of God in Jesus Christ.

As a church of the word the Christian community is
dependent on the gospel, and seeks to listen, to be attentive.

There have undoubtedly been times when there has been too much emphasis on the sermon in the Church, on words, on the intellect, on rhetoric and on moral instruction. But the abuse does not take away the proper use. The preaching of the word and the hearing of the word, a word of forgiveness and reconciliation, a word of life, the life of Jesus Christ, will always be central. Where the word is not heard, the gospel begins to be forgotten. The effective preaching of the word remains one of the great challenges of our time.

We shall have much to say later about the role of the Church in society. Here I want to recall the importance of the Church in the individual Christian life. From New Testament times individuals are drawn by the grace of God to the gospel, to repentance and the acceptance of the forgiving and reconciling power of God. God's love involves justice and peace and a relationship with God and our neighbours. This is the process known to the tradition as justification and sanctification. It is based on God's righteousness, and his grace which comes to us undeserved. The promise of the gospel is not a theological formula but a reality for our everyday lives. How to make this promise more of a reality throughout our lives is part of the task of Christian living. It may be impossible, but it is seen to happen within the Church in every generation of Christians. It is linked both with worship and with service in a kind of ever-changing dynamic. It is not a matter of legislation but of grateful response. Faith, hope and love may be anything from empty catchwords to profound reality. It is the task of members of the Christian community to deepen their awareness of this reality and to make it a reality for others.

The notion of Christian community may be expressed in different ways in different contexts. It may be expressed through meeting together for prayer and worship, around the centre of word and sacrament. It may involve the structures of the Church at local or national level. It may involve church-based organisations which seek to strengthen the fellowship of church members, and also to create a fellowship of service to the local community in various ways. It may also mean the service which individuals can render, based on their Christian commitment, within their professional organisations and in voluntary organisations which have no church connections. For the latter, worship is a stimulus to commitment within perhaps an entirely secular context.

Schillebeeckx sees 1 Peter as 'an invitation to vulnerable love for others' (*Christ*, 229). Herein lies the Christian hope. This is a hope which is grounded in suffering for others, so that these others may be led to reflect and even to be converted, 'to be brought to God' (3.18), just as through the suffering of Jesus, Christians and sinners are brought closer together. 'As long as there is still a real history of suffering among us, we cannot do without the sacramental liturgy: to abolish it or neglect it would be to stifle the firm hope in universal peace and general reconciliation' (836).

4. Particularity

The Christian Church is the Church of Jesus Christ, the Church of the love of God, brought out of and sent into the world by God, to serve as an instrument of his love for humankind.

I wish to reflect here on the actuality of the Church as an ecumenical endeavour. As an example we shall look particularly at Reformed ecclesiologies and their connections. Other denominations exhibit similar features. Reformed ecclesiologies are those expressions of the understanding of the Church which reflect the historical particularity of the Reformed witness. They are developed from the central features of the theology of the Reformation in the tradition of John Calvin – the lordship of Christ, the centrality of the authority of the Bible, and the place of the visible Church in worship and in service.

Reformed ecclesiology lays stress on the true preaching of the Word and the right administration of the sacraments. It has also cherished pastoral care, and the importance of the link between belief and discipleship. It affirms continuity with the Church of the New Testament, of the apostles and the Fathers, and also with the Reformers. It seeks catholicity together with evangelical truth. It looks forward to development, *semper reformanda*, under the guidance of the Spirit and in discipleship to Jesus Christ its Lord.

In matters of church polity and ministerial order Reformed ecclesiology is agreeable to the existence of a reconciled diversity. The limits of diversity are the limits of faithful service in Christ, and they include internal and external constraints. Discipleship rules out exclusive sacramental practice, the marginalisation of the oppressed, and the celebration of justification as self-justification.

Within the constraints of the divine love, a reconciled diversity of ecclesiological understanding and practice is to be welcomed, as a sign of the diversity of the gifts of the Spirit. On this basis the table of the eucharist is open in the Reformed tradition to all people in full communion with any branch of Christ's Church. Though it is not, of course, the prerogative of reformed Christians alone, openness in Christ is of the esse of Reformed ecclesiology.

Within this framework we may now seek to construct some central elements of a Reformed ecclesiology. None of these elements is exclusive to Reformed Christians, but they express a perspective which the Reformed tradition has been historically concerned to stress. It goes without saying that this project has to be seen in the light of full commitment both to the WCC and to particular agreements with other traditions, e.g. the Leuenberg process in Lutheran-Reformed agreement.

We begin with Calvin on the Church. The main lines of his view are readily set out. How is faith to be awakened and strengthened ? For this purpose God has given us the Church. He has given us pastors and teachers to preach the gospel, and sacraments to strengthen our faith. Such is the divine plan for us, and we should be faithful members of the Church. It is true that the Church is both visible and invisible, and includes some who are bad and others who are good. The visible Church is important. As he put it in a famous sentence, 'Wherever we see the Word of God purely preached and the sacraments administered according to the institution of Christ, we must not doubt that there is a church.'[3]

[3]Calvin, *Institutes*, 4.1.9.

The Church must preach the word and administer the sacraments. It must also help its members to develop in their sanctification. This is the element of pastoral care, of strengthening in discipleship. One central aspect of this is the maintenance of ecclesiastical discipline. Whether the love of God or man can or should ever be compelled is of course a vital question. The motive however was the pastoral concern. Christians should have the right religious attitude and the right moral practice. Wendel said of discipline 'it belonged to the organisation and not to the definition of the church'.

The basis of the Church is prescribed in scripture, but the external forms are subject to expediency – a balance never wholly defined. The spirit offers diverse gifts, and to these correspond diversities of ministries – pastors, doctors, elders and deacons. The Church is always under scripture, which is infallible. Unity among Reformed Christians is always preferable to schism. Niesel commented that for Calvin the Church is a living organism, a communion of mutual service (*Institutes*, 4.1.3). This is not an exclusively Reformed view, but it is stressed by Calvin. There is indeed an invisible Church, consisting of all the elect, living and dead. But there is also a true, visible Church. Discipline is important, but not actually one of the marks of the Church.

The Church is the Church of Jesus Christ, dependent on the Holy Spirit. External disciplines and ceremonies may be subject to change. There may be a diversity of ministries. But all must be subject to the judgement of the Word of God. The visible unity of the Church throughout the world is an important goal.

Calvin's teaching was to be taken up in different ways in the various reformed traditions. In Scotland for example, the *Confessio Scoticana* reflected Calvin, but also Bucer and other scholars, as well as Scots theologians. Here the Reformation sought, as Calvin had done, to go back to its apostolic roots, restoring the Church from corruption. Later, political issues were to play an ever increasing role in settling the shape of the ecclesiology. Presbyterian and Episcopalian structures, puritan, Enlightenment and pietist influences, battles for jurisdiction between Church and state, and many other factors shaped the tradition. There were secessions and reunions, resulting in

Reformed churches today with different sorts of ethos, and various degrees of internal pluralism.

The twentieth century has brought new challenges to the Reformed church, not least in the struggle with Nazism. At Barmen Reformed and Lutheran Christians expressed a common faith. 'The Christian church is the community of brethren in which Jesus Christ acts presently in word and sacrament through the Holy Spirit.' But as the next sentence makes plain the Church is not infallible, is always dependent on Jesus Christ. 'As the church of pardoned sinners, in the midst of a sinful world it has to witness by its faith and obedience, its message and its order, that it is his alone, that it lives and desires to live only by his consolation and by his orders, in expectation of his coming.'[4]

As far as the continuation of Reformed/Lutheran witness is concerned, we may note the inclusion in the continuing Leuenberg process of the specific practical implications of the priesthood of all believers, the relation of this to the ordained ministry in the life of the Church, the pneumatological aspects of ecclesiology, and historico-critical and hermeneutical problems of the biblical foundations of ecclesiological statements.

As a preliminary response we may reflect that all Christians share in *diakonia*, ordained Christians are a technical support for the others, the Spirit is always the Spirit of the crucified and risen Lord, and it produces Christlikeness, and that all ecclesiological statements are made within the ongoing tradition of the gospel.

We now turn to fresh reflection on the understanding of the marks and attributes of the Church in the present. The Church is God's Church. The fellowship of the Holy Spirit is the medium of the grace of the Lord Jesus Christ, through which we are sustained in and through the love of God. The Church is one, holy, catholic and apostolic. These are eschatological pointers, to which its particular manifestations rarely correspond completely, but they remain central in pointing to God's purpose for his Church.

[4]Barmen, cf. Niesel, *Reformed Symbolics,* 357f.

The Church in Jesus Christ is one. It is called to express more fully that unity which it has. There should doubtless always be differences in theory and practice. But in central affirmations and in discipleship there ought to be unity. To unite with other Christians is not of course just to swallow them up: we shall come to speak of practical ecumenism again. The Church is one.

The Church is holy. The holiness of the Church is in the first place not the holiness, the transparent goodness and love of its members, but the holiness of Christ. If the members fail to respond to the great invitation, then they are members in name only. The Church is catholic. It encompasses the whole of our planet. Its concern is equally with the people of North and South, East and West, rich and poor.

The Church is apostolic. It is only as the bearer of the witness of the time of the events concerning Jesus that the Church can communicate a distinctive message to humankind. Though it must be rooted in the being of God, the Church as such belongs to the created world and remains a highly fallible community. Apostolicity is not a permanent endowment but something to which the Church is constantly recalled by the Word.

We may note too the conviction, deeply rooted in the tradition, that the Church is indestructible. The promise is there as long as there are human beings alive, and it continues beyond physical death. God promises always to be with his people, however difficult conditions may become. However unfaithful we may be, God's promise remains with a visible community. This indestructibility is also the hope of the Church. The creation awaits the divine perfection and consummation, which is the fulfilment of the role of the Church as a central instrument of God's love in the present. Thy Kingdom come.

We come to the understanding of ministry. The Reformation brought a new understanding of Christian discipleship as the priesthood of all believers. We must not see the clergy as the *real* Church. All Christians are constantly invited to a mutual ministry to one another and to all humankind. This is based on God's gift through grace of the Spirit of the risen Christ.

In addition to this universal ministry there has been since New Testament times a variety of particular ministries. People have been dedicated and employed, full or part time, to preach the word and administer the sacraments, to conduct pastoral work in congregation and community, to offer leadership and direction. Such ministries have taken different forms in different places and cultures.

The basic elements of such a structure are the ministers, men and women, at local congregational level. These may be priests and deacons, ministers, elders and deacons, bishops, priests and deacons, or other combinations. In some churches the central unit for administrative, liturgical and other purposes will be the presbytery, presided over by a chairman or moderator and including an equal number of ministers and elders, or a synod presided over by a superintendent or a bishop. Different structures encourage the use of authority and power, wisely or unwisely, in different ways. The basis of ministry remains not what we do but what God does.

The service of the ordained minister is to seek to become an instrument of God's love in Christ for the world. At the same time, this ministry is not a virtuoso performance but takes place within the mutual ministry of all Christians in and for society. Ministry is not effectively carried out through consensus on the definition of church order. It has to be grounded in worship and in service. In worship, ministry takes place within the common stream of adoration, confession, thanksgiving and intercession. It also means preaching. If the Word is not heard as a living word, the Church may die of boredom.

The ordained ministry is understood within the Reformed tradition as a ministry of word and sacrament. Calvin followed Augustine in describing a sacrament. 'One may call it a testimony of divine grace towards us, confirmed by an outward sign, with mutual attestation of our piety towards him' (*Institutes*,4.14.1). In his classic threefold structure of signification, there is the word of God's promise in the institution, then the matter or substance, that is, the Christ with his death and resurrection, and finally the effect, the benefits of Christ, the life in Christ (*Institutes*,4.17.1).

How is it possible to reflect this tradition today? Jesus Christ, we suggested, is the one sacrament of the Church in the primary sense. Baptism and eucharist are understood in the light of the primary sacrament of Jesus Christ. John the Baptist prepared the people of God for God's coming. People repent, and receive a baptism by water. Jesus was baptised to assume the ministry of the servant of God. After Pentecost all who join the churches are baptised. This is the baptism of the Spirit, as well as water baptism. It marks repentance, but also the placing of the baptised in the household of God. It is a work of God, and it also marks the natural response in repentance of those who hear his invitation. Those who come, come to something that is already there, as children or as adults.

Constitutive of the new humanity is the fact that it is not destroyed by human death. In the life of Jesus the Kingdom of God was inaugurated and it goes on for ever. Through Jesus Christ humanity is incorporated into the eternal life of God. This incorporation is both a reaffirmation of the created order as part of the new creation and a reaffirmation of life beyond the created order, in the communion of the saints with God. The new humanity includes the eschatological peace of God, which passes all understanding. But this does not mean it is entirely incomprehensible. For it is characterised by God's own self-giving love. But its realisation goes beyond all that we can conceive in this life. Fullness of life is the fulfilment for which God has ordered his creation.

25

The Church of the Future

1. Oekumene

In the last chapter I have sought to consider a particular tradition, the Reformed tradition. It seems to me however that nothing that has been said would be unacceptable to the Lutheran tradition (hence the Leuenberg agreement), though of course the Lutheran tradition has its own historical memory and distinctive style, and would quite rightly wish to enrich this in the future.

Perhaps more surprisingly, I do not see our previous reflections as being incompatible with the Anglican tradition, though again the same considerations apply as with the Lutherans. Anglicans have no wish to be turned into Reformed Christians overnight, any more than Reformed Christians wish to be instantly Anglicanised.

Clearly, in searching for a more adequate expression of visible unity there has to be movement on all sides. No tradition can be regarded as the norm, the *principium*, the *fons totius unitatis* or whatever. We still have a very long way to go in exorcising the belief that in ecumenical relations, 'it is more blessed to give than to receive'. *We*, whoever we are, have to be prepared to receive, even when that can be a painful process. There is a great deal of nonsense involved in hiding behind 'the need to endure the pain of our divisions', which is often a mask for tribal prejudice. But all must be prepared to receive. A striking instance of the difficulty of such an achievement is provided by the WCC's Baptism, Eucharist and Ministry (BEM) document, which confronted traditional Protestantism with some hard choices but failed to confront traditional Orthodoxy and Catholicism with the same demand for a tough critical engagement with the past. It is indeed much easier to give than to receive.

I return to a Reformed/Anglican discussion. It appears to me that nothing of the Reformed perspective sketched above would have presented any difficulty to Cranmer, or indeed to many later generations in sympathy with his approach. To Anglicans more influenced by the historical impact of the Oxford Movement, which we discussed at an earlier stage, the mention of Calvin would hardly be a commendation, and the tone and style of ecclesiological reflection might be different, in general and in detail. But I seriously doubt if there remain doctrinal differences sufficient to warrant continuing confessional separation. This is not to say that there may not remain other factors, theological and non-theological and matters of ecclesiastical administration, which will continue to divide for the foreseeable future.

To make real progress in such areas requires vision and determination. In considering the whole question of the future of the Church I have found valuable hints in Peter Walker's *Rediscovering the Middle Way,* which though written by a diocesan bishop, might equally well have been produced, *mutatis mutandis* by either of the Baillie brothers in the Reformed tradition.

> To discourage, indeed to be nervous about, new insights into the truth is, as Hort warned his church long ago, not life but death, and it is inevitably to lose the future which the church is about. And the distressing thing about the present impasse, and such it seems to me, is not only that men and women of good will and concern, and of conscientious regard for truth, find themselves alienated: it is that the Church loses its direction, locked into a pre-occupation with the past. (89)

The book ends with a recall of the Church of England to the essentials.

> At its most faithful, it has refused to make absolutes of other things, and has distinctively gone back to that which is none

other than the central mystery entrusted to the Church's keeping: God's great condescension – that God was in Christ reconciling the world to himself and committing to us the ministry of reconciliation. (136)

God was in Christ reconciling the world to himself. All Christians are irrevocably committed to a ministry of reconciliation. The churches share common problems, both in their internal structures and in relation to the communities which they seek to serve. They need to reach out to nations in which most people no longer go to church services. They need to find new ways of preaching the word effectively and administering the sacraments to God's people as the body and blood of Christ. They need to find better ways of reaching out to other churches in fellowship.

As I see it, one of the most profound contemporary contributions to the understanding of the Church has come from Edward Schillebeeckx, in a progressive Catholic tradition. Schillebeeckx is aware of the urgency of the task, and of the lack of awareness of urgency in many areas of the Church. Sometimes,too, it is helpful to look at the Church's more radical critics, in order to remind ourselves that the *status quo* is not the only conceivable position. Here I find it helpful to consider the argument of Don Cupitt's study, *Radicals and the Future of the Church.*

2. A Radical Church

Don Cupitt posed sharply the question of how far in a postmodern age a church is possible. He noted that in the sixties and seventies a radical church seemed like a possibility. But now, like the patriarchate of Constantinople as he sees it, the Church is declining, becoming more conservative, but consolidating its most reactionary and autocratic pretensions. His study is five-sixths analysis, one sixth solution.

Cupitt said of the churches in the 80s, 'They have largely disinvested in critical theology, and are instead taking up various forms of theological populism' (9). 'Reform is not in sight. The church appears locked into long-term decline, growing rigidity and a slide into fantasy and the cult mentality.' Cupitt believes that God is not external to us, but is basically as way of reflecting on the self. This is not a position which I share. But he does say things about the Church which are well worth considering.

He is strongly critical of the power of the clergy. 'So far as the people who control it are concerned, the church is about one thing only, spiritual power, and power is never surrendered voluntarily' (71). As for the role of women, 'existing doctrine is and was designed to be highly sexist'. What is to be done? 'We can see clearly that the liberal ideology is mythical and has collapsed'(167). Neither the Bible nor the creeds could be central to a radical church, but there could be sacraments, a common meal for a common fellowship. 'In general the design-requirement for a future church is not to create a new pattern, but to open a space for plurality, for humanity and for spiritual freedom.' (172)

There are viewpoints in the volume with which one may not agree. But there is an awareness of a need for real change rather than cosmetic rearrangement. I do not consider that we can or should reinvent the Church. As I see it, the Church is God's Church, or else it is nothing. It is of course also our Church, and it occasionally needs to be turned inside out. And since we human beings all look at the Church in different ways at different times, from Catholic Peru to Protestant Germany, as teenagers, as families, as single people, as men, as women, and so on, it needs to be a broad church, capable of welcoming us as we are, and leading us again to God.

Sometimes there is need for clear-cut change. But usually only God can change the whole, and it is up to us to look after the details. The art of the possible is often the most humane way of ordering the affairs of humankind.

Since the European Enlightenment we have seen the development not only of a secular culture but also of a radically pluralist culture on our planet. But the pluralism also contains new monochrome cultures and new fundamentalisms. We have blueprints neither for God nor for the eternal truths of reason. Yet neither are we completely at sea on the accidental truths of history, inventing our own existence and values at will. Exploiting people is always wrong. Caring for our fellow human beings is always right. Caring for the Church may involve taking risks. For the Church, Jesus Christ remains always and ultimately the way, the truth and the life, even though in faith we may see this way, truth and life through a glass darkly.

In the world of theology Bonhoeffer taught us in his life and in his death about the secular meaning of the gospel. Rahner taught us about the value of true spirituality. Barth reminded us of the sovereignty of grace, Gutierrez of the bias of the gospel towards the poor. In the churches too there are different cultures, catholic and sacramental cultures, conservative evangelical cultures, liberal academic cultures, hierarchical and grass roots cultures. These cultures speak different languages, but they are not always incapable of translation and mutual support. Within these cultures there are good and bad developments, authentically Christian and not so authentic pressures. What matters is whether they point to the character of Christ as this comes through the tradition of the gospel to us.

Testing the spirits is never a simple thing and it requires constant attention, sensitivity, listening. But despite colossal failures there remains a remarkable stream of constructive and original Christian witness of astonishing variety in the churches in every century. There is every reason to turn the Church inside out from time to time for the sake of the gospel, so that we can see in a new way the depth of God's love. *Ecclesia semper reformanda*, to use the language of the Vatican.

3. A Participating Church

God is love, not love in general but love characterised precisely through the life, death and resurrection of Jesus Christ. The Church is the Church of the love of God. This is not a formal statement. It is the heart of the nature of the Christian community. The Church can be understood in terms of numerous models. But these are useful only as they illuminate the centre.

Avery Dulles analysed various ecclesiastical structures in his excellent *Models of the Church*. These structures included the understanding of the Church as institution, as mystical communion, as sacrament, as herald and as servant. All have advantages and disadvantages, and may be combined to point to the centre in different ways. I should like to develop this suggestion further, in considering the relation of the understanding of God to the understanding of the Church.

God in Christian perspective we have understood as the God of creation and redemption, of Israel and of Jesus. The Church is the place where Christians become aware in word and sacrament of the hidden presence of God. The Church is the fruit of the pattern of the life of Jesus, who turned to the disadvantaged, who supported the unsupported. The Church is the fruit of the death of Jesus, the legacy of a man dying in agony for ultimate truth. The Church is the fruit of the resurrection, of the new creation in the Spirit. The Church is the Church of the triune God, and it is there for all humankind.

The model of the body of Christ has been much used in recent ecumenical study, notably in the BEM document. It has also been much criticised, often with the not unjust suggestion that in practice it has favoured a hierarchical and even juridical understanding of church structures. Against this a trinitarian model of ecclesiology has sometimes been preferred, stressing the community of faith and the complete interdependence of one member of the Church upon another. In our earlier chapter I gave prominence to the understanding of the Church as the Church of the crucified and risen Christ. It remains to explore the significance of the understanding of the Church as the Church of Jesus of Nazareth.

As we have already seen, the picture of Jesus which is emerging from what is sometimes called the 'third Quest' continues to produce surprises. It is increasingly clear that the world into which Jesus came was a world of tension, of terror and counter-terror, in which Jew and Roman co-existed uneasily. Within this darkness, Jesus produced and produces grounds for hope. Without a political programme, he was and is a threat to political powers, not least in his quite uncompromising concern for the most vulnerable in society.

In Jesus' life and work, there was no neat division between the concerns of the Church and of the world. In a modern pluralistic age there are echoes of such a situation, where the Church is no longer a privileged and protected body. Pluralism works in different ways. In some areas there are still large self-sufficient communities within a pluralist culture, predominantly impervious to their surroundings, with the advantages and disadvantages that this brings. There is the possibility of remaining uncontaminated by alien values. There is the danger of self-absorption and neglect of the missionary and diaconal roles of the Church. In other areas there is a much greater interaction between church and wider community. Here both the consciousness of the need and the capacity to act for the wider community may be much greater. But the Church may be in danger of losing confidence in its values and becoming simply an uncritical echo of current cultural trends.

We cannot avoid living in a pluralistic world. This is the challenge which we have to face with careful reflection and consistent action. These are problems with which ecumenical bodies and national church organisations have to engage. But they are also, and perhaps in the end more decisively, the issues which local Christian communities must manage successfully if they are to be instruments of God's love in his world. In some countries these communities will still be able to operate in their traditional ways as sections of national churches with a widely recognised public position. In other areas they will function more as a thin network of worship and service, more like a helpline in voluntary social work than like a public corporation.

In considering Christian reflection in this framework I have found particularly useful comment in Peter Hodgson's *Revisioning the Church – Ecclesial Freedom in the New Paradigm.*[1] This study considers the ecclesial consequences of the understanding of God in *God in History,* which we discussed earlier.

Hodgson traces three great paradigms or patterns in the Christian tradition, the classical, the modern and the post-modern. The post-modern paradigm includes a cognitive crisis in philosophical rationality, and a historical, socio-

---

[1] P.C. Hodgson, *Revisioning the Church,* 104. Cf. too the emphasis on the Church as communion and as sacrament of salvation in Walter Kasper's *Theology and Church.*

economic, political and religious crisis. The certainties of classical and Enlightenment thought and culture have gone. A new theological agenda, and a new theology of the Church, are required.

Reflection on elements of the classical paradigm and in Enlightenment thought indicates that these can be neither absolutised nor ignored. A new consideration of the spirituality and historicality of the Church stresses the sociality of the Church, as a means of interpretation, sacramentality and caring and justice. Much can be learned from the preferential option for the poor and from feminist ecclesial vision. Christianity must be a truly global religion, accepting religious pluralism. This leads to a new theology of ministry. Ministry is leadership, but leadership in nurture and in enabling participation rather than hierarchical domination.

Ecclesia is divine gift and human activity. 'As a mediating, spiritual reality, ecclesia is unambiguous but fragmentary: it participates in the saving power of the basileia (God's world-transforming redemptive rule), disclosing it unambiguously but actualising it only fragmentarily, because the instruments of actualisation are historical and finite' (104). As such, ecclesia becomes a critical principle of praxis.

I find Hodgson's distinction between the unambiguous and the fragmentary particularly apposite. The Church exists and works only as a witness to and in the service of Jesus Christ. But its discipleship is most effective when most sensitive to the changing and varied needs of the plural and complex society within which it is set. It has to create spaces for reflection on the source of its discipleship, for meditation and prayer. It must also always be open to the people of the world in their urgent, often unexpressed but often desperate needs.

The role of the Church in society has never been confined to raising consciousness about matters of political and social ethics. It has a long and remarkable tradition of pastoral care which has extended well beyond the boundaries of individual congregations. This ministry, of clergy and of individual members of congregations, has been the prototype of the 'caring profession' over the centuries, and remains a vital area of the Church's service.

We live in a world in which wealth, beauty, physical and mental health are increasingly emphasised as the norms for human flourishing. Diatribes against materialism are often tedious, and the gospel encourages us to enjoy the potential of the created order to the full. But this enjoyment should not involve the neglect af those who are disadvantaged, through chance circumstances, through poverty or illness. Apart from contributing to the solution of ethical problems raised in modern medicine, the pastoral care of the sick remains a continuing and important task. It is necessary to promote and sustain a consistently high level of health care in a world in which the prizes often go to the strong in disproportionate measure. It is also vital that individuals who are ill should be supported with care and friendship on a short term and on a long term basis. Here the Church will always have a distinctive and indispensable task of service.

Pastoral care has a preferential option for the poor and for the sick. But it is concerned for the whole Christian community, in encouraging a life of discipleship. and of relationship in the light of the gospel. In society at large it is committed to offer a quality of concern for others which reflects faith in the God who is love.

The whole question of the wider responsibility of Christians to act as a therapeutic community is sensitively dealt with by Stanley Hauerwas in his *Suffering Presence. Theological Reflections on Medicine, the Mentally Handicapped and the Church.* He explores the relationship between physical and mental suffering, and the scope and limitations of different sorts of medical practice for the wellbeing of society. He underlines the great need for understanding and support for the mentally handicapped and the retarded in society, reminding us again of the extent and the gravity of human suffering.

That we avoid the sufferer is not because we are deeply unsympathetic or inhumane, but because of the very character of suffering. By its very nature suffering alienates us not only from one another but from ourselves, especially suffering which we undergo, which is not easily integrated into our ongoing projects or hopes. To suffer is to have our identity threatened physically, psychologically, and morally.

Thus our suffering even makes us unsure of who we are. It is not surprising, therefore, that we should have trouble with the suffering of others. None of us willingly seeks to enter into the loneliness of others. (175)

4. The Church of the Reconciliation

The Church expresses human response to the gospel of Jesus Christ. Response varies, according to the culture in which it is expressed. But it ought always to be centred on the gospel. That is to say, the Church is always evangelical. There can be few words so often misused, abused and hi-jacked in the Church as the word evangelical. There has always been discussion about the essence of Christianity. But however we may differ in our interpretations, Christians seek always to respond to the God who is identified through the self-giving love of Jesus Christ.

We can learn by exploring to the full our sometimes conflicting interpretations. But we have a primary duty to see to it that our tensions are constructive rather than destructive tensions. Jesus Christ is not a weapon to be used in bludgeoning others into submission. Here church history calls us to repent of our sin in sackcloth and ashes. The voices of thousands of men and women murdered in the name of a particular interpretation of the gospel, in civil wars, in crusades against heretics and heathen, the women drowned as witches, the men drowned as anabaptists, the silenced and the vanished in our own century cry out against this inversion of true evangelism.

Evangelical means open, open to conservative and liberal Christians alike, and to all our fellow men and women, not least the marginalised and the victims of institutional violence. It requires attention to the unconditional compassion of God, to forgiveness and reconciliation. Evangelical includes neither cheap grace nor cheap slogans. It costs. Evangelical demands catholic sensitivity to the unlimited love of God. If we are to have Christian renewal it will certainly not come through closing hearts and minds. I was a stranger, and you took me in. Evangelical also includes a recognition that in fact we learn from each other, and that integrity is not a personal monopoly for any of us. That, of course, is a challenge to us all.

The Church in God's purpose is, as Luther said, the creature of the gospel. It is there to manifest the reality in human terms of God's overwhelming love. In God there is a boundlessness of love, not as domination but as solidarity with the fragile and the vulnerable. A bruised reed he will not break. It is not the sort of vulnerability which can be experienced as a threat, making the fragile feel even more fragile and insecure. God's love bears all the encompassing effectiveness of God. As the Church understands Jesus Christ as God's word and sacrament for the world, so the Church is to be there as a sign of this word of promise and as a manifestation of the substance of the sacraments of grace. It is also a pointer to the realisation of God's peace in the future.

The Church as an empirical social institution has a history, a long history which can be examined. This history is partly a history for which we may give thanks, of selfless devotion to the way of Jesus Christ, of light in darkness, of caring when no one else cared. It is partly also a history for which we must ask forgiveness, a history in which natural ferocity has been enhanced by religious fervour, in which hundreds of thousands, perhaps millions of lives have been crushed explicitly in the name of the Christian gospel.

When the Church prays for the guidance of the Spirit it has to remember that its interpretation of the guidance of the Spirit has often been much less than infallible. The Spirit is always, as we have seen already, the Spirit of the crucified and risen Christ. The fruits of the Spirit are manifested in Christlikeness, in compassion, patience, gentleness and humility. In this sense the Church to be Church is always charismatic, and the charisms are indissolubly bound to the character of Christ.

In the book of Acts the Church appears as the ecclesia, the assembly of the people of God, in some ways a continuation of and a parallel to the synagogue, the people of God in the Old Testament. The whole question of the relation of Church to synagogue remained and remains an unsolved question, with tragic consequences for the Jewish people, culminating in the Holocaust, the greatest and we must hope the last triumph of the kingdom of darkness, in our time. The New Testament is full of rich and varied imagery to describe the Church. The centre is not however the imagery but the life, death and resurrection of Jesus of Nazareth.

Though we have seen, notably in the case of the Son of Man sayings, how difficult it is to pinpoint the *ipsissima verba* of Jesus, we have also seen that we can make statements about him with a considerable degree of probability. The picture which emerges is more of challenge than of comfort.

Jesus came into a society torn with all sorts of violence and conflict, a Jew immersed in Judaism. This society had many layers, of varying degrees of sophistication. It included a totalitarian regime, and a number of religious and secular power groupings whose members were prepared, as always in such circumstances, to use all means at their disposal to secure their own power and to promote the destruction of their enemies. Within this minefield Jesus used tact, diplomacy and firmness of purpose to preach the gospel of the coming of the Kingdom of God, to offer God's forgiveness, to act on behalf of the marginalised and the victims of institutional violence, and to confront the political and religious authorities with the demands of unconditional love. He was arrested and his followers scattered. He was condemned as a traitor and executed barbarously. God raised him from the dead.

The Church is constantly called into the way of discipleship, after the pattern of this, one decisive life. It is also constantly reminded of its basis in crucifixion and resurrection. It is always the Church of the crucified one, always in solidarity with the exploited, the abused, the murdered. It is always empowered to bring light out of darkness, however improbably. For it is a sign, not our sign but God's sign, of the effective power of resurrection, in new creation. There is still a very long way to go. But forgiveness, reconciliation and unconditional love are already a reality. In the eyes of faith, the grace of the Lord Jesus Christ, the love of God and the fellowship of the Holy Spirit are just there, often despite almost all appearances to the contrary.

As the Church of the Spirit the Church is one. Its oneness is that of its obedience to the Spirit. There are however the numerous different organisations, each with its different structures, especially of ministry. This diversity, born of different cultural developments, need not in itself be a problem. The difficulties arise from the fact that each denomination in practice tends to regard its own claims as exclusively correct, over against other forms of ministry. Each group tends to regard assimilation to its own pattern and power structure as the ideal and often the only appropriate ecumenical structure. In this way a diversity of worship, of work in the wider community and of internal organisation which ought to be creative becomes instead a source of destructive tension at every level. Instead of witnessing to the manifold nature of the work of the Spirit it becomes a monument to human capacity for alienation. This is nowhere more clear than in dissension concerning the ministry of women in the Church.

We have discussed the oneness of the Church. It is remarkable how divisions about the nature of church structures mirror differences on the method and content of theology. Once again the gulf between creative and destructive disagreement is clear, and this is very much to the disadvantage of the whole Christian enterprise. There is perhaps no overriding reason for the Church to be one in organisational structure. But it should at least be one in charity.

Similar considerations apply to the other major traditional images of the structure of the Church. The Church is holy, it is asserted. This should in turn be reflected in the fruits of the spirit in Christian life. Once again the patterns of discipleship may be reflected in different ways in different cultures and traditions. What is not needed is a rivalry between different patterns of goodness.

The Church is catholic. It is, as exploration of each of our models emphasises, concerned with the welfare of all Christians, and indeed of all humankind. Concentration on the particular local community may enhance the life of a local group. But this should not lead to a loss of the universal perspective. It is a typical but unfortunate feature of the prevailing denominational rivalry that catholic is an attribute monopolised by one denomination. The Church is also, and quite rightly, Protestant, Orthodox, Baptist, Episcopalian and Congregationalist. It is these things, eschatologically, as the Church of Jesus Christ. As divided groups it can only partially realise any of these aspirations.

Denominational churches do not of course live entirely in worlds of their own. They are immersed in and influenced by a wider society. If they lose their distinctive identities they are in real danger of vanishing, through becoming colourless communities with a vague message and a lack of strong commitment. If they retreat into their traditions, develop a fortress mentality and a deeply conservative ethos in all things, then they may in fact gain in membership. But they risk losing that truly catholic concern for humankind which is at the heart of the gospel.

In the Church as in society in general, there are often conflicts between concern for individuals and concern for society. The Christian Church is clearly deeply committed to concern for both. The gospel is preached to each individual human being. It is a call to faith and to response. It is an invitation to individuals as individuals. God is experienced in faith, we said, not as a vague concept but as the God who brings new life, who brings forgiveness and reconciliation. This gift of faith is from God.

There is an important element of complexity and even of paradox in a contemporary Christian understanding of Church and society. We understand the whole created order to be brought into being by God, and dependent upon God for its fulfilment. But in many countries Christians form a small minority of the population. Where Christians have been in a large majority they have often proved historically to be insensitive to the rights and values of the minorities, and so our desire for a wider spread of the gospel is not a desire for the return of an imperious and insensitive Christendom. Minorities may be more sensitive to the role of the Christian community in seeking to witness by persuasion, invitation and example rather than by diktat. On the other hand, minorities can also become rather self-obsessed, develop an inferiority complex and fail to contribute responsibly to society as a whole. Balances need to be struck between caesaro-papalism and sectarianism throughout church history. A particular community has to nourish its own internal life in order to be of service to others, but that wider concern must remain at the centre of the agenda. At the same time, the service of the love of God always needs to be advanced by means and attitudes which are themselves consonant with the self-giving love of God. Otherwise, as history constantly reminds us, nothing worthwhile is achieved.

Jesus died on the cross for the whole world. Those who follow Christ, the way of the cross, must die to the world and find a new life in Christ. They must take care not to be overwhelmed by the values, concepts, claims and duties of this world. But they are also sent out into the world. They are given the task of communicating in word and action the Christian gospel in this world now.

The Church is a worshipping community, in which Jesus Christ is present and active. Here the Church waits on God, who is present in word and sacrament. Through the presence of Christ the congregation becomes part of the body of Christ. Waiting for God involves recollecting the presence of God in the past, recorded in the scriptures. It involves thanksgiving in praise and prayer, in confession and petition, in intercession for others, within and outside the Church. Worshipping and waiting, the Church participates in the new creation yet to come. Anticipating the new creation, the members of the community may seek to become instruments of that peace which God intends as the fulfilment of his purpose for the created order.

Churches like all social institutions need structures. These structures have included from almost the beginning ministers, persons dedicated to working for the community at local or regional levels, often on a full time basis. Different patterns have emerged in response to local needs at different times. I want to consider now the nature of these patterns of ministry.

Central to the purpose of the whole Christian community is service, *diakonia*. In this sense there is a diaconia or priesthood of all believers, in the service of Jesus Christ and dependent on the Holy Spirit. Ministry has sometimes been inadequate, sometimes a travesty, sometimes exemplary. Ministry involves authority, spiritual authority. But this authority involves temporal power in society, and can be used with or without responsibility, as church history amply demonstrates.

The development of church law followed the increasing complexity and pluralism of administrative structures, in a continuing dialogue between theory and practice. In the early Church there was manifold complexity and diversity already. The Middle Ages, the Reformation period, the European Enlightenment and the proliferation of different approaches, radical and conservative, in the so-called Third World have produced an almost infinite variety of patterns in ministry. This diversity may be regretted and ignored. But it has existed. I believe it points to an awareness that the pattern of effective Christian ministry may be very different in different times and places. Some structures may be better than others in different circumstances. None is of the esse of the gospel.

However structured, the Christian ministry, which is not the ministry of Christ though it is based on this, always involves the basic tasks of a ministry of word and sacrament and of pastoral care in congregation and community. It also involves a contribution to the wider work of the Church and the churches.

Ministry involves the leading of worship, as a central and vital part of the life of the Christian community and of its witness. Adoration and confession, thanksgiving and intercession, prayer and preaching and the sacraments will always be at the centre of Christian life. Where these elements are neglected there is a serious impoverishment of the community. Not the least serious of temptations to which the minister is vulnerable is the temptation to preach boring sermons, lead ill-considered prayers and celebrate the sacraments without due care – often simply because of the considerable pressures of the contemporary parish.

In all this discussion of Church and ministry I presuppose a complete equality of the ministry of men and women in the Church. One has to note that even churches where equality is theoretically complete have a great deal to do to translate theory into consistent practice.

The centre of a church which is grounded in God's love must be attention to the source of its life in God. Here its love is rekindled and its faith is inspired. From attention come thanksgiving, forgiveness, and reconciliation as fruits of the

Spirit. From attention to the love of God come the traditional marks of the Church in unity, holiness, catholicity and apostolicity. Without attention these too easily become sources of destructive rather than constructive tension, grounds for exclusive rather than inclusive attitudes.

5. Repentant Compassion

I have emphasised the communal nature of the Church, Christian life as life together. But this is only possible as a source of enrichment for humanity when the Christian life of the individual is developed. Each is a child of God. However such individualism, far from banishing social concern, should in my view drive Christians to greater efforts to ensure the individual development of all human beings, the starving in Africa and Asia and the neglected in Europe and in America as well as the culturally and materially enriched. The gospel is not opposed to the enjoyment of the benefits of creation in material and cultural riches. It is however implacably opposed to these when they serve as barriers to devotion to God and our fellow human beings. God's love means justice and fairness in all things. Precisely attention to the life of the individual as grounded in the reality of the forgiveness of sins and faith in the resurrection and the life everlasting may turn us to the social dimensions of the gospel. The life of the Christian carries on into the Kingdom of God, which already affects present reality.

There is then a vital and integral connection between the life of the Christian in its most private and individual dimension and in its social commitment. It is precisely because Jesus Christ has died for the forgiveness of my sins that he has lived, died and risen for all humanity. Concern for human rights, for the dignity, worth and freedom of every individual, is of the essence of evangelical Christianity. That is why the persecution of minorities who are already marginalised by some Christians throughout history is literally damnable. The physically and mentally ill, lepers and AIDS victims, prisoners, often women and children, people of minority faiths, homosexuals, Jews, and Gipsies, have been the subject of endless institutional violence. If it seems unnecessary to list the victims, we have to remember that until recent times theological reflections were too often a seamless framework of triumphalist satisfaction. Repentance is not simply an attribute of old-fashioned theology. It has to be at the centre of an imaginative approach to the future of the faith.

The past, the track record, is an index of the need for repentance. It is also a sign of hope and a record of faith. We believe that God has used past generations as instruments of his love, and he communicates again to each generation through human contact. The shared experience of grace is the source of faith, of hope and of committed and sustained action. In this way the Church helps people towards a deeper knowledge of God, and enables people to respond to the invitation of the gospel, to an awareness of the sense of the presence of God. God communicates with his people and leads them as pilgrims on their journey, supporting them on the way. For through Jesus Christ God has been there. God is there, as hidden, loving, sustaining presence. This is our understanding in faith.

The Church is a community of people called to serve God in discipleship to Jesus Christ, seeking the guidance always of the Spirit. It is present in human history in many different forms at different times and in different places. Its service is always the same, to love God and humanity after the pattern of the character of Christ. But the forms of this service vary, as the shape of society changes and people's needs change and are variously expressed.

The Church is there to worship God, and to draw renewal of strength and commitment from meditation, through word and sacrament, and through fellowship among its members. The bounds of the Church are not rigidly defined, for God is present to and equally concerned for all his creatures, even where they may not acknowledge that presence. The Church must always be an open Church, ready to share, to listen, to serve. It must have a preferential option for the poor, the sick and the marginalised.

This cannot be said too often, for in history the Church has often exercised a preferential option for the rich, the powerful and the popular. The Church must reflect with care on its tradition, seeking perspective from its past as well as its present for informing its concern. The tradition calls for repentance as much as for as pride. The greater the tradition of the various churches, the greater the need for repentance, it sometimes seems. The gospel of God's love has often itself been a weapon rather than a source of nurture and support. But the Church cannot and need not repent of the gospel. It is called to attend ever more closely to the gospel, in love for God and for all humankind, and to express God's love with ever greater sensitivity, understanding and commitment.

After this section was written I read Edward Schillebeeckx's *Church – The Human Story of God.* I am very much in sympathy with his stress on the servant role of the Church amid the reality of human experience in the world today. 'People have Christian experiences in and through human experiences with men and women in our world history, within the natural environment in which we live, but always in the light of the faith content of the Christian tradition of experience' (25). He goes on to stress that 'the Church is an actual minority which is there to serve a majority and is not concerned with winning as many souls as possible for itself' (184). For, always, 'The coming of the Kingdom of God is a grace, but a grace which is effective in and through human action and not outside it, above it or behind it.'

Faith and praxis are always related, and always seeking a better articulation of that relationship. The sense of the presence of God, creator and redeemer, is part of the gift of the Spirit within the Church and the world. Making that presence visible in human community, through the charitable presence of Christian concern, is faith's response to the invitation of the gospel. It continues, unvarying in its scope but always changing in its form, throughout human history. It is the response to God in Christian perspective. This response to and through the Spirit, in church and wider community, is the subject of our next chapter.

26

The Spirit and the Human

1. The Humanum

Consideration of the work of the Spirit in the world leads inevitably to further reflection on the Christian understanding of man, of the human. The tradition speaks of man as God's creature, made in the image of God. A distinction is then usually drawn between the old man, fallen Adam, and the new man, restored in Christ, usually seen as man as churchman. It is perfectly possible to follow this route and to give a comprehensive account of the Christian understanding of man. The understanding of God outlined in these pages suggests a rather different approach. God is creator and reconciler. God is there as a self-differentiated God, Father, Son and Spirit. All humanity *is* potentially reconciled through the Spirit of the risen Christ, even if the eschatological fulfilment is still outstanding between the times, even if there is still sin and evil in the world. It is indeed in the light of this reconciliation that the enormity of sin, of alienation, becomes clear. It is not indeed that man is only man in relation, as God is in relation. But man is precisely a self as man in the context of relationship. Being and authenticity are realities, sustained through the medium of the divine-human relationship. Man may then be seen through the twin foci of the old and new creation narratives, neither without the other. In the new the old is fulfilled and also radically transformed. Yet the transformation is only recognisable through the reality of faith.

In considering the action of the Spirit of God we have been reflecting on the Christian life in relation to the Church and to society. This brings us again to the question of the nature of man, man in relation to God and his fellow men and women. For it is in relation to the Spirit that the Christian understanding of man is most naturally worked out. There is no more intimate friend of human nature than the Holy Spirit, as Karl Barth strikingly and paradoxically put it. There is an intimate connection between pneumatology and anthropology. This is the basic reason why we may not, *pace* the early Karl Barth, leave the realm of the human to Feuerbach's reductionist analysis.

In Christian perspective God alone can give genuine autonomy of selfhood to his creatures. He does not put pressure upon them as we exert pressure upon each other. As there is no symmetrical correspondence between God and man, so there is no simple correspondence between the divine spirit and the human spirit. God invites human beings to participate in the life of faith, and through faith in the fruits of the Spirit. These are characterised in the attributes of Christ, expressed in many ways, and summed up in the famous Pauline list of patience, long-suffering, kindness, the parameters of charity. How are these fruits of the Spirit exercised in relation to human capacities? Sometimes these have been related specifically to the soul, or the conscience, or to a sense of historicality, existential self-realisation or to other concepts. I am not sure that any such specific link is conceivable, at least, as a definitive explanation of how the Spirit works. The Spirit blows where it will. It is of course entirely proper to use imagination to develop certain areas, such as conscience in relation to spirit. The basic Christian question remains whether the human characteristics under consideration do or can contribute ultimately to the exercise of charity or not.

2. Human Reconciliation

The Judaeo-Christian tradition has reflected on humanity as in one sense the crown of creation, God's final and central creation, made in the image of God and destined to be fulfilled in God. This centrality of man has had good and bad effects. It has encouraged people to develop a sense of responsibility for the created order. It has also led man to think of himself as the primary and even the sole object of God's care, and so to emphasise a tendency to egoism. Christians reflect that God was in Christ reconciling the world to himself. God became man. The purpose of reconciliation is fulfilled in the human. In the reconciliation, it may be thought, cosmic reconciliation is achieved, in that the centre of cosmic creation is restored. In redemption through the sphere of the personal, it may be thought, the physical order is recreated in the person in its highest form. God's activity is best understood through the analogy of moral agency, reflecting the ultimacy of the moral will. There may well be some truth in all these considerations. Yet they can clearly lead to an anthropocentricity which may take away from a theocentric view of God and the universe, and to that extent to a domestication of the understanding of God. There is also in Christian reflection an opposite tendency, to feel that it is necessary to denigrate man in order to glorify God, and so to paint a picture of man as either a passive lump of stuff in God's hands, or an unreservedly wicked and sinful creature. It is of course true that our century has seen more murders of man by his fellow man that most previous centuries in history. But there have also been countless examples of lives lived in selfless devotion to the welfare of others. Above all, for Christians there will always be the reflection that whatever man may be or have been, through Jesus Christ the human condition has been and will be transformed.

It is sometimes said then that we must look at humanity only in a theocentric or a Christocentric way. But in reality human beings reflecting on man are bound to take into account all human study of man. Even Karl Barth, after all, often associated with radical theocentricism, was an avid reader of the newspapers. Theologians might well feel able to take on board Addison's *Spectator* motto: *Quicquid homines agunt, nostri farrago libelli.*

What is much more controversial, however, is the manner in which general anthropological data is to be related to the theological subject matter. Hence the impassioned debates about the scope and limitations of revelation in determining a theological anthropology, e.g. in the famous Barth-Brunner debate about the image of God in man. It also raises the issue of the significance of the religious as such in human behaviour, in its various manifestations. To what extent does the gospel itself raise questions about a Christian understanding of man and indeed a general anthropology? Is it the case that a theological anthropology should reflect only or chiefly on matters first raised by a secular anthropology? If not, where are further sources of information to be found?

The Christian understanding of God does not entail a highly particular account of man as such, as a kind of divinely given philosophical anthropology. It involves certain central beliefs about the nature of man as God's creature, man created, redeemed and reconciled potentially through God. These beliefs may be expressed and their implications explored with the aid of various existing philosophical and other cultural frameworks. Some frameworks may be such that they lead to accounts of man which directly contradict central Christian beliefs, e.g. racist and fascist views of man. These will be denied by Christians. But that still leaves the possibility of articulating central beliefs about man in the light of God in such a way as to allow the widest scope for the exercise of human imagination in its cultural and social diversity.

I have summed up the centre of the Christian understanding of humanity elsewhere like this. 'In Jesus word and history are united in the disclosure of the ultimate meaning of humanity as the capacity to give and receive love, love which always involves speech and action and takes place within the reality of a concrete historical situation.' How may we remain faithful to this faith while engaging in dialogue with non-Christians? 'I suppose perhaps by speaking of a quality of corporate life and corporate concern which, though it derives from God's love, may be hoped to be capable of commending itself in the long run on the basis of its own human credentials, because it reflects the truth of what God has created us to be, and keeps open for us.'[1] The Spirit leads people into response to God's

---

[1] *Theology of the Love of God*, 134.

love, as part of God's continuing fulfilment of the consequences of redemption. In the light of this basic fact we may then see the numerous anthropological perspectives in philosophical and theological traditions in perspective.

In the Old Testament narratives man is part of the created order, but has a unique status. He is a free creature, free for the service of God and his fellow men. But there is a contradiction in his nature, which leads him to disobey God's will. He aspires to become equal with God, to overstep his limits, and is led into rebellion against God. Through Christ alone comes salvation. In the Old Testament man is distinguished from other animals through being created in the image of God. In the New Testament Christ is the image. Through the image fellowship with God is restored. There was much discussion in the tradition of distinctions between image and likeness. Basic to this line of thought is the belief that image is connected with right relationships, with God and man.

For the Fathers the centre of the understanding of man was often the relationship of the soul with God. For Luther it was justification by faith. For Barth it was the humanity of God in Jesus Christ. For Rahner it was obediential potency for the hypostatic union. For Pannenberg the key is man's sense of history, personal and social.

There is of course a sense in which all human activity forms a clue to the nature of man, especially as this has been analysed in reflection through the ages, in art and in the natural sciences, in literature, philosophy and the social sciences. This applies equally to the worst as to the best manifestations of human behaviour, and all shades between. This spectrum is evidence of the genuine autonomy which God gives to the created order, and of the awesome responsibility which it brings.

Research into the phenomenon of the human goes on in very many areas of academic study, notably in the life sciences but also in the arts-based subjects. Throughout history people have struggled to express what they regarded as the essence of the human. Philosophy, literature, art and history, bear testimony to the enormous diversity and fertility of this representation. More recent developments, especially in the nineteenth century, in anthropology and ethnology, psychology, psychiatry and sociology have produced a wealth of scholarly investigation of human characteristics and behaviour. The explosion of medical science in the modern period has yielded a continuing fund of new knowledge about the human body. This plethora of information makes it increasingly difficult to produce a unitary philosophical anthropology of the sort that was possible for Aristotle and even for Aquinas.

It is characteristic of the twentieth century that it is particularly in the tradition of German philosophical idealism that such attempts have continued to be made, e.g. by Max Scheler and Helmut Plessner, More typical of Anglo-Saxon thought is John Passmore's *The Perfectibility of Man*, which chronicles views of man through the ages without producing any sort of key to or essence of the human.

3. Theological Anthropology

Theological assessments of this material have varied, as theological attitudes to culture in general have varied. What has Athens to do with Jerusalem? The Greeks have been contrasted with the biblical authors, the law with the gospel, the philosophers with the theologians. However, a glance at the history of this discussion shows that, as one might expect, the preoccupations of the theologians, even in opposition, often mirrored and were dominated by the philosophical concerns of the day. Plato and Aristotle had been particularly concerned with the origin and role of the soul in mankind. The soul is central to consideration of man in the early Church. This concern was linked directly to the biblical passages which spoke of the image and likeness of God, a distinction which was to play an important role from Irenaeus on, enabling a distinction to be made between man in a fallen and in an original state. In this way it was possible to bring in the paradox of the human condition as reflected in the biblical narratives, namely that man is God's good creature, yet is also capable of behaving ruthlessly towards his fellow human beings.

Augustine marks a turning point in the understanding of man, at least in the West. Augustine was aware of the dangers of undue optimism about human motives and values. For him all is corrupted, body, soul and spirit, by original sin, transmitted in unbroken succession from the Garden of Eden by the act of procreation in every generation. These ideas were not new, but they were now to achieve a classical status, hammered out and linked to a strict doctrine of predestination, of the good to heaven and the bad to hell, in the controversy with Pelagius. This understanding, in which sin was understood as individual rather than social, and salvation correspondingly individual, dominated the West from Aquinas to Luther and Calvin.

Luther stressed that man can know himself as man only in the light of justification by faith. He learns who he is from God. This close connection between knowledge of God and knowledge of man was to be emphasised also by Calvin. Man was for Luther *simul iustus et peccator*. For Calvin he was totally alienated from God by sin, then reconciled with a genuine sanctification through the Holy Spirit.

The precise implications of justification and sanctification were to be the subject of intense scrutiny in the new scholasticism of Reformed and Lutheran orthodoxy. In reaction there developed a new interest in a theology and philosophy of Christian experience.

This theological interest in experience corresponds to a new philosophical interest in man as an autonomous being, notably in the work of Locke, Descartes and Hume. Here is a philosophical anthropology for its own sake. Hume's *Treatise on Human Nature* was a fundamental study of the nature of the human and of human knowledge. These searching studies were to be the springboard for a new continental philosophical anthropology which has flourished especially in Germany for the last two hundred years, from Kant and Herder to the present. Such a philosophical anthropology helped produce a new dimension in theology, in the theology of consciousness which was to have a profound influence in the nineteenth century. A rather different anthropological reflection in the work of Hegel brought forth the reaction of Kierkegaard, and a critical re-examination of the whole period from Descartes to

Hegel by Barth and Bultmann. Pannenberg's anthropology represents yet another substantial critique of the entire previous development.

'There is no question of importance whose decision is not comprised in the science of man. In pretending to explain the principles of human nature we in effect propose a complete system of the sciences.' So said David Hume, and his sentiments were to be echoed in reflection by his friend Adam Smith on man in his social environment. The study of man was no longer to be a matter of metaphysical speculation, but of empirical, biological observation. However, in the hands of the great German philosophers the enterprise was to be expanded to include man as the measure of all things, in a new transcendental philosophy. Meaning in the universe is to be defined in terms of intelligibility, in relation to the scope of the human imagination.

What is man? He is *homo creator, homo sapiens, homo ludens,* a number of things at once. Marx and Freud, Darwin and Durkheim, Gehlen and Geertz, and many others working in expanding areas of the social sciences have greatly enlarged our understanding of man in his changing cultural environment. Man's individuality as a unique person is crucial to his well-being. His ability to relate at various levels to his fellow men is also crucial. The balance between the free development of selfhood and the development of genuine community is often difficult and always central to human flourishing.

What then are the central characteristics of human nature, in Christian perspectives. Anthony Dyson has produced an excellent succinct list.[2] Human nature is created. It is social and political. It is sexual. It is culture creating. It seeks equality among persons. It is part of nature. It is religious. It is moral. It is unfulfilled. It involves mystery and contradiction. For Christians it is redeemed in Christ. It is to be fulfilled in new creation.

Keeping this short list in mind, I now want to look at the most ambitious of modern theological anthropologies,

[2]A.O. Dyson, art. 'Anthropology' in *New Dictionary of Christian Theology* (SCM).

Pannenberg's *Anthropology in Theological Perspective*.[3] Anthropology is crucial to theology. That is Pannenberg's first axiom.

> Theologians will be able to defend the truth precisely of their talk of God only if they first respond to the atheistic critique of religion on the terrain of anthropology. Otherwise, all their assertions, however impressive, about the primacy of the God-ness of God will remain purely subjective assurances without any serious claim to universal validity. (16)

In the tradition of German philosophical anthropology Pannenberg finds a decisive clue to man in his exocentricity, in the fact that he finds his centre outside himself. Human beings need relationship. They are deficient beings who need language and culture. The deficiency, according to Herder, gives rise to a quest for direction which mirrors the image of God in man. The image is not a state of primitive perfection but a drive towards improvement.

For Pannenberg this means that the openness of human beings to the future and to each other has a religious dimension. We reach beyond the world, presupposing a religious reality in every moment of perception. (Against Pannenberg one could suggest that even if we hope for this reality, it may not in fact be there.) In this dialectic of need and fulfilment consciousness of identity arises. But the self tries to impose its identity on other selves. Here is *concupiscentia*, hubris, selfishness. Empirical human nature is selfish. But essential to human nature itself is the God-given drive to relate. Because we are by nature selfish, we naturally need redemption.

In Part II of Pannenberg's work we come to the person as a social being. Man is more than a collection of random molecules. His identity is formed through the development of a basic trust (220). This is the natural, anthropological correlate of faith in God. Lack of trust, bad faith, is the correlate of alienation, from God and man.

This understanding of identity provides a clue (Part III) to the meaning of culture as a whole. Meaning in culture is

---

[3] Cf. E.Farley, *Good and Evil*, and C.Taylor, *Sources of the Self*.

expressed through thought and language, often through myths. These myths are important for the understanding of social structures, for the role of property, work and economics, for the understanding of sexuality, marriage and the family, for the relation between political order, justice, and religious institutions. The concept of the Kingdom of God is a clue to how these institutions may develop in the way most fruitful for mankind, according to their destiny in God.

How then are anthropology and theology connected? Human history is unfinished, relations are still incomplete. Therefore anthropology cannot produce any ultimate clue to God's nature. But in the historicity of Jesus of Nazareth the destiny of humankind was revealed. Therefore there is an element of fulfilment in unfulfilment. Here is the role of spirit. The human being is a creation of the Spirit (528), anticipating the final fulfilment of identity. The human community is an anticipation of the community of the persons of the Trinity.

It is appropriate that we should consider the Christian understanding of man at the end of this study. For the gospel is directed towards all humankind. It is in the light of the Christian understanding of reconciliation as well as creation that we may reflect on the nature and destiny of man. We do not have a divinely given detailed blueprint of the human, any more than we have of God or of creation. On the other hand, a theological anthropology which is simply an echo of secular anthropology is at best superfluous and at worst a denial of the centrality of Christ as the source of new creation.

The concept of the image of God has been widely considered to indicate a degree of priority for man within the created order. This may sometimes have led to a disregard for animals, the natural order and the environment, on the assumption that man has a divinely-given right to use everything in creation for his own immediate and exclusive benefit. But of course this need not be the case, if we regard the image as inclusive rather than exclusive. In any case, the image is fulfilled in Christ. This may lead us to consider that the character of Christ, in loving concern rather than in exploitation, has environmental and cosmological as well as personal dimensions. Most commentators in the theological tradition on man have explored the contrast between the positive and negative sides of the *imago Dei* concept, in attempting to come to terms with the Fall, the need to understand what appears to be a permanent contradiction in humanity between choices of good and evil, instances of selfless concern for others and entirely selfish brutality. Reflections upon biblical understandings of man will lead us to consider the entire biblical narrative as an account which focuses upon the central structuring elements of the gospel. Within this however it remains open to us to reflect again on the images which have been formative in the Christian understanding of the human.

27

Fall and Freedom

1. The Human Reality

Nondum considerasti quanti ponderis sit peccatum. Readers accustomed to a more traditional sequence of theological topics may have remarked on the absence in the preceding pages of a formal treatment of sin. Some might even detect an old fashioned liberal minimising of the gravity of sin, and so of the wonderful nature of redemption.

I want here to focus specifically on the reality of sin. But I should want to insist that, just as the love of God is the leitmotif of all Christian theology, in creation and redemption equally, so the all-pervasive nature of sin is present as a counterpoint, though definitely and decisively in a minor key, throughout this study. It is too convenient to deal with sin in an isolated and easily manageable block. This is indeed to underestimate the nature of sin, and is cheap grace. It is often a particular shortcoming of theologies which pride themselves on majoring on sin.

How are we to understand the Fall, and the reflection upon sin and evil which it involves? The reality of the human predicament, of evil, human wickedness and human tragedy, has occupied some of the best minds, not only in theology but in literature, poetry, art. music and all the humanities, since the beginning of civilisation and doubtless before that too. It is not hard to list causes for the evil that men do to each other. It is impossible to find a single ultimate root. Beyond evil action from malicious motives in the realm of the personal, there is the whole realm of tragic accident, involving the natural world,

387

the natural disasters which continue to engulf mankind, and which God does not prevent. The Genesis narratives see man's fall from paradise into a hard world as a consequence of disobedience to God, explicitly in relation to an eating of the tree of knowledge of good and evil. The tradition from Augustine has seen a mechanical transmission of original sin from Adam and Eve through every generation. This has had the advantage of emphasising the universality of sin, of a turning away from God. But it has had the twin disadvantages of complicating sexual relationships with a continuing complex of guilt, and narrowing sin to individual actions, so that the social implications of the human predicament may be ignored.

As far as the results for moral conduct of belief in original sin in this tradition are concerned, there would not appear to be much to choose between medieval man who accepted the narrative without question and modern man who does not accept it. The presence of tragic evil based on human malice remains, despite all attempts to educate man out of it. In the Old Testament narrative the law is given as a guide to conduct according to God's will. But this is constantly broken. God makes a series of covenants with his people, to no lasting avail. The concept then arises of God's salvation of a righteous remnant, to be saved by the coming of a messiah who will personally fulfil the law, and who will be the culmination of the prophetic and priestly traditions of Israel. It is in the whole narrative of Israel's story, in its several strands, with its contradictions and variations, rather than simply in the *imago Dei* passages, that we may hope to find clues to the Old Testament understanding of man. This narrative includes liturgy, poetry and song, not least in the book of Job and in the Psalms.

What are we to make of this biblical narrative? In an illuminating discussion of theological anthropology in Hans Frei, David Kelsey has drawn attention to three families of conceptual schemes.[1] For the first group the defining characteristic of human personhood is its capacity for intentional

---

[1] Kelsy, 'Biblical narrative and theological anthropology' in G. Green (ed.), *Scriptural Authority and Narrative Interpretation*, 125ff.

action. To know a particular person's 'unsubstitutable identity' is to know his typical action. The second set of concepts involves an 'ascriptive centre or focus of intentional activity', the self-differentiated person constituted by the dialectic between the inner and the outer person. The third group considers the self-manifestation in an alienating socially constructed cultural world. These concepts may be brought together in cross-reference through narrative. The biblical narratives offer 'the distinctly Christian version of a larger class of sacred narratives expressive of human consciousness' sense of its own inner coherence and meaning' (133). Narrative offers a uniquely individuating description of a person.

Theological anthropology provides 'a thoroughly theocentric view of personhood'. It has to relate concrete communities of persons to Christian claims about God, authorised by the biblical narratives. But the anthropology itself is not authorised by scripture. It is nonfoundational. It is not a source of ready made solutions to problems but an ongoing process of dialogue and discussion.

The concepts of man in the biblical narratives are developed further in the New Testament, both in the gospels and in the Pauline and Johannine literature. Here the Old Testament motifs are echoed and often reshaped. Man is to be understood in the light of God in a new way, in the life and teaching of Jesus and in reflection on Christ as the second Adam, the source of new creation, the light of the world. In the light of Jesus' teaching about the Kingdom, and in the light of faith, in reflection about Jesus' life and death and resurrection, a Christian understanding of man as reconciled to God through the forgiveness of sins, and the abundance of grace, is reached. In the light of Christ the darkness in much of human nature is seen in greater depth. In the cross the reality of evil in much human action, individual and collective, is focused. Through the resurrection God's victory over evil is achieved, and this has permanent consequences for a Christian understanding of man.

The Christian understanding of the human is seriously realistic. but it is neither gloomy nor pessimistic. It is based not on man's past failure, but on the reality of the resurrection and the promise of the fulfilment of the Kingdom of God. Against this perspective the monstrous evils done by man to man in our own century do not come as a totally unexpected surprise. But they may not be allowed to overwhelm a human perspective. God has already in Christ died out upon evil on the cross, and in the resurrection he has overcome evil. This affirmation lies at the heart of all that Christian faith has to say about the human condition. In seeking further elucidation of the meaning of resurrection we are driven back to the lineaments of the life and teaching of Jesus in the gospel narratives. God is there for the outcast and the lepers, the marginalised in society. Concern for the frail and the vulnerable is absolutely central to any Christian understanding of man. Conversely, when such a concern is absent, the Christian understanding of man is ignored or contradicted.

In this perspective it is necessary to spell out the consequences both for individual lives and for the life of the individual within society. In considering the Church as Christian community we have already said something about man as individual in the light of the gospel. God creates faith, response to his presence in the context of forgiveness and reconciliation, justification and sanctification. God issues an invitation, which is taken up in faith's response to the gospel. This is a universal invitation. Even though it has not been taken up universally, yet it still has universal and momentous consequences.

As God's creature, man has always been precious in the sight of God and the object of God's providential care. This care is reaffirmed, both in the history of his relation to Israel and in the new creation of man through the events concerning Jesus. God has shown in the most direct possible way his concern, not only for Christians, or for the religious, or for any particular group, but for all humankind. Because of Jesus Christ, we may understand human rights as God-given rights. These are not just freedom from oppression, injustice, etc. They are also freedoms for, positive freedoms inaugurated in the resurrection of Christ. These freedoms of man, which stem from the freedom of God's love in Christ, have important individual as well as social dimensions.

Human beings as individuals are the subject of God's loving concern for all things. Man is neither to be isolated from his fellow men nor herded together as a collective or a mere number in a collection of statistics. Where his individuality is lost, due to circumstances of great hardship or deprivation, this is clearly contrary to the values of the Kingdom, and is to be resisted. God's love is not a sentimental benevolence which is indifferent to evil, and those who seek to be instruments of his love can scarcely be content with a situation in which individual liberty and development are suppressed. Since man is created to relate in love to God and to his fellow men, civil and religious liberty are essential consequences of a Christian understanding of man as individual.

It must be stressed however that a Christian understanding of the unique worth of the individual before God does not enshrine a commitment to a particular political ideology. Not every sort of individualism is consonant with a Christian understanding of man. Much supposed defence of individual freedom is merely a licence to selfishness disguised as freedom.

Concern for man as man in society also arises from the heart of the Christian understanding of God. Man as churchman is called to co-humanity. The same applies with equal force to man in society at large. The Kingdom of God is a social kingdom, to be fulfilled in the communion of saints. It is no accident that Christian theology has been one of the springs of the modern disciplines of social science and economics. Human beings live not only as individuals but together with one another in society. The nature of society affects the way in which we live, and there may be insights to be gained from correlating our understanding of society with our understanding of theology.

The whole question of the relationship between theology and community, culture and society, which we have already considered in relation to Liberation Theology and to the idea of a local theology, raises basic questions about the nature of society, which in turn provoke further theological explorations.

Conceptions of society, as debates among sociologists demonstrate, are subject to constant change. Habermas' wide ranging critique of the sociological tradition in the *Theory of Communicative Action*, especially of Weber, Mead and Durkheim, results in a new perception of 'modernity'. Action in society is to be understood as communicative action, seeking goals in a process of reaching agreement with others. Habermas' conception of society, as the 'lifeworld' of a social group, and as a set of integrated systems, reflecting outside influence on the life-group, was developed in dialogue with Adorno, Horkheimer, Parsons and Marx, and has in turn been widely criticised.

It does not seem to me that we can look to the sociologists, or indeed to any particular discipline, to help us to construct the ideal critical framework for theological reflection. The sort of theological demolition work that was done, e.g. on Ebeling's theology by Hans Albert in the late 1960s, in the tradition of the Frankfurt school, appears with hindsight to have missed much that was of continuing value through the sweeping application of dogmatic presuppositions. But a critical awareness of the complexity of the society with which theologians are concerned is both valuable in itself and a source of critical questions about the social dimensions of theological work. A good example is John Milbank's *Theology and Social Theory*, which produces not only a useful reminder of the complexity of social theory over the centuries but a perceptive critique of recent theology, notably George Lindbeck's *The Nature of Doctrine*.

In Christ man is recreated in the image of God, as new woman and man in the new creation. This has profound consequences for all Christian thinking about man as individual and in society. The pattern of Jesus' life and action of self-giving concern for individuals and social groups provides an historical paradigm for the treatment of persons in relation, as individuals or in small or large groups. Jesus' relations with religious and political authority have consequences for both politics and religion. Jesus brought a new dimension of forgiveness and of reconciliation to both, and the characteristic reaction of both was, and often is, to reject forgiveness and reconciliation. Yet these are of the essence of the gospel. Ours is a world in which man's inhumanity to man, expressed either as open brutality or as a tacit self-interest and disregard of others, is as common today as it has ever been.

Jesus' resurrection retains cosmological and geophysical significance for our planet and its inhabitants. In the resurrection Jesus' victory over death is made effective. On that basis it is not necessary to maintain a dualism of good and evil

as the way the world is. God's power in powerlessness is
effective, though its ultimate triumph remains eschatological.
A further consequence of the outpouring of the Spirit of Christ
is the mind of Christ in those who have faith, though Christians
remain all too fallible. Nevertheless there is the promise of the
reality of grace to lead humankind into the way of justice and
peace, of goodness and truth. There is even the possibility of
being in Christ. To the extent that all society is now in Christ,
nothing in the realm of the human lies outside the influence
of the risen Christ. This is not ground for Christian cultural
imperialism, but an affirmation that there are no limits to
God's self-giving love in human society.

It is perhaps desirable to reconsider the momentous
consequences of the Christian claim that in Christ there is new
creation. These are no less momentous than the claim that
God is creator. They do not mean that everything in society can
be understood only in the light of Christ, so that all theology
is a Christological monologue. But it does mean that the Spirit
of the risen Christ is the background, if not the foreground, of
all Christian thinking about the past, present and future of the
human race. Much Christian thinking about man, in the
recent theological tradition more than in the past, has been
too narrow. In an open theological anthropology, all things
human are to be understood in the light of Christ.

2. Spirit and Psychology

The Christian understanding of God includes the
understanding of the Spirit and of humanity in Christian
community and in society. The reality of personal experience
of God is part of the reality and the truth of the God of
Christian faith. Pneumatology is a central part of theology. It
is related to Trinity and Christology, but also and very
significantly, to anthropology.

Personal experience of God occurs in church, and is central
to the understanding of the Church. But God touches the life
of human beings at all levels, and here developments in the
human sciences can help us to reflect on religion in many
different ways.

Modern psychology is one tool which continues to open up new information about the workings of our minds. Provided that this is used critically, it can be a valuable adjunct to theology. An excellent exploration of this dimension is provided by Don Browning in his book, *Religious Thought and the Modern Psychologies: A Critical Conversation in the Theology of Culture.*

Browning reflects on the ethical and metaphysical consequences of major contemporary psychologies. Different anthropologies embody different sorts of vision. Freud and others use deep metaphors which embody important philosophical commitments. The humanistic psychologies of Rogers, Maslow and Perls have their own metaphysic of self-actualisation. Skinner's notion of the common good, Jung's view of self-realization, and Erikson and Kohut's understandings of generativity and care are pregnant with underlying value systems. Browning stresses the need for critical psychological theory.

Such a theory may lead to a genuine theology of culture.

> By taking their images of human fulfilment seriously as practical constructive responses to the forces of rational capitalism, I can then justifiably evaluate these responses. For the Christian, theology provides a way of evaluating these deep metaphors, of evaluating their metaphysical adequacy and of influencing their further direction.

Scholars are no more exempt than other mortals from a certain impatience with the variety and complexity of human nature. Like scientists eager to announce the discovery of cold fusion, they are given to believing that they have found the key to human behaviour when they have only found some very minor clue. Don Browning's work reminds us of this complexity, which pneumatology must address in considering the influence of the Spirit in the life of human beings. As with other areas of what we deem to be knowledge, our contemporary sophistication will no doubt appear to our successors as highly primitive in many important respects.

Our experience of God within the Church and in all areas of our lives is, as we have seen, mediated through experience of the culture in which we live. It takes place, in the standard phrase, in, with and under our cultural environment. Yet it is still experience of God. This pneumatological dimension, balanced by the Christological dimension, may prevent our view of God from becoming an abstraction from the reality of the God of Christian faith.

It is in the pneumatological dimension of talk of God that we may see the important element of *coincidentia oppositorum* in traditional Catholic and Protestant understandings of God. Both are concerned to stress that talk of the Christian God is not simply a matter of entertaining the possibility of the existence of some remote and abstract deity. For Catholics the reality of the presence of the Spirit in the Church as sacramental community has been central. For Protestants the faith of the individual believer has been the source of knowledge of the God who forgives and justifies. Both of these emphases are entirely proper and are complementary. The Spirit, as the spirit of the crucified and risen Christ, is the mediator of the divine reality, in, with and under human response.

In this chapter I have deliberately taken a different path from that of many traditional systematic theologies in juxtaposing discussions of the Spirit in the Church and the Spirit in the world. This has disadvantages. It is clearly useful on occasion to speak about Christians in the Church as such, and about Christians in society. Here I want to underline the integral connection and mutual dependence of the spheres of Christian worship and Christian service.

It is very often held against nineteenth-century Protestant Christianity that it led to a bourgeois, middle class faith which was in many ways no better than simple moralism in a wider social context and an exclusive élitist club in its narrower ecclesiastical structure. There is something in this charge. But I think the charge itself masks a much deeper problem, which is as endemic to twentieth-century traditional Catholicism and Protestantism as it is to nineteenth-century liberalism. It is this. The Church is called to manifest the fruits of the Spirit. What it often manifests is a false piety which is a deeply worldly and ultimately cynical echo of secular values, both at an 'establishment' and at a populist level. The classic example is the Nazi church in Germany in the 1930s, which supported Hitler because he promised a return to strict moral standards, coupled with an emphasis on family values, and a crackdown on all dissidents and social minorities, notably the Jews and the Communists. But to focus on this example may itself be an easy and convenient accommodation. Wherever, *ubique, undique et ab omnibus*, the human rights of minority groups in society are denied and people are marginalised and persecuted, where the Church uses well sounding words to evade its duty or even to subvert it, there indeed are the accents of Caiaphas, there Christ is in a sense recrucified. That is why all racism, and every sort of prejudice, notably too in relation to the rights of women, is utterly contrary to the gospel.

Of course the Church does exhibit these prejudices all too often. It is condemned. There is also divine forgiveness. But this forgiveness imposes a new obligation to seek radical renewal. That is why, in my view, the charge of the bourgeoisification of the Church is not too severe, but much too limited

3. Engagement in Society

A church which is serious about its ecclesiology must be equally serious about its commitment to the world, in terms of ethical theory and practical action. If forgiveness and reconciliation are central to ecclesiological and ecumenical self-understanding, they are no less central to the Church's mission and discipleship in the world.

One particularly good example of such a close relationship between mission and reconciliation was shown in the Church of England's 1984 *Faith in the City* report.[2] The Introduction sets out the problem. The quality of life in the inner city is often much lower than elsewhere, and things are getting worse. The underlying factors are unemployment, decayed housing, substandard educational and medical provision, and social disintegration. There is poverty, powerlessness and increasing inequality. It is our view that the nation is confronted by a grave and fundamental injustice in the Urban Priority Areas. The report is addressed first to the Church of England and then to

[2]There is a considerable discussion of *Faith in the City.* Cf too *Faith in the Scottish City,* ed. R.O'Brien et al., New College, Edinburgh, 1986. Cf. too now *Faith in the Countryside,* Church of England, 1990.

'Christians throughout this country'.

The first chapters characterise Urban Priority Areas. Urbanisation is today usually not a sign of hope but of deprivation. The main indication of decline is unemployment. There is also physical decay of the housing stock, social disintegration – more petty crime, and a polarisation in the city between the haves and the have-nots. The reasons given by the clergy for poor church attendance were 'ignorance of the Church and Christianity' and 'perception of the Church as irrelevant in their lives'. There was too little ecumenical co-operation.

We come to 'Theological Priorities'. How do we serve our neighbours in need? We may have to question current economic slogans, to produce action which promotes community. What about a theology for Urban Priority Areas? There is no single 'Theology of the City'. But Christianity means solidarity with suffering humanity and concern for the justice of God. It is perhaps striking that only one of the pages in the report is devoted to a paragraph of constructive theology. The need is to develop a church which is local, outward-looking and participating. The report considers church organisation. Parish boundaries should be related closely to neighbourhoods, and there should be constant attention to the challenge of racial discrimination and disadvantage. There should be exchange between UPAs and other parishes,

A chapter on 'Developing the People of God' pursues this further. There must be new emphasis on the role of laity, of women, of local non-stipendiary ministry, and on proper clergy training and support. There are real dilemmas for families. How is a church which truly participates in the urban community to be supported? Church buildings should be shared, and a Church Urban Fund set up.

Part III of the report was addressed to the nation. The 1977 White Paper, *Policy for the Inner Cities*, identified the problem, but little has been done and assistance has been cut in real terms. Action is needed on employment, education and the physical environment. 'We have lost a decade.' An interesting point here is the call for a greater priority for the outer estates in urban policy initiatives.

We come to the key areas of poverty, employment and work.

Unemployment produces poverty. It is wrong to regard only market transactions (irrespective of their social usefulness) as adding to national wealth. We must recollect our national tradition of collective altruism. A chapter deals with housing, homelessness, the crumbling physical condition of the housing stock, and suggests an increase in public housing. We cannot blame people for being unemployed and poor.

The report is concerned with health. Disease is underpinned by unease. This leads on to social work and community work. A section on 'Education and Young People', opens with a striking quote from a headmaster. 'Unemployment has dealt us a stunning and crushing blow. There is little motivation. Truancy is high.' Teachers and youth workers need much support. The last chapter deals with 'Order and Law'. Frustration may lead to crime. 'There is smouldering anger and quiet despair.' Policing must be more humane. In conclusion, we are called 'to change our thinking and action in such a way as to help us to stand more closely alongside the risen Christ with those who are poor and powerless. We have found faith in the city.'

It seems to me that this report is not 'the answer' to the problem of the UPAs, in the sense that following its recommendations will eliminate the deprivation and disadvantage. Human nature is such that there will always be deprivation and disadvantage, even if all were to start out equal on a given day. Nevertheless, and despite all the criticism which has been and can be made, in my view this remains an excellent report. It is indeed a committee document, representing a number of points of view, and so sometimes mentioning the trivial in the same phrase as the fundamental. It is very much a Church of England orientated report, but it does have wider substantial implications. It did echo a fair number of left-of-centre political slogans which were recently the flavour of the month. But it is difficult for commentators on a scene with political implications to maintain an abstract impartiality, and perhaps it is better not to pretend to one. This way we know where we are.

Since I am a theologian and not a politician or sociologist, let me pick out what I regard as an important sentence from the section on theology.

> We believe that God, though infinitely transcendent, is also to
> be found, despite all appearances, in the apparent waste lands
> of our inner cities and housing estates, that men and women
> are created to glorify God in and through his creation and to
> serve their fellow human beings in the power of his love.

Most people with a little common sense will realise that the
deprivation of decades is not to be removed overnight, or even
over a ten-year period, with the aid of a grand design, however
powerfully imaginative. The problems are too entrenched, and
even too diverse, for that. Most Christians also realise that an
invocation of the Holy Spirit which seeks to ensure that we shall
become supermen and superwomen overnight is also likely to
be less than helpful. But if we are then content to say nothing and
do nothing, then we really have disregarded the gospel.

What we should pray for, it seems to me, is not that we should
become in some way less human but more human. We need to
be more sensitive to the suffering of our neighbours, and at
once more relaxed and more constant and consistent in our
response to their need. As far as the Church is concerned, it is
obviously not enough for concern for the poor and the deprived
to be isolated in a sectional interest. Much more relevant is that
this concern should be reflected in the central administrative
and financial areas of the Church. Otherwise no effective
action will be taken. This is, as far as I can see, a problem for all
Christian bodies.

As far as the inner city is concerned, Christians have a duty
in respect of their church organisations. They also have a
Christian duty as citizens. It is clear that a society which
polarises its citizens between the haves and the have-nots is not
a Christian society. Here is a new barbarism, whether not it
affects to support traditional Christian values. There are of
course important obstacles to progress on the national scene.
Many of our citizens are not Christians. Some would agree with
a Christian understanding of justice as fairness. Others would
not. If taxation is used to redistribute resources, people who
create economic wealth may simply emigrate to countries
where the tax system favours the rich. In that sense the world

is indeed a global village, and individual national churches can have only a limited effectiveness in encouraging a change of attitudes and of practice.

Again looked at on a global scale the urban deprivation of Britain is nothing like as bad as that in India or parts of Africa, where starvation is a commonplace daily occurrence. It is necessary to fight deprivation both at long range and at short range, abroad and at home. There are also at least two important strategies. There is the importance of local contact. Without people 'on the ground' in such areas there can be no immediate assistance where it is immediately needed. This is an immensely needed and continuing area of service. But there is also the need for long term assistance, in economic and social terms. This can only come from action by government and the leading financial institutions of a nation.

The whole question of the Church's response to the marginalised in society, neglected and shunned for whatever reason, is an issue on which Christian consciousness still has a very great deal to learn, and does not find the learning process an easy one. At the same time, there is need for a continuing dialogue with the more traditional partners, the great national institutions, with which the churches have lived in uneasy harmony since the earliest times.

4. Politics and Ethics

The relation of church to society inevitably raises the question of the gospel and politics. All sorts of good and bad examples of such relationship will quickly come to mind. Once again there is a necessary correlation, though not always a simple and direct relation, between Christian understanding of the nature of God, the standards of behaviour and the lines of policy which the Church may engage with in dialogue with politics. The Church can be identified strictly with neither the religious, of whatever faith, nor the agnostic nor the atheist in society. It is concerned with the welfare of all mankind in the light of salvation through Jesus Christ.

The Church is integrally involved in all dimensions of human culture, whether these are based on the sciences or the humanities, whether they are expressed through art or literature, social life or politics, whether they express the ethos of modern international business communities or of particular local ethnic roots. The Church always has a prophetic role, to call humanity to realise the fruits of the Spirit in every sphere which God has made possible for us. It also has a pastoral or enabling role, to work within these cultural frameworks to free us from the tribal inhibitions which repress our response to the catholic invitation of the gospel, so that our relationship with God and each other may be brought to maturity.

God's act of creation and reconciliation continues in the work of the Spirit in the Christian community, the Church. It is also continued, in a parallel and overlapping manner, as it were, in the work of the Spirit in the world, in anticipation of the fulfilment which God intends for the created order. We can say little of this area of God's influence, for it remains mysterious in many ways to us. We know that God's purpose is to bring about the establishment of his peace, of love and justice, of perfected community between creator and creature. It is reasonable to believe that wherever in human development there is a movement towards values, institutions and practice in which these values of the gospel are more closely reflected, there is the guidance of God's Spirit among his children. The achievement of these goals is never straightforward, and is usually fraught with setbacks and disasters. But the eschatological vision of God's Kingdom provides a light for orientation on the way, and a promise of effectiveness, a candle that shall not be extinguished.

There is an important area of interaction between the work of the Spirit in the sphere of Christian worship and community, and the work of the Spirit in the world. That is in the sphere of Christian ethics, personal and social. It might be thought that personal ethics was purely a church matter, and social ethics purely a matter for relationships with the outside world. But the Christian is also a citizen, and the social organisation of the Church is enmeshed in the structural constraints of all structures involving human co-operation. There is therefore a constant interaction between the gospel and all human ethical theory and practice.

This precisely does not mean, as Karl Barth strikingly pointed out, that there is a large hiatus between Christian doctrine and Christian ethics.[3] We do not abandon the word of the holy book for the word of the holy man, finding new axioms apart from the word of the gospel. The word of the gospel is for all mankind in every sphere of life, not just the doctrinal sphere. Equally, the word of the Bible and the tradition has to be related to the often highly complex issues which are unique to a modern technological society, with its immense powers for good and evil in human life.

God is creator and reconciler, sustainer and director of the entire created order. As such he is concerned for the ultimate good of all his creatures. His salvation is indeed that ultimate good, the final goal to which we are all directed. Studies in Christian ethics seek to spell out in detail the principles of ethics in the light of faith, and enquire into the insights, appropriate behaviour and understanding generated by the gospel.

Discussion of ethical principles goes back to the tradition of ancient philosophies. These discussions are frequently framed within the sphere of small local societies, such as the Greek city-state. They concern the conduct appropriate to individuals and the community. They raise the widest of issues, of merit and responsibility, of the nature of justice and the nature of the good, of the need for law, of punishment for offenders, of the conflict between the rights and duties of the individuals and of the society in which the individual is placed. With some exceptions, they are not concerned with the planet Earth as a single society, with common problems.

Concern with the planet as a whole is characteristic of modern ethical discussion, among Christians and non-Christians. God is the God of all human beings equally. He is concerned with this planet, and indeed with all created matter. Christians have become aware that ethical discussion cannot be concerned simply with rules of behaviour in local communities, as often seen in studies up to and including the nineteenth century. They must be concerned equally with global issues, in a world in which there are real threats to global human existence.

---

[3]K. Barth, *Church Dogmatics*, 1.2, 782ff.

5. Acute Issues

Most notably the planet is confronted with the twin threats of nuclear war and starvation as the result of population explosion. There is also a serious problem of environmental pollution and destruction threatening to upset the ecological balance through deforestation, land erosion, acid rain, breakdown of the ozone layer. Till recently these were matters, it seemed, for apocalyptic visionaries rather than sober observers. Now they are imminent problems, in twenty or thirty years they may be actual catastrophes.

None of these global threats reduces the necessity of tackling the remaining issues of ethics, personal and social, upon which the life of society has always depended. Honesty and integrity in personal relationships, in financial and political involvement, remain as central as ever. Problems of justice and equity in every sphere of individual and social life require constant resolution. Priorities in the distribution of national resources need to be assessed. The appropriate political and executive decisions need to be made and implemented. Where there is a clash of values and needs in matters of medical and social ethics, solutions have to be found. In the lives of individuals, relations in the circles of family and friends, and in professional life, have to be forged. Individual character is shaped and matured. In all these areas response may be shaped by reflection on the character of the Christian God as the source and the goal of our human striving. [4]

Here I mention a single case, which has become a major contemporary problem. I refer to the abuse of drugs. How do we look after those most at risk in our society ? In his study *Protecting the Vulnerable* R.E. Goodin concludes with the following illuminating prescriptions (206).

> Preventing exploitable vulnerabilities: No one should be forced into an exploitable or dependent position, insofar as this can be avoided. If people are placed in such a position (either through personal choice or through natural or

[4]Central to the Church's task is pastoral care in general, at a congregational level and beyond this in society, in affirming people as people. Awareness of sin is bound up with forgiveness and affirmation.

social necessity), vulnerabilities /dependencies should be reciprocal and, ideally, symmetrical among all those who are involved. In no case should they be so severe and asymetrical that one party has exclusive, discretionary control over resources that the other needs to protect his vital interests.

Protecting the vulnerable: Where people are particularly vulnerable to or dependent on you, for whatever reasons, you have a special responsibility to protect their interests. Where they are vulnerable to you individually, you must seek to produce this result directly through your own efforts. Where they are vulnerable to a group of you, the group as a whole is responsible for protecting their interests; and you as an individual within that group have a derivative responsibility to help organise and participate in a co-operative scheme among members of that group to produce that result.

The drugs problem is a particularly difficult issue, because it involves all kinds of social connections. There is indeed a valid argument that the individual may act as he or she chooses in the privacy of the home, provided that no harm is being done to any other person, even if the individual may be damaging his or her own health. Against this there is the equally valid argument that, if the individual's activity, which may be addictive, damages health and may be ultimately life-threatening, or contributes to a fashion which damages others, then society's interest may take a priority at the expense of individual liberty. The individual as a creature of God is free, but not free to exploit or harm others.

Addiction to drugs by the individual involves connection ultimately with large international gangs of drug dealers, whose activities are notoriously pursued with the utmost ruthlessness and disregard for human life. The issue then becomes an instance in which the freedom of the individual is constrained by concern for the welfare of society. In a similar way the freedom of the individual to express anger under the law is constrained by prohibition from using physical violence upon others in this expression. For the Christian, the basis of this position is the self-giving love of God, which creates true freedom for all his creatures, freedom to relate to God and man on the pattern of the character of Christ.

From these considerations it becomes clear that Christians will always be strongly committed to the rule of law. The contrast between the law and the gospel is not an invitation to antinomianism in social relationships. Often in history there have of course been unjust laws, and here Christians are bound to work by constitutional means to seek improvement. So the laws supporting slavery were finally repealed, and capital punishment, once seen as enjoined by God, has been disappearing gradually from civilised societies, even where there has been the occasional relapse.

The God of Christian faith is a God of justice. But justice involves not only legal considerations. For the gospel, it involves social justice. This does not mean that God is a God of the poor more than of the rich. It does however mean that social conditions which militate against the welfare of some sections of society, whether in areas of health, education, housing and opportunity in society in general, are not conditions with which Christians in community can rest content.

God's justice, as the justice of reconciling love, has vast implications in all areas from morality in personal and in business relationships to the morality of relations between nations. Perfect love casts out fear. This is not a state of affairs to be brought about overnight. It is a perspective within which to build up mutual trust over a period.

The establishment of a relationship of trust between individuals, between social groups and between nations, is a most important step in all ethical matters. A further step is that such trust is not betrayed, for this represents then a major reversal. But trust in itself will not solve ethical dilemmas. There may be, though there is not always, a high degree of mutual trust and respect in many of the issues involving medical ethics. But there may remain a basic uncertainty and even disagreement about, for example, the rights and wrongs of abortion or questions of when intensive care treatment should cease and how the discomfort of some dying patients may be eased. In all these areas the commitment of the gospel to unlimited compassion remains the basic guideline.

28

New Creation

1. Cosmic Re-creation

The resurrection of Jesus Christ signifies for Christians the inauguration of the new creation. This does not mean that the old creation is abolished. But it is transformed through reconciliation, and looks forward to God's completion. Issues of individual and social ethics, of belief and practice, are inextricably related in the perspective of God's reign. This is an insight explored recently in a powerful manner in the World Council of Churches' studies on justice, peace and the integrity of creation. We have spoken of creation and cosmology, and creation and anthropology. In the light of reconciliation we must explore the interrelations of the cosmological and anthropological dimensions of the work of the Spirit in the world.

We begin to see that there is an increasingly close connection between our human goals and the state of our natural environment. Nowhere is this more strikingly illustrated than in the emergence of the so-called 'greenhouse effect'. How does our understanding of God help us to relate to this type of challenge?

The God in whom we trust is not a solitary being, remote from us. God is involved with the created order, and especially with humankind. God is creator, redeemer and sanctifier, simultaneously. God is complex, beyond the complexity of the cosmos. God is present to faith, open to childlike trust.

Christians understand God to be the source of all that is, sustaining and maintaining the whole structure of the physical cosmos. God is the creator of all life, and particularly of human life. How are we to understand God's relation to the universe, and his plans for its future? We know that the universe in which we find ourselves came into being several billion years ago. We know roughly how it has developed. We think we can predict roughly its physical development till it disintegrates in the long term future. It is reasonable to expect that a similar process takes place in all other universes. Such is the physical history of the cosmos.

The history of life on earth occupies a mere fraction of a second on the time scale of the life of the universe. It is a most astonishing and fruitful development. At one level it involves the growth of community, joy and goodness. It also includes endless waste, disaster and evil. Against this background of risk, contingency and ambiguity, on a cosmic as well as on a human level, faith affirms the active presence of God's love as the source and goal of creation. How are we to think through a theological response to the greenhouse effect? The theologian's vision of God's creation cannot offer an alternative cosmology to the cosmologies of scientific research. It may be, though theories change from decade to decade, that our universe will develop towards its end in masses of crushed and burnt out matter. But before that time God may have countless positive developments in store for the created order. The Christian doctrine of creation affirms that God has created the physical cosmos. Within this God has given humankind a responsibility for its development towards the fulfilment of the abundance of life. This is centred on the New Testament understanding of love, of agape, within the physical structures of creation. It also affirms that God's final fulfilment in love for mankind is eschatological as well as temporal. All men are mortal. The time may come when humanity, in whatever finally developed form, may vanish from the universe as the conditions for sustaining human life disappear. Other forms of life may appear. But Christianity affirms in the face of future physical destruction, for us as individuals now and for humanity in the future, God's loving presence to humankind as a continuing spiritual relationship.

Let us consider the basic shape of the greenhouse problem.[1] There appears to be a warming effect on the earth. It may be accelerating. The climatological changes may be beneficial to some parts of the world, at least in the short term, and hazardous for other parts. We do not know for certain the rate of change or the exact effects. Things may be better or worse than we expect. We don't know what other changes may follow the greenhouse phenomenon. Much seems to centre on the role of carbon dioxide absorption and emission in the oceans of the world.

How are we to evaluate and react to this effect as Christians? The greenhouse perspective might well be thought to be a challenge to the basis of belief in a loving God. After all, to allow earthquakes, hurricanes and ice ages might be a divine oversight. But to allow the whole world to heat up uncontrollably could be thought to be undoubtedly careless.

A traditional, and indeed even a modern response to the problem would be to point to human sin, and wilful destruction. After centuries of preoccupation with the sins and sensibilities of individuals, we have woken up to the corporate character of sin, especially against the environment. We are seeing the 'greening' of sin, in our generation. But this would be too simple an analysis. Though there has indeed been a conscious exploitation of nature to make financial profits, much of the production of the greenhouse effect has been entirely accidental, unobserved, certainly not the product of wilful malice or premeditated evil. Until recently, the consequences of the spread of CFCs or of carbon dioxide in the atmosphere were simply not realised. Knowledge has brought about a new situation. But it is crucially important not to blame people for actions whose consequences they could never reasonably have predicted.

How does Christian faith view the human future? Perhaps we may say, with both trust and uncertainty. Most Christians will agree that St. Paul's affirmation, that nothing can separate us from the love of God in Jesus Christ, belongs to the heart of the gospel. This is, as they say, the bottom line. God's loving

---

[1] Cf. *Scorching Heat and Drought: A Report on the Greenhouse Effect*, Edinburgh 1989.

presence is there for every human being who is, who was, who will be. Many, perhaps most, human beings are not conscious of this presence during their natural lives. But this presence will never be withdrawn.

We have not yet addressed the question of whether God could allow the human race to come to an end, through natural disaster or self-destruction. Might God be expected to mount a special rescue operation to ensure the physical preservation of the human species? We do not know. Faith believes that the reign of God has begun in the life of Jesus and it continues for ever. Whether the future fulfilment of this state includes the continuance of human life on earth Christians have never been able to decide. I do not think we have evidence for a conclusion either way.

There remain a number of issues in urgent need of attention. The reign of God is understood by Christians as a reign of peace, of justice, of love. Given this paradigm of God's Kingdom, we have a responsibility to act, in relation to the created order and to human beings, in a way consonant with this peace, and consonant with the character of Christ.

There does not have to be a conflict between concern for human beings and concern for the integrity of creation. We have long realised that the dominion over nature understood in the theological tradition has to be modified in the direction of stewardship and responsibility in creation, not only for the sake of future human generations but because of respect for creation as God's creation. Human beings have a natural tendency to regard themselves as the sole beneficiaries of creation. There is a difference between being stewards and being predators of the universe.

There is also the dimension of concern for our fellow human beings. This itself demands respect for the natural environment, without which there will soon be no possibility of human flourishing. There is something of an analogy between discussion of environmental issues and discussion of war and peace. In times of limited warfare it was perfectly possible to live by a doctrine of the Just War. The possibility of global nuclear conflict, and the ensuing probability of nuclear winter, render such theories unworkable. It was possible until recently to argue that the benefits of industrialisation usually outweighed the disadvantages. Now the threat of global pollution faces all humanity, rich and poor alike.

The God of Christian faith is a self-giving God, whose character is shown definitively in the life, death and resurrection of Jesus Christ. For God, to be is to be self-giving, in solidarity with all humankind. Our love is sometimes also self-giving, courteous, compassionate, rejoicing in the well-being of other people. But often it is none of these things. It is confined to those with whom we feel special ties. Others are excluded, even neglected. The greenhouse effect reminds us vividly that the welfare of each is bound up with the welfare of all, that we flourish or perish together. We may reject such views, sticking to a fierce individualism. But concentrations of ultraviolet light or carbon dioxide gas are no respecters of individual choice.

A warming effect may bring benefits to some parts of the world for a time, such as more rain or better crops. But the effects of related phenomena, such as the thinning of the ozone layer or the accumulation of carbon dioxide, appear to bring only universal hazard. To wait for others to act first, as in the much less drastic case of unleaded petrol, is to court disaster.

Knowledge brings a responsibility to act to those who are aware of the problem. The increasing speed of global pollution adds urgency to the need for action. It is true that it might take a hundred years to produce complete disaster, and that new techniques may be found to mitigate the effects of current trends. But man is not superman. Humankind is a fragile species, whose fragility is actually increased by exploding population, with all the shortages, constraints and tensions which this brings in its train. Before God man is sometimes at least made aware of this fragility. Man may also become aware of the strength which he is given through faith, to cope with formidable problems against the odds.

The hidden presence of God is the ultimate reality for human existence. It has been a source of inspiration and encouragement to millions of people through the ages. But God's love is not always manifestly effective in this world. It is often weak and powerless and its fulfilment is still to be seen. This must be a source of continuing sorrow in God. God remains involved in all the history of the created order, its natural and its human history, guiding it to fulfilment in his eschatological peace. In this process he uses men and women as the instruments of his love, wherever they are ready to be open to his service, continuing to invite them to response, to discipleship.

In our multi-cultural world there are inevitably rivalries and tensions, political, social and economic. These tensions are often destructive. To combat the greenhouse and other effects we need constructive tensions which will operate for the common good. In that development Christians will see the light of the gospel, shining through the darkness.

For faith the central clues to God are the events concerning Jesus. Here God is involved in the destruction and reconstruction of life. The lines between animate and inanimate matter in the natural sciences are far from clear cut. The Easter proclamation 'I am the resurrection and the life' understands God as the ground of re-creation and renewal within the world of sentient, intelligent persons. In God there is power to restore human personhood after it has undergone the physical processes of decay. This is the character of the God of resurrection. God's love is inclusive, humble, patient. It is also ceaselessly active, ultimate and effective.

Against this background it might seem that the Christian task is not to overcome the world but to cherish it. The grand design we can leave to God. Our task is to begin with precise attention to the particular human tasks which we can identify, quantify, and act upon. It is imperative to tackle the problems of the environment with realism. Christian realism includes faith.

We return to these particular human tasks. As in most other areas of life, the simplest matters are the hardest. We neither have nor need a new green gospel. We must turn from pure self-interest to concern also for others, in corporate finance, in national policy, in international relations. The greenhouse effect reminds us again of our mutual dependence on this planet. The Christian gospel is concerned with the humanity of all humankind, and with care for God's whole creation.

2. Integrity and Creation

Environmental issues drive home to us the fragility of the equilibrium within which we are privileged to enjoy life on earth. Yet of course life continues to be anything but enjoyable for millions on our planet, because of humankind's numerous self-inflicted disasters. We do not normally inflict these upon ourselves, but upon other people.

Recent studies of justice, peace and the integrity of creation have focused upon hunger and poverty in the world, upon the huge inequalities of opportunity in every direction. The resources to abolish poverty are there, but the will is lacking. The frameworks to establish justice are well-known, but the implementation is halted, because of special interests, individual and local, national and international. Even in so-called developed countries the ease with which vast communities can be isolated and overlooked is frightening. The task of attending to poverty and to life-threatening malnutrition in many areas of the world is something which, clearly, will be with us for decades if not centuries, and by which Christian faith is directly and immediately challenged.

One way of finding the resources to meet this challenge is to avoid wasting resources by cutting back on the all pervasive armaments races which obsess different countries at different levels. Perfect love casts out fear. God is a God of love and not of hate. Yet again human practice testifies to rivalry developing into more rivalry, national, ethnic, religious and other, and to mutual destruction. We cannot speak of the God who is love in this century without recalling that more people have been murdered in our time than in any other period in human history, and mass murders have been committed by a surprisingly large number of nations.

It is clear that sensible and balanced programmes of staged disarmament are a clear priority in a world understood as the theatre of God's new creation. Apart from reinforcing the absolute necessity for a phased abolition of nuclear weapons, a Christian understanding of reality, taken seriously, necessitates world-wide attempts to stem the huge growth of the small arms industry, upon which many countries rely as a consistent source of external revenue.

We have already noted the explosion in the drugs market, with its enormous economic ramifications. Christianity affirms love, and in so doing opposes all such exploitation of one human being by another. In the spheres of education and health, housing and employment, and in all vital areas of our community life, the gospel sets an agenda, of fairness and caring, which we dare not ignore if we wish to call ourselves Christian. This is as much a consequence of understanding God as any other exploration in the detail of systematic theology.

A caring society is concerned with health. This involves attention to detail, as in all else, and here too priorities and sound practice in the many difficult decisions called for in modern medicine. The Christian centre is the understanding of the human being as a person redeemed through Jesus Christ. Neither traditional prejudice, nor contemporary expediency, nor sentimentality, is appropriate. God's love is equally directed to all humanity, and nothing can separate us from his love.

The understanding of God has consequences for our view of social relationships. Integrity and patience, trust, forgiveness and reconciliation are often painfully difficult to achieve in our relationships. Yet these are the pattern of the character of Christ. They are all the more crucial, and sometimes even harder to achieve in our intimate relationships, and in the context of marriage. The basic concept of respect for persons has developed and been given depth within the Christian tradition. The Church is often seen as crassly insensitive in its approach to human personal relationships. It is vital to reaffirm that Christian understanding in this field is rooted, not in the mechanical repetition of Levitical codes, but in the love of God. Our task is not to be judgemental, but to live out forgiveness and reconciliation, acceptance and support.

A community of the resurrection, as an anticipation of the new creation, is a community which takes God's promise of reconciliation as the basis of reality. It retains this faith, often despite almost all appearances. It plays a full part in all the affairs of society quietly, not seeking the triumph of a religious imperialism. It trusts in God to direct humankind to goodness wherever it is open to the divine love.

Our concern in this study is with the understanding of God. Where a community shares in the same background, culture, and convictions, it may be possible to suggest an understanding of God which all in that community will find illuminating. There are at least two problems with such a view today. First it is increasingly clear to Christians that the gospel is concerned with all humankind equally, and must take account of the needs and aspirations of all for whom God has brought reconciliation. Secondly it is obvious that there is tremendous pluralism, cultural, religious and social, throughout the planet, and this too must be reflected in a Christian understanding of God.

Theology since the Enlightenment has often been thematic. It has focused upon key terms – experience, the Word, authentic existence, the secular, liberation. Each of these key terms has illuminated central issues, but only at particular times and in particular areas, in Europe and Africa, in America and Asia . Even here the cultures have been so polarised that what made sense in one context simply proved obscure in another.

One response to this pluralism has been a retreat to a new fundamentalism, whether religious or secular, conceptual or cultural, or indeed, often ecclesiological. Only this perspective, only this denominational ecclesiology is to be considered. These fixed perspectives may be foundational or antifoundational, fideist or non-fideist.

Such a response is not irrational and has strong sociological and anthropological claims to be an appropriate response to pluralism, and the danger of complete relativising of all values. It may well represent a strategy for the Church as a temporary measure, to establish new intellectual and cultural foundations. But ultimately it is emphatically not, in my view, what the Christian gospel in theory and practice is about. For the God who loves is concerned for all humankind, not exclusively but inclusively. To this extent we may share the intention of John

Hick in his recent Gifford Lectures volume, *An Interpretation of Religion*. We must seek to relate our understanding of the hidden love of God, Father Son and Spirit, to all that is human, wherever this is according to the character of Christ and not in opposition to it. We may work from any particular tradition or approach, but we shall only approach the fullness of God's reconciliation as we integrate something of the richness of the whole catholic tradition into our own perspective, offering this as a contribution to a common Christian pilgrimage, which is part of the human pilgrimage towards fulfilment in God.

God is God. God is not a mirror image of the sum and substance of the human. Yet in Jesus Christ he has entered into permanent direct engagement with humanity. This means that our understanding of God has far reaching consequences for our understanding of humanity as new humanity in the light of God's reconciliation. We cannot anticipate the eschaton, but we may not accept as inevitable the age-old oppression and marginalisation of a great proportion of the human race – usually women and children. However misguided some of their labours may have been, the nineteenth-century missionaries who wandered the face of the earth, often into probable death, to bring the love of God to those who were in need of it, were in many ways on the right lines. We may feel superior to them in their simplicity. But we fall far short of their grasp of God's love and its practical consequences for the great anonymous mass of suffering humanity.

Concern for humanity is usually too large a concept for fallible mortals to cope with. We begin with great ideals, and end by coercing people into the patterns we choose for them, often bringing about endless misery. Human beings are usually more successfully employed in attempting to cope with particular problems, for individuals and for social groups. Each human being is loved by God, and each case of exploitation is directly contrary to God's will for humanity. This means that the understanding of God has consequences for all areas of life, for social policies, economic structures, education, health, everything. God's will is certainly not to be identified with any party political programme. Yet the priorities of the Kingdom are always before us in considering the arrangements of society.

We look back at the history of mankind and see ourselves as enormously advanced and sophisticated. No doubt our ancestors thought the same. But if we do not destroy ourselves, humanity may continue indefinitely, and human self-understanding may also increase indefinitely. Self-understanding does not always increase regard for others, as the continuing atrocities which blacken our history demonstrate. But the potential for greater self-understanding, and of more informed concern for others, increases. A more informed concern may enable us to act more effectively as instruments of God's love, through the power of the Spirit. As we seek a better understanding of the human, we may reach a more mature appreciation of the humanity of God in Jesus Christ. It is through the Spirit that we understand the Son, who is the mediator of the Father's love towards us. There is indeed a reciprocity between the love of God and the love of man. The key to understanding this force is Jesus Christ, the hidden presence of ultimate reality within the created order.

We come back to our understanding of God as the basis for our understanding of humanity. It is through the nature of God that the cosmic process begins. It is through God's love that humanity is produced, cherished and redeemed. It is through God that we are invited to respond in love to our fellow human beings, and to develop in the life of the Spirit. This is the nature of God, not that we first loved God but that God first loved us.

The twentieth century has seen organised murder on a scale never before experienced. It has also reflected, with the benefit of knowledge never before possible, on the social and cultural implications of this dark side of our planet, both in the destruction of the lives of individuals, for all sorts of reasons, mental and material, and the destruction of nations. It is hardly surprising that many people have given up belief in God, often not through arrogant self-assertion but through weary despair.

It is true that the medieval world was often a place of cruel and wanton wastefulness, and that nevertheless people believed. It is true too that there have been movements towards God in our time, notably in Catholic Poland, a land which suffered more than most from total war. And there has been a resurgence of religious fundamentalism, Christian and non-Christian. But for many people today faith has been washed away, or almost washed away, in an ocean of grief, in a world full of unnecessary suffering and mindless waste of lives, aspirations, talents, commitments and affections. It might be possible for them to cling stubbornly to old loyalties and obligations. But gradually the point begins to disappear, the reality of the bond of faith to atrophy. Not with pleasure, but with sad reluctance, the reality of assent begins to lose its substance. There remains openness, but a new sense of living presence is needed.

This is a point where the sense of God as the God of Jesus Christ, and as the Spirit of new creation, may provide clues to renewal. God who has endured and has brought light out of the darkness of the cross may speak to all who have borne echoes of that darkness in their lives. The hope of light comes from the ground of the resurrection. The Spirit bears this experience and encompasses those who recognise its shadow in their own lives. The Spirit communicates the reality of grace as a healing and restoring presence through all humankind. Christians believe that this presence will be recognised eschatologically by non-Christians, in some way entirely mysterious to us, as the presence of the God of Jesus Christ.

3. The Church and Humanity, Unity and Diversity

In this study I have deliberately linked closely together the various areas of the third article of the ancient creeds, the work of the Spirit. I have discussed the Church, its nature and its mission, and then gone on at once to consider again the relationship between Church and society, and the area of social ethics. I have then returned to consideration of the understanding of man, of the human, in the light of the gospel. It is of course entirely proper for these various dimensions of the work of the Spirit to be considered separately in their own right. I have chosen to highlight the integral connections between these areas.

I do not myself consider that there should necessarily be one pattern for structures of the Church throughout the world. The notion of reconciled diversity appears to me to be of central importance. This does not mean however that 'anything goes'. On the contrary, the various structures within the denominations must be prepared to make the often painful discovery that their own traditions are often inadequate, and that they must be prepared to receive from others as well as to give to others.

In different parts of the world different church patterns may be appropriate. In some areas the gospel may most effectively be manifested through ancient traditional liturgies. In other parts much more modern forms of witness, perhaps through denominations of comparatively recent origin, may be most effective. I do not think it profitable to take sides in absolute terms between concepts of the Church as outpost of piety in society and as integral part of the community. Different patterns may be appropriate in different places at different times. In some areas the very large parish or cathedral church may act as a colourful focus of the gospel in metropolitan areas. In other contexts the country church may still be an integral part of rural society, or the industrial mission charge may work effectively through various sorts of house groups or community centres. Different solutions work at different times in different areas, sometimes at different times in the same area. What matters is not the triumph of particular ecclesiastical tastes, but the service of the gospel among humankind.

In my view, the existence of different church traditions and the need to respect these, while seeking to learn from each other in moving towards the unity which we seek, means that among the forms of church government and doctrines of the sacraments and the ministry there should also be the positive and proactive acceptance of reconciled diversity.

Similar considerations apply to the understanding of the human and the social order. The Christian gospel underlines the absolute truth of love in relation to all human beings. Where there is exploitation, marginalisation of minorities or indeed neglect of majorities, where there is injustice, the gospel is actively opposed to such treatment. The gospel actively promotes love on the pattern of the character of Christ, everywhere, by all people and at all times. Beyond this the pattern of human life in individual and social relations may take innumerable different forms in different places. Here the notion that there is one pattern of Christian anthropology or sociology is just as erroneous as the belief that there is one definitive Christian interpretation of history, or of politics, or of any other human discipline. It is not so. That it is not so is part of the freedom of the gospel, the glorious liberty of the children of God.

There is indeed a clear connection between Christology and anthropology. It is through reconciliation in Christ that the Church as the community of the new creation is born. Through the Church and in the world, spreading out ever more widely since the life, death and resurrection of Christ, the Spirit works to produce new creation out of the old creation, created for God yet alienated from God. The new humanity is central to the new creation.

Constitutive of the new humanity is the fact that it is not destroyed by human death. In the life of Jesus the kingdom of God was inaugurated and it goes on for ever. Through Jesus Christ humanity is incorporated into the eternal life of God. This incorporation is both a reaffirmation of the created order as part of the new creation and a reaffirmation of life beyond the created order, in the communion of the saints with God. The new humanity includes the eschatological peace of God, which passes all understanding. But this does not mean it is entirely incomprehensible. For it is characterised by God's own self- giving love. But its realisation goes beyond all that we can conceive in this life. Fullness of life is the fulfilment for which God has ordered his creation.

Bibliography

Adorno T. *Negative Dialektik*, Frankfurt 1966
Armstrong A. H. *Introduction to Ancient Philosophy*, London 1947
Arpe C. *Substantia*, Philologus 1940
Baillie J. *The Sense of the Presence of God*, Oxford 1962
Balthasar H. U. von *The Glory of the Lord*, Edinburgh1982
Barr J. *Explorations in Theology 7*, London 1980
Barth K. *Church Dogmatics*, Edinburgh 1936-69
Berkhof H. *The Christian Faith*, Chicago 1979
Bonhoeffer D. *Letters and Papers from Prison*, London 1953
Bonhoeffer D. *Creation and Fall*, London 1959
Bonhoeffer D. *Christology*, London 1966
Borg M. *Jesus, A New Vision*, San Francisco 1987
Bowker J. *The Sense of God*, Oxford 1973
Brown D. *The Divine Trinity*, London 1985
Browning D. *Religious Thought and the Modern Psychologies: A Critical Conversation in the Theology of Culture*, Chicago 1987
Browning D. A. *Fundamental Practical Theology*, Minneapolis 1991
Brunner E. *Dogmatics*, London 1949
Buckley M. J. *At the Edge of Modern Atheism*, Yale 1987
Bultmann R. *Jesus Christ and Mythology*, London 1960
Campenhausen H. von *Tradition and Life*, London 1968
Carnley P. *The Structure of Resurrection Belief*, Oxford 1987
Chadwick O. *The Spirit of the Oxford Movement*, Cambridge 1990
Chadwick H. *Boethius*, Oxford 1981
Chadwick O. *The Secularisation of the European Mind*, Cambridge 1975
Childs B. *Old Testament Theology in a Canonical Context*, London 1985
Church of England: *Faith in the City*, London, Church House 1985
Church of England: *We Believe in God*, London, Church House 1987
Cobb J. and Griffin D. *Process Christology*, Belfast 1977
Creel R. E. *Divine Impassibility*, Cambridge 1986.
Cupitt D. *Taking Leave of God*, London 1980
Cupitt D. *Radicals and the Future of the Church*, London 1989
Dalferth I. U. *Theology and Philosophy*, Oxford 1988

421

422   *God in Christian Perspective*

Davidson D. *Essays on Actions and Events*, Oxford 1980
Davies P. C. W. *God and the New Physics*, London 1983
Denney J. *The Death of Christ*, London 1902
Dillistone F. W. *The Christian Understanding of Atonement*, London 1968
Dillon J. *The Middle Platonists*, London 1977
Dorrie H. *Der Platonismus in der Antike*, Stuttgart 1987
Driver T. *Christ in a Changing World*, London 1981
Duke J. O. and Streetman R. F. *Barth and Schleiermacher, Beyond the Impasse*, Philadelphia 1988
Dulles A. *Models of the Church*, Dublin 1976
Dyson A. O. art. 'Anthropology', in *Dictionary of Christian Theology*, London 1983
Ebeling G. *Dogmatik Des Christlichen Glaubens I-III*, Tübingen 1983
Edwards P. ed. *Encyclopaedia of Philosophy*, New York 1967
Fackenheim E. *God's Presence in History*, London 1970
Farley E. *Good and Evil*, Minneapolis 1990
Farrer A. *Interpretation and Belief*, London 1976
Fergusson D. *Rudolf Bultmann*, Oxford 1992
Fergusson D. *Christ, Church and Society*, Edinburgh 1993
Finley M. ed. *The Legacy of Greece*, Oxford 1981
Fiorenza E. S. *Foundational Theology*, New York 1986
Flew A. *God and Philosophy*, London 1966
Ford D. *Barth and God's Story*, Bern,
Frei H. *The Eclipse of Biblical Narrative*, London 1974
Frei H. *The Identity of Jesus Christ*, Philadelphia 1975
Gadamer H. G. *Hegel's Dialectic*, London 1976
Gerrish B. A. *The Old Protestantism and the New*, Edinburgh, 1982
Gerrish B. A. *Schleiermacher, a Prince of the Church*, London 1984
Gerrish in FL. Battles ed. *Reformatio Perennis*, Pittsburgh 1981
Gilkey L. *Naming the Whirlwind*, Minneapolis 1969
Goodin R. *Protecting the Vulnerable*, London: University of Chicago Press, 1985
Green G. ed. *Scriptural Authority and Narrative Interpretation*, Philadelphia 1987
Greenwood D. C. *Structuralism and the Biblical Text*, Berlin 1985
Greg R. and Groh D. *Early Arianism*, London 1981
Grillmeier A. *Christ in Christian Tradition*, *I* and *II*, London 1965
Gunton, C. *The Actuality of Atonement*, Edinburgh 1988
Gunton, C. and Hardy D. W. ed. *On Being the Church: Essays on the Christian Community*, Edinburgh 1989
Gustavson J. *Theological Ethics*, Oxford 1981
Guthrie, W. K. C. *The Greek Philosophers from Thales to Aristotle*, London 1967

Habermas J. *Legitimation Crisis,* London 1976

Habermas J. *The Theory of Communicative Action I* and *II,* London, 1984, 1987

Hart K. *The Trespass of the Sign,* Cambridge 1989

Harvey A. E. *Jesus and the Constraints of History,* London 1982

Harvey A. E. ed. *God Incarnate, Story and Belief,* London 1981

Harvey Van *The Historian and the Believer,* London 1967

Hauerwas S. *Suffering Presence. Theological Reflections on Medicine, the Mentally Handicapped and the Church,* Edinburgh 1988

Hauerwas S. *Naming the Silences,* Grand Rapids 1990

Hebblethwaite B. L. *The Incarnation,* Cambridge 1987

Hebblethwaite B. L. *The Ocean of Truth,* Cambridge 1988

Hebblethwaite B. and Henderson E. ed. *Divine Action,* Edinburgh 1990

Hegel F. *Phenomenology of Spirit,* Oxford 1977

Hendry G. *Theology of Nature,* Philadelphia 1980

Hengel M. *The Cross of the Son of God,* London 1986

Hepburn R. W. *Christianity and Paradox,* London, 1958

Hick J. *Evil and the God of Love,* London 1966

Hick J. *An Interpretation of Religion,* London 1990

Hodgson P. and King R. *Christian Theology I,* New York 1982

Hodgson P. *God in History: Shapes of Freedom,* Nashville 1989

Hodgson P. *Revisioning the Church – Ecclesial Freedom in The New Paradigm,* Philadelphia 1988

Hollenweger W. *The Pentecostals,* London 1972

Houghton R. *The Passionate God,* London 1981

Jeanrond W. *Text and Interpretation as Categories of Theological Thinking,* Dublin 1988

Jenkins D. *The Contradiction of Christianity,* London 1976

Jenson R. *The Triune Identity,* Philadelphia 1982

Joest W. *Ontologie der Person bei Luther,* Göttingen 1967

Johnson R. A. *Rudolf Bultmann,* London 1987

Jüngel E. *Paulus und Jesus,* Tübingen 1967

Jüngel E. *Death,* Edinburgh 1975

Jüngel E. *God as the Mystery of the World,* Edinburgh 1983

Jüngel E. *Theological Essays* ed. J. B. Webster, Edinburgh 1990

Kasper W. *Jesus the Christ,* London 1976

Kasper W. *The God of Jesus Christ,* London 1984

Kasper W. *Theology and Church,* London 1989

Kaufman G. *God the Problem,* Cambridge, Mass. 1972

Kaufman G. *Theology for a Nuclear Age,* Manchester 1985

Kelsey D. *The Uses of Scripture in Recent Theology,* London 1975

Kenny A. *The God of the Philosophers,* Oxford 1979

Kippenberg H. *Concepts of Person in Religion and Thought,* Berlin 1990

Kitamori K. *Theology of the Pain of God,* London 1958

Klostermaier K. *Hindu and Christian in Vrindaban,* London 1969

Knitter P. ed. *The Myth of Christian Uniqueness,* London 1988

Knox J. *The Death of Christ,* Nashville 1958

Kretchmar *Die Trinitatslehre,* Tübingen 1956

Kung H. *Does God Exist?,* London 1980

Lampe G. W. H. *God as Spirit,* Oxford 1977

Lampey, *Das Zeitproblem in den Bekenntnissen Augustins,* Regensburg 1960

Langford M. *Providence,* London 1981

Lindbeck G. *The Nature of Doctrine,* London 1984

Link C. *Hegel's Wort, Gott Selbst ist Tot,* Theol. Stud. 114, 1974, 37ff.

Lucas J. A. *Treatise on Time and Space,* London 1973

MacGregor G. *He Who Lets Us Be,* New York 1975

Macintyre A. *After Virtue,* London 1981

Mackey J. P. *The Christian Experience of God as Trinity,* London 1983

Mackinnon D. *Borderlands of Theology,* London 1968

Macquarrie J. *Jesus Christ in Modern Thought,* London 1990

Macquarrie J. *In Search of Humanity,* London 1982

Martin D. and Mullen P. *Strange Gifts,* Oxford 1984

Mascall E. He *Who Is,* London 1943

Mascall E. *The Openness of Being,* London 1971

McEvenue S. 'The Old Testament Scripture or Tradition', in *Interpretation,* July 1981

McGrath A. *The Genesis of Doctrine,* Oxford 1990

McIntyre J. *The Christian Doctrine of History,* Edinburgh 1957

McIntyre J. *Faith, Theology and Imagination,* Edinburgh 1987

McIntyre J. *The Shape of Christology,* Edinburgh 1992

Mellor D. H. *Real Time,* Cambridge 1981

Meyendorff J. *The Orthodox Church,* London 1964

Meyendorff J. *Byzantine Theology,* London 1975

Meyer Ben, *The Aims of Jesus,* London 1979

Michaelson C. 'The Real Presence of the Hidden God' in P. Ramsey ed. *Faith and Ethics*

Milbank J. *Theology and Social Theory,* Oxford 1991

Mildenberger F. *Gotteslehre,* Tübingen 1975

Milet J. *God or Christ,* London 1981

Miller D. E. *The Case for Liberal Christianity,* London 1981

Mitchell B. *The Justification of Religious Belief,* London 1973

Moltmann J. *The Way of Jesus Christ,* London 1990

Moltmann J. *The Crucified God,* London 1975

Morgan R. ed. *Lux Mundi, Essays on the Incarnation,* Bristol 1988

Morgan R. and Barton J. *Biblical Interpretation,* Oxford 1988

Morris T. V. *The Logic of God Incarnate,* London 1986

Morris T. V. *Anselmian Explorations,* Notre Dame 1987

Morse M. The Unattached, London 1965

Murphy R. *Social Closure, the Theory of Monopolization and Exclusion,* Oxford 1988.

Newlands G. *Hilary of Poitiers,* Bern 1978

Newlands G. *The Church of God,* London 1984

Newlands, G. art. 'Love' in *Dictionary of Pastoral Care,* London: SPCK, 1985

Newlands G. *Theology of the Love of God,* London 1980

Newlands G. *Making Christian Decisions,* London 1985

Niebuhr R. *Experimental Religion,* New York 1972

Niesel W. *Reformed Symbolics,* Edinburgh 1962

Norris C. *The Contest of the Faculties: Philosophy and Theory after Deconstruction,* London 1985

O'Collins G. *Interpreting Jesus,* London 1983

Ogden S. *The Point of Christology,* London 1982

Olofsson F. *Christus Redemptor et Consummator,* Uppsala 1979

Owen H. P. *Christian Theism,* Edinburgh 1984

Pannenberg W. *Jesus – God and Man,* London 1968

Pannenberg W. *Basic Questions in Theology I–III,* London 1970

Pannenberg W. *What is Man?* London 1970

Pannenberg W. *Anthropology in Theological Perspective,* London

Pannenberg W. *The Apostles' Creed,* London 1972

Pannenberg W. *Christian Spirituality and Sacramental Community,* London 1983

Passmore J. *The Perfectibility of Man,* London 1970

Peacocke A. R. *Theology for a Scientific Age*

Peacocke A. R. *The Sciences and Theology in the Twentieth Century*

Peacocke A. R. *God and the New Biology,* London 1986

Peacocke A. R. *Science and the Christian Experiment,* Oxford 1971

Peacocke A. R. *Intimations of Reality, Critical Realism in Science and Religion,* Indiana 1984

Peacocke A. R. *Creation and the World of Science,* Oxford 1979

Pelikan J. *The Christian Tradition,* London 1971-89

Peukert H. *Science, Action and Fundamental Theology,* London 1984

Phillips D. Z. *Faith after Foundationalism,* London 1988

Polkinghorne J. *Science and Providence,* London 1989

Polkinghorne J. *Science and Reality,* London 1991

Polkinghorne J. *In Nature 293.37, Nov. 81*

Preller V. *Divine Science and the Science of God,* Princeton 1967

Pullinger D. *Scorching Heat and Drought,* Edinburgh 1989

Quinton A. *The Nature of Things,* London 1973

Race A. *Christianity and Religious Pluralism,* London 1983

Rahner K. *Mysterium Salutis II,* Einsiedeln 1967

Rahner K. *Theological Investigations XVII,* London 1963-84

Ramsey M. *Holy Spirit,* London 1987

Ratschow H. *Gott Existiert,* Berlin 1966

Ratschow H. *Der Angefochtene Glaube,* Gütersloh 1957

Richard L. *A Kenotic Christology,* Washington DC 1982

Richardson A. and Bowden J. *A New Dictionary of Christian Theology,* London 1983

Ricoeur P. *Essays in Biblical Interpretation* ed. L. S. Mudge

Ritschl D. *Memory and Hope,* New York 1962 ?

Robinson J. A. T. *The Human Face of God,* London 1972

Robinson J. A. T. *Where Three Ways Meet,* London 1987

Robinson J. M. Review of Jüngel, *Paulus und Jesus,* in *Interpretation* 18, 1964, 346ff.

Rohain in NZSTh. 22(80), 282f.

Rorty R. *Philosophy and The Mirror of Nature,* Oxford 1980

Rowland C. C. *The Open Heaven,* London 1982

Rowland C. C. *Radical Christianity,* Oxford 1988

Ruether R. *Sexism and God-Talk,* Boston 1983

Russell R. J., Stoeger W. R. and Coyne G. V. ed. *Physics, Philosophy and Theology: A Common Quest for Understanding,* Notre Dame 1988

Schillebeeckx E. *Jesus,* London 1979

Schillebeeckx E. *Christ,* London 1980

Schillebeeckx E. *Church – The Human Story of God,* London 1989

Schillebeeckx E. *The Understanding of Faith,* London 1974

Schüssler Fiorenza E. *In Memory of Her,* London 1983

Schreiter R. *Local Theologies,* London 1985

Shaw D. ed. *In Divers Manners – A St. Mary's Miscellany,* St. Andrews 1990

Sheenan T. *The First Coming,* New York 1986

Shepherd J. J. *Experience, Inference and God,* London 1975

Shoemaker S. and Swinburne R. *Personal Identity,* Oxford 1984

Shoemaker S. *Self Knowledge and Self Identity,* Ithaca 1963

Simon U. *Atonement: From Holocaust to Paradise,* Cambridge 1987

Smith R. G. *The Doctrine of God,* London 1970

Sobrino J. *Christology at the Crossroads,* London 1978

Sobrino J. *The True Church and the Poor,* London 1985

Sokoloski R. *Presence,* in J. Phil 77, 634f., 1980

Stead G. C. *Divine Substance,* Oxford 1977

Stroup G. *The Promise of Narrative Theology,* London 1981

Stuhlmacher P. *Historical Criticism and the Theological Interpretation of Scripture,* Philadelphia 1977

Surin K. *Theology and the Problem of Evil,* Oxford 1986

Sutherland S. *God, Jesus and Belief,* London 1984

Swinburne R. *The Coherence of Theism,* Oxford, 1977

Swinburne R. *Responsibility and Atonement,* Oxford 1989

Sykes S. W. *The Identity of Christianity*, London 1984

Taylor C. *Sources of the Self*, Cambridge 1989

Temple W. ed. *Doctrine in the Church of England*, London 1938

Theissen G. *On Having a Critical Faith*, London 1979

Theissen G. *Lokalkolorit and Zeitgeschichte in den Evangelien*, Göttingen, 1989

Theissen G. *The Shadow of the Galilean*, London 1987

Thistleton A. *The Two Horizons*, Exeter 1980

Thomas O. C. *God's Activity in the World*, Chico, Ca.,1983

Thompson Events, in Phil. Rev. 1978

Tillich P. *Systematic Theology*, London 1953

Toedt H. E. *The Son of Man in the Synoptic Tradition*, London 1965

Torrance T. F. *Space, Time and Incarnation*, London 1969

Tracy D. *The Analogical Imagination*, London 1981

Vesey G. ed. *The Philosophy in Christianity*, Cambridge 1989

Vielhauer P. *Aufsätze zum Neuen Testament I, II*, Munich 1965-79

Walker P. K. *Rediscovering the Middle Way*, London 1988

Ward K. *A Vision to Pursue*, London 1991

Ward K. *Holding Fast to God*, London 1982

Ward K. *Rational Theology and the Creativity of God*, Oxford 1982

Ward K. *Divine Action*, London 1990

Ware K. T. *The Orthodox Church*, London 1963

Webb C. C. J. *God and Personality*, London 1918

Webster J. *Eberhard Jüngel*, Cambridge 1986

Wendel F. *Calvin*, London 1953

Wiesel E. *Night*, London 1981

Wiggins D. *Sameness and Substance*, Oxford 1980

Williams B. *Problems of the Self*, Cambridge 1973

Williams R. D. *Arius*, London 1987

Williams R. D. *Person and Personality*, Downside Review 94 (1976), 253ff.

Yarnold E. *The Second Gift*, Slough 1974

Index

429